T0316313

Work, Locality and the Rhythms of Capital

Employment and Work Relations in Context Series

Series Editors

Tony Elger
Centre for Comparative Labour Studies
Department of Sociology
University of Warwick

Peter Fairbrother
School of Social Sciences
Cardiff University

The aim of the *Employment and Work Relations in Context* series is to address questions relating to the evolving patterns and politics of work, employment, management and industrial relations. There is a concern to trace out the ways in which wider policy-making, especially by national governments and transnational corporations, impinges upon specific workplaces, occupations, labour markets, localities and regions. This invites attention to developments at an international level, marking out patterns of globalization, state policy and practice in the context of globalization and the impact of these processes on labour. A particular feature of the series is the consideration of forms of worker and citizen organization and mobilization. Thus the studies address major analytical and policy issues through case study and comparative research.

Recently published titles:

Changing Prospects for Trade Unionism: Comparisons between Six Countries
Peter Fairbrother and Gerard Griffin

Trade Unions in Renewal: A Comparative Study
Peter Fairbrother and Charlotte Yates

Work and Employment Relations in the High Performance Workplace
Gregor Murray, Jacques Bélanger, Anthony Gilles and Paul-André Lapointe

Unionization and Union Leadership: The Road Haulage Industry
Paul Smith

Reshaping the North American Automobile Industry: Restructuring, Corporatism, and Union Democracy in Mexico
John P. Tuman

Trade Unions and Global Governance: The Quest of Trade Unions for a Social Clause
Gerda van Roozendaal

Globalization, Social Movements and the New Internationalisms
Peter Waterman

WORK, LOCALITY AND THE RHYTHMS OF CAPITAL

The Labour Process Reconsidered

Jamie Gough

Routledge
Taylor & Francis Group
New York London

To John Leask,
and to workers throughout the world organizing
against neoliberalism

First published 2003 by Continuum.

711 Third Avenue, New York, NY 10017, USA
2 Park Square, Milton Park, Abingdon, Oxon OX14 4RN

Routledge is an imprint of the Taylor & Francis Group, an informa business

First issued in hardback 2017

British Library Cataloguing-in-Publication Data
A catalogue record for this book is available from the British Library.

ISBN 978-0-8264-6284-8 (pbk)
ISBN 978-1-138-43461-5 (hbk)

Library of Congress Cataloging-in-Publication Data
Gough, Jamie.
    Work, locality and the rhythms of capital/Jamie Gough.
        p. cm. — (Employment and work relations in context series)
    Includes bibliographical references and index.
    ISBN 0–8264–6284–7
        1. Industrial location. 2. Space in economics. I. Title. II. Employment and work relations in context.

    HC79.D5 G67 2002
    331–dc21   2002073326

Typeset by YHT Ltd, London

CONTENTS

Acknowledgements   x

Chapter 1 INTRODUCTION   1

1.1 Factory stories   1
1.2 The main themes of the book   9
1.3 The context: capital's offensive and its uses of space   12
1.4 Fragmentation versus collectivity of workers   14
1.5 London as the site of study   16
1.6 Theory and case study   17
1.7 The structure of the book   18

PART I WORK IN LOCALITIES

Chapter 2 LOCAL ECONOMIES   25

2.1 Workplace, locality and world: the problem of scale   25
2.2 Difference and materialist dialectics   29
2.3 A key structure: the labour process   30
2.4 Work and workers in localities   36
2.5 The built environment and local production   39
2.6 Competition between localities through the labour process   40
2.7 Demand and local economies   42
2.8 Socialization, conflict and contradiction in local economies   42

Chapter 3 THE DYNAMICS OF LABOUR PROCESSES IN PLACE   49

3.1 Introduction   49
3.2 Raising labour productivity: technological change versus intensification?   49
3.3 Cutting costs   54
3.4 Production and the product   57
3.5 Cooperation and conflict, the universal and the partial   61
3.6 New geographies of the labour process?   63

Chapter 4 LOCATING THE WORKPLACE   65

4.1 Paradigms of workplace location   65
4.2 Stimuli to workplace change   66
4.3 The dialectic of the labour process and capital accumulation
         within workplaces   67
4.4 Firms' use of place and space   69

PART II MANUFACTURING IN A METROPOLIS

Chapter 5 MAKING THINGS IN A CAPITAL OF CAPITAL   75

5.1 London and 'manufacturing'   75
5.2 The difficulties and logics of manufacturing in London   76
5.3 Five cultures of London manufacturing   79
5.4 Historical dialectics of productive structure and products   89
5.5 Oligopoly, surplus profits and locality   91
5.6 Long waves in London's manufacturing   93
5.7 Geographical spread, decentralization and archaeology of London
         manufacturing   98
5.8 Local coherence in London manufacturing?   101
5.9 British manufacturing decline and crisis   103
5.10 Manufacturing in Britain and London in the period of study,
         1976–81   106
5.11 Theoretical threads   108

**Chapter 6 FROM RAGS TO RADAR: A SLICE OF LONDON
MANUFACTURING**   111

6.1 Exemplifying theory   111
6.2 The workplaces and data described   112
6.3 Categorizing the labour process   115
6.4 The specialization of London: second cut   118
6.5 The divided and dividing labour market   120
6.6 Work and buildings   133
6.7 Competition and profitability   139
6.8 Forms of capital   143
6.9 Was London manufacturing 'backward'?   144

PART III CHANGES OF THE LABOUR PROCESS IN SPACE AND THEIR RHYTHMS

Introduction to Part III   148

Chapter 7 STRUGGLES OVER INCREASING PRODUCTIVITY   151

7.1 To stay or go? Location and raising productivity   151

Section A: Change in situ
7.2 Changing mechanization   152
7.3 New machines and new skills   156
7.4 Changing things around: the micro-geography of production   158
7.5 Intensification of work   159
7.6 Intensification by changing the workforce   162
7.7 Productivity and divisions   164

Section B: Change through relocation
7.8 Consolidation onto more advanced plant   165
7.9 Changes in site number and size due to dynamic labour processes   166
7.10 Relocation to improve the quality of premises   168
7.11 Intensification through relocating to a new workforce   169
7.12 Relocations to discipline workers   174
7.13 Conclusions: locations and times of increasing productivity   178

Chapter 8 THE PRODUCT MATTERS   181

8.1 Products, production and labour   181
8.2 Improving the quality of production   181
8.3 Design work, technical rents and division of labour   185
8.4 Changes in products and the expansion of capital   187
8.5 How product change alters the labour process   188
8.6 How the labour process shapes product change   190
8.7 Relocation to facilitate change in products   191
8.8 Major technical change in products and the social division of labour   193
8.9 Conclusions: products, labour processes and space   194

Chapter 9 THE COSTS OF CUTTING COSTS   196

9.1 Cost cutting and its causes   196

9.2 Redistributing income: wage cuts in situ during the recession   197
9.3 Wage cutting by changing the workforce   199
9.4 Relocation to cheaper labour   201
9.5 Working for the machine: longer hours and overhead costs   202
9.6 Increasing the scale of the workplace   203
9.7 Limiting the scale of production   205
9.8 Conclusions: the costs of cutting costs   208

PART IV THE LABOUR PROCESS, CAPITAL ACCUMULATION AND BEYOND

Introduction to Part IV   212

Chapter 10 CHANGING LABOUR PROCESSES AND CHANGING PLACE   213

10.1 The labour process and location   213
10.2 Labour process change and relocation   214
10.3 The choice between in situ change and relocation: patterns and first cut explanation   216
10.4 Do labour processes have intrinsic dynamics?   217
10.5 The dynamic tendencies of the labour process   218
10.6 Relocation pressures, second cut: different labour processes   226
10.7 Labour process change and class relations   228

Chapter 11 RHYTHMS OF CAPITAL, THE LABOUR PROCESS AND SCALE   231

11.1 The varied rhythms and varied scales of accumulation   231
11.2 Reinforcing accumulation   232
11.3 Overaccumulation   235
11.4 Underaccumulation   238
11.5 Contradictory spatial accumulation and structured paralysis   239
11.6 Accumulation and devalorization: the creative destruction of value   240
11.7 Conclusion: the labour process, class control and socialist politics   242

Chapter 12 WORKING ON THE ROLLER-COASTER: THE BUSINESS CYCLE AND SPACE   245

12.1 The cyclical time and shifting spaces of work   245
12.2 The business cycle   247

12.3 The business cycle, scale and the workplace 250
12.4 The business cycle and labour process change: evidence and explanation 251
12.5 Cyclical switches in the causes and spatial forms of labour process change 258
12.6 The cycle as contradiction 259
12.7 The business cycle, space and the labour process: some conclusions 262
12.8 Accumulation rhythms: why time matters to space 263

Chapter 13 DIFFERENCE, FRAGMENTATION AND THE ASSOCIATED PRODUCERS 269

13.1 Divisions and socialist strategy 269
13.2 Relations between workers, relations between the classes 272
13.3 Differences and cooperation between workers 273
13.4 Struggle against capital, struggle against difference 275
13.5 Competition within the product-industry and beyond 280
13.6 The big smoke: workers' struggles and divisions in a metropolis 284
13.7 Conclusions: fragmentation, difference and socialism 289

APPENDICES

Appendix 1 The business cycle in London manufacturing in the period of study 298
Appendix 2 Some troublesome terms in spatial economic change 302
Appendix 3 Relocation and change in floor space 303

Bibliography 304
Index to major threads of the argument 318
Subject and author index 319

Acknowledgements

I would like to thank Roger Leigh and David North for permission to use survey data collected for the research project on London manufacturing which they directed in 1978–82. Thanks also to Michael Jacobs for his diligent and resourceful work as a research assistant for the present work. Most of the analysis on which this book is based was carried out with a personal Research Grant from the Economic and Social Research Council, number D00232147. I am very grateful to my colleagues in the Division of Geography and Environmental Management at the University of Northumbria for giving me the unscheduled sabbatical during which the first draft of this text was written, and to the Department of Economics at Sydney University for providing me with accommodation, warm hospitality and support during this sabbatical. I am deeply indebted to Tony Elger and Aram Eisenschitz for making many detailed and insightful suggestions for improvements to the first draft of the book, most of which I have attempted to implement. Thanks also to Dave Etherington, Teresa Hayter and Clive Morphet for very useful comments. While these suggestions led to major improvements, the responsibility for the book's faults remains mine. Finally, my gratitude and love to my household at Great Russell Street, to John Leask, and to other friends for putting up with my distraction and absences while working on this book, and for their encouragement in continuing with it.

1 INTRODUCTION

1.1 Factory stories

The situation of workers in capitalist societies is one of fragmentation and individualization: each worker has individually to sell his or her ability to work to an employer, competing for the available jobs with other workers. This individualization has been countered by trade-union and other collective forms of organization, which put pressure on employers, including via the state, to meet collective needs of workers. These forms of organization always have to combat multifarious forms of division and antagonism between workers. This problem has been deepened by the worldwide strategy of neo-liberalism inaugurated in the 1970s, which exacerbated every type of division and competition between workers not merely as an effect but as a key aim.

Divisions between workers have many roots, but a central one is the qualitative differences in labour processes and their dynamics which workers experience in their daily working lives. These are the subject of this book. Consider, for instance, the following examples, taken from the study of manufacturing firms in London in the late 1970s and early 1980s on which this book is based:

- A clothing firm, under increasing pressures from low-price imports, and facing difficulties in recruiting sufficiently skilled workers at the wage offered, reduces its factory workforce and takes on homeworkers who are in more plentiful supply in the Cypriot communities of north-east London and whose cost is lower. Around the same time, work in the factory is changed from each machinist making a whole garment to part work, in order to be able to employ lower skilled workers.
- A factory that assembles standardized electronic goods experiences chronic difficulties in holding onto workers in the low skilled, low paid

work it undertakes, affecting production quality. Management is unwilling to increase wages; mechanization to displace labour is not financially viable at the volumes made, and the firm considers moving to another part of London where the manager believes there is less competition for labour. A sharp recession resolves this problem for management by increasing unemployment and thus easing recruitment.

- A large, multisite firm producing electronic capital goods wishes to diversify its product range into new niche markets. It chooses to site part of this expanded production at its long established London factory because of the variety of production equipment located there and the diversity and high level of skills and experience of the workforce.

- A specialist scientific instruments firm is seeking to introduce a new product line. This, however, requires some new production equipment and corresponding new labour skills. The firm decides not to proceed with the diversification due to the cost of equipment and difficulties in holding skilled labour. This puts the future of the firm in jeopardy.

- A large brewing firm owns an old brewery in inner London. It has invested in a large state-of-the-art brewery in the south-east, outside London, which, however, is operating at well under capacity. The labour force at the London site has longer experience of negotiation with management, and the site is valuable. The firm closes the London brewery and transfers its production to the new plant, thus increasing its utilization. There is no organized resistance to the closure despite the shortage of alternative employment for many of the workers.

- A printing firm with a single site in London is seeking to expand its output. Rather than expanding at its existing workplace, it opens a new site in another part of London. This is because management believes that the strong unions in the London printing industry become still stronger as the size of the workplace increases, and because the new capacity will use production equipment that is new in significant ways and that will require negotiation with the unions.

These events happened in the same city, during the same period, and with the same macroeconomic conditions. Yet the experiences of the workers concerned were, on the face of it, completely different. Some were, for the moment at least, in a relatively secure position, while others were faced with incipient or immediate threats. These threats were themselves varied: pressure on wages, deskilling, changes in tasks, relocation of the job, or outright loss of employment. Moreover, before the restructurings were initiated, the factories were enormously diverse in terms of wages, skills, hours and sections of the labour force employed. The result was to isolate each group of workers from others within London and elsewhere. London at that time had the largest single concentration of manufacturing workers in Britain, yet for the most part each group of workers faced its employers alone. The diversity of their experiences made it difficult for workers to recognize commonalities in their situation even with others within the same city and, *a fortiori*, to develop unity against their employers.

Yet behind these differences are commonalities. All the workers were hired, allocated tasks and compelled to do those tasks at a certain pace and quality in such a way as to (attempt to) make their employer a reasonable profit on capital. Many faced intensification of work, albeit in different modes. All faced competition from other factories, whether near or distant, based on some combination of price and quality. All were subject to waves of investment and disinvestment at the level of factory, industry and territory as capital undershot or overshot production capacity relative to demand. These commonalities, and others that we shall see shortly, might provide the basis for recognition of common experiences and thus for common action; but these would need to take account of workers' different situations. As David Harvey (2000: 83) has written, '[t]he socialist cause ... [requires] a serious discussion of the relations between commonality/difference, the particularity of the one and the universalism of the other.' The starting point for this book is, then, the political need to grasp, in theory and practice, the *commonalities* of waged work within a given territory at a given time, and how they cut across, but also give rise to, very real *differences* within it.

What are the most significant processes that might enable us to think about the kinds of workers' experiences described above both in their commonalities and their differences? A key starting point is the *labour process*, which includes the material processes of production, the allocation of workers to production tasks, the control of workers by management within these tasks, and – crucially – the interrelations between these. The main labour process within the clothing industry, for example, consists of skilled workers using the old and slowly changing technology of the sewing machine to produce potentially varied types of garment, working at a discrete machine and at a pace set, immediately, by their own skill and initiative. The labour process in the assembly of standardized electronic goods consists of semi-skilled workers using simple tools, working at a pace that may be set by an automated flow of the product between stages of assembly. The stories of the factories in these two industries are contrasted partly because of these labour process differences: the employer in electronic assembly was concerned above all with obtaining a cheaper and more plentiful supply of labour through relocation, unconstrained by the need to keep or access a skilled labour force; in contrast, the clothing firm sought to alter its labour process in such as way as to decrease the skills needed by each worker while remaining in situ. In both brewing and printing, the skilled nature of the work and the bargaining power this gave to male workers had been a basis for them to build up, over many decades, relatively strong union organization, which the employers then sought to side-step using both technical change and relocation. Brewing and printing differed in the degree of integration of the labour of different workers and the consequent minimum efficient scale of operation: the printing firm could consider fragmenting production between different sites in London (as could the clothing employer), whereas the brewer had constructed its large plant outside London in order to obtain economies of scale, and needed to move production to it in order to realize those economies in practice.

The labour process, then, is the immediate site and material medium of the relation between capital and labour. The particular form of the labour process affects the strategies of labour control and technical change that management is impelled, and able, to adopt. It shapes the forms of work-places and the daily preoccupations and culture of management. For workers, the labour process concerns the material form, healthiness, interest and sociability of their work. It enters strongly into their ability to organize collectively and the kinds of sanction that they can use against the employer. While the labour process is embedded in its existing locations by buildings and equipment and by access to particular labour forces, tensions within it may lead to employers attempting to shift these locations.

The labour process contains a further element, *employment relations* – the wages, work-related benefits, hours and security of jobs. These have dense connections to the organization of work – though they do not uniquely determine each other. Thus the deskilling of work and shift to homeworkers by the clothing firm was facilitated by the fact that workers in the London clothing industry had little expectation of secure employment, and many were working without written contracts and so had no legal rights on redundancy. In contrast, in electronic capital goods employers often put a high value on workers' continuity of employment in order to ensure the technical quality of production, and in our story the firm was reinvesting in its London plant to exploit this; security of employment, wages and conditions consequently were better in this industry than in clothing.

The varied jobs constructed by the labour process are not assigned randomly to those seeking jobs; and the differentiated capacities of workers used in production are produced outside production in social life. Thus a further part of the picture is the *production of 'labour power' – the ability to do particular wage work – and the matching of particular types of labour power to particular jobs.* Clothing, brewing and printing all involve skills that potentially give bargaining power to workers; the fact that unions were weak in the London clothing industry but strong in brewing and printing had a lot to do with the fact that the former industry employed mainly women from minority ethnic communities whereas the latter industries employed mainly white men. Clothing workers' bargaining power was further reduced by the fact that women in these communities often learned machining skills within the home, giving employers a ready supply of at least partly trained labour. In contrast, the skills required by the scientific instruments firm depended substantially on formal training and learning on the job, whose provision was inadequate in London, thus threatening the viability of this firm's labour process. The reproduction of labour power is strongly rooted in particular places and differentiated by neighbourhood, locality and region. The problems of recruitment for the scientific instruments firm, for example, were exacerbated by the fact that many men with manual skills had moved out of London to the surrounding Home Counties in search of a better lifestyle. The consumer electronics firm could hope to find a more abundant supply of non-skilled labour by relocating – and thus maintain its existing labour processes – because many areas of London had substantial unemployment. The clothing firm exploited the captive labour force of the Cypriot communities in north-east London, most of whose members were spatially immobile because of their *social* ties within their communities. The *geographies* of labour power and its reproduction were therefore crucial.

We have here, then, another promising element in exploring differences in workers' bargaining power. Labour power is reproduced through household work and leisure, which makes use of housing and goods and services supplied by both the private and public sectors. These produce 'segments' of labour power differentiated by gender, ethnicity and age, skill and attitudes, and unevenly distributed in space. These supplies of labour power then impact strongly onto the ways in which firms develop labour processes, including their locations. The forms of work and employment relations of these labour processes reciprocally have fundamental effects on social life: the social reproduction of the Cypriot communities in London – their incomes, gender relations, housing, and so on – were strongly affected by the clothing industry. We have, then, dense interconnections between work techniques, work organization, employment relations, and social life that simultaneously shape differentiated workers' experiences *and* their social identities, outlook and culture.

The labour process is strongly bound up with the type of *products* it produces. The long runs of identical electronic consumer goods enabled the employer to design low skill tasks, whereas the variety and internal complexity of products in electronic capital goods, clothing and printing meant that employers benefited from workers who were skilled and experienced. Some workers in the latter industries could take some interest and pride in what they were producing – which was hard in electronic consumer goods. *Change* in products was also important. It was the diversification of the product range in the electronic capital goods firm that led management to select the production characteristics of the London factory. The new products could then reap design rents, which would enable management to pay wages sufficient to retain the necessary skilled labour. In contrast, the increasing standardization of beer was an element in the shift of production to the new out-of-London plant. Understanding varied experiences of work, then, requires us to think about products too.

The stories also suggest the importance of another element, the *premises and land* used for production. Brewing production was relocated partly because of land prices in London and the land-intensive nature of this labour process. Setting up a new site in the printing firm was constrained by the need to find premises suitable for this kind of production. Clothing manufacture, on the other hand, was so little constrained by premises that it could be carried out in workers' homes. Premises, then, could be important in the development of the labour process, and connected the latter to the wider built environment of the locality.

Our workplace stories were constructed not only by what happened locally – in the factories, in the workers' residential communities – but by *the forms and geographies of competition*, the workplaces and workers against which they were competing. The London factory producing electronic consumer goods, for example, was competing against workplaces in cheaper locations in Britain and, even more sharply, in East Asia; this was one reason for management's strategy of low skill and low wages and its consequent relocation intentions. In contrast, the capital goods factories, due to the technical requirements of the product, were competing with producers in other developed countries, many with higher wages; and the printer was competing with others in London because of the quick turnaround times for their products; pressures of deskilling and wage cutting were therefore less intense (though not absent) in these two factories. The evolution of the London workplaces, then, was profoundly affected by the product and production strategies of their rivals, strategies that were conditioned by the latters' geographical locations. Conversely, the geography of competition was a function of the product and labour-process strategies predominating in the industry.

The *type of firm* owning the workplace could also be significant. Both the scientific instruments firm and the clothing firm were undertaking or considering drastic change partly because they had little capital with which to pursue their existing activities. The brewing and electronic capital goods firms, in contrast, were multisite, making it easier for them to select between the qualities of different labour forces, production facilities and localities and thus exploit geographical difference. These different forms of the firm were themselves constructed over time by the production and product characteristics of the respective industries: the simple and divisible production technology of the clothing industry allows small, low-capital firms, whereas in electronic capital goods the large research-and-development requirements and the large-scale and complex products give rise to many medium and large firms. There is evidently, then, mutual construction of labour process, product activity and form of capital.

A further important element suggested by the stories is *the rhythms of investment*, the uneven pace of investment in time, the cumulative growth or decline that are so characteristic of capitalist economies. The consumer electronics firm, for instance, benefited from the recession due to increased available labour power, and this changed the firm's production-location strategy. The brewer overinvested in capacity, leading to cuts. These were selective, retaining particular fixed capital and labour forces and cutting others, and thus *qualitatively* changing the labour process. The scientific instruments firm suffered from the excessive aggregate investment across the London economy, which had contributed to shortages of particular kinds of skilled labour. Conversely, the clothing firm benefited from the accumulation over decades of sector-specific skills in the London Cypriot communities. At the plant level, the electronic capital goods firm built on existing capacity, skills and accumulated experience, so that the rhythm of accumulation was here a self-reinforcing one. Moreover, as we shall see, the factory stories were influenced by a 'long wave' of stagnation and low productive investment in the world economy.

We see here, then, the importance of waves of investment and disinvestment. These were focused on varied spatial scales. The cumulative growth of the electronic capital goods factory was specific to the workplace. The overinvestment of the brewer was internal to the firm. The shortage of skilled labour for the scientific instruments firm was generated within London, and to some extent Britain as a whole, whereas clothing industry skills were accumulated in a particular part of London. The business cycle and the recession were national and international in scope. There were also many resonances between the rhythms at these different spatial scales – the brewer's overcapacity, for instance, was worsened by the recession. We need, therefore, to consider *varied scales* of accumulation rhythms and their mutual resonances, including rhythms not only in production but also in the reproduction of labour power.

Finally, we can draw out from these elements a more abstract distinction that will be central to this book: the contrast between *the material form of production and reproduction* on the one hand and *their specifically capitalist nature* on the other. The labour process consists of technologies and tasks with their unique material nature, but it is also a way of extracting surplus labour and making a profit. The first is particular, the second the universal aim of capital. The labour process is thus *particular use values of production* but also *abstract exchange value and capital.* These two aspects can sometimes be in harmony, sometimes in conflict. In the electronic capital goods firm, for example, the material effectiveness of production privileged the London site and investment was made there despite its relatively high costs. In the clothing and printing firms, however, productive logic implied keeping production in the existing factory, whereas the impulse to cut costs (clothing) or keep capitalist discipline over labour (printing) produced dispersal of production that would jeopardize productivity. In these cases, productive efficiency conflicted with capital accumulation.

Productive efficiency often benefits from strong linkages within territories between aspects of production and reproduction, which I will term *socialization*; the ties between firms and skilled labour within London are an example. However, socialization in place often comes into conflict with the mobility of goods (clothing from East Asia for example), of capital in its money form, of knowledge (disinvestment from electronic consumer goods in Britain), or of labour (the migration of skilled workers out of London). This tension between socialization of material dependencies motivated by productivity and spatial mobilities powered by exchange value and profit will be a key focus of this book.

The contrast between use value and exchange value is crucial for the question with which we started: the unity and fragmentation of labour. Jobs and their evolution over time are differentiated by their endlessly varied material nature. At the same time, there are processes common to them by virtue of their being jobs in capitalist firms. The former considerations differentiate and separate workers, the latter are common and potentially bring them together. These two aspects cannot, in the end, be separated. There may, for instance, be important commonalities in the development of such things as skills and intensity of work, and there are differences in profit rates and capital mobilities between different kinds of firm. These potential unities and differences will be central to our concerns.

1.2 The main themes of the book

The aim of this book is to develop an analysis of production change in place, its material nature and its class relations, with a particular concern for the differences and commonalities between workers. We shall be concerned with 'structures', but these contain the active strategies and consciousness of both management and workers. The conceptual themes that I have drawn out of the factory stories suggest that this project will involve developing dense relations between a set of processes; these are pictured in Figure 1.1. The book investigates and develops these relations in different registers: through analysing the behaviour of a large set of individual workplaces over a five year period; through examining the long term development of the London manufacturing economy; and through developing the analysis of production and class relations in place in modern capitalist economies in general. The analysis is done in such a way as to inform a politics of workers' self-activity and struggle.

In Figure 1.1 I have divided the relevant processes schematically into three groups, 'the labour process', 'capital accumulation' and 'the local economy'. I have done so because these are usually treated separately, and each has its own distinct literature. The project of the book is to destabilize these separations by developing as many relations as possible between the elements shown; some of these relations have been under researched and under theorized to date. I therefore hope to suggest to labour process theorists, to political economists and to geographer-urbanists some ways in which their studies can and should be more closely interwoven. Figure 1.1 also emphasizes another distinctive feature of the book, its focus on the contradictory relations between the productive logic of material use values *and* the abstract and fantastic qualities of exchange value and capital accumulation.

All studies have to balance richness of dialectics against focus and manageability (Ollman, 1993). The centre of the book's discussion is the *labour process*, and the other structures are woven around it. This choice is related to the book's political problematic. The labour process is the immediate site for the relation of capital and labour, of their mutual dependence and their antagonism. It gives particular resources to management and to workers and

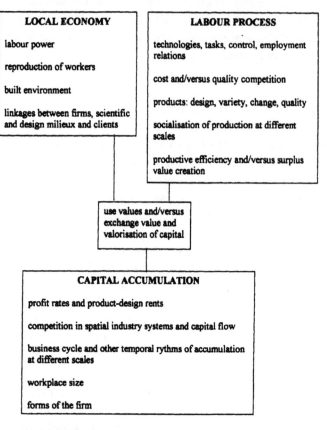

Figure 1.1 *Subject matter and themes of this book.*

shapes their daily concerns, identities and cultures. As I have already hinted, it enters powerfully into the construction of labour power (and through it social life), product development, built environments, industry competition, and the form of the firm. The labour process will thus be the guiding thread.

As the analysis of the factory stories suggests, geography is central to this analysis. The workplace is the immediate unit of study, but this was embedded in processes and structures at larger spatial scales: local markets in labour power and premises, systems of reproduction of people, and local ties between firms and institutions, and at higher spatial scales the spaces of competition within the industry varying from London to the globe, and equally varied geographies of the firm. Firms were subject to pressures from these spatial structures, but also used them actively through relocations of production, a major focus of the book. The relations between workers were equally affected by these geographies. Workers were reproduced in particular local communities, to which they had ties of varying strength. They competed against other workers who were sometimes close-by, sometimes distant, and these distances were bound up with particular *forms* of competition (cost, skill, quality, and so on) and particular possibilities for anomie or cooperation. Relocations of production could be used by management to discipline or to replace workers. A central argument, then, is that the labour process, capital accumulation and their politics are *inextricably geographical.* The book develops in detail a theoretical approach for such analysis, which develops new relations between class-production dynamics and geography.

The different geographical scales of analysis raise the problem of what is internal and what is external to each scale, and the relations between these. The question of whether (and in what senses) workplace change comes from within the firm or from external forces on it is not only analytically but politically important, because painful restructuring is typically blamed on external constraints. The same happens when local change is blamed on 'globalization'. In developing the theory of local production, I shall give particular attention to distinguishing *and* relating internal and external causes, what is intrinsic to the structure in question and what is contingent. This will concern not only structures of different spatial scale but also those related in other senses, for example production and reproduction.

The empirical study is based on a longitudinal survey of 379 workplaces selected from twelve manufacturing industries in London, giving data on production, its change, and associated relocation decisions over the five year period 1977–81. The availability of this very rich data set was one reason for the choice of case study. The analysis uses a detailed typology of the direct labour process to make systematic comparisons between the dynamics of different labour processes. This is a novel approach. The non-geographical labour process literature has focused on particular sectors, firms or workplaces, studied either singly or through comparisons of two or three cases; systematic comparisons of the dynamics of different labour processes have been rare.[1] However, Massey and Meegan (1979; 1982) carried out two pioneering studies arising from geographers' concern for differences within and across territorial economies, which compared different forms of labour-process change across a range of manufacturing sectors within Britain. The present study similarly undertakes a systematic comparison of change in varied labour processes during a particular period and set within a particular territory, London. It extends Massey and Meegan's research by examining individual workplaces rather than national industries, thus mitigating the problem of structural diversity within the latter (cf. 1982: 195–6);[2] by using a more elaborate typology of labour process change, enabling more of the diversity of such change to be appreciated; by using a systematic typology of the *initial* labour process, so that the constraints on possible paths of production change can be analysed more systematically; and by examining the relation of changes in labour processes to the structures shown in Figure 1.1. This, then, is the first study to compare a wide range of labour processes and the full variety of their dynamics within a particular locality.

Various rhythms of accumulation were important in the case study. The period marked the beginning of full-blown neoliberalism in Britain and was one of deep and far-reaching restructuring in manufacturing industry, providing a good basis for studying labour process change. The period fell into two phases of the business cycle, a weak upturn in 1976–9 and a sharp recession in 1980–1. The workplace data were collected separately for these two phases – another useful feature of the data set. As hinted at in the factory stories, labour process change and relocations associated with it were very different in the two phases of the cycle. A major part of the book is devoted to investigating this relation; this is the first systematic study of the relation of the business cycle to a wide range of labour process change in space. This theme is set alongside analyses of the relation of the labour process to long waves and other forms of cumulative growth and decline at varied spatial scales. The influence of these diverse rhythms of accumulation on the labour process is a central theme of this book.

Having outlined the book's themes, I now consider its political context: the long-term spatial-economic-political situation, and the questions for workers' strategies that it raises.

1.3 The context: capital's offensive and its uses of space

In 1979 the Conservative Party won the British general election, defeating a Labour government weakened and discredited by its conflict with the trade unions during the previous 'winter of discontent'. The new government implemented a sharply deflationary policy designed to discipline unruly labour and inefficient firms. It relaxed controls on the export of capital, putting further pressure on domestic producers through an exodus of investment money. It increased the rate of taxation through regressive means, claiming that this would encourage everyone to work harder – the poor by cutting their rewards, the rich by increasing them. This regime combined with a world recession to achieve the sharpest downturn in the British economy since the 1930s. In two years output fell by 7 per cent and registered unemployment rose from 1.3 to 2.8 million. Whole industries were eliminated from Britain, and the geography of industrial production was radically altered. For those who remained in employment, management was not slow in taking advantage of the situation to hold down or reduce wages, intensify work and reorganize production (Elger, 1991).

This economic and political trauma forms the historical context of the present study. But while 'Thatcherism' launched itself with a particularly violent and extreme exhibition of its philosophy and powers, the processes it employed at its birth were typical of the capitalist world during the long wave of stagnation of the last 30 years. Low average rates of profit have compelled firms and industries to restructure their work processes, products and forms of internal organization. Wage restraint and speed-up, already introduced as profitability declined in the 1960s, have been supplemented by abrogation of previous work agreements and continuous change in work arrangements in the name of 'flexibility', the declaration of 'management's right to manage', attacks by both management and governments on trade unions' influence and rights, weakening of legal controls on terms and conditions of work, and reform of social security to press the unemployed into low wage jobs (Pollert, 1990; Levidow, 1990). These changes have been integral to neoliberal strategy, which has sought to discipline labour and depoliticize the economy through the sharper imposition of value relations (Bonefeld, 1993). The impact of these measures has not been limited to incomes and the delimited time of waged work: for many they have produced a profound sense of loss of control and self worth, and chronic anxiety (Pelaez and Holloway, 1990; Sennett, 1998). They have underpinned an increasingly individualistic culture in which the fantasy is, to quote Thatcher, that 'there is no such thing as society, only individuals and their families' (Geras, 1998).

Geography has been integral to this crisis. Decreasing barriers to trade, increasingly internationalized finance, and in some industries greater spatial choice in location have all increased the competitive pressures on firms. Management has been able to use the threat of redundancies to extract concessions from their workforce on wages and working practices. The competition of capital has thus been translated into competition between workers. These globalizing tendencies have not been the result merely of changes in communications and information technologies, nor of freeing of markets in the interests of efficiency. Rather, they have to a large extent been a *class strategy* adopted by capital to discipline both labour and individual firms and to reassert the rule of value: globalization has been an integral part of neoliberal strategy (Swyngedouw, 1992; Moran, 1998). The dominant discourse of 'globalization', in which firms, localities and nations 'have to' become leaner and meaner or risk extinction, has facilitated this political strategy.

Yet globalization has not eliminated the role of local economies. To the contrary, local networks of dependencies – local 'socialization' – and the consequent differences between localities have become *more* important for capital. Intensified competition has led many firms to seek closer local linkages with other firms, greater attention to reproduction of their labour force and to local infrastructures, and greater political influence on the local economies in which they operate. Many firms have espoused local in place of district or national bargaining, tying rewards to labour more closely to the profitability of the particular workplace. Global pressures have underpinned ideologies of 'the locality versus the world' within which labour has been encouraged to cooperate more closely with management's projects. This local solidarity for competitiveness has facilitated cooperation between industry, labour, communities, government and quangos in ways which were previously politically difficult (Gough and Eisenschitz, 1996a). Thus the rediscovery of the local economy has not been powered merely by the productive logic of local socialization (Scott, 1998) but also by the class relations that localism promotes. These politics have been underpinned by the fact that most workers continue to have social ties to their locality, albeit of very varied forms and intensities (Cox, 1998). The generally greater mobility of production *in relation to* the mobility of workers (Massey, 1996) then gives capital power over labour.

Global flows and socialization within localities are, then, mutually dependent, though, as we shall see, there are many tensions between them. The interweaving of restructuring at different spatial scales and its impact on labour processes and industrial relations is a major theme of this book.

1.4 Fragmentation versus collectivity of workers

The offensive of capital against labour, both globally and in particular localities, has had success not only in holding down wages and intensifying work but also in weakening the collective organization of workers – reducing union density, restricting legal action, eroding cultures of solidarity and fostering passivity (Martin, Sunley and Wills, 1996). The weakening of the unions has allowed management to change the rules, and the new work practices, in turn, have often been designed to further weaken the possibilities for collective consciousness and action. These developments raise pressing questions about how labour can rebuild its organizations and develop new cultures of solidarity.

Academic theorization of the tensions between fragmentation and collectivity of workers has been thin. Postwar Marxism gave insufficient attention to the sources of fragmentation of the working class. It was too readily assumed that the socialization of production within capitalism creates a solid basis for collective action and consciousness of workers, albeit unevenly realized in practice. In the late 1960s and 1970s the left generally believed, on the basis of impressive displays of working-class solidarity in many countries, that the barriers to mutual understanding and support among different groups of workers were relatively minor and therefore did not need theorizing.[3] This view was to suffer an abrupt reversal of intellectual fashion. From the 1980s, the dominant currents on the left, under the pressure of capital's offensive and labour's defeats, abandoned a perspective of working-class unity. Following suit, most left intellectuals sought to theorize the infeasibility of workers' political unity, on the grounds, variously, of technical features of the division of labour, the displacement of workplace by consumption identities, the division of the working class by 'non-class' forms of oppression, or an *a priori* rejection of 'grand narratives' such as class (see, for example, Laclau and Mouffe, 1985; Hall and Jacques, 1989; for a critique see E. Wood, 1986).

A more grounded approach to thinking about divisions in labour is labour market segmentation theory (Gordon, Edwards and Reich, 1982; Peck, 1996). This seeks to relate differences in workers' roles within production to differences in their roles in social life. However, the production-side distinctions are usually very broadly drawn – between 'core' and 'peripheral' workers, or the secure and the casualized, for example. I therefore develop this approach by a more detailed consideration of the production differences that divide labour, including different labour processes, different types of *change* within them, variation in profitability, and different intensities and forms of competition within industries. These are related to differences in the reproduction sphere and to divisions of gender and ethnicity. Capital accumulation plays a major role in creating segmentation, and I draw out this moment more strongly than is done in much of the segmentation literature.

Overall, I seek to theorize the competition between workers, whether as individuals, members of social groups, or employees in workplaces and local economies, and the way this is constructed by the movement of capital in space. This competition produces contradictory pressures to both individualization and collectivity. Divisions between workers are deepened by the very different resources, pressures, identities and concerns given by the varied competitive conditions, labour processes, labour markets and residential communities in which they participate. These kinds of diversity make it difficult for workers to recognize commonalities in their situation even with others within the same territory, and, *a fortiori*, to develop unity of action against their employers (Gough, 1986; 1992; Martin, Sunley and Wills, 1996: 149–51; Harvey, 2000: 46–7). Such differences have always posed problems for the trade-union movement; they have appeared in a sharp form in recent attempts at community based unionization across diverse sectors (Jonas, 1998; Wills, 2001). But they present barriers to all projects for collective action of workers across occupations and industries.[4]

Nevertheless, common processes and structures underlie these differences and give the potential for mutual comprehension and solidarity. Territories, and localities in particular, can thus be sites where divisions are reproduced, or ones in which collective consciousness and organization can be built (Massey, 1993). They can generate indifference to, or competition with, workers in other territories, or the politics to overcome these. The conclusion of the book is concerned with how the fragmentations of labour might be overcome and collective control of the economy built.

1.5 London as the site of study

London has a paradoxical relation to the current long wave of stagnation of the world economy. On the one hand it has seen this period's characteristic erosion of working and living standards. This has been manifest particularly in the decline in manufacturing employment absolutely and relatively, a rise in unemployment concentrated in poor neighbourhoods, an increase in casualized and low paid service employment, and deterioration of the social infrastructure and large parts of the physical infrastructure. On the other hand, London has been the centre of rapidly expanding financial and business services (Budd and Whimster, 1992; Thrift, 1994), of design and the media, of yuppie jobs and lifestyles. These 'core' sectors have led to problems of inflation, congestion and disrupted reproduction, which have fallen disproportionately on firms and workers *outside* the core (Friend and Metcalf, 1981; King, 1991; Sassen, 1991; Fainstein, Gordon and Harloe, 1992). In short, London has manifested both under and overaccumulation. While this book's focus is on manufacturing, it explores the ways in which this has been influenced by London's core activities. This exemplifies our theme of the relation between rhythms of investment and disinvestment.

Much writing on the neoliberal metropolis has been centred on its growing economic and social inequalities (Friend and Metcalf 1981; Sassen, 1991; Fainstein, Gordon and Harloe, 1992). I develop this issue by investigating the genesis of inequality in differences in labour processes and forms of competition within industries, and the politically disempowering effects these differences have. The book thus makes a distinctive contribution to the literature on metropolises by examining the articulation of value processes, the labour process and reproduction, and the divisions in labour that result.

While London manufacturing has experienced rapid employment decline, it should not be regarded as a mere vestige, as a historical curiosity. At the time of the study, London still had the largest single concentration of manufacturing in Britain. Nor were these merely mature or obsolete industries – in many of them world output was increasing. Nor had the ties of these sectors to London been lost through technical change: they remained strong, but in many cases had been disrupted by the region's development. In short, we are not looking at a 'marginal' manufacturing economy, but rather one whose 'centrality' has been deeply contradictory.

London contains a particularly diverse set of manufacturing industries, and thus provides good opportunities to compare the dynamics of different types of labour process, products, labour power, and competition. London also poses, with particular sharpness, the political problem of the heterogeneity of workers' experiences and identity. Whereas, in towns dominated by a particular industry, workers' and residents' organization is facilitated by shared culture and concerns (Urry, 1985), in large urban areas with diverse sectors collective organization may be weakened by apparent lack of commonality. The metropolis is therefore a good site to explore diversity of work and work identities.[5]

1.6 Theory and case study

This book both develops abstract theory and gives a concrete account of production in a particular place and time; how are these related? In the approach adopted here, abstract concepts and concrete empirical data have a *mediated* relation. Concrete instances are developed from abstract structures through their melding in increasingly complex combinations and, crucially, through the working out of their contradictions. Concrete instances are constructed by the mutual modification of abstractions rather than simply by their addition, so one does not necesssarily find simple correlations between 'causes' and 'effects'. This contrasts with empiricist and positivist approaches where there is assumed to be a one-to-one and immediate relation between concrete and abstract.

In one sense this is a study of a single case – a particular local economy at a particular time; in constructing it only loose and implicit comparisons with other cases are made. But the study also involves systematic comparison between the behaviour of numerous workplaces with different types of labour process, where quantitative patterns are explored. These modes of analysis are combined in the discussion, but the former predominates in Part II and the latter in Parts III and IV.

At the same time as the concrete account is constructed from abstractions, the abstractions themselves are refined. Thus the case study is also a process of development of theory. The book seeks to relate a large number of elements both theoretically and concretely (Figure 1.1), so the account of London manufacturing is built up gradually at different levels of historical and spatial abstraction, while the theoretical work is done by traversing the case study along varied trajectories. Some theoretical themes are developed through multiple 'cuts' (cf. Harvey, 1982), where a problem is treated successively at different levels of abstraction and sometimes also different spatial levels, with one 'cut' building on previous ones.[6]

1.7 The structure of the book

Part I develops a theory of local economies and of workplaces within them, and critiques some existing theories. Chapter 2 analyses local economies and their relation to both larger (global) and smaller (workplace) scales of the economy. It shows how structural features of workers, workplaces and local economies can be related to markets, competition and capital flows, and thus how internal and external processes, in both a logical and a spatial sense, can be distinguished and related. In this framework, the nature and relations of some key structures – the labour process, labour power and local infrastructures – are explored, and contradictions and rhythms of accumulation in local economies examined. We shall be centrally concerned with difference, and I argue that common structures can be used to analyse difference rather than counterposing the two. Chapter 3 discusses the labour process and its relation to product activity. It introduces the relation and tension between the labour process and capital accumulation, and between the use value and exchange value aspects of production. Different forms of labour process change are explored, and models of the labour process critiqued.

Chapter 4 theorizes the dynamics of workplaces on the basis of the discussion in the previous two chapters. Workplace change is pictured as responding to local and non-local stimuli, which can result in successful accumulation or in underaccumulation or overaccumulation within the workplace, paralleling these rhythms in local economies. Firms have a choice of developing their labour processes either through restructuring in situ or by using relocation. Part I is written as abstract theory; exemplification is to be found in the remainder of the book.

Part II examines manufacturing industry in London. Chapter 5 explores the historical construction of the specific types of labour process, product, firms, final markets, labour power and industrial relations found in London, and examines long-term waves of growth, decline and restructuring. Chapter 6 presents a snapshot of London manufacturing during the period of study, 1976–81, drawing on the primary research. The structural attributes of the workplaces studied – their labour processes, product types and form of capital – are presented, and forms of competitive pressure on them analysed. The local markets in labour power and premises are analysed using primary data. Some distinctions in these structures are developed as typologies, which are used in the subsequent analysis.

Part III presents and theoretically constructs the forms of labour process change and spatial behaviour of the study workplaces in the periods of expansion (1976–9) and recession (1980–1). It explores how these are conditioned by structural features of the workplaces, especially the labour process, and by structures of the London and larger scales introduced in Part II. The three chapters of this part discuss particular types of labour process change and how they were achieved in contrasted ways in situ and through relocation. Chapter 7 discusses the ways in which firms sought to raise labour productivity, including fixed investment, intensification by changes in management control and intensification through changing the workforce. Chapter 8 discusses change aimed at improving the product or the quality of production. It argues that labour process theory needs more fully to incorporate consideration of these aspects of the product, and discusses the dialectic of process and product across local economies. Chapter 9 presents the strategies of firms aimed at cutting costs, whether through changing the scale of production, downward pressure on wages, or changing sections of the workforce used. It is argued that cutting costs is more difficult than is often supposed and can conflict with maintaining volume productivity or quality, contradictions which are particularly acute in metropolises.

The final part of the book, Part IV, considers some overall patterns in the case study and draws out further theoretical points. Chapter 10 considers the dynamic tendencies of different labour processes. It examines systematically the relations between different dimensions of labour process change, and between spatial and non-spatial modes of effecting these changes. Chapter 11 considers the relation between the labour process, capital accumulation and the socialization of production, and the ways in which these generate different rhythms of accumulation. These dynamics at different spatial scales – the workplace, the firm, and the local economy – not only interact but are structurally similar to each other. Chapter 12 considers how labour process change and spatial change both vary over the business cycle. It argues that the business cycle deserves more attention from both labour process theorists and economic geographers, and shows how it is an internal structure, and not merely an external condition, of spatial labour process change. On the basis of Chapters 11 and 12, I argue for the need to develop theoretically the relations of the labour process to temporally uneven accumulation.

Finally, Chapter 13 returns to the political problem with which we started: the barriers to workers' cooperation and struggle posed by the heterogeneity of jobs. Building on the previous theorization of locality, it develops an understanding of the fragmentation of workers both by differences within the labour process and the competition of capital. It discusses how a politics for labour could confront this fragmentation and the contemporary offensive of capital and build collective resistance and positive control over the economy. I discuss this kind of politics within the labour process, product-industries, and metropolises, and draw out the implications for the socialist project.

The book can be read with different emphases. To those with a concern for detailed labour process analysis Chapter 3, Part III and Chapter 10 will be of particular interest. Parts I and IV present more abstract considerations of labour processes, capital accumulation and space. Part II and section 13.6 deal with general features of London and metropolitan economies. A guide to major strands of argument running through the book is given in the subject index.

NOTES

1. There are exceptions, but they use very different kinds of distinction of labour processes and its change from the present study. For example, P. Edwards (1986) has discussed labour process change in relation to workplace industrial relations regimes. Steiger (1999) uses a typology of

aspects of the employment relation and skill, but his explicandum is the rate of exploitation, not qualitative labour process change.

2. Massey and Meegan's first study (1979) examined labour process change within seventeen large firms.

3. One needs to go back to Lenin or Trotsky to find major Marxist writers centrally concerned with the political fragmentation of workers and with means of overcoming it, a thread subsequently largely lost in the thought of the official communist parties. The regulation approach, which originated in the latter tradition, tends to understand workers' organization as functionally integrated into the regime of accumulation; labour politics has then either to find a benign productive regime to support, or must voluntaristically invent one (Lipietz, 1992). The *contradictions* of work and worker identities and the possibilities for self-transformation are not theorized in this approach (Gough, 1996b).

4. In popular, as distinct from academic, left discourses, 'divisions among workers' are now usually thought of as social divisions of gender, ethnicity and age, or differences in wages and job security. Differences arising from work processes tend to be neglected.

5. Two major research programmes in the 1980s on localities in Britain (Cooke, 1989; Rubery and Wilkinson, 1994) examined the employment outcomes of local production, but did not go deeply into the dynamics of the latter nor focus on labour processes. The localities researched were mostly medium-sized towns with a limited range of industries, as was the important work of the Lancaster research group, in contrast to the highly diverse metropolis studied here.

6. There are further discussions of method in sections 2.1, 2.2 and 6.2, the introduction to Part III, and section 10.4.

Part I
Work in Localities

2 LOCAL ECONOMIES

2.1 Workplace, locality and world: the problem of scale

In the introduction we saw that both global and local scales can be important in understanding workplace change. In recent years there have been some important investigations of the relations between these scales (for example Swyngedouw, 1992; 1997; Howitt, 1993; Massey, 1993; Jonas, 1994; 1996; Cox, 1997; Harvey, 2000). However, no framework has been put forward which is adequate for the present study, that is, to understand detailed change in individual workplaces within a particular territory in the context of larger scales. As Neil Smith (1989) argued on the basis of a survey of radical economic geography to that date, there is a need for theoretical work that integrates the spatial-economic behaviour of workplaces (location theory) with an analysis of uneven development at varied scales. Smith argued that such an understanding of scalar economic relationships needs to be founded on the fundamental processes of capitalist economies (what he termed a 'return to theory'). The concrete analysis of particular workplaces in particular places and times can then be thoroughly theoretically informed – and informing. More than ten years later, this theoretical gap remains. In this part of the book I accordingly develop a framework for thinking through a set of scalar relations rooted in fundamental capitalist processes: between the workplace and key elements of the local economy such as labour markets and property, between the workplace and the 'sectors' to which it belongs, and between local and global economies.

The problem of scale has two theoretical-political dimensions:

- *A problem of causality and power.* In what sense can the behaviour of workplaces, firms and local economies be attributed to processes respectively 'internal' and 'external' to them? This is a key political, as well as theoretical, question. Much political-economic debate consists in apportioning 'blame' for failures between these levels: firms blame local, national or global conditions for their failures, governments blame management or labour within particular firms or industries for those same failures, and so on. For labour, the question of at which spatial and organizational level to act is a pressing concern: whether to act as an individual (watching out for your own job, switching to a better one elsewhere), or to act collectively with workers in the same workplace, firm, district or industry, or more widely still? At what spatial level are the adequate levers to be found?

- *A problem of specificity.* Academic writing in recent years has been centrally concerned with difference, for example with the specificity of particular types of firm, industry or locality *vis-à-vis* larger aggregates. Yet it is impossible to speak of what this 'difference' is without resort to concepts that span those differences. Concrete difference, then, has to be constructed from abstract categories, but how can this be done in a non-reductionist way? How can a politics be developed that both enables unity of workers around common problems and common structures of the global economy *and* that is adequate for the individual worker or distinct groups of workers and sensitive to their particular situations?

Mainstream theory has given some answers to these questions, but they are misleading.

Neoclassical economic theory understands the relation between individuals, firms and the economy as a whole through partial or general equilibrium theory: in the absence of market 'imperfections' there is a harmony between the aspirations of individuals and firms on the one hand (utility or profit maximization) and the behaviour of economic aggregates on the other. Urban economic analysis then focuses on land markets because these are seen as the problematic element of local economies due to the inherently monopolistic nature of land, but neoclassical economics gives no account of the historical and social constitution of the worker, consumer or firm; the specification of their properties is not only one-dimensional but is prior to the economy and society as a whole. The part-whole dialectic is thus radically truncated from the first. Moreover, the weak notion of the economic whole in neoclassical economics, where it appears merely as an aggregation of interacting parts, is manifestly inadequate in understanding local economies. Durable structures and arrangements such as the built environment, physical and social infrastructures, business culture and industrial relations traditions cannot be thought about within this framework.

Keynesian and institutionalist theory, in its many different paths, takes economy-wide processes somewhat more seriously. The market 'imperfections' that are the focus of Keynesian theory are socially constructed (for example 'animal spirits', risk aversion, segmented labour markets) or represent inherently social interactions (flows of demand between different parts of an economy, the relation between finance and production). In the analysis of local economies this tradition has focused on flows of demand (Myrdal, 1957), transaction costs understood as an imperfection of market exchange (Scott, 1988), and on durable ties between actors within a local economy, for example within 'industrial districts' (Lorenz, 1992; Grabher, 1993). These approaches have given important insights, but the relations between worker, firm, local economy and global economy still remain *external* ones. This is because these units are regarded as fundamentally related through exchange in markets, albeit that these exchanges are 'imperfect'; neoclassical economics is still the foundation of Keynesian theory. The social nature of the economy is thus always secondary to markets, and the social *constitution* of the worker, firm or local economy is missed.

A third perspective on the relation between firm and economy is that of the *systems or behavioural theory of the firm* (Hayter and Watts, 1983; Taylor and Conti, 1997). The firm is in interaction with its 'environment', and each is a distinct system. This approach was developed in reaction to perceived theoretical inflexibilities of neoclassical and Keynesian approaches, particularly in dealing with large firms. It allows the theorist to specify the relevant attributes of the firm, its environment and their geographies in an 'open' – in practice eclectic – fashion. The crucial problem, again, is that the nature of firm and environment are given separately *prior to* their interaction; there is no sense that they may be constituted by common processes.

In contrast, the tradition of *Marxist theory* is to regard the nature and dynamics of firms, and of larger units of the economy such as industries or local economies, as fundamentally constituted by economy- and society-wide processes. There are certainly different ways within Marxism of conceiving these relations;[1] I will use the concept of *internal relations* (Ollman, 1993; Harvey, 1996). Rather than starting from the atoms of the economy (workers, consumers, firms) and aggregating them, the economy as a whole, and indeed the society as a whole, is understood as a totality. The parts, aspects and structures of the totality are 'moments' of it and moments of each other: each part is constituted by the others. Social actors such as individuals and firms are thus constituted by the social relations into which they enter; thus capital and labour do not exist except in relation to each other, and both are constituted by their relation. This does not lead to a functionalist analysis in which the parts serve the smooth functioning of the whole, since the processes constituting the totality are assumed to be contradictory, that is, they are intrinsically unstable and dynamic. Nor does an internal relations approach mean that one needs to know everything in order to understand anything, or that the parts of the social whole have no differentiation or integrity (*pace* Sayer, 1995). Investigation is always necessarily centred on a particular region of society, selected by the interest of the analyst or social actor, and other parts are called into the analysis on the basis of their proximity (Ollman, 1993). Moreover, in the Marxist as distinct from idealist and postmodern conceptions of internal relations, the individuation and naming of the parts of society is not arbitrary: processes and the social units they define are based on the material nature of human life and on the forms of consciousness that both reproduce and change these. In consequence, some internal relations are stronger and more formative than others.

Within this approach, I shall use the term 'structure' to denote both *social relations*, such as the capital-labour relation, and *social processes and dynamics*, such as the tendency to the overaccumulation of capital.[2] Contrary to common usage, structures here are not static but always already dynamic, open to struggle and integrally involving it (Gunn, 1989). Such structures are mutually constituting; for example, the tendency to overaccumulation of productive capital arises partly from capital's attempts to free itself from excessive dependence on living labour, thus reproducing labour's subordination to capital.

Such structures then enable us to conceptualize the scalar links between workplaces, industries and local and global economies as internal relations. A particular social relation may imbue each of these spatial levels of the economy. The capital-labour relation, for example, operates at the global level (as ubiquitous processes of exploitation and formation of capital and labour), at the local level (the use by locally located capital of local labour power; specific local industrial relations practices), and at the workplace level (the firm's particular use of its labour force). Each of these spatial levels is essential to how this social relation works. Relations within the workplace are founded on the ubiquitous capital-labour relation; they are influenced by markets in capital and labour power at every spatial level from the world to the locality; and the workplace's industrial relations are specific, differentiated forms of those at higher spatial levels.

Conversely, the larger scales depend on the smaller. Capital is inherently *private and parcelled*, and workers are constituted as *individual* sellers of labour power. In contrast to exploitation in precapitalist class societies, this privatism is central to how the capital-labour relation works through the competition of firms and of workers which it generates. Thus it is not merely that the concept of the capital-labour relation can be 'applied' at different spatial levels. The workplace, local economy and global economy internalize a common relation. Moreover, this relation is constituted simultaneously at these different spatial levels. The common counterposition of 'micro' and 'macro' is thus fundamentally misleading. The task of the present study, to relate workplaces to larger economic scales, can thus be based on an internal relations approach.

2.2 Difference and materialist dialectics

Within this framework, how can one theorize difference? It is a truism that we live our lives as particular individuals and collectives in particular spatio-temporal milieux, and that abstractions in themselves are no guide to practice. All social theory must therefore be open to particularity, to situation, to conjuncture. The question is *how* difference is to be grasped. The post-modern denunciation of 'grand narratives' and 'essentialism' is based on the assumption that the use of abstractions necessarily obliterates empirical detail and texture. Now, this is certainly true of much deductive empiricism, in which abstractions are developed in an *a priori* fashion; thus the neo-classical notion of the firm is inherently incapable of being the basis for a rich account of concrete firms. But this is not true of all abstractions. The abstract structures proposed by Marxism can be developed dialectically to produce difference. Schematically, this occurs in four ways.

(a) Social relations of power constitute and thus differentiate social actors – capitalists from workers, men from women, and so on. Similarly, many social processes are about the creation of polarities: the processes of spatial uneven development create differences between local econo-mies, for example.

(b) Many social differences *appear as* distinct and fundamentally hetero-geneous structures (Derrida's *différances*). A relevant example is the distinction between the spheres of production and reproduction respectively, associated with a plethora of differences from their forms of time regulation to their property relations. Much social science is content to treat production and reproduction dualistically, as funda-mentally distinct systems, which may then have secondary interaction with each other (for example Castells, 1996: 14–17). In the internal relations approach, however, production and reproduction, and their difference, are *constituted by* their mutual relation. Capitalism creates a particular divide between these realms defined by value and non-value production; reproduction depends on the division of labour and rewards within wage labour; production depends on the types of labour power reproduced outside it; and so on. Thus it is not merely that heterogeneous structures come into interaction, but also that the difference between these structures is constructed by their mutual relations.

(c) Structures meld with each other in ways that are spatially and temporally specific. Structures can then be specified at different levels of spatial and temporal abstraction. These differentiations of structures are not counterposed to their abstract forms but are developments of them.

(d) The *contradictory* nature of structures produces tensions and dilemmas which allow a range of possible paths to be followed. The capital-labour relation, for example, is contradictory in that capital seeks both to exert discipline over workers and to elicit active cooperation from them. This tension gives rise to endless dilemmas for both management and workers, and the articulation of discipline and cooperation pans out in very different ways in different settings and over time in the same setting (see further Chapter 3). Thus contradiction gives the opportunity for both structural difference *and* for agency, conscious strategy and choice.

In these ways difference can be developed out of abstract structures, providing these are understood as materially-based, relational and contradictory. The postmodern rejection of 'essentialist' abstraction is based on the positivist premise that there must be a *one-to-one* and *immediate* relation between concrete and abstract, producing accounts that are descriptive or, at best, taxonomic. In contrast, the approach adopted here can *explain* difference and reveal its limits and its dynamics.

2.3 A key structure: the labour process

With these preliminaries, we can now consider the constitution of local economies. Our starting point and central thread is the labour process. Interest in the labour process in the developed countries was re-awakened in the early 1970s by sharp workers' struggles. Following Braverman's influential though controversial *Labour and Monopoly Capital* (1974), there was an explosion of study and debate within a variety of theoretical and political perspectives (for overviews see S. Wood (1989a), Thompson (1989), Knights and Willmott (1990), Berberoglu (1993) and Wardell, Steiger and Meiskens (1999)). Marxists in particular sought to go beyond traditional industrial sociology by analysing the organization of work as class relations governed by capital accumulation (Braverman, 1974; Conference of Socialist Economists, 1976; Gorz, 1978; Levidow and Young, 1981), a project that I follow.

Facets of the labour process

The labour process, in the sense used in this book, has five aspects (following Friedman, 1986):

(i)   the *technical nature* of the production process: the material forms of production technology, raw materials, transformations performed on them, and final form of the product;
(ii) the *tasks* necessary to carry out these transformations, including the nature of the human capacities used;
(iii) the *control of labour by management*, including the allocation of tasks to jobs (the 'technical division of labour'), the means of imposing discipline on workers with respect to both the speed and quality of work, the resistance of workers to this discipline, and the resultant unstable forms of negotiation of labour tasks;
(iv) *employment relations*, including the segment of the labour force employed, hours of daily or weekly employment, security of employment, and the allocation of types of workers to such differentiated jobs;
(v)   the *relations between workers within work*, including communication necessary to progress the work and that sought by workers for their own purposes, set within the unequal statuses arising from the division of labour.

These aspects of the labour process are internally related moments of a single structure. Thus the forms of control exerted by management are chosen to be most appropriate to the given material nature of technology and its associated tasks; indeed, only some control strategies may be at all feasible given a particular technology. Conversely, technology and tasks are themselves shaped by management with the aim of improving its control (Marglin, 1978). For example, a flow line may be introduced as a means of better regulating the speed of work (Palloix, 1976; Aglietta, 1979); production technology or the product itself may be designed with the aim of deskilling the associated tasks (Noble, 1979; Cooley, 1986); or, with given technology, tasks may be redesigned in order to increase their speed or decrease their skill requirements. Thus while technologies of production and products are largely developed by designers separately from the direct workers, these designs are partly built around management's control aims (Hales, 1980). Nor, contrary to geographical systems theory, are technologies simply formed 'outside' the firm in the scientific 'environment' or the world industry and subsequently adopted by the firm: firms are active developers of technology even where they do not have their own research and development, because technology is moulded to control.

The skills necessary for carrying out a particular task are distinct from the skills attached to jobs: the latter are particular sets of the former, which emerge from struggles over control, worker autonomy and employment relations. Control and employment aspects of the labour process are also mutually dependent. Management selects segments of the labour force (by gender, age, and so on) to fill jobs of particular skill and autonomy, not simply on the basis of their 'skills' but what management thinks those workers will tolerate; the latter is itself shaped by historical practices in particular territories and by expectations of the workers concerned. The logic does not run simply from the nature of the job to the segment selected; the skills and autonomy of jobs are shaped by the segment of the workforce employed. Indeed, even production technologies, and *a fortiori* tasks and jobs, may be shaped by the section of the labour force employed, for instance by its gender (Cockburn, 1985). Job specifications are connected with labour segment also through hours of work and security of employment. Socially and geographically defined segments of the workforce have different capacities to work particular hours and to bargain over hours and job security. Moreover, job skills, hours and security are linked. Hours and security of work constrain the type of skills that can be acquired and for which the employer is prepared to give training, whereas management may make concessions on hours and security in order to hold skilled workers.

The interactions between workers are conditioned by managements' control strategies. Tasks and the technical division of labour may be designed by management in such a way as to require interaction and coordination between workers, thus enhancing flexibility when problems arise, or they may minimize such interactions in order to isolate the worker and enhance management's control of task coordination. Employment relations can be designed to encourage collective identity among workers (as part of the firm rather than as part of a class) or to foster division. These relations are an important basis of workers' collective organization and in turn a product of it.

The notion of the labour process is useful in underlining the mutual construction of these aspects, which otherwise tend to be dealt with by separate academic and technical discourses (industrial engineering, work design, production management, industrial sociology, labour market theory, and so on). This is not to argue that the labour process is a smoothly functioning articulation of its different aspects – to the contrary. In the discussion above, none of the aspects of the labour process simply *determines* the others. A given machine will constrain the tasks performed with it, but the range of uses made of it may vary widely and the associated jobs even more so. Attempts by management to increase speed of work may be pursued either by imposition of more direct supervision and measurement or on the contrary by allowing greater worker autonomy over the detailed scheduling of the work process (cf. section 2.2 (d); P. Edwards, 1986). Jobs of a given type may be filled from different labour force segments at different times depending on management's control or labour market strategies. These indeterminacies arise because all aspects of the labour process are conflictual, and because of the many contradictions and dilemmas that run through it. Thus the labour process is an *unstable* interpenetration of its different aspects: internal relations of distinct elements are not mechanical fits.

The labour process, class relations, and conflict

Running across these aspects of the labour process is a distinction between concrete material forms and general social relations, or in traditional Marxist terminology the forces and relations of production. On the one hand we have the material form of workplaces, machines, products, tasks and workers' capacities, on the other the relations between management and workers and among workers, the directly social and political moments of the labour process. The forces of production are use values, always particular and concrete.[3] The relations of production, by contrast, are centred around the production of value and the struggle to extract surplus value. The enormous variety of the use values of production results, in part, from the complexity of the natural world and its elaboration by technical development, but we have already seen that these material aspects of the labour process are shaped by the specifically capitalist social relations in which they are set. Moreover, the social relations of different labour processes have much in common despite their material differences (Spencer, 2000). Our analysis needs to maintain this theoretical tension. The relations between the material and the social aspects of labour processes will be a central focus of this study.

The labour process is the key site of labour's disempowerment within capitalism. In distinction to previous class societies, the ruling class is not guaranteed a surplus by political arrangements prior to production; capital therefore has to ensure *through its control of the labour process* – 'the real subsumption of labour' – that more value is produced by the workforce than it is paid in wages (Burawoy, 1985). The labour process is thus the site for the creation of surplus value and hence for capital accumulation (Cohen, 1987). By the same token, the labour process is inextricably a matter of power and politics. Indeed, capitalist society is unique among class societies in that political power is located and reproduced within production itself, rather than in military and legal institutions. Labour is subordinated to capital through its dependence on the wage, the need to compete for jobs, and the need for (potential) employers to be profitable enough to provide those jobs. Labour is then subordinated within the labour process itself both because of workers' need to hold onto their job *and* because the firm reproduces itself only through the production of adequate surplus value. Thus the subordination of labour within capitalism is located in the labour market *and* the labour process. It is in the first place economic rather than juridical and private rather than public (E. Wood, 1995: Ch.1).

The power of capital within and through production is nonetheless always and everywhere contested. This has caused many labour process theorists to avoid the notion of managerial 'control'; the original work of Braverman, in particular, has been extensively criticized for occluding the subjectivity and active role of workers (for example Isaac and Christiansen, 1999). I use the notion of control because, as just noted, the creation of surplus value requires a minimum degree of control by capital over the work process. I take 'control' to be a chronic *project* of capital rather than a 'structural given'. Individual or collective resistance to the creation of surplus value is always present, and indeed 'control' is necessary partly because of this resistance (R. Edwards, 1979; Herod, 1997). Nor does 'control' imply that workers take no initiative within the work process, as we explore further section 3.5. In a more passive mode, workers may substantially consent to the targets set by management and thus sustain them (Knights and Collinson, 1985). There are complex hermeneutics between management and workforce such that overt control, resistance, compliance, and active consent construct each other and evolve over time (P. Edwards, 1986). The agency of workers is, then, crucial to understanding labour processes. However, as Smith and Thompson (1999) have emphasized, in focusing on workers' interventions we should not lose sight of the ways in which they are materially founded.

Much labour process literature since the 1980s has sought to emphasize workers' ways of coping day-to-day within the workplace, their actions as individuals, and their self-identities. In an influential work, Burawoy (1979) argued that workers cope by playing games that may even lead them to exceed managerial targets. Much writing has concerned forms of individual resistance that have little impact on the organization of work or extraction of surplus value. These processes have been developed in Foucauldian work to argue that workers may adopt identities that are incompatible with collective action, and indeed that their individual actions make them collude in their own oppression (Knights, 1990). This ends up closing off possibilities of broad *collective* action and, *a fortiori*, collective control (Gibson-Graham, 1996). However, as Martinez Lucio and Stewart (1997) have argued, this neglects the socialized and collaborative nature of production, both within workplaces and between them – expressed in the social definition of value in Marxist theory. This gives the potential for collective consciousness and resistance.

These points have important implications for understanding the politics of production. Much work on industrial organization has used an institutionalist approach within which production organization and labour markets are *shaped by* political and cultural structures (Granovetter and Swedberg, 1992). This approach has a Weberian premise, that there is an economic/production system and a cultural/political system that exist prior to their external 'interaction'. Production is then constituted in the first place by abstract 'markets' and technological change, so that at the most fundamental level it is apolitical and acultural. But we have seen that the labour process is a process of exploitation, and is always conflictual, so that politics and culture are *intrinsic to it* rather than an external influence upon it (E. Wood, 1995: Chs 3 and 4; Spencer, 2000).

The labour process and space

From the mid-1980s labour process theorists increasingly argued that the dynamics of work are bound up with industrial and political structures beyond the workplace. The influences on production strategies of national and local labour markets and their segmentation have been investigated (Littler, 1979; Kelly, 1985; Friedman, 1990). Final product markets shape management's organization of the work process (Edwards and Scullion, 1982; Kelly, 1985). And the labour process needs to be set within a wider set of political relations (Burawoy, 1985; Cohen, 1987; Thompson, 1989; Eldrige, Cressey and MacInnes, 1991). In the rest of this chapter and in Chapter 3

I discuss some of these wider connections and their spatiality. In doing this, however, as Thompson (1990) has argued, it is important not to lose sight of the ways in which labour power, product markets and so on are not autonomous areas of management strategy but both shape and are shaped by the labour process; the latter will thus remain central to the analysis.

Localities vary enormously in their ensembles of labour processes, and this specialization is being deepened rather than diluted by intensifying global flows. Even within a particular industry, or with the use of a particular production technology, the labour process can vary greatly between different localities. At the core of this differentiation is the local rootedness and durability not only of fixed capital but also of managerial control and employment relations. These are developed in relation to other elements of the local economy, to which we now turn.

2.4 Work and workers in localities

We have seen schematically how the labour process is shaped by workers' skills, attitudes, organization and resistance, and by social divisions within the labour force. How is this labour force produced within and outside of production?

One literature in which this has been addressed is labour segmentation theory. Early work (Berger and Piore, 1980) investigated the construction of differences within the labour force by the use of labour by employers, with causality running from production to labour power. Later work has included the reverse causality, arguing that the reproduction sphere plays a key part in producing differentiated labour power, and moreover that this labour power can then influence the development of the labour process (R. Edwards, 1979; Gordon, Edwards and Reich, 1982; Kelly, 1985). These dialectics operate not only at national but also at local levels (Peck, 1996). These 'horizontal' divisions within labour, however, need to be understood in their internal relations with 'vertical' power relations between the classes.

Let us start with the 'sphere of reproduction' – households, neighbourhoods, purchased consumer commodities, and state services. This involves a complex set of social relations that are centred around unpaid labour within households and its strongly gendered division of labour. With the freedom of the labourer within capitalism, reproduction is in the first place the reproduction of *people*, not potential workers; but a considerable amount of reproduction labour is deliberately directed towards shaping people's employment capacities, and much of the rest has this as an unintended consequence. The labour process is dependent on this local reproduction of labour power (Vogel, 1983; Barrett, 1988).

The reproduction sphere produces labour power which is strongly socially differentiated. People's work capacities are constructed in the long term by their household incomes and those of their neighbourhoods. Moreover, the labour power of people of different gender and age is differentiated by the social relations of households, in both the long-term formation of capacities and short-term constraints on their waged employment (Barrett, 1988; Hanson and Pratt, 1995). These differences form the basis for the use by firms of different 'segments' of the labour force.

The reproduction sphere is differentiated by locality. This is so partly because of processes proper to that sphere itself: particular local traditions within the home, the dynamics of gendered household labour, racial discrimination in housing provision, or specific local forms of welfare provision (Walby and Bagguley, 1989; Bagguley et al., 1990; Watson, 1992). However, the reproduction sphere is also strongly shaped by local production. Income from wages obviously affects reproduction practices and outcomes. The spectrum of local employment and its segmentation affect gender, 'racial' and inter generational relations within the home and neighbourhood. The skills, status and security acquired in waged work strongly affect people's identities, outlook, ways of life and relations with other local people. Production based skills, or the expectation of acquiring them in the future, affect the use made of public services and thus the development of those services themselves. The local specificities of the reproduction sphere, then, are not only *sui generis* but also strongly constructed by local production.

An implication is that labour power is not simply an exogenous input into production, as it is portrayed in neoclassical and systems approaches, but is partly constructed by production itself. Much radical work has argued that localities in the contemporary economy are distinguished above all by their labour power and reproduction spheres (Castells 1977; Swyngedouw, 1992). But the latter is largely produced by local production; it is *the interrelation of the two* that differentiates localities.

The labour process and the reproduction of labour power are, then, internally related in myriad ways; indeed, we may speak of them as a single, differentiated structure. This structure has a particular geography: daily commuting distances constrain most workers' links between the two spheres, and the reproduction sphere coheres primarily on the basis of daily personal contacts and use of services. Thus local distance and local area are intrinsic to the internal relations between labour process and reproduction sphere. Since they inherently involve space, we may term structures of this type 'spatially effective structures'.[4] The relation between labour process and reproduction sphere is thus a 'locally effective structure' – one within which locality plays a constitutive role.

For two social structures to be internally related, their relation must have a certain durability. Many of the elements that make up the reproduction sphere have this durable quality. The role of cultural tradition and habit is significant because many workers spend a large section of their lives within the same locality, although this tends to be less true the higher the person's income. Cultures of worker collectivity, in particular, benefit from such continuity (Thernstrom, 1984). But even in localities with high labour migration, as in parts of London, the qualities of the reproduction sphere are perpetuated by other means: the qualities and prices of consumer services and social and physical infrastructures, and the influence of the production sphere. Thus local culture may be transmitted not only directly between generations but indirectly via the economic and physical conditions of the locality.

Despite these forms of inertia, local reproduction spheres change continually. Due to the dynamism of capitalist investment in production and its constant restructuring, it is often this sphere that leads change. This frequently creates dissonance with the supply of labour power and with the traditions of the local reproduction sphere more generally. Contradictions in the labour process-reproduction nexus can also erupt through change originating in domestic gender relations, household formation, housing, transport, public services, youth culture, and so on. Once again, terming the labour process-reproduction nexus a 'structure' does not imply that it is functional or free from contradiction. Policies aiming to influence production, and those directed at the reproduction sphere, are often deflected from their aims precisely because of the interpenetration of the labour process and reproduction, so that policy may be pushed into addressing both simultaneously (Eisenschitz and Gough, 1993: Ch.6).

Locally distinctive industrial relations are produced by this *combination* of production and reproduction (Warde, 1988, 1992; Peck, 1992; Jonas, 1996). Local labour processes, and the forms of competition playing on them, strongly shape industrial relations. Attitudes to work, capitalist discipline and workers' solidarity are also reproduced in social life, differentiated by locality (Wills, 1998). Local gender relations (themselves arising from the production-reproduction nexus), as well as constraining women's access to jobs, can produce distinctive attitudes to work and trade unionism among men and women respectively (McDowell and Massey, 1984). Local divisions between ethnic groups profoundly affect industrial relations for both dominant and oppressed ethnicities (Waldinger, 1986; Maguire, 1988). Locally particular conditions of reproduction such as high housing prices can affect workers' attitudes to wage bargaining. The social as well as the production sphere is thus central to the formation of relations in production. Locality can be as much a resource for resistance by workers as a site for their discipline and control (Massey, 1996; Herod, 1997; Isaac and Christiansen, 1999).[5]

While labour markets and industrial relations are strongly constituted by locally effective structures, they are nevertheless set within *national* practices of production and reproduction (Smith and Thompson, 1999; Edwards and Elger, 1999). The degree of local variation differs between countries. Indeed, in each country, this spatial unevenness affects class relations and is thus an integral part of the national labour regime.

2.5 The built environment and local production

Industrial premises and physical infrastructures are an important – though usually neglected – part of the technical aspect of the labour process. As with labour power, the built environment and labour processes within a locality are mutually constructing. Structures of provision of the built environment (Ball, 1988) vary significantly between localities. These supply industrial and commercial premises to firms according to anticipated demand; wider physical infrastructures are also developed partly in response to firms' needs as well as those of residents. The stock of the built environment is built up over a long period and has a large inertia because of both its physical durability and its financial depreciation over a long period – that is, both use value and value reasons. The stock is thus a locally differentiated product of the history of the labour process in the locality. The local prices of land are also in part determined by production, whose local profitability feeds through to ground rent (Roweis and Scott, 1981). Thus production and the local built environment are strongly internally related.

Once again, this nexus is unstable and dynamic. Changes in local labour processes, as well as merely quantitative changes in output, can create serious mismatches between production demands and the built environment. Even for slowly changing and long-standing types of labour process, if their profitability is low the building stock can become inadequate due to lack of upkeep or diversion to alternative uses. Property developers and their financiers may then boycott the area, causing further deterioration. The land market can also cause disruption: if a firm, sector or labour process develops a locationally associated rate of profit below that of the average for the area, it will find itself under pressure from land price. Thus the 'locally effective structure' encompassing labour process and built environment is contradictory. Again, this manifests itself in difficulties in policy: policies for industry are sometimes deformed by their repercussions in the property market, and initiatives in the built environment are often derailed by the dynamics of the occupier producers.

2.6 Competition between localities through the labour process

One of the directions taken in the 'widening' of labour process studies has been to take account of the form and intensity of competition within the industry (Friedman 1977; 1990; Terry, 1989; Marchington and Parker, 1990).[6] It is argued that managements will attempt to change the labour process, and will do so in particular ways, as a function of the competitive pressures acting on the workplace. This insight has important implications for local economies.

Competition *presents itself* as an external relation. Independent firms act in response to the actions of competitor firms that are outside of their control and thus appear as an external force. This is the conception of competition in neoclassical economics. The kernel of truth here is that investment in industries does indeed develop through the decisions of individual firms, which are mostly uncoordinated *a priori*, and coordinated *a posteriori* only through highly uneven valorization and devalorization. Similarly, local industries face apparently external competition from rival localities.

Competition may thus appear as the result of actions of known competitors, but it also seems an external force beyond *anyone's* control, appearing as the fetishistic mechanisms of value and capital valorization. Firms in an industry producing a particular product – what I shall call a 'product-industry'[7] – have their costs of production commensurated by competition, giving a value to their product which then imposes itself on each firm. Profit rates on capital also tend to be commensurated, causing capital flows into and out of the industry's firms and workplaces. The system thus imposes norms on each firm that *abstract from* its particular labour processes, labour and local roots – something that is often the cause of strong political resentment. This abstraction is not simply a theoretical process of ignoring inessentials. Rather, it is a 'determinate abstraction' effected by material social processes, in this case inter firm competition and capital accumulation (Marx, 1976 ed.; Gunn, 1989).

But competition is also, crucially, *internal* to the workplace, firm or locality.

It arises from the institution of private capitalist property, which internally constitutes all scales of the economy from the firm to the globe, and which are measured against each other through value and capital valorization. More concretely, capitals compete by means of *internal* processes and class relations. Local sectors compete through altering relations of control within the labour process (section 2.3), by product innovation and its attendant labour process changes, through collective policies on training or the built environment (sections 2.4 and 2.5), through restructuring firm ownership and internal controls, and through conflicts between productive and money capital. Competition, then, is not only an external relation but a set of class conflicts *internal* to firms and local sectors (Bryan, 1985; Gough, 1991).

The local sector may react to competitive pressures within the product-industry in two different modes. It may attempt to adjust its locally specific structures so as to bring them *closer* to those in a 'more successful' locality. An alternative mode of adjustment is for the local sector to *differentiate* itself from the rest of the product-industry, with the hope that this will yield higher-than-average rates of profit. Thus the determinate abstractions effected by competition may push towards either homogenization or differentiation of the industry (Smith and Thompson, 1999; for examples see Rainnie, 1984; Marsden, Lowe and Whatmore, 1992). The path taken by a particular local sector depends on its class relations. For example, in localities where labour organization is weak, capital may be inclined to cheapen wages and casualize employment, with impacts on the labour process and the reproduction sphere; whereas where labour is strong, capital may choose strategies centred around product innovation, skill upgrading or mechanization.

Through these processes, taking place continually within every locality, the product-industry as a whole changes. Relative growth rates of localities shift, and some localities drop out of the system altogether while others enter it. The dominant accumulation paths within the industry change, as some prove more successful than others, and hence too the reference points for local sectors. Product specialization between localities shifts. In short, the spatial division of labour is constructed through structural processes internal to localities, including social struggles. These shifts then define new average costs of production and average profit rates on capital, taking us back to our starting point. The dynamics of a product-industry and its spatial form can thus be understood as a dialectic of *external competition and commensuration within the industry* with *the locally specific and locally effective structures that make it up.*[8]

This analysis has vital implications for the politics of local sectors. In selling restructuring to workforces, capital often appeals to forces which it portrays as external, impersonal and beyond control: the actions of competitor localities, technological change, or low average profit rates (these days often referred to vaguely as 'globalization'). These are portrayed as something other than what is transacted within the workplace, firm or locality itself. But the latter are formed by structures that are not 'out there' but ubiquitous, equally there *and* here (section 2.1). Competition is realized through changes in the structures of local sectors that are, in their basic form, ubiquitous – even though the local variation of these structures makes them more difficult to recognize as such. Moreover, the externality of competition is premised on a ubiquitous structure, private capitalist property. The competitive struggle between industries in different localities is thus always also class struggle within each, although capitalist discourse always focuses on the former rather than the latter.

2.7 Demand and local economies

Demand, like competition, appears from the viewpoint of a firm as an external constraint, and is figured in this way in neoclassical economics. However, the picture changes completely if one changes scale: the larger the scale, the more strongly is demand a function of production – an internal relation that, again, greatly complicates economic governance.

In the case of large local economies, a substantial part of the demand for manufactures may be local and hence derive from local production: contracting within the local sector or between manufacturing sectors, sales to local non-manufacturing enterprises, or sales to local consumers. Demand for, and thus growth of, local sectors is then a function of (i) the range and character of local sectors, derived from the agglomeration dynamics of the region, and (ii) the incomes and tastes of local consumers, derived from locally specific class, gender and other social relations arising from both production and reproduction spheres. We shall see that such socially created local demand was important in shaping many London manufacturing sectors. Demand flows within the locality, then, are important not only in a quantitative sense (the local multiplier), but as expressions of the qualitative character of the local ensemble of production and reproduction relations.

2.8 Socialization, conflict and contradiction in local economies

Local economies in capitalist societies are constituted in the first place by the fragmented interests of firms and persons based on their private property.

Yet these are coordinated through webs of non-market ties, the 'socialization of production' to use the classical Marxist term. Indeed, we should widen this notion to include non-market coordination of the reproduction sphere and its links to production. Socialization does not merely link but *constitutes* the social actors in a locality (in other words, the social actors become internally related). Partly because socialization proceeds through conscious, political arrangements rather than 'natural' market exchanges, it is prone to political conflict. I examine in turn the elements of socialization, how it contributes to accumulation, and how both socialization and local accumulation may be disrupted.

We have already seen the importance of the internal relations between labour processes, labour power, the reproduction sphere, and the built environment. The relations between local firms, too, may be closer than merely short term exchanges of goods and services, and may include long-term contracting arrangements, collaboration on product design, granting of credit, the winning of a reputation, or collaboration to provide common services (Camagni, 1991; Grabher, 1993). What the firms *are* is, then, strongly a function of their mutual relations. Local scale is, here, more than a container for these relations, because local distances facilitate these close forms of interchange, and rootedness in the locality motivates them. Similarly, there may be particular business cultures – characteristic accumulation paths – within the locality that involve not only pervasive *ideas* about how to do business but particular *relations* between firms, infrastructure providers, labour and so on, these practical relations giving the culture durability. These relatively durable local class relations and forms of social power may then also be understood as locally effective structures.

Local socialization can contribute positively to long-term, sustained capital accumulation within the locality. This has been emphasized since the 1980s by the 'new regional economics', which has focused on the productiveness and competitiveness of industrial districts, 'learning regions', 'networked regions', and so on (Amin and Thrift, 1995; Scott, 1998; Storper, 1998). This literature has, however, focused on relations between firms and institutions, neglecting relations between capital and labour, between workers and between residents. A better conceptualization is Harvey's (1985a; 1985b) notion of the 'structured coherence' of the local economy, which includes not only inter firm relations but the full range of class and social relations. These are underpinned by what Cox and Mair (1988; 1991; Cox, 1998) term the 'local dependence' of social actors, which leads to projects to sustain their mutual relations and hence to powerful ideologies of locality. All of these conceptions point to the ability of local socialization to sustain accumulation; to this extent, these local relations are 'coherent' from the standpoint of capital. Sustained accumulation then enables the elements that contribute to it – fixed capital, labour power, harmonious industrial relations, infrastructures, and so on – to be well reproduced and hence contribute to further accumulation, a circular process I will refer to as *reinforcing accumulation.*[9]

However, local socialization may produce weak accumulation or actively impede it. Local social relations may contain tensions that lead to internal disruptions both 'political' and 'economic'. Local capital may find it difficult to mould local conditions to its needs. There are varied sources of such failures. Firstly, the *relation between local socialization and wider socio-economic structures* may break down. We have seen how this may occur in competition of the locality within a product-industry. Local reproduction relations and services are always dependent on structures at higher spatial scales, and these may come into conflict with the local practices. Much local politics, then, consists of mediating *between* local and non-local processes (Cox and Mair, 1991). Secondly, *contradictions internal to particular structures of the local economy* may break through. For example, local relational subcontracting may be disrupted by firms wishing to maintain commercial secrecy or to use a new product to expand their own production (Gough, 1996a). Such disruptions are particularly difficult to deal with when they span distinct local structures (that is, when they occur within locally effective structures). Changes in housing or in household formation, for example, may disrupt the supply of labour power sought by local capital (cf. sections 2.4 and 2.5).

Difference and coherence: the heterogeneity of local sectors

The different requirements of local sectors for labour power, infrastructures and economic culture can also create disruptions. There may be periods of peaceful coexistence between capital in these industries through a social and/or spatial parcellization of the locality between them, but conflicts between them are endemic, particularly in times of stagnation or rapid restructuring. These conflicts may be resolved by the dominance of a particular large employer, as in the classical company town, or a dominant local industry, which may succeed in imposing particular class relations on the locality. The dominant sectors of capital may be able to exclude inward investment by heterogeneous sectors (Beynon *et al.*, 1989). Large firms or even whole local sectors may shift their location in order to be able to achieve better dominance over the new locality.

However, what is hegemonic in a locality and gives it coherence may not be a particular sector but a particular tradition of class relations and cultural practices. Thus, for example, many 'peripheral' regions are marked by disciplinary industrial relations, branch plants and weak inter firm relations, permanently high unemployment, low wages and poor reproduction, irrespective of the particular product-industries present. In contrast, parts of central Italy (the 'Third Italy') are marked by skilled labour, consensual industrial relations, strong inter firm collaboration, and politics dominated by locally based firms, across a heterogeneous set of product-industries (Brusco, 1982; Garofoli, 1991). In both these examples there is a commonality of *labour process* within the localities – of Fordism or Taylorism in the peripheral regions, of flexible specialization in the Third Italy. A labour process of a particular type forms the dominant structure of the local economy, and from this spill out particular types of labour power, inter firm relations, and reproduction sphere.

However, none of these forms of coherence may be achieved. The labour processes, infrastructure requirements and political strategy of the local industries may be too heterogeneous, or business may be too weakly coordinated (Leys, 1985; Gough, 2002). As we shall see, this has been true of London. Such heterogeneity can result in permanent, unresolved conflicts between the various sectoral capitals. This incoherence may be exacerbated by conflicts between sections of the labour force employed in different sectors, for example over the different reproduction needs of well paid and poorly paid workers, or those of women and men.

Underaccumulation and overaccumulation in localities

Local socialization can also be disrupted by an excessively weak or strong pace of overall accumulation. Slackening investment caused by the tensions already discussed impacts negatively on infrastructures and the reproduction sphere as well as production itself, and may also impact on local suppliers. Whereas in neoclassical theory this would always produce immediate recuperative mechanisms – falling local factor prices, and a rise in inward investment attracted by them – in reality it further disrupts socialization, and thus tends to lead to further reductions in investment. I will refer to this kind of cumulative process as *underaccumulation* in the local economy.

Disruption may occur through the *strength* of local investment. Rapid investment may outrun the supply of labour power, training facilities or communications infrastructures. Strong demand for labour power can give bargaining power to workers, which they use to change work processes or employment conditions to their benefit. Rapid accumulation in particular sectors may force up wages or land prices in ways that severely disrupt other sectors. These are cases of *overaccumulation* in the local economy.[10] Again, rises in prices do not in the short, or even long, term result in corresponding falls in investment and recuperation of the problems. On the contrary, local overaccumulation can be chronic, resulting in qualitative changes to structures of the local economy.

Local economies, then, may be given coherence, but may also be disrupted, by the dialectics of the local socialization of production and reproduction *with* competition in wider product-industries. The rhythms of capital accumulation in the locality – reinforcing accumulation, underaccumulation and overaccumulation – then sustain local labour processes or cause them to be restructured.

This way of thinking about local economies has a particular relation to the history of urban theory. In the 1970s and 1980s there was considerable work by Marxist geographers on the value relations of localities, including rents and locally variable prices, flows of investment capital and the vicissitudes of fictitious capital (for example Rose, 1981; Roweis and Scott, 1981; Edel, 1981; Harvey 1982; 1985a; 1985b). This work did not however concern itself closely with particular labour processes and industries. The latter became the central core of urban geography from the 1980s. But this work, particularly that of 'the new regional economics', has increasingly neglected value processes and class relations (Gough 1986; Lovering, 1990; Peck, 1992; Eisenschitz and Gough, 1996). The approach outlined here, and developed further in the rest of the book, attempts to bring the concerns of these two literatures into creative contact with each other, linking the study of labour processes and local socialization to spatial value relations.

Having examined local economies, we now focus more closely on one aspect of them: tensions and change in the labour process.

NOTES

1. 'Rational choice marxism' in particular conceives of individuals and firms in a framework borrowed from neoclassical economics.
2. For a discussion of the many, quite different senses in which the term 'structure' is used see Gough (1991).

3. I employ the term 'use value' in its Marxist sense: not simply the usefulness of something, but an entity as concrete, material and sensuous.

4. See Gough (1991), where I refer to them as 'spatial structures'. I argue there that many important structures involve space *at a high level of abstraction*, as against the view (for example, Sayer (1985)) that space enters social processes only at a concrete and contingent level.

5. Burawoy (1985) was concerned centrally with this nexus of labour process and reproduction of labour power in particular territories. He argued that labour process theory had been too narrowly focused on the workplace, and neglected employment relations, the reproduction of labour power, worker organization, and the institutional regulation of these. He termed the latter processes 'the production regime' and 'apparatuses of production', and distinguished these conceptually from the labour process and 'relations in production'; he argued through case studies that the same labour process could have varied implications within different national 'production regimes'. The labour process *is* deeply interconnected with territories' reproduction spheres. But Burawoy's conception of the labour process includes the technical and task aspects only; in effect, the political, class and control aspects of the labour process are removed into the 'production regime'. In Althusserian fashion, Burawoy thus proposes a relative autonomy between the 'economic' and 'political' moments of production (Gartman, 1983). I therefore do not use Burawoy's conceptual distinction.

6. The literature sometimes refers to 'the importance of product markets'. This can mean at least three different things, with distinct implications for the labour process: (i) the forms of the product (variety, changeability, etc); (ii) the intensity of competition in the final market; and (iii) the stability of demand. Here we are concerned with (ii).

7. I use this term because, as we shall see, 'industries' can be defined on the basis of their production characteristics (section 6.3).

8. Sayer (1995) has argued that the division of labour and the capital-labour relation respectively are distinct processes operating in different dimensions with their own specific dynamics and properties and distinguishable effects. It is true that private capitalist property and relations of exploitation are distinct features of the capitalist mode of production. But they construct each other at a high level of abstraction. Their dialectic within a product-industry, traced here, means that they do not have their own specific dynamics nor distinguishable effects. See Gough and Eisenschitz (1997).

9. In neoclassical approaches these relations are referred to as 'positive externalities', in Keynesian approaches as 'virtuous circles'. Both these terms are too weak, in that they imply an interaction of externally related elements rather than their mutual construction.

10. In traditional Marxist theory these are referred to respectively as the overaccumulation of capital with respect to labour power, and disproportionality between sectors. We see here that these processes may be strongly locally specific and locally embedded. See further section 4.3.

3 THE DYNAMICS OF LABOUR PROCESSES IN PLACE

3.1 Introduction

This chapter examines change in the labour process, the barriers it encounters, and the conflicts it involves. I develop a set of conceptual distinctions and relations between different forms of labour process change. These will provide the categories for analysis of the London case study, where more of their interrelations will become apparent. The labour process dynamics discussed here are 'structural' and therefore infuse all spatial scales (section 2.1). They will thus provide us with a guide to changes in production in world industries, in the London economy *and* in individual workplaces within it. The focus here is on the dynamics of the labour process itself, but these are related to labour markets, to competitive and financial pressures, and to products, in line with the interdependencies discussed in the last chapter.

3.2 Raising labour productivity: technological change versus intensification?

Capitalism, in contrast to earlier modes of production, involves unprecedented *powers* of the ruling class to initiate changes in the labour process, but also unprecedented *compulsion* on it to do so. This is true in all the aspects of the labour process introduced in section 1.3. In the *employment relation*, the freeing of labourers from ties to particular members of the ruling class gives unpredecented forms of freedom not only to the labourer but also to the ruling class. Capital can hire and fire labour free from ties other than the wage relation, can change the sections of the workforce employed, can tap into differentiated workforces by using the unprecedented mobility of production, and can vary the terms and conditions of employment free from constraints of custom. Using the power given by these employment relations, capital has subjected workers to more intense and elaborate forms of *control* within the work process than in any previous mode of production. Indeed, this control is *necessary* in order to (attempt to) ensure that the value produced by the workers exceeds the value of the wages paid to them. This control is the basis for dynamic change in *production technology and tasks.* The real subsumption of labour enables capital to implement the radical changes in tasks associated with new technology, to ensure that new fixed capital will be used over sufficient hours and with sufficient intensity and care. The aggregate effect of productivity increases in consumer commodities is then to lower the value of labour power and hence increase aggregate surplus value. Thus continuous technological change helps to realize surplus value for both individual and aggregate capital.

These potentials and pressures to change the different aspects of the labour process are inscribed in capitalism, but their relative importance and their articulation has been the subject of much debate. Marx (1976 ed.) distinguished between two different methods by which capital can extract more surplus value from a given workforce, 'relative surplus value' and 'absolute surplus value'. *Relative surplus value* uses new production technology to increase the value produced per labour hour. By contrast, *absolute surplus value* involves an increase in the actual or effective hours of labour performed by the worker. This can be achieved by (i) lengthening the working day; (ii) reducing the 'porosity' of the labour process, the time during which the worker is idle; or (iii) increasing the speed at which the worker performs a given task, which may be construed as an increase in effective time worked. The latter two methods can be described as different forms of 'intensification of work' (Palloix, 1976).

In terms of our aspects of the labour process, relative surplus value *in the first place* involves changes in technology and tasks, while absolute surplus value involves changes in control, tasks, or the employment relation (Table 3.1). The caveat 'in the first place' indicates that change in the different aspects of the labour process are always mutually dependent, as we shall see shortly. The application of new production technology, reduced porosity or increasing speed of work all increase the value produced per hour, that is, labour productivity.

For Marx, relative rather than absolute surplus value extraction is the most important form of labour process change since it is the most *characteristic* of capitalism: constant technological innovation, the application of science to production, and the development of ever-more elaborate machinery are the

Table 3.1 *Marx's distinction in forms of labour process change*

Form of change	Aspect of labour process		
	Fixed capital, technology, tasks	Control	Employment relation
Relative surplus value	Technical change, task change to increase productivity	–	–
Absolute surplus value	Decreased porosity via new machinery	Decreased porosity, increased speed; both = intensification	Lengthening of working day

most obvious features differentiating the capitalist labour process from that in earlier modes of production. This argument, however, is problematic because, as we have just seen, capitalism introduces important changes in the dynamics of the control and employment relations as well as of technology. A quantitative argument is more defensible: that change in production technology can achieve far greater increases in surplus value than either pure intensification or lengthening of the working day. For given production technology, there are strict limits set by human physiology on the extraction of absolute surplus value, because neither the intensity of work nor the working day can be indefinitely extended. Historically, these limits impelled capital to turn to relative surplus value extraction; and, in the very long run, it is technical change that has produced the enormous increases in productivity under industrial capitalism (Maddison, 1979). For these reasons, it is sometimes thought that a strategy of absolute surplus value has become obsolete, at least in the advanced countries, and is confined to an ever-shrinking sector of marginal, backward firms, or of sectors which are fated to shift to the Third World. Some orthodox Marxists have criticized a focus on intensity of work and wage cutting in economic geography as a reversion to the ideas of Smith and Ricardo (Jenkins, 1984).

In part this debate is about differences between labour processes: some are more susceptible to relative or absolute surplus value extraction respectively. But the discussion of the labour process in Chapter 2 suggests that changes in production technology, tasks, control and employment relations are not simply alternatives but are *internally related*. Even though changes in productivity between year x and year y may be accounted, through comparative statics, as due to change in production technology, the *processes* by which such change takes place may integrally involve the control and employment aspects of the labour process. Moreover, the balance between them may be a function of financial considerations or the labour power available. We therefore need to consider the *interrelations* between relative and absolute surplus value extraction. Absolute surplus value plays an important role, even in contemporary developed economies, for a number of reasons:

(i) A given production technology can be used with wide variation in intensity of use. There are large differences in productivity in the use of the same manufacturing process technology in different advanced countries and in different firms (Pratten, 1976; Gertler, 1997). In sectors where leading-edge process technologies are freely available on the market, rather than developed or monopolized by particular firms, these differences in the intensity of use can be crucial in competitive survival.

(ii) Effective control of labour by management is often crucial to decisions to introduce new technology. Effective control means that the firm can negotiate the associated changes in tasks within the workforce, and be confident that the new machinery will be efficiently used. The high rate of fixed investment in Japanese manufacturing has been due in part to management's strong control of the labour process. Thus relative and absolute surplus value extraction are *dynamically* linked.

(iii) Technical change is often the *means* to intensify labour. New production technology may be designed to intensify the work process. This is true of the production line, for example, which both decreases porosity and automatically sets the speed of work (Aglietta, 1979); process plant, with its automatic flows of fluids, has similar effects. More subtly, production technology that separates workers spatially within the workplace and lessens their routine interactions with each other may socially and politically atomize the workforce and thus facilitate control.

(iv) A complex and controversial question is the links between technology, skill and control. New production technology may be designed to reduce the skills required for discrete tasks. In the Taylorist strategy this is expected to improve managerial control over the work process because management gains knowledge relative to the worker. The work rate can be more easily quantified, facilitating payment by results. The employment relation may also be changed: lower wages may be payable to less skilled labour, and less skilled workers can be more easily hired and fired (Braverman, 1974). But there are barriers to such deskilling, and important processes leading to upskilling (S. Wood, 1982; Sayer and Walker, 1992). Since already deskilled tasks are the easiest to (further) mechanize, lower skilled jobs tend to be faster replaced by mechanization. Productivity or quality of production in using new technology may require the same or higher levels of skills, especially in the first period of use. Reduced skills, casualization and cheapening of labour may lead to worker dissatisfaction and lowered intensity of labour. Nevertheless, there is a powerful tendency for management to appropriate conception of work processes to the extent that productivity and quality considerations allow (Thompson, 1989; Armstrong, 1988).

(v) Even where the design of new technology does not lend itself to intensification, the *process* of its introduction may give management the occasion to increase control. New technology may require newly designed tasks – or management may plausibly be able to claim that it does; and this gives an opportunity to design tasks of greater intensity or that facilitate management control. We shall see this process in relocations in the case study.

(vi) In many labour processes for long periods of time there is little substantial technological change. This is true of sectors as diverse as clothing, building, and many personal services. In these sectors, particularly ones where price is crucial and quality competition is muted, absolute surplus value is a common reaction to competitive pressure.

(vii) Even where change in production technology is *technically* possible, financial conditions may inhibit it. In 'long waves of stagnation', the rate of investment declines (Mandel, 1978a); it declines in downturns of the business cycle; and it tends to be low in sectors experiencing over-capacity.[1] In these conditions, firms may seek to compete through absolute surplus value strategies. For example, I noted in the introduction how the present wave of stagnation has elicited intensification, wage cutting and casualization. This points to connections between the labour process, profitability and accumulation of capital which will be a focus of this book.

(viii) Changing conditions in the market for labour power can make absolute surplus value extraction an important element of strategy. For a local sector, rising unemployment, immigration, or a move by women into paid employment in the locality can create opportunities for capital qualitatively to change the workforce. This may be encouraged by slow rates of change in production technology, (vi). Such change may be used to change employment relations – to casualize jobs or lower wages, but it can also be used to intensify work. The rate at which a person is prepared to – or indeed able to – work is strongly a function of their habits, cultural norms and expectations; it involves powerful notions of what is right, dignified, reasonable. These attitudes are strongly differentiated by gender, by ethnicity, by age, and by family and community work histories. Change in the social layer from which the workforce is drawn can therefore make a big difference to the work intensity that can be imposed. Such local change may be limited in time and give only a one-off fillip to profits, but in other cases it may be repeated, for example through further rises in unemployment or through immigration of a new ethnic group. Thus change in ethnic group has been used repeatedly in the clothing industries of metropolises in the developed countries.

(ix) Just as world financial conditions may affect rate of technical change, so may conditions in markets for labour power. If a product-industry throughout the world is able to use strategies of intensification and change in the employment relation, then the aggregate pressure for change in production technology may be lessened. This may be true, for example, in the clothing industry and in some personal services. Thus it is not simply that a slow rate of technical change encourages absolute surplus value extraction, but also that a sectoral norm of absolute surplus value may slow down technical development.

There are, then, complex relations between changes in production technology and absolute surplus value extraction as ways of raising labour productivity.[2] One is not in a simple sense dominant over the other; nor are they clear alternatives. Restructuring within a workplace will often involve a politically difficult interplay between the two aspects. The relation between them will vary with the technical possibilities for change in mechanization, with the politics of skill in the workplace, sector and locality, with financial conditions in the workplace or wider economy, and with conditions in the relevant markets in labour power locally or globally. We shall see these complexities in the variety of labour process norms in London manufacturing in Part II, and in the variety of ways of increasing productivity in Chapter 5.[3]

3.3 Cutting costs

Increases in labour productivity cut unit costs; but costs can also be reduced in other ways. These do not have the potentially large long-term impact of

Table 3.2 *Forms of labour process change studied in this book*

Form of change	Aspect of labour process		
	Fixed capital, technology, tasks	Control	Employment relation
Productivity increase	Technical change, tasks	Intensification directly within the labour process	Intensification by changing workforce, change in rewards
Pure cost cutting	Capacity utilization; economies of scale	Dis/economies in control	Wage cuts; changing workforce

relative surplus value creation. But they can nevertheless be vital to the workplace in the short term; the short term can make the difference between extinction and survival, and, as post-Keynesians point out, can affect the subsequent evolution of the workplace (Clark, Gertler and Whiteman, 1986). In the case study, I shall make a basic distinction between productivity-raising change and 'pure' cost cutting (Table 3.2).

Pure cost cutting can be achieved through wage cutting or by changes in scale of production. Specifically:

• Wage cuts

Employment relations may be changed in order to prevent wages rising or to reduce them ('wage cuts' for short). The ability to impose wage cuts on the existing workforce depends on the balance of forces between labour and capital at different spatial levels; the negative impact on worker cooperation that management anticipates; financial pressures at all spatial levels and hence the threat of redundancies or workplace closure; traditions of militancy and union organization; and the perceived penalties of being made redundant, often related strongly to employment trends in the local economy (see further section 12.3). In cases where some of these pressures are unfavourable to management, firms may seek to cut wages by change in the social groups from which the workforce is drawn: this can enable not only intensification but also wage cuts, if the wage norm of these groups is lower.

• Hours and capacity utilization

Management may seek to use capacity more fully by extending the weekly hours during which it is used. Fixed capital is depreciated not only by physical wearing out but by time (Harvey, 1982), so this reduces unit costs.

- Increasing workplace size

Economies of scale at workplace level have been studied by industrial organ-ization specialists (Pratten, 1971); they are of central importance in debate between Keynesian and neoclassical economics; and they underlie several Keynesian-based models in economic geography. They have, however, had relatively small place in the labour process literature, which has tended to focus on qualitative issues.[4] Nevertheless, labour process change may be directed towards gaining such economies. The scale of production may be increased for efficiencies of fixed capital, to elaborate the division of labour, or to lower porosity.

- Decreasing workplace size for better control of labour

Management may limit or even decrease employment within the workplace in order to gain better control of labour. As the size of workplace grows, the direct personal exercise of authority that owners call 'family atmosphere' weakens, and workers tend to see themselves more as a group and a potential collective. This can affect both the control of management over the work process and the balance of forces in negotiations over wages and conditions (reflected in the frequency of strikes in workplaces of different sizes: Prais (1978)). As is always the case with spatial variables, the size of workplace does not have an *unmediated* effect on industrial relations. For instance, in large firms recent management strategies have been centrally concerned with deepening sectional or individual divisions, fostering identification with company aims, and creating a 'family atmosphere' *without* cutting workplace size (T. Smith, 1995). Nonetheless, manipulating the size of workplace can be a useful tactic for management.

Whereas measures to increase productivity have a legitimacy based on their 'efficiency' and 'productiveness', despite their often negative effect on workers, cost-cutting measures tend to have weaker legitimacy. Wage cuts simply redistribute income from labour to capital. Limitation of the work-place size cannot avoid being seen as a political measure rather than a 'productive' one. When hours or shifts are extended to employ plant more fully, this may be seen as workers being subordinated to the 'requirements of the machine'. Cost cutting, then, may face ideological barriers that pro-ductivity increases do not. Cost-cutting strategies and their use of space are examined in detail in Chapter 9.

3.4 Production and the product

The early debate on the labour process in the 1970s and early 1980s, following Marx, was concerned with the means used to reduce labour time in the production of a given product; the design and quality of production of the product were largely abstracted from. This is problematic, however, because the material nature (use values) of labour processes are inextricably bound up with those of the product. Moreover, competition between firms depends sharply on qualities of the product. Some work on the labour process since the 1980s has considered products in such aspects as variety, batch size and changeability (Kelly, 1985; Marchington, 1992; Benders, 1995), but this has not been theorized in a systematic way.[5] In particular, concern with qualities of products needs to be better integrated into a Marxist framework, opening up value analysis more fully to the material nature of the labour process.

The quality of production of manufactured goods (unlike some services) can be controlled by inspection at the end of production, with defective products being scrapped or returned for correction, but this has obvious costs and possible errors. Firms therefore take measures to ensure quality of production through choice of machinery, design of tasks, supervision and organization of the work process (Marchington, 1992), rewards and discipline of labour, or recruiting a more reliable workforce. Thus all aspects of the labour process may be brought into play (Table 3.3).

The design of products is, in general, as central to competition as reduction of cost and price, though the balance between the two obviously varies between products. Product innovation can reap technical rents, and, more defensively, is necessary to avoid obsolescence; it is thus central to the way in which

Table 3.3 *Product considerations and labour process change*

Form of change	Aspect of labour process		
	Fixed capital, technology, tasks	Control	Employment relation
Production quality	Technical change, tasks	Supervision, worker commitment	'Better' workers, changing rewards
Product change	Different processes, tasks	Continuous reorganization, worker commitment	Workers with different skills or multiskills

firms and local economies position themselves in the value flows of product-industries (section 2.6). Product innovation is itself a labour process, carried out in particular spatial divisions of labour within and between firms and institutions (these are explored for the case of London in Part II). Product innovation also has many implications for the labour process in direct production. On the one hand, given labour processes constrain the type of new products that can be introduced without an overhaul of production, and this may be an important determinant of product innovation. The most obvious constraint is machinery. In some cases this may be usable in a very wide range of products; this can be true both of simple machinery (sewing machines) and of complex (CNC machine tools). In other cases machinery is dedicated to a narrow range of products, particularly for high volume production (most process plant, much flow line machinery). But the skills of the workforce can equally be the key constraint (Benders, 1995). Moreover, management-worker relations within the work process can affect the introduction of new products, through the willingness of the workforce to undertake reorganized tasks and to contribute their experience to planning them. Thus the labour process in all its aspects constrains product innovation (Table 3.3).

One may also look at the question from the other direction, the effect of product innovation on labour processes. The product cycle theory (Vernon, 1966) proposed that products in the early stages of their life cycle are manufactured using skilled labour, product-flexible machinery, and an elaborate and ever-changing division of labour including numerous subcontractors; the industry at this stage was therefore tied to established centres of related industries. Later in the product's life the rate of change in its specifications would slow down, and production volumes would be larger, allowing production with dedicated machinery in vertically integrated workplaces that were more footloose.

One problem with the product cycle model is that products intended for the mass market are now typically designed for mass production from the start. Conversely, even mature products may have their specifications changed frequently to mitigate price competition, sometimes resulting in a major change in design that gives a boost to final markets. Some industries' products are by nature varied and never become standardized, something we will see clearly in London manufacturing. Moreover, high-volume production can incorporate product flexibility through appropriate machinery, control of labour and range of tasks in each job. Investigation of the link between product change and labour process thus needs to go beyond the product-cycle theory.

The management of the labour process, then, may be as much directed towards improving qualities of the product as to the increases in labour productivity examined in section 3.2. Yet in both cases labour is being directed with the aim of increasing revenue per worker-hour. How, then, can we link them? A product of superior design or one that is better-made may require more labour time to produce and thus have greater value and price. This greater value added is sometimes the firm's aim in product quality strategies. In other cases the aim is technical rents: if the superior product produces a monopoly or oligopoly, it may sell above its 'price of production', reaping a surplus profit. In general, then, better product quality is associated with higher prices, sometimes as increased value, sometimes as higher profit rate. In contrast, strategies aimed at reduction of unit costs lower the firm's prices, and if generalized lower values. Accordingly, I shall refer to the enhancement of product quality as improved *value productivity*, in contrast to those aimed at reducing labour times which I shall call *volume productivity*. These two aims are practically enmeshed with each other, and are often in conflict.

Qualities of products can impinge on the labour process in another way, through shaping cultures of work and workers' identities. This point has been extensively discussed in recent work on face-to-face service work, where the product is itself a social relation to the customer (for example Halford and Savage, 1997). Though less direct, the nature of manufactured products can also influence work ideologies. Workers doing bespoke work, those with craft traditions, or producing upmarket products, may take a particular pride in their work. The 'quality' of the product may enable it to reap a technical or design rent that can give both an economic and cultural superiority to the workers. Product types are not only locally variable but substantially locally derived (section 2.7), so these product associated ideologies can be specific to the locality. We shall see many examples of this link in the case study.

In Part II, using the history of London manufacturing, I explore how labour processes and product strategies construct each other over time, enabling technical rents to be captured. In Part III these relations are examined in detail through the case study. We shall see how different labour processes both constrain product innovation and pose particular problems for quality control, and on the other hand how product innovation impinges on labour process change. The case study suggests that this dialectic can have particular spatial and temporal dynamics.

An epoch of 'quality'?

Themes of production quality and product innovation have been prominent in business and industrial organization strategy since the early 1980s, reflected in such notions as 'total quality management' and 'continuous improvement' and specific measures such as quality circles. Some have interpreted this increased stress on quality as part of a shift from a paradigm of Fordism to an emerging epoch of post-Fordism or flexible specialization.[6] A more grounded explanation is that the increased emphasis on quality arises, through various mediations, from the long wave of stagnation. Whereas poor quality may not be a severe liability when markets are expanding, it is exposed by sharper competitive conditions. Moreover, as the risks of investment have increased, large fixed capital outlays have become less attractive compared with modifications to labour processes to achieve better quality of production and innovative capacity. The shifting balance of class forces has helped in developing this new emphasis. Whereas in Japan the defeats of the labour movement in the 1940s and 1950s enabled firms to elicit a high degree of cooperation from their workforces in product innovation and quality assurance, in North America and Western Europe this was achieved – although patchily and provisionally – through the defeats of labour and higher unemployment from the 1970s. This shifts the explanation away from technological change and organizational innovation *per se* towards conditions of capital accumulation and class relations; this will be our focus in examining product strategies.

The theorists of a new epoch argue that production change is also being powered by *demand* for greater variety in products. Little systematic evidence has been presented for this trend. In consumer products, rising real incomes may lead to greater product variety, but this would not produce a qualitative shift. It is easy to cite sectors of consumer goods and services where there is greater differentiation and others where massification proceeds apace. Culturally, there are processes promoting both differentiation and homogenization in consumption. The widening income differentials produced by the long wave of stagnation may be promoting both greater product differentiation with the growth of income differences *and* more cost-competitive standardized products for those on stagnant and falling incomes. In machine goods, to the extent that machines are becoming more product-flexible there would be a trend towards greater standardization in products. The effect of long-term consumption shifts on product variety is therefore unclear.

In undertaking the case study of London, then, I shall assume that questions of product quality have become more important as a means of competition during the present long wave of stagnation but I shall not assume any new paradigm of production-product innovation or of consumption.

3.5 Cooperation and conflict, the universal and the partial

Across the forms of labour process change so far discussed, we have seen the importance of both cooperation and conflict between management and labour. These active roles of the social agents need further scrutiny. Friedman (1977; 1986) distinguished two ideal-type forms of industrial relations, 'responsible autonomy' and 'direct control'. In a regime of responsible autonomy, workers have substantial leeway in determining how they work minute by minute, an input into the design of their tasks, and often some control over the division of tasks between workers. They are expected to be self-motivating, because their interests coincide to a large extent with those of management: what is most pleasant and interesting for them is also most productive and efficient. Tasks typically embody considerable skill, and this gives workers both authority and bargaining power to reproduce their autonomy from management. In a regime of direct control, by contrast, management dictates the division of labour and the form of tasks, and exercises close supervision over the detailed process of work. Workers are assumed to have directly opposite interests to management, namely to minimize effort, and hence require continuous compulsion. Though tasks may still require considerable skill, management attempts to minimize task complexity in order better to know and control them and to minimize workers' bargaining power. Whereas with responsible autonomy workers actively contribute to product innovation and ensuring production quality ('mining the gold in workers' minds'), direct control implies that product quality measures are designed by management and imposed on workers.

These forms of control link to employment relations. Responsible autonomy tends to fit with secure employment and predictable hours and remuneration, in order to earn workers' loyalty and ensure use of their accumulated knowledge. This implies employment of relatively privileged sections of labour. Direct control, however, inclines capital towards casualized contracts and payment by results as disciplinary threats to workers, and implies employment of the least powerful social groups. The contrasted forms of class relation within production thus connect to different relations within the local social sphere (cf. section 2.4).

These two regimes are, of course, extreme cases, between which is a continuum of possibilities; and the strategies may be applied differently to tasks, control and employment relations (Friedman, 1986; 1990; P. Edwards, 1986). But it is not merely that there are alternatives: underlying the contrast between responsible autonomy and direct control is a contradictory unity. In *all* workplaces, capital is impelled to maintain a discipline sufficient to ensure that a surplus is produced (section 2.3). At the same time, because human beings are active agents, capital must elicit a minimum of willing cooperation from workers. Management can never know, let alone enforce the use of, everything that workers know, nor can they formalize and capture their tacit skills (Manwaring and Wood, 1985). There is thus a tension at the heart of the labour process; and while different technologies, different states of class struggle and different competitive conditions may favour one side or the other of this tension, it is always and everywhere present (Cressey and MacInnes, 1980; Hyman and Elger, 1981).

These contradictions are related to contrasts we have already encountered between use value and exchange value sides of the labour process, and between the forces and relations of production (section 2.3). Development of the forces of production to meet human needs is furthered by a responsible autonomy of workers, using their creativity while at the same time producing efficiently in value and volume terms. This is the 'universal' side of the labour process, that which operates in the interests of society as a whole and that prefigures socialism (Meszaros, 1971). In contrast, the moment of direct control is driven by the specific dynamics that *capital* imposes onto an industrial society – the 'partial' side of the capitalist labour process.

Speaking of a *contrast* between the universal and partial moments of the capitalist labour process might be taken to imply that one could choose one side or the other. Social democratic and Keynesian strategies, for example, believe that a responsible autonomy 'model' can be achieved systematically and stably. The partial aspects of capitalism can be tamed, its productive aspects accentuated, and capitalism can be rendered as a progressive 'industrialism'. This would imply an eventual identity of interests between capital and labour, so labour should cooperate with capital in pursuing this goal. In reality the two sides of the labour process are always present. The domination of workers and the compulsion to maximize the value of assets are inherent in capital. Even the development of production technology is marked by capital's partial interests (section 3.3). Moreover, as Friedman pointed out, cooperation and discipline are dependent on each other. For example, labour's cooperation with management in Japan since the 1950s has been premised on the strength of capital's domination. The two sides of the labour process are therefore not merely contrasted but intertwined, that is, they form a genuine contradiction.

As we would expect from the discussion of difference (section 2.2), this contradiction gives rise to great variety. The tension between consensual and disciplinary class relations is played out in many different ways. All of these are provisional and potentially unstable not merely as a result of external influences but due to the tension between the universal and partial aspects of the labour process which underlies them.

3.6 New geographies of the labour process?

A number of academic schools have argued that the geography of the labour process is currently being restructured into durable, even epochal, new configurations. Analysts of the 'new international division of labour' (Frobel *et al.*, 1980) and the 'new spatial division of labour' (Hymer, 1972) proposed that labour processes of particular types were being separated in space and assigned to regions and countries with characteristics favourable to capital. These models had the merit of showing how space can be actively used by capital and some *tendencies* in the connection between the labour process and territorial economies. But this literature tended to underestimate the continuing strength of the socialization of production within territories, particularly in the developed countries (Jenkins, 1984; Gordon, 1988; section 2.8). Moreover, these models neglected differences between labour processes, and have a schematic view of the relation between production and product innovation related to the product cycle theory (section 3.4).

Since the mid-1980s, the high degree of mobility of productive capital in these models has been criticized by authors who diagnose a new era dominated by more-or-less strongly integrated regional production complexes and networks. These are usually seen as combining task and product flexibility with close inter firm relations and substantial institutional regulation (Piore and Sabel, 1984; Leborgne and Lipietz, 1988; Best, 1990; Scott, 1998; Storper, 1998).[7] This literature suffers from the mirror-image problem, in that it attributes excessive stability to territorial networks and cooperative industrial relations, and plays down the disruption of these by capital mobility, value processes, and class struggle (Pollert, 1988; 1990; Levidow, 1990; Peck, 1992; Gough, 1996b; Lovering, 2000; Perrons, 2000). Correspondingly, it looks for one geographical pattern, the regionally integrated sector set functionally within international networks, and neglects others. But global-local relations involve chronic instabilities and can produce very varied paths for local industries (Thrift, 1988; Amin and Robins, 1990).

The present study, then, does not assume that the present period is characterized by any particular model of the labour process and its geography. This does not mean an unguided empiricism, but rather an exploration of the fundamental contradictions of class relations, labour processes and their geography as they are manifest in a particular time and place.

NOTES

1. However, as we shall see in Chapter 12 *intensive* investment may hold up in times of low profitability.
2. The lengthening of the working day, which increases value produced per worker but not 'labour productivity' as defined here, has not figured in this account. Its most significant instance in the developed countries in recent decades may be the increase in two-wage households with the increasing wage work of women, changing household work and consumption norms, and effectively increasing the waged working day *of the household.*
3. The distinction between relative and absolute surplus value can be drawn in a number of different ways. For example, intensification can be included in relative surplus value because it raises labour productivity and thus reduces the hours necessary to reproduce the labourer. Wage cutting can be included in absolute surplus value in that it is a means of increasing the rate of exploitation without increasing productivity, hence at the expense of the labourer. These two changes of definition would bring Marx's distinction into line with that used in this book, namely between productivity-raising change and cost cutting.
4. A notable exception is the study of Massey and Meegan (1979) in which economies of scale in production was one of their two broad forms of production change, the other being cuts to capacity. In fact, firms whose main change was cuts to capacity also achieved scale economies by relocations to larger factories.
5. For example, in his comprehensive account of the field, Thompson (1989) has no systematic discussion of the relation between labour processes and product innovation.
6. For critiques see Clarke, 1988b; 1992; S.Wood, 1989b; Gough, 1996a and b; Bonefeld and Holloway, 1991.
7. The new regional geography is largely based on various models of 'post-Fordism', on which see note 6.

4 LOCATING THE WORKPLACE

4.1 Paradigms of workplace location

Having examined local economies and labour processes, we can now return to our starting point of the workplace (section 2.1). This scale of analysis has its own specific political importance. Most workers' daily experience is contained within particular workplaces. Workers' collective organization is mostly (though not exclusively) built up from the workplace level, and the workplace is in all cases an important site for struggle. And the workplace is for firms a key unit of production when planning investment and disinvestment. This chapter considers the workplace and its location, and thus lays the basis for the study of workplaces in London.

The weaknesses of the neoclassical, Keynesian and systems approaches discussed in section 2.1 led Marxist and radical geographers from the 1970s to develop new theorizations of workplace location, focusing on relations neglected in the former theories: class struggle, investment flows and labour processes (Massey, 1976; Walker and Storper, 1981; N. Smith, 1989). One, continuing, strand of this theorizing has focused on transnational companies and their geographical investment decisions (Newham CDP, 1977; Dicken, 1992), though much of this work has not gone much beyond behavioural theories of the firm. More sophisticated accounts sought to theorize spatial investment flows within firms in relation to production processes (Walker and Storper, 1981). Friedman (1977) and Massey and Meegan (1979) showed how labour processes conditioned firms' spatial investment decisions. In particular, firms may use relocation to increase control of labour and avoid militant workforces (Gordon, 1984).

However, since the 1980s radical economic geography has shifted its focus to (one might say, become fixated on) relations between firms and institutions within and across industrial clusters, and consequently lost interest in both the labour process and individual workplace dynamics. In recent years an interest in production relations within the workplace has been revived by work on trade union organization and action (Martin, Sunley and Wills, 1996; Herod 1998). But there is a need to reconsider the relations between workplace location, the labour process, class struggle and investment flows. I do this by extending the analysis of the last two chapters. I first consider how pressures for workplace change can arise from different scalar logics. Forms of workplace change are then examined. The relation between *quantitative* growth or decline and *qualitative* change within workplaces is discussed, continuing our examination of the relation between capital accumulation and the labour process. Finally, I focus on how managements use workplace (re)location to resolve the pressures and conflicts they face.

4.2 Stimuli to workplace change

Workplace change is obviously connected to change at larger spatial scales. The framework so far developed allows us to conceive this more precisely. A workplace changes partly because of contingent external influences such as demand. It also changes because of internal tensions within the structures that form it such as the labour process. But these tensions may be the same as those that operate within larger economic units and spatial scales, and in that sense are both internal and external. Thus we have seen that there are structures *common to* workplaces, local economies and larger units of the economy (section 2.1), and that there are 'locally effective structures' that *span* the workplace, the local economy and local society (sections 2.4–2.9). These structures are formed and altered in relation to competition within product-industries (section 2.6). The impulses for change in a workplace can arise in each of these moments:

- Tensions may arise from *within the structures that form a workplace*. In particular, we saw in the previous chapter how the labour process is inherently unstable and dynamic. Similar tensions may be found in other workplaces, but they take a unique form in each one.
- The workplace may change in response to *change within the local economy*. Developments in the local politics of reproduction, the supply of labour power, the built environment or local industrial relations impact on the workplace. Note that these changes are not simply external to the workplace or local sector, since, as we saw in Chapter 2, they arise in a large part from the production system itself.

● Tensions may arise *within the product industry* to which the workplace belongs. These may originate in changes in externally given final markets. But they may also arise from changes in the structures and strategies of firms and local sectors within the product-industry.

In the case study of London we shall see examples of all three of these types of scalar process. Note the congruence of these forms of disruption of *workplaces* with those of *local economies* discussed in section 2.6; this similarity arises because of the contradictory structures common to these different spatial scales. These Stimuli lead to change in workplaces, to which we now turn.

4.3 The dialectic of the labour process and capital accumulation within workplaces

Workplace change is both quantitative and qualitative. How are these enmeshed with each other? This concerns a key theme – the relationship between the quantitative accumulation of capital and the qualitative use values of the labour process.

Output and employment in the short term depend on the competitive performance and profitability of the workplace, determined by the pressures on it and the ways in which the firm respond to them. Competitiveness and profitability are also the major factors determining investment in the work-place, thus influencing long-term output and employment trajectories. These quantitative changes in output, however, can also have their own *qualitative* effects. Recall that *local economies* have quantitative growth paths with distinctive qualitative effects: they may grow in a way which sustains and reproduces their coherence – 'reinforcing accumulation'; their competitiveness may decline and cause them to spiral into 'underaccumulation'; or their rapid growth may give rise to compounding problems of 'over-accumulation' (section 2.8). Within our approach it is not surprising to find analogous dynamics occurring at the *workplace* level:

(i) Successful competition can lead to new rounds of investment in fixed capital, training, managerial resources and technological innovation (sections 3.2, 3.4). 'Fair' wages, employment relations and forms of labour control, enabled by good profitability, can win harmonious industrial relations, active cooperation of labour within the work process, and a stable workforce which builds up its expertise over time. Strong competitiveness and stable output facilitate stable relations with suppliers and cooperation of various sorts with other firms (possibly in the same locality: section 2.8). Growth in output may lower costs in the short to medium term by increasing capacity utilization, while in the long term growth in fixed capital and employment may yield economies of scale of various kinds (section 3.3). The combination of these outcomes then in turn reinforces the competitiveness and profitability of the workplace. We can call this trajectory '*reinforcing accumulation*' at the workplace level.

Notice that, in contrast to neoclassical accounts, competitive success is far more than a selection of the right 'factors of production' in the right proportions, and does not rest on a static optimality but is *inherently dynamic* (Storper and Walker, 1989). It is also *holistic*, involving many aspects of the workplace's operations and their mutual coherence, in an analogous way to the coherence of local economies (section 2.8). This contrasts with many Keynesian (especially behavioural) approaches, which focus on particular aspects of the workplace. Notice, too, how strongly *social* this dynamic is, in the sense that it rests on, and reproduces, particular social relations within the firm and with outside agents.

(ii) Poor competitiveness can lead to an unravelling of the coherence of the workplace. Low profitability can lead to underinvestment in fixed capital, training and innovation. If poor wages and conditions result, then industrial relations may be soured, workers may cooperate less with management or 'soldier' to avoid redundancy, or turnover of labour may increase thus reducing experience and loyalty. Relations with other firms may be treated in a short-term and cost-cutting manner, thus weakening their productive efficiency. Capacity utilization may be low, and economies of scale may be lost. We then have a downward spiral of *underacccumulation*, which again is dynamic, holistic and social.

There may be recuperative elements in this dynamic. Evident decline of the workplace may have a disciplinary effect on labour, enabling management to cut wages, intensify work or restructure tasks. A smaller workforce may improve management control (section 3.3). Subcontractors' prices may be bargained down. Many British manufacturing workplaces, despite being relatively uncompetitive and investing at a low rate, seem to have held on through these kinds of processes, often over decades (Williams, Williams and Thomas, 1983). Yet these countertendencies to decline do not amount to automatic equilibrium-restoring mechanisms of a neoclassical kind: they depend on unpredictable conflicts within the firm, contingent economic and political conditions in local and national economies, and the particulars of the labour process. While some workplaces may hang on through under-accumulation, many others will fail.

(iii) Although based on strong competitiveness, growth of the workplace may in time undermine it. Over-investment in workplaces is a chronic condition within capitalism not simply because final markets are unpredictable but because the quantity of ongoing investment else-where in the product-industry is unknown by each firm as it makes its investment, leading to overcapacity across the industry. Moreover, business secrecy means that strategies being adopted elsewhere are unknown so that many firms invest in inferior ones. Growth may also lead to exhaustion of the local pool of suitable labour. Steady or increasing employment and a low turnover of labour may embolden workers to be more demanding when negotiating over wages, condi-tions, tasks and technical change. Growth may also require increase in space, a need for qualitatively different premises, or increased demands on local physical infrastructures, all of which can disrupt production. Increased output may also increase the bargaining power of sub-contractors or run into supplier bottlenecks. We can refer to these contradictions of growth or workplace size as *overaccumulation within the workplace.*

Thus, just as with local economies, there is a dialectic between qualitative and quantitative sides of the workplace. The use values of the labour process (technologies, tasks, management control, employment relations) and capi-tal accumulation within the workplace (profitability, investment or dis-investment) construct each other over time, and these can take the paths of reinforcing, over- or underaccumulation.[1]

4.4 Firms' use of place and space

The various pressures on workplaces, and tensions generated by their growth paths, may be addressed by very different management strategies towards the labour process (Chapter 3). One aspect of such strategies is the locational decision whether to remain in situ or to relocate. It should already be evident that this decision is not separable from decisions on aspatial structures: location decisions are an integral part of labour process strategies (Walker and Storper, 1981).

Relocation of a workplace may resolve pressures on it in a number of ways. A move to another locality can provide a new set of social relations in which to operate, which may include labour power (its skills, price, attitudes, and so forth), premises, physical infrastructures, potential long-term interfirm linkages, business culture or local politics (Chapter 2; Storper and Walker, 1983). In particular, different union organization in the two places may be an important motive (Massey and Meegan, 1979; Peet, 1983; Gordon, 1984). Relocation may also be aimed at repositioning the workplace within supplier and final markets.

Relocation may be motivated not so much by the different qualities of the old and new localities as by the *newness* of the new location and the opportunities this gives management for making changes in the labour process: it is the move itself that counts. If the workers in the new location are new to the firm or industry, then management can have a relatively free hand in changing forms of control, tasks and production technology. Workers are rendered as *abstract* labour power, free of knowledge of particular work processes, free of particular habits of work. Even if a substantial part of the workforce moves with the workplace, as is usually the case in local moves, the necessary changes in layout and (usually) production technology can legitimate wider changes in tasks and forms of control. Whereas relocations motivated by the qualities of the two localities are examples of capital's use of *place*, moves aimed at facilitating reorganization through the relocation itself illustrate capital's exploitation of *distance* (Harvey, 1985b).[2]

Management nevertheless often prefers to make changes in situ. Workplaces are locally embedded, albeit to very varied degrees: dependence on a local pool of skilled labour, or on workers who have workplace-specific skills and habits; plant that is difficult or expensive to move; long-term dependencies on local suppliers and business services; use of particular physical infrastructures; beneficial participation in a particular business culture, local information networks or local politics (Grabher, 1993; Cox, 1998). These locally effective structures are not merely 'linkages' of the workplace but give to it some of its durable characteristics (cf. sections 2.4, 2.8).

This local embedding may have exchange value as well as use value aspects. Plant has to be financially depreciated as well as physically used, and this responsibility may be difficult to transfer to another firm through sale. Even owner-occupied premises may be hard to sell at sufficient price, and they may be owned for reasons of finance rather than use. The firm may have credit worthiness with local banks or suppliers that would be jeopardized by relocating. Thus with spatial ties as with workplace dynamics, the labour process and the valorization of capital are entangled with each other.

Workplaces may also remain in place because of location related prices, as mapped by (neo)classical location theory. Finally, the process of relocation always has costs, some of which are the buying out of the ties just described, as in redundancy payments or accelerated depreciation of fixed investments.

All these ties give the workplace a geographical inertia. Management may then have to find ways of making changes in the labour process with the existing workforce. This is often politically more difficult than relocating to a new workforce, but in building on accumulated experience and the workplace's local embeddedness it may reap better rewards – 'reinforcing accumulation'. Alternatively, the firm may attempt to change its workforce qualitatively without relocating (cf. sections 3.2, 3.3). Remaining in situ may also mean renegotiating relationships with local suppliers and credit sources and it may require the firm to have an active intervention into the politics of the local economy (Cooke, 1989; Eisenschitz and Gough, 1993: 155–8).

Precisely because of the political difficulties of change in situ, capital often uses the *threat* of relocation to persuade labour to cooperate in restructuring. A firm may threaten its workforce with rundown of production, closure, or a relocation outside the locality if concessions are not made. This threat can also be made by capital collectively in a local sector or even across the local economy, using discourses within which failure to improve competitiveness will be penalized by relocation or shift of whole sections of the local economy (Ross, 1983; Johnston, 1986; Clark et al., 1992). These play on the local ties and consequent relative immobility of most workers (Cox, 1998). Thus even apparently non-spatial workplace change in situ is internally related to geographical uneven development and spatial mobility.

Our discussion of workplace change has so far made no reference to openings, that is, production new to the firm initiated at a green-field site or production of a new type initiated at a brown-field site. These may be carried out by either existing or newly-established firms. (For a map of these rather confusing 'components of change' see Appendix 2.) I have left consideration of openings to this point because there were few in London manufacturing during the period of the study, so that we shall be concerned mostly with the dynamics of existing workplaces. The origin of openings lies partly in the competitiveness and profitability of local sectors (Chapter 2), mediated by minimum efficient scale and barriers to entry into the sector. Openings by newly established firms are constrained by the resources of potential owner-managers – capital or access to it, sectoral knowledge, networks of business contacts, and by the internalization of the appropriate social relations – being your own boss and being the boss of others. These resources are not *sui generis*, but are created by national and local socializations of production, labour processes, and business cultures (Waldinger, 1986; Storey, 1988; section 6.8 below). Indeed, entrepreneurship is at base *a set of social relations,* whether to former co-workers, to future workers, to other businesses or to political actors. These internalize moments of status and gender as well as class and financial gain.

Relocation is the most visible, but not the only, way in which the division of labour between localities changes. The spatially uneven decline and closure of workplaces on the one hand, and their opening and expansion on the other, usually account for a greater proportion of change in the location of production than overt relocations. I shall refer to such change as *spatial shifts*. Our case study is limited to one locality, so we shall not examine such shifts directly, but rather the opening, growth, decline and closure of workplaces in London in competition with other localities. The relocations in the case study, however, provide a window onto direct comparison of London with other localities.

The material of Part III is arranged according to these locational workplace dynamics. Each of the three chapters considers an aspect of labour process change as a function of the initial labour process. They consider how and why such change was carried out in situ and through relocation respectively. These will enable us to see how aspatial and spatial means can be used to the same end, while grasping the specificity of these locational strategies. This way of presenting the case study emphasizes the role of space, whether as place or distance, in labour process reproduction and change. It also shows that relocation is not simply a question of movement from one local set of 'factors of production' to another but is premised on the initial labour process and strongly intertwined with changes in that labour process and with capital accumulation. I shall, then, use analysis of workplaces to examine the nexus of labour process, accumulation and locality.

NOTES

1. An aspect of the relation between production and capital accumulation is the relations between the financial sector and industrial firms. I do not investigate this relation in this book, although I am concerned with financial *moments* of industrial firms (profit rates, investment flows and fictitious capital). The relation of industrial dynamics to the finance system has been neglected in recent economic geography; for exceptions see Fagan (1990; 1991).

2. Some geographers now use 'space' in distinction to 'place', denoting distance in distinction to territory. In this book I use 'space' and 'spatial' to denote both distance and territory.

PART II

MANUFACTURING IN A METROPOLIS

5 MAKING THINGS IN A CAPITAL OF CAPITAL

5.1 London and 'manufacturing'

In this part of the book we examine manufacturing in London. The account will draw on the theorization of local economies given in Chapter 2, further elaborate it, and show its usefulness in understanding a particular locality. Chapter 5 gives a history and anatomy of London manufacturing, while Chapter 6 develops this through examining the nature and situation of the surveyed workplaces in the late 1970s.

This chapter first argues that manufacturing in London should be understood in relation to the city's 'core' activities of finance, business services and government, and thus Britain's world role. The historical development of five broad sectors of manufacturing is traced, distinguished centrally by their labour processes, product activities, industrial cultures and worker identities. It is argued that London has afforded particular opportunities for manufacturing to reap surplus profits, which then react back onto production relations. Long waves of development in London manufacturing are traced in both their value and use value aspects, and successive waves of spatial decentralization are explored. The socialization of manufacturing in London is examined, and this is related to the politics and evolution of British manufacturing as a whole. A central concern is relations between scales – from the world economy to Britain, the London region, the city itself, and sectors and areas within it.

The category 'manufacturing' requires comment. The definition of manufacturing used here is the conventional one found in official statistics, which is somewhat arbitrary. Labour processes that transform materials in form or spatially go well beyond this category because they include the utilities, transport, building industry and most consumer services (production of meat pies in factories is manufacturing, that in cafes is services). Production services carried out by manufacturing firms are 'manufacturing', while those contracted out to specialist firms are not. Nor is the conventional distinction between manufacturing and services one of their time and space performance: some manufacturing is timely and is performed at the customer's location (see section 5.3 below), while many services are now performed at a distance from the customer and with time gaps till consumption. Nor does the labour process provide a clear distinction: manufacturing – as we shall see for London – includes bespoke work and strong worker autonomy, resembling traditional personal services, while most contemporary services produce an essentially standardized product with little worker autonomy (Sayer and Walker, 1992: Ch. 2). We may thus expect the approach to labour processes given here, and many of the specific tendencies found, to be applicable also to 'services'.

In the developed countries, starting variously from the 1950s to the 1980s, manufacturing as a proportion of total employment has been in secular decline. Part of the reason for this lies in the official demarcations of 'manufacturing' just considered, which have tended to reduce 'manufacturing' employment by increasing amounts over time.[1] Part of the relative decline, however, has been due to certain differences in the labour processes in respectively manufacturing and services, particularly personal and informational ones, such that the rate of labour productivity increase in manufacturing has been higher over a long period. These dynamics have, however, been strongly differentiated by locality, and it is to the specificity of London that we now turn.

5.2 The difficulties and logics of manufacturing in London

What one could call the 'core' functions of London have always been non-manufacturing ones: since the rise of mercantile capitalism London has been one of the top two or three world centres of trade, banking and insurance as well as the centre of national government. These were the key activities of London as the centre of the most powerful empire in the world from the late seventeenth century to the First World War. This power remains very substantial to this day, and has been supplemented in the twentieth century by London becoming a key organizing site for international money capital and the main site for British corporate headquarters (Hamilton, 1991). These functions are the core ones of London in that they are both the most durable and the most immobile.

This stability arises not only from the geographical inertia of financial industrial districts and government bureaucracies but also from the extraordinary political centralization of the British ruling class. Since the Glorious Revolution the ruling class has been exceptionally well integrated, with a strong sense of itself as a disciplined and well coordinated collective. From the late seventeenth century there was a union of aristocratic landowners and gentry engaged in capitalist agriculture with merchant capital (Anderson, 1964). From the late nineteenth century British industrial capital became organizationally more integrated with the City and itself developed an overseas orientation (Fine and Harris, 1985). Atkins (1990) has shown that this strong integration of the ruling class has both been expressed in, and reproduced by, its geographical centralization in central London. This has then further anchored the core economic sectors.

Government, trade and finance are also 'core functions' in the sense that the other activities of London have flowed from them. Most directly connected have been the legal apparatus, medicine, and the media, in which London has not only been the largest centre but has contained the most specialist, senior and politically powerful sections of those industries. Together with Oxford and Cambridge – also located in south-east England – it has been the major centre of scientific research and the university system. And as the principal place of residence of the British ruling class, much visited by its overseas counterparts, and with an exceptionally large and high-income middle class, London has also been a world centre of luxury consumption.

Manufacturing, then, appears as an annexe to these core functions. But further, manufacturing in London has faced distinctive barriers arising from the core activities. The first are costs. The high profits of the nexus of activities around trade, finance and business services, and the enormous weight of luxury consumption, have together generated high land prices. For some sections of London labour these have fed through to higher wages, for other sections to poor housing and inadequate reproduction services. The surplus profits of the core functions and the luxury spending of the elite have also constructed a segment of the London labour force, extending into the manual and clerical working class, with high wages and salaries ultimately derived from the core. High land prices and wage levels have then posed potential cost problems for manufacturing. In these senses, then, there is chronic overaccumulation in London (section 2.8).

A second problem for London manufacturing is the heterogeneity of the London economy. The variety of sectors in which workers can find employment makes it difficult for manufacturing industries to manage their workforces. More generally, it makes the political regulation of the economy difficult. There are potential conflicts between manufacturing and the 'core functions', including the City. This is not primarily because of an allegedly distant relation between banking and industrial capital in Britain (see further section 5.9).[2] Indeed, we have already noted the integration between large banking and industrial firms in London, and the London region has been the preferred location for foreign inward manufacturing investment (Dunning, 1958; Hamilton, 1991). Rather, the requirements for labour power, reproduction and transport facilities of the core and of manufacturing have not necessarily coincided. I argue below that political regulation since 1945 has functioned to benefit the core rather than manufacturing.

How, then, has manufacturing been able to survive and prosper in London *despite* these adverse cost and political conditions? Part of the answer is that manufacturing has supplied *final markets linked into London's core functions* (cf. section 2.7). As well as luxury consumer markets, it supplies firms and government institutions within or attached to the core. Moreover, due to its imperial role, since the early modern period London has been the most populous city in Europe, and since the late nineteenth century this has provided a strong market for mass-produced goods. London has also been the centre of wholesaling, linked to its mercantile role. Location in London has had the advantages of close productive and informational contact with the market, and speed of delivery. Capital goods and luxury consumption have been more closely bound by market ties to London than mass consumer goods production: the former are more specialized and more spatially differentiated than the latter, and tend to require closer and faster contacts.

Manufacturing has also been linked to London as one of the world's largest *transport hubs*, arising from London's role as international trading entrepôt and largest point of entry for goods into Britain, cumulatively reinforced by national transport infrastructures. These, too, are a product of London's imperial role. They have supported manufacturing both in ready access to raw materials and components and in shipment to distant markets.

Manufacturing has been further anchored in the capital through its *productive structures*, developed from London's manufacturing specializations. In many industries pools of sectorally specific skilled labour were built up, including technicians, designers and managers. The latter form integrated milieux, with flows of information between individuals and movement of personnel between enterprises, and which encourage new firm formation (Hall, 1962: Ch. 7). Many of these sectors have the character of the 'industrial districts' first outlined by Marshall (1919). Technicians, designers and managers in these districts have also often had crucial interchanges with firms, government and individuals linked to the core functions. These sectors, then, involve locally effective structures through which firms, the interfirm division of labour, labour power and sectoral knowledge are mutually constituted. Because these structures are *locally* effective, there has been 'reinforcing accumulation' in situ despite the problems of a London location.

5.3 Five cultures of London manufacturing

These processes have shaped five types of manufacturing that have been important in London over a long period. I shall outline how these 'broad sectors', as I shall term them, have been attached to London, and how this is bound up with their specific structures – labour processes, products, types of firm and inter firm relations; class, gender and 'racial' relations and identities; and forms of competition and valorization (for a summary see Table 5.1).[3] These are best seen as sets of processes, as cultures, running through the London economy, rather than as sharply distinct sectors. Indeed, particular product industries and parts of them have shifted between the broad sectors over time, and the composition of each broad sector has changed historically.

(i) Craft and low-mechanization production of consumer goods

From the late middle ages, London was a centre of craft production of luxury consumer goods – clothing, shoes, jewellery, furniture, books and so on. A London location was necessary for bespoke production for upper- and middle-class clients, and for the designers and skilled workers to keep abreast of fashion, including international fashion. From the mid-nineteenth century rising real wages nationally and an exploding population in the capital itself (from 1.1 to 6.6 million over the century) generated mass markets for these goods. This was served to a large extent by production in London, much of it based on 'sweating' – a fine technical division of labour to deskill tasks, casualized employment to reduce workers' bargaining power and respond to market fluctuations, putting out to a vast network of small workshops and homes, and the use of female and child labour. Sweating, in the sense of deterioration in working conditions, first occurred on a large scale during the depression of the 1830s and 1840; the present wave of stagnation has seen its return (Part III; Friend and Metcalf, 1981). From the early nineteenth century well into the twentieth century, the division between the luxury and mass trade took a geographical form: the former was located in the West End of central London, the latter in the working-class East End, though substantially organized by wholesalers based in central London.

As we have seen in Chapter 3, pure absolute surplus value extraction, of which sweating is an example, is unstable in the long term in the face of competition from lower cost locations; this has been true of these London sectors. Some sectors have disappeared in London, as with the removal of the shoe industry to the Midlands in the early nineteenth century (Massey, 1984) and the relocation of the textile and leather industries over that century (Green, 1991). But in other sectors a substantial fraction of the industry has remained, through a number of processes:

- In some cases intensification and cost cutting have been renewed by using the successive waves of migrants, such as Eastern European Jews in the late nineteenth century, Bangladeshis, Cypriots and Turks from the 1960s. These supplies of labour have not been contingent but rather a function of London's nature as centre of an empire and its role as the major international transport hub.
- Sometimes remaining in London has been enabled by bringing production into medium or large factories, with consequent efficiencies through quality control, control of throughput, and accumulation of workers' experience, as occurred in a part of the clothing industry in the late nineteenth and early twentieth centuries (Hall, 1962). But in itself this does not provide a long term dynamic competitive advantage.
- Mechanization has either been slow, or, where it has been substantial as in the furniture industry, has qualitatively shifted a part of the sector to mechanized mass production, as we see below.
- In other cases production has remained in London through the importance of rapid changes in design and short turnaround times in serving the city's market. This timeliness can obtain in down- as well as up-market production, as in the production of 'street fashion' in London. Indeed, one of the specificities of London (and some other metropolises) is the strong place of high fashion, at least in its 'flash' forms, in working-class culture, and the ability of high fashion to experiment in and learn from the local mass market. Thus 'value productivity' (section 3.4) based on qualities of the product – in this case both design and timeliness – can yield surplus profits, which enable a London location.
- In sectors where mechanization has been least or slowest changing, production is often more efficient using labour with substantial skills rather than a high division of tasks between workers, and this has tended to anchor the industry to London's experienced workers.

- Where production has remained organized through an elaborate division of labour between local firms, whether for specialization or for overflow subcontracting, this also has rooted the industry. But in some cases – clothing and furniture are examples – these linkages have been partially replaced by integrated production in larger workplaces.
- London's role as a national and international transport hub has been important, in enabling access by buyers to luxury production, international exchanges in the design milieux, and export of upmarket products. These same infrastructures have also facilitated imports.

These processes produce highly differentiated industrial relations and worker identities within this broad sector. Sections of the industries employing men such as furniture and printing have had strong union organization and have sustained strong craft worker identities. Women, who have predominated in sectors such as clothing and toy making, in general have had just as significant skills, but many of these skills have been learned in the home, thus culturally devaluing them; and women's position in the reproduction sphere has inhibited strong unionization and prevented them from enforcing recognition of their skills. In another dimension, the differentiation of the broad sector from luxury to cheap products has been aligned with differentiation of skill levels, security of employment, and unionization. Hence insecure employment and marginalization have existed alongside high-status craft identities.

(ii) Craft production of capital goods and their components

The scientific and medical milieux of London have been the basis for, and themselves been reinforced by, advanced technology manufacturing. From the sixteenth century London was the centre for the production of mechanical and optical scientific and medical instruments, and from the late nineteenth century an important centre of electrical instrumentation. From the nineteenth century the design expertise for these industries was decreasingly a matter of individual innovators and increasingly created by interactions between the manufacturing firms themselves, the universities and research institutes, and between scientists, technologists and skilled manual workers, forming a combined private-public milieu. The London location of these sectors was further cumulatively reinforced by the rich networks of component suppliers and testing facilities. Early productive capacity and expertise in instrumentation was then the basis for successive *changes* in products and production techniques. There were major changes in product on the basis of similar technologies, for example from cars to aircraft. There was also continuity of the productive structure through revolutions in fundamental technologies, from mechanical to electrical to electronic capital goods (Martin, 1966: 35–9). From the 1970s the design and production of specialist, especially capital, electronic goods, together with associated software design, have grown, not in London itself, but close by in the 'Sun Belt' of southern England (Hall *et al.*, 1987).

Military procurement, centred in London, was another key component of this broad sector. Military spending of the British state has been exceptionally high due to its imperial role. Given the complexity of armaments in both their technologies and potential uses, designers and managers of manufacturing firms have benefited from being able to have regular face-to-face meetings with military personnel and associated civil servants. Military procurement has provided a soft (though fluctuating) market in the form of cost-plus contracts and the covering of cost over-runs (Kaldor, 1982). This circumstance was a major factor in the growth, at various periods, of shipbuilding, aerospace, radio, telecommunications and many types of instrumentation in London and the south-east (Hall *et al.*, 1987: Ch. 9; Lovering, 1991). The state-owned factories of the Royal Ordinance were also strongly centred in London.[4]

We thus have a large set of *overlapping* industrial districts (Martin, 1966: Ch. 5) with a major state input. The relations between technologists, skilled workers and managers, and at the institutional level between firms, universities, government research and development and production facilities and the military bureaucracy, substantially constitute each other – a set of powerful locally effective structures.

The technological dynamism of these sectors has enabled surplus profits in the form of technological rents to be reaped (or built in, in the case of military procurement), so that the higher costs of a London location have not been a major problem. In its turn this broad sector has been a major contributor to those higher costs. Correspondingly, firms have not been under great pressure to reduce wage costs, but rather have pursued value productivity through process and product innovation. This has enabled relatively harmonious relations between firms and a largely skilled, male workforce, an important component of London's labour aristocracy – a continuity in identity with artisans in the instrument industries of the early modern period.

(iii) Jobbing firms and service manufacturing

London has long had a vast array of manufacturing firms which service local firms and institutions: components and systems for the building industry; shop and display fittings; iron and steel structures of all sorts; electrical and electronic fitments to buildings; media hardware; business printing; and reproduction of electronic media. This production has fuzzy boundaries with sectors that are conventionally classified as 'services' such as building firms, carpenters, mechanics, electricians and plumbers, and firms often operate across these boundaries. This broad sector makes distinctive use of time and space: all of the work is timely, and much of the work is done on the customer's premises, so that the London market has to be served from local premises and with local labour. There are thus similarities with the timeliness of fashion goods (i), and with the need for local face-to-face coordination in both groups (i) and (ii).

The time and space nature of this work is also integral to its labour processes. Products are often bespoke, and much of the work is fitting to buildings; thus the general level of skill is high, the technical division of labour low, and workers perform complex sets of tasks. Workers tend to have a considerable degree of autonomy in carrying out their work, all the more so because much of it is spatially separated from the firm's workplace and often done without supervisors. Throughout the sector the quality of production is a key competitive question; in some cases design of the product is also important, but this has less weight than in the two broad sectors already considered. The nature of the labour process just described makes it difficult for management to ensure quality of production, putting reliable and experienced workers at a premium. Surplus profits are generated on the basis of timeliness, of quality of production, and sometimes of an oligopoly of London suppliers.

The substantial skills learnt on the job, until recently through apprenticeships, and the high pay have encouraged men to monopolize these jobs, sometimes spuriously justified by their physical characteristics (see Cockburn (1983) for the case of printing). Worker identity has been constructed along a spectrum from the responsible craft worker proud of his work to the cowboy proud of what he gets away with, both poles built on a masculine autonomy from management. In some sectors, the timeliness of the work has given workers strong bargaining power against management, enabling them to cream off part of the surplus profits reaped by the firm: national newspaper setting and printing is the classic case, but it is true also in some firms related to the building industry.

Nevertheless, casualization and instability of work has been common in this broad sector. This is due partly to final market characteristics – the one-off nature of most of the work, and the highly cyclical nature of the building industry to which much of the sector is linked. It is also due to the ease of entry, given that machine and plant requirements are mostly fairly simple and capital requirements low, with consequent large instability in individual firm output and high rate of closures.

Indeed, this broad sector shares some characteristics with the craft consumer goods sector: high skill content of tasks and/or jobs, low fixed-capital intensity, and ease of entry (this last feature distinguishing them from craft capital goods with their demanding product design). These characteristics give rise to a common trait across these sectors, namely a wide differentiation in the *quality of firms* in a broad sense – quality of labour process organization, worker skills, design, production quality, stability of output, profit levels, and wages and conditions. This differentiation in quality arises from contradictions of the sector structures, and is not simply an overlay (section 2.2). On the one hand quality competition is important (in product design or production quality), whereas on the other the relative ease of entry allows a high proportion of inexperienced firms. The proliferation of firms produces intense competition that, combined with high London factor prices, then tempts firms to pursue low-quality, low-cost strategies using poorly trained workers. The reproduction of the high-quality firms depends on holding their skilled and experienced workers, a task that is more difficult in a large metropolitan economy, and on the maintenance and circulation of reputation, which, in the case of jobbers especially, may be difficult given a high turnover of managers in customer firms. Both owners and workers in these sectors then tend to have an acute sense of the 'good' and the 'bad' firms in their local industry, from the reputable, long-established firms with an artisanal identity to the cowboys, and workers are similarly differentiated between 'the rough and the respectable'.

Another common thread in the class relations of the jobbing and craft consumer goods broad-sectors is a movement of men between the roles of direct worker and entrepreneur. Workers' knowledge of the whole production process, contacts with buyers or customers as part of their work, and relatively low capital requirements, facilitate this transition (see further section 6.8). If the firm fails, as many do, the entrepreneur returns to the role of direct worker. This two-way flow functions to blur the identities of male worker and entrepreneur, sometimes approximating the role of the traditional 'ganger'. This reinforces consensual industrial relations, at least in the smaller firms (cf. Solinas, 1982).

(iv) Fordist production

A further broad sector is made up of substantially mechanized mass production industries producing standardized consumer and intermediate goods in large volume. These employ mainly semi-skilled labour, and use continuous flow of the product between stages of production, sometimes automatic; in some cases components are produced within the firm or workplace, sometimes involving a higher level of skill. This form of production emerged in the developed countries in the second half of the nineteenth century, and in this century was taken forward by the innovations of F.W. Taylor and Henry Ford; I shall refer to it as 'Fordist'.

While Fordist production has been important in London manufacturing, it did not dominate it, even during the era sometimes dubbed 'Fordist' (cf. Meegan, 1988). It has developed principally from evolutions within the three craft-based broad sectors already considered. One path has been a transition from craft to mass production *of the same general type of product*. In expanding final markets, products and their components and modules have been standardized and their design simplified. An increased technical division of labour has been introduced, enabling deskilling. Simplified tasks and standardized products have laid the basis for increased mechanization. Thus in the interwar period the wooden furniture industry began to shift from craft methods to mechanization of component production and flow line assembly, and from a highly vertically disintegrated industrial structure to integrated factories (Hall, 1962). Similarly, there have been shifts from craft production of metal structures to the mass production of steel building components, heating equipment and ducting, while, as in the furniture industry, retaining a large subsector using craft methods. The car industry in London emerged initially on a craft basis from the mechanical and precision engineering sector, broad sector (ii), but then made a transition to mass production in the interwar period.

In contrast, in other cases, *a new type of product* has been mass produced from the beginning (cf. remarks on the product cycle model in section 3.4). Nevertheless, these mass production sectors had a basis in the craft production sectors of London. The electrical industries are a case in point. The mass production of standardized electrical *consumer* goods that exploded in London between the wars had part of its roots in the milieu of scientists and technicians in electrical engineering and the skilled manual workers producing small-batch electrical *capital* goods, part of broad sector (ii). Although these skilled workers formed only a minority of the workforce in the mass production of the new electrical appliances, they were nevertheless essential to it (Hall, 1962; Martin, 1966). After the First World War London was the principal centre in the country for electrical engineering, and this was one of the main reasons for the subsequent concentration of the mass production sector there.

The principal work process in the Fordist sectors, repetition of single or narrow range of tasks in a flow line, was the basis for the growth of new forms of employment relations in London manufacturing. The academic literature on Fordism has been so strongly focused on the car industry that it is often assumed that flow line workers are male. This was true, however, for only a part of Fordism in London. In the sectors where the general type of product remained the same in the transition to mass production, the initial skilled workforces, overwhelmingly male, while not able to resist deskilling (Braverman, 1974), were nonetheless able to maintain a male monopoly of jobs. In some sectors, such as furniture and steelwork, the new semi-skilled workers maintained the strong unionization of the craft industries; in others, such as mass production of cars, unionization had to be fought for; Ford's plant at Dagenham took 20 years to become fully unionized. Where there was less or no continuity in type of product, as in the electrical durables sector, management was able to use women workers for the new semi-skilled assembly jobs, and on this basis was able to economize on wages and to tap into a large pool of labour power in the expanding outer suburbs.

Compared to the previous dominant form of manufacturing employment for women in London, craft consumer goods, Fordist jobs have been paradoxical. On the one hand, they have been less skilled and creative and more monotonous, compared with the relatively high (though variable) skill level and worker autonomy in sectors such as clothing and parts of toy making. Given that the skilled jobs in mass production have usually been monopolized by men, they have offered less possibilities for working up to more skilled and more senior positions. On the other hand, women's jobs in Fordist production have generally been superior in security, work-related benefits, unionization and wages. The usual equations between high/low skill, high/low wages and high/low security do not apply for women working in twentieth-century London manufacturing.

There was, then, a certain continuity in production and labour power of the new Fordist industries with older manufacturing sectors. But Fordism was less strongly tied to London than the craft sectors had been. The minimum efficient scale of production of particular products increased, and output had to be realized over markets of increasing scale; from the targeting of the strong London market in the interwar period, these expanded to national or, particularly from the 1960s, international markets. Moreover, the use of semi-skilled labour power, and training on the job to often firm-specific skills, tended to free firms from ties to London's skills and enable use of cheaper labour power elsewhere. Dependences between sectoral firms tended to be less, given the higher degree of vertical integration within mass production workplaces and firms. Proximity of production to the design and technical milieux of London was less important with long runs of standardized products. This was reinforced by the fact that liaison between designers and production workers was less important in Fordism given that, following Taylorist precepts, the work process of the semi-skilled workers was determined *a priori* rather than developed with their input. In addition, the larger firms carrying out mass production had the volumes to justify, and the resources to implement, a separation of sites for technical and design work on the one hand and direct production on the other (Massey, 1984). Finally, although much craft production has been, and still is, carried on in multistorey flatted factories, Fordist production typically required single storey operation, with correspondingly greater sensitivity to London's high land prices.[5] Thus the socialization of production within localities characteristic of the craft industrial districts of London was replaced by the Fordist firms socializing production within the factory or within the firm, weakening attachment to place. In consequence, much of the mass production initiated in London has subsequently decentralized to other British regions or abroad.

(v) Process plant production

Our final broad sector is of process plant production using automatic flow of material (gas, liquid or solid) between stages of production in a single, integrated plant. This sector has been strongly linked to London as a port through which the raw materials have been brought in (so that London has some similar sectors to Liverpool or Hull), but also to London as a large market, in which the products are sold to final consumers or to downstream manufacturers. The longest standing industries in this category are in food and drink, in paper production, linked into London's printing and publishing, and in timber. From the late nineteenth-century oil refining, chemicals and pharmaceuticals grew rapidly. The packaging for London's manufactures has also been produced with process plant, from the longstanding board and glass industries to metal boxes and tins in the late nineteenth century.

These, rather than Fordist production, were the first mass production industries in London. The degree of skill and responsibility of jobs has varied greatly. Skilled maintenance work, similar to that in broad sector (iii), has occupied a large part of the workforce. Monitoring of flows of material through particular stages of production may be high or low skilled, depending on the plant design (Nichols and Beynon, 1977). As in Fordist production the skilled/non-skilled divide has been strongly gendered.

The labour process of process plant has facilitated trade union organization in a number of ways. Most of the workforce has been employed in large plants. Even more than in Fordist production, the whole plant has been organized around continuous flows so that local disruptions are serious, exacerbated by the high value of fixed capital. Some process industries, such as brewing, had union organization which grew out of craft labour traditions, while those which took off in the late nineteenth century were organized by the 'new unionism' of non-craft workers.

The spatial stability of the process industries resulting from the ties of port and final markets has been reinforced by the inertia of the productive capacity itself. The large capital cost of process plant and its integrated nature have inclined management to modify plant in situ rather than start from scratch on new sites. As with Fordist production, however, increasing economies of scale have enlarged the scale of markets required and reduced the market ties to the region, facilitated by transport improvements. For example in the 1960s the brewers moved to much larger scale plant, and to supplying regional and even national markets rather than local ones. In most process sectors these developments have resulted in consolidation onto fewer sites and extensive closures of older plants, but the inertia of fixed capital, plus the greater role of skilled labour, have tended to make this process slower than in Fordist production.

Thus all five broad sectors originate in, and are to varying extents reproduced by, the core activities of the capital. This gave London manufacturing a remarkable strength and stability over a long period: in both 1861 and 1951 the proportion of manufacturing in London's total employment, 32 per cent and 36 per cent respectively, was only slightly less than in England and Wales as a whole (Hall, 1962: 21). However, we have also seen that London manufacturing has faced specific difficulties by virtue of its proximity to the core activities; its relation to the core is thus *contradictory*. Moreover, the broad sectors are very varied in their forms of reproduction in place and their extent of reinforcing accumulation. This diversity then tends to make collective projects of both capital and labour within manufacturing more difficult.

These brief histories exemplify the way in which the evolution of industries is developed by the internal relations of labour processes with other struc-

Table 5.1 *Some characteristics of the broad sectors of London manufacturing*

	Labour power	Local interfirm relations	Final market ties to London	Local physical infrastructures
Craft consumer goods	Skilled manual, designers	Strong	Luxury and mass consumers	National and international passenger
Craft capital goods	Skilled manual, technicians	Strong, including in design	State, industrial HQs, medicine, scientific institutions	Ditto, plus port and airport
Jobbing	Skilled manual	Some	Firms and institutions	No
Fordist production	Semi-skilled, minority skilled	Weak or moderate	Consumers and firms	National and international goods
Process plant	Mixed skilled and non-skilled	No	Consumers and firms	Port

tures that we examined in Part I: the work of product and process innovation; the form of the firm (size, capital, type of owner); gender relations; accumulation and overaccumulation of capital (ease of entry, proliferation of workplaces, scale economies and overcapacity); and the appropriation of value (surplus profits, design and technical rents). Two of these dialectics deserve further comment.

5.4 Historical dialectics of productive structure and products

In the long-term evolution of manufacturing sectors in London one can discern an interplay in which given productive structures elicit new products while existing products elicit new productive structures (Walker, 1989a). An example of the first of these processes is the evolution of the broad sector of complex capital goods. On the basis of a set of overlapping industrial districts in instrumentation and optics, there was not only technical change within a particular type of product (watches or lens grinding for example) but innovation of new types of instruments and movement into products with qualitatively new scientific bases, from mechanical to electrical to electronic. The networks of specialized firms and research institutions, and the scientists, technologists and skilled manual workers within them, were able at certain times to change the nature of the product on the basis of the pre-existing productive structure, although modifying the latter in the process. The ability of industrial districts to make continuous modifications within a particular type of product is well-documented (Sabel, 1989; Camagni, 1991); less well-recognized is the ability over very long time periods to shift to wholly new types of product while retaining the same general form of productive structure. Thus the capital goods craft sectors in London have not usually evolved towards more standardized forms of production methods, as in the product cycle model (section 3.4), partly because the products continue to be produced in small volumes, but also because radical innovation and diversification of specialized products has emerged from the given productive structure. A variant of this process is where a new product selectively uses *one* aspect of the existing productive structure in a new way, as when Fordist production of electrical consumer durables drew on London's craft electrical engineering skills.

The given production structure can also lead to a narrowing of the product range rather than its diversification. In some of the craft industries the productive structure has changed little over a long period whereas the range of products produced has narrowed: the clothing industry in the twentieth century has increasingly specialized in fashion garments, the craft-based furniture sector has specialized in 'reproduction' furniture, and the printing industry has increasingly concentrated on complex, short run and timely work. These product trajectories have been based not only on the nature of local markets but on the comparative advantage of the existing labour processes and productive structures.

The converse process is where the type of product produced in the locality remains fixed and the production system changes. We saw this process in the conversion from craft to Fordist production in wooden furniture and some steel structures. The constancy of the type of product in this sort of transition is often taken for granted; but the ability of firms to change products while maintaining production methods, as just discussed, shows that there is something to be explained here. Firms were committed to the product type either because their existing labour processes could *not* be adapted to different products, or because they wanted to stick with final markets and customers with which they were acquainted. The result was major changes in the production structure of the sector, with all the conflicts that that involves. Sometimes this has led to the exit of the sector from London, as in the disappearance of textiles, ships and heavy engineering in the nineteenth century (Green, 1991). In other cases it resulted in the introduction of major new types of production structure to London.

Firms, then, may become committed either to particular labour processes and productive structures *or* to particular product types and markets; these alternatives produce different forms of historical trajectory within local economies. Whereas Massey's (1984) theory of a succession of 'layers' of local economies focused on continuity (and transformation) of their stock of labour power and traditions of industrial relations, we see here that continuity may also be constructed by other threads such as productive structure, products and market activity.

5.5 Oligopoly, surplus profits and locality

We have seen that local labour process strategies are developed in dialectics with competition within the relevant product-industries (section 2.6). An important moment in this process is the *rate of profit* within the industry or in particular firms within it. A number of labour process theorists have argued that where surplus profits (profits higher than the national or international average) are reaped these can allow looser forms of managerial control. Surplus profits have for the most part been seen as arising from oligopolies associated with large or 'monopoly' capital (Baran and Sweezy, 1968). Thus Friedman (1977) distinguished 'monopoly' and 'competitive' sectors of the contemporary economy, the former distinguished by large capital requirements (and hence large firms), consequent high barriers to entry, and thus a higher than average rate of profit (Andreff, 1984). Because they reap surplus profits, firms in the monopoly sector have more leeway than 'competitive' firms in opening and closing plants and in the time horizons for profitability. They also have greater ability to grant good wages and conditions to their workforce and to maintain employment during downturns, through a redistribution of part of their surplus profits; they are more likely to adopt elements of 'responsible autonomy' (Friedman, 1990). All these characteristics potentially affect their geography. Richard Edwards (1979) made a similar distinction between 'core' and 'peripheral' firms, and argued that the former tend to adopt 'bureaucratic' rather than direct modes of control. Burawoy (1979) went further and argued that the twentieth- century industry *as a whole* is dominated by monopoly competition, which allows for a 'hegemonic' form of control, including workers themselves actively constructing consent to their exploitation.[6]

Friedman's 'monopoly' sector and Edwards's 'core firms' would include most of the London Fordist and process plant sectors. In the periods of take-off of these sectors they tended to offer relatively good wages and conditions based on high rates of profit. In some cases the latter were due to oligopoly, but in others to technological leads. But we have seen that subsequently surplus profits in these two broad sectors have come under pressure in London due to weak ties of innovation, rising scale economies, consequent weakening of market ties to London, and tendencies to overcapacity. Thus the scale of capital requirements of the labour process does not ensure surplus profits. Indeed, *within London*, scale of production has tended to *undermine* their profitability.

On the other hand, our history suggests the importance of sources of surplus profits *other than* capital requirements and the size of firms (Marchington, 1992). The broad sectors of labour-intensive consumer goods, craft capital goods and jobbing firms have been able – albeit with great instability and variation between firms – to reap rents from design, process and product technology, timeliness, spatial monopoly, and reputation (Pred, 1965). These are typically reflected in higher value added per employee in London manufacturing than in the rest of the country (Buck *et al.*, 1986: Ch. 4). These rents have then enabled the high prices of land and labour power in London to be met (and reinforced), giving good wages and conditions in *some* firms in these broad sectors. Notice that the space and time of production have been crucial to these surplus profits: durable local information and supply networks, local designers and technologists, timeliness in delivery, and site-specific work. These structures vary with locality: London is distinctive in the historical importance of rents associated with product design, product quality, bespoke work (including for specific sites), and timeliness. Surplus profits may be not only locally *generated* but locally *specific* (cf. section 2.6).

These forms of surplus profit may also be associated with specific forms of control. In many craft firms, surplus profits have enabled workers to win a substantial degree of responsible autonomy. Conversely, in those sectors where profit rates are lower than average, such as clothing, disciplinary forms of control are common. However, this causality is not simple: as Marchington (1992) has pointed out, firms or sectors with chronic low profitability may be able to use the threat of bankruptcy to exploit a considerable degree of responsible autonomy. This indeed appears to have been the case in some London clothing firms.

Thus surplus profits can impact in important ways on the labour process, but their sources are wider than those understood within the traditional Marxist theories of 'monopoly capital'. They depend not on economies of scale and firm size but also on product innovation, spatial ties to clients, and timeliness, and are thus more locationally and temporally dependent than traditional theory suggests. In particular, surplus profits are generated by locally effective structures, and these may be specific to the locality. Local labour processes, especially those of metropolises, can be strongly influenced by these surplus profits.[7]

5.6 Long waves in London's manufacturing

The historical evolution of sectors so far discussed has been modulated by long waves of accumulation, which have in some cases been associated with major qualitative changes in London manufacturing. The case study is set within a long wave of stagnation of the (inter)national economy, but also within a long decline of employment in London manufacturing which started a decade before that in Britain as a whole. An investigation of these waves in London provides another cut on the dialectic of labour processes and capital accumulation and suggests some of the tensions that informed the case study. There is no extant study of long waves of the London economy, and the treatment here is exploratory.

The relations between value categories, labour processes, technological innovation and wider political relations are highly controversial among theorists of long waves, not only between institutionalists, post-Keynesians and Marxists but also among Marxists themselves. I adopt here a 'theoretically light' approach, sufficient for the present purposes, drawn from Marxist work (Mandel, 1978a; Gordon, 1980; Bowles, Gordon and Weisskopf, 1986; Marshall, 1987). I assume that the average rate of profit is central to the propagation of long waves, in particular in affecting the rate of extensive investment. Long upward waves depend on arrangements within the labour process and broader socializations broadly beneficial to capital. The upward wave once initiated is propelled both by relative surplus value extraction and by strong demand. Upward waves are undermined by a rising organic composition of capital, by conflicts between deepening socialization of production and private appropriation and freedom of investment, and by increased bargaining power of labour. Conversely, downward waves recuperate accumulation through devalorization of capital, breaking up of the entanglements of the socialization, and disciplining of labour. Long upward waves centre on new growth sectors (the 'carrier waves'), and strong accumulation helps to build appropriate socialization of these sectors; but the emergence of these sectors does not account for the expansion.[8]

These processes have complex implications for long waves within regions. Large-scale long waves obviously impact externally onto each regional economy through the average rate of profit and through demand. Some, but not all, of the processes generating large-scale long waves operate also *within* regions: the relations between accumulation, labour processes, industrial relations and the socialization of production are structural ones in the sense introduced in Chapter 1, and therefore operate within regions as much as at higher spatial scales (see further section 12.3).[9] Sectors of rapid growth or decline are often concentrated in particular regions due to their territorial socialization, and these can produce regionally specific long waves (Marshall, 1987). I explore these mechanisms by examining firstly the impact on London manufacturing of rhythms of investment, prices and demand (value aspects of long waves), and secondly the impact of regional socialization on sectoral growth and decline (use value aspects).

Long waves in their value aspects

Investment rates and employment in London manufacturing have to some extent tracked those in British and international manufacturing. Thus in the national wave of expansion in the 1890s and 1900s manufacturing in London expanded strongly, while in the present long wave of stagnation much of the contraction of capacity in London shares the generalized crisis of British manufacturing. But long waves of the (inter)national economy can have paradoxical effects on London manufacturing, tending to generate counter waves to the national ones. This may occur through three value processes:

- Accumulation and local prices

During national booms, the strength of London's core activities and consumer spending create tight markets in most labour segments, further inflate prices of land and labour power (exacerbated by land speculation), and worsen congestion of infrastructures – in short, they exacerbate overaccumulation. This puts particular pressures on manufacturing sectors facing cost competition, especially sectors using low paid workers, because in booms the latter have a better chance of finding employment in non-manufacturing sectors. Reproduction of skilled labour power also tends to be undermined by poaching from non-manufacturing sectors and by inflated costs of living. This is part of the explanation why London manufacturing employment declined earlier and faster than that in Britain as a whole during the 1950s and 1960s, given that demand for London's industries was generally strong during this period (Dennis, 1978; Fothergill and Gudgin, 1979).

Conversely, international waves of stagnation may alleviate the local cost pressures on London manufacturing by reducing growth in the core. Thus stagnation in the 1930s may have facilitated the growth of the new consumer goods industries in London by providing a large available workforce for semi-skilled work and relatively cheap land for space-intensive Fordist factories. However, the core sectors tend to be less adversely affected by waves of stagnation than others, at least since the substantial detachment of the City from the domestic industrial cycle from the 1870s (Marshall, 1987: 111–12, 159–60, 195–6). This has been the case in the present wave of stagnation: since the 1980s there has been strong growth of the City, with negative impacts on non-core sectors (Sassen, 1991).

● Investment rhythms and spatial shifts

To the extent that spatial shifts in sectors are powered by new fixed investment, periods of stagnation, characterized by lower investment rates, would tend to have slower spatial shifts. If we think of London manufacturing as under permanent cost pressures, then shifts away from London due to these pressures may be slowed by stagnation. Buck *et al.* (1986) argue that this has been the case in the present wave of stagnation. But there are problems with this argument. Spatial shifts of sectors can be effected not only by new fixed investment but by selective closures, particularly during waves of stagnation (Massey and Meegan, 1979; 1982: Ch. 8). London manufacturing may then contract faster in such periods if its workplaces are weakly competitive. Moreover, while extensive fixed investment does tend to decline, intensive investment may hold up (as it did in Britain in the 1980s), and this may deepen lack of competitiveness in London firms. More concrete analysis of a wave of accumulation is therefore needed to determine which of these contrary processes is paramount.

● Final demand

Important components of the demand on which London manufacturing depends may hold up better in long waves of stagnation than that for manufactures in general. As already noted, the core functions of London tend to be less affected than the rest of the economy. Moreover, there tends to be a shift in distribution towards those on higher incomes, which are disproportionately centred in London, as during the 1980s and 1990s. Idle capital may flow into speculation in the built environment (Harvey, 1982), and London tends to be a strong focus for this speculation, the 1980s again being a case in point; this benefits those sections of manufacturing in the city linked to the building industry. Thus, in a period of stagnation, demand adds to the price processes discussed above in privileging manufacturing in London compared with other locations.

Long waves as sectoral growth and decline

Entangled with these value processes are waves of *sectoral* growth and decline *partly* propelled by (inter)national waves. There have been major waves of investment in London in sectors that were rapidly growing at the national or world level, and which were new to London either in their broad type of product or in labour process or both (section 5.4). Thus from the 1890s there was a wave of investment in chemicals and food processing, using large scale process plant; in the interwar period until the 1950s the boom sectors were in cars, aerospace, and electrical consumer and capital goods; and, if we widen our focus to the London region, there has been a boom in specialist electronic goods since the 1970s. The need to distinguish these regional waves of sectoral innovation from national waves of growth is indicated by the fact that they have taken place in both upward and downward waves of the national economy (Marshall, 1987).

The local socializations of emerging industries may be more easily created in regions where the most characteristic social relations of the previous wave are not strongly present. Thus in the case of London one might argue that investments in process plant and Fordist production may have been sited in London, not because of an absence of strong trade union organization, but partly because of the *type* of union organization traditionally dominant there: craft unionism within a fragmented industrial structure, rather than collective organization in large workplaces such as was present in northern industrial regions. On the other hand, as we have seen, some growth industries were strongly centred in London because of their *continuity* with existing forms of local sectoral socialization (section 5.4). Thus the food and chemical process plant sectors emerged partly from earlier forms of processing of raw materials from the docks as well as from attraction of final markets. Electrical capital goods and aerospace emerged from the productive capacities of earlier mechanical machine and instrument-making sectors, and the former in turn were the basis for the contemporary electronic industries of the London region. We have seen that mass production of cars and electrical consumer goods, although radical departures from previous production structures in many respects, drew on technical knowledge of products and on skilled labour from earlier sectors. Other forms of standardized mass production emerged by virtue of continuity in product type and marketing knowledge. Thus successive waves of new sectors, product types and labour processes in London and its region have emerged there through continuities in productive structures or through modifications or selective use of earlier structures.

A different argument on the geography of growth sectors has been developed by Storper and Walker (1989). New sectors may initially emerge in many different locations because these sectors have to create most of the conditions for their own growth. These locations may be either existing industrial regions or non-industrial ones. The former may have advantages in that certain structures useful for the new sector may be formed out of older structures of the region (entrepreneurs, component suppliers, labour power), but they are not essential in general. Sectors formed in different localities often have substantially different production structures, and in the next stage of development of the industry the least profitable of these are shaken out. This perspective would imply that the new growth sectors of London formed rather fortuitously; and it is not clear within Storper and Walker's approach why London's productive structures might have been more successful than those elsewhere. I have suggested, to the contrary, that the new growth sectors had very substantial bases in existing forms of sectoral coherence; Storper and Walker's caveat concerning the possible role of inherited industrial structures needs making more strongly.

The relation between growth sectors and existing economy in London is thus contradictory. On the one hand new sectors have emerged in considerable continuity with earlier ones, either through production structure or products. On the other hand, in some dimensions, such as forms of unionization, it may have been the *difference* between the new and old structures that made London attractive. In some periods manufacturing has expanded in a wave of high profit rates and investment, which also fuelled expansion of the core, whereas in others manufacturing expansion may have benefited from slowdown of the core activities.

The decline of London manufacturing sectors has been equally paradoxical. Decreasing employment has seldom been due to (inter)national decline of the sector, but rather to shifts to other parts of Britain or, latterly, abroad. These shifts have in many cases accelerated during long upward waves, as new socializations of the sectors have been constructed in other regions and as the cost pressures in London discussed above intensified. These processes may account for the sharp decline during the mid-Victorian boom of textiles, shipbuilding and heavy engineering in London (Stedman Jones, 1971), and for the rapid decentralization of Fordist and process plant production during the postwar boom. In these cases growth of industries in other regions propelled by long expansions has exposed the characteristic weakness of London production.

Growth sectors in London, once inaugurated, have built up supporting locally effective structures and benefited from reinforcing accumulation (sections 2.4, 2.8). But these processes may also go into reverse. As a sector begins to decline, networks of local suppliers are weakened. The temptation of firms to skimp on training is exacerbated, and keeping skilled workers within the industry is made more difficult by worsening wages and conditions *given* the variety of other opportunities in London. Thus, paradoxically, declining demand for sectoral labour power can *exacerbate* skills shortages. These processes of underaccumulation tend to be most acute in the craft sectors, less so in Fordist and process plants given their wider and less dense linkages and their greater use of internal labour markets. However, problems of labour supply may be lessened in periods of stagnation. Thus, following Storper and Walker, the development of both growing and declining sectors may be read as evolutions of technological capabilities; but they are also always evolutions of class relations.

5.7 Geographical spread, uneven accumulation and archaeology of London manufacturing

As population and production in the region have grown in the very long term, the characteristic social relations of London manufacturing so far discussed have been remarkably constant. Outward shifts of residence and jobs have contributed actively to renewing these relations both in long-standing sectors and in growth industries. However, patterns of reinforcing, under and overaccumulation have been highly uneven both between sectors and between successive rings of development within the region. Again, we have combined dynamics of accumulation, labour processes and socialization in space.

From the early nineteenth century to the First World War what is now inner London was built up through successive rings of development. In the interwar period a population and employment boom greatly expanded outer London. These outward waves of development involved three processes. First, some craft capital goods, jobbing and process plant production moved outwards. Second, those parts of the craft sectors that from the 1890s were converting to Fordism tended to shift to outer London, not only for access to land but also to tap new sources of semi-skilled labour while still being able to use sectorally skilled workers who had moved to suburbia. Third, from the 1920s, Fordist factories producing new products set up in outer London.

Growth and decentralization developed a cross-like pattern of industrialization, with bands running northwards along the Lea Valley, eastwards down the Thames, southwards down the Wandle Valley, and westwards and north-westwards into Middlesex. The northwards and eastwards expansion took the sectors previously concentrated in east London, especially those derived from down-market craft consumer goods, while westwards expansion took those derived from craft capital goods earlier located in Clerkenwell and the West End, including electrical industries (Hall, 1962: Ch. 8). The difference of class relations in East End and West End manufacturing in the nineteenth century was thus detectable as an east/west contrast in the twentieth, and the same contrast extended into the Home Counties after the Second World War; the socializations of sectors remained territorial even as they expanded outwards. As a result, in the period since the Second World War, manufacturing employment has declined faster in east than in west London, and since the 1970s manufacturing in the eastern Home Counties has been weaker, both quantitatively and qualitatively, than in the west (SEEDS, 1987).

After the Second World War, the outer boundary of London was frozen by the imposition of the Green Belt; development could take place in the rest of the south east region (ROSE), but was channelled into designated New Towns and Expanded Towns and, as it turned out, on the fringes of other existing settlements. Manufacturing developed in ROSE in broadly the same types of sector except being light on craft consumer goods production. Just as outer London had in the interwar period, ROSE offered advantages of somewhat lower land prices, land availability, local supplies of skilled manual workers, technicians, managers and owners who had already decentralized, a new ostensibly conservative suburban identity, no continuity of workplace or industry trade unionism, as well as better road (and subsequently air) transport infrastructures. At the same time firms were close enough to London to be a part of its informational, marketing, design and technological milieux, parts of which were anyway expanding into ROSE itself. The shift from London to ROSE was hastened by land use and regional policies (section 5.8 below), but it was essentially driven by social and economic processes. Since the 1970s a further spatial wave of development has taken place: the most information-intensive part of the electronics industry has been overwhelmingly centred in the 'Sun Belt' triangle lying to the west of London. It is essentially a continuation of the craft, high technology part of the electrical industry of (outer) London and is anchored to the London region for the same reasons (section 5.3 (ii)). But it has grown outside London because of the prior decentralization there of many technicians and managers and some skilled manual workers, the availability of land for 'business parks', and the opportunity to construct an elite production and consumption space in a pseudo-rural setting (Hall *et al.*, 1987; Allen, Massey and Cochrane, 1997). Thus many of the locally effective structures of London manufacturing have in essence been retained during expansion outwards; indeed, expansion has played an active role in reproducing them.

It has not been, however, simply a matter of a spread of London-type industry into ROSE; particular sectors in London declined, and since the 1950s total manufacturing employment has also declined. It is tempting to see this as simply the decline of older vintages of investment; but this does not explain why renewal of investment within London was not more common. I discuss some problems of labour power and built environment in the next chapter, and the variation of pressures with the labour process is analysed in Part III. Here the most acute pressures may be briefly mentioned (Martin, 1966: 230; Buck *et al.*, 1986: Ch. 4). In sectors transferring to more land-intensive methods, or with rapidly growing output, firms were often constrained by the size of their existing site (Fothergill and Gudgin, 1982). Skill shortages were often a problem, particularly in the craft sectors. The high costs of London weighed especially on sectors competing with firms in the development areas (Martin, 1966: Ch. 10) or low cost countries, and those unable to reap quality rents based on London location, particularly in Taylorist or Fordist production (cf. section 5.4). Congestion of goods traffic was an important difficulty for many firms. These problems sometimes led to lack of upgrading of processes and products. Thus in the 1960s London manufacturing weakened in sectors which nationally were experiencing rapid productivity growth (Buck *et al.*, 1986). In the craft sectors this was sometimes exacerbated by the disintegration of industrial districts (section 5.5), a decline of *collective* productiveness. The impact on accumulation was varied: some sectors were able to achieve profit rates similar to or greater than those nationally though their growth was constrained; others, especially those exposed to sharp cost competition, had lower rates of profit (Moore *et al.*, 1982; Fothergill and Gudgin, 1982).

Aside from shifts to ROSE and decline through contraction and closures, some manufacturing also relocated out of the south-east (Buck *et al.*, 1986: Ch. 4), though relatively little to the development areas (Dennis, 1978). This was largely less-skilled and Fordist production where costs were crucial. Some firms maintained their high skill operations in London when decentralizing others (Martin, 1966: 125 and Ch. 12; Massey and Meegan, 1979).

These contradictory relationships to London and the resulting outward shifts of production have been inflected by the long waves of development. The boom in outer London manufacturing that started in the interwar period slackened in the 1950s. The international boom of the 1950s and 1960s exacerbated the cost and supply difficulties of London. The generalized crisis of the British economy since the 1970s has tended to relieve the particular cost and labour market pressures on London manufacturing, but the neoliberal globalization that arose from the crisis gave London renewed importance as a finance and business centre, so that inflationary pressures remained strong, especially from the 1980s. The powerful wave of development in electronics from the 1970s took place largely outside the boundaries of London itself; but the London *region*, including the south-east and the Sun Belt, continued to be the most dynamic manufacturing area in Britain. Thus the long history of expansion and decentralization of manufacturing in the region has been marked by sharply uneven development: overaccumulation deriving from core functions has adversely affected manufacturing in inner rings and caused underinvestment in many sectors, while in successive outer rings there has been cumulative reinforcing accumulation.

The result of all these processes was that during the long boom manufacturing employment in London declined absolutely and relatively to the country as a whole: in Britain registered manufacturing employment was the same in 1968 as in 1951 but had declined by 33 per cent in London, the largest contraction of any of the conurbations; it peaked in Britain in the mid-1960s but in London in the late 1950s. Manufacturing as a proportion of all employment in London stood at 36 per cent in 1951, but by 1976 had declined to 21 per cent. However, with the onset of the long wave of stagnation manufacturing employment in London did not fare significantly worse than in the rest of the country: in 1968–81 it declined by 30 per cent in Great Britain and by 33 per cent in London.[10] The discussion above suggests some possible reasons for this change: rising unemployment gave greater ability of management to recruit and hold workers, to hold down wages, and to reorganize and intensify work; spatial cost differentials lessened; and there was a relative strengthening of demand for goods produced in London, particularly upmarket products, those related to construction, and suppliers to the core.

5.8 Local coherence in London manufacturing?

We have seen that industries in each of the broad sectors have grown and been anchored in London through varied forms of sectoral socialization.

Some of these extend out into the reproduction sphere and into local politics. For example, the craft- and labour-intensive production of consumer goods has been sustained by successive waves of immigrants, many of whom were strongly dependent on their communities for work; by gender relations that, although varied, have tended to provide employers with 'suitable' female workforces for both factory work and homeworking; and large-scale provision of public housing in inner boroughs that made it possible for a low paid workforce to remain in London. Similarly, the suburban built environment and social life probably contributed positively to the interwar boom in outer London manufacturing. More recently, Sun Belt manufacturing has benefited from an uneasy balance between sufficient new urbanization and the maintenance of a 'rural' landscape, as well as from (largely publicly provided) infrastructures of training, motorways and airports.

However, there have been limitations. Even in the craft sectors, firms have been more weakly coordinated, both economically and politically, than in many industrial districts on the continent – a characteristically British trait (Hirst and Zeitlin, 1989). Sectors in London have lacked even the limited degree of coordination that has been built up in some provincial industries in the process of lobbying for regional aid. It is even harder to find evidence of coordination of capital in London manufacturing *as a whole*. The London Chamber of Commerce and Industry has been notably weak. Planning of land use and infrastructures since the Second World War, at least until the late 1960s, has tended to damage manufacturing in the capital while benefiting the core activities (Leigh *et al.*, 1982a). Relocation of non-confirming industry from residential areas was more rigorous in London than in other conurbations, though much was directed to new units within the city (Martin, 1966: 233). Industrial Development Certificates were required for expansion of manufacturing premises, though exporters and armaments production tended to be treated lightly – a *de facto* industrial policy (Martin, 1966: 231). In contrast, office development permits were not seriously applied due to the perceived importance of London's financial and control functions (Buck *et al.*, 1986: Ch. 3). Housing regulation has had adverse effects. The outer London boroughs, mostly controlled by the Conservatives, were allowed to refuse to build public housing, thus damaging the reproduction of the semi-skilled workforce and tending to raise house prices across the board. The Green Belt has raised the price of housing in London substantially (Hall *et al.*, 1973), with more serious effects on manufacturing than the high-profit core functions. Transport subsidies disproportionately benefited the radial passenger transport links by rail, which serve the core functions of central London rather than manufacturing (GLC, 1985: Ch. 20). In contrast, policy has benefited manufacturing in ROSE: the New and Expanded Town programme after the war, and lavish infrastructure spending and pragmatic land use planning since the 1960s.

This history of 'anti-manufacturing policies' could be interpreted as a result of a London-wide regime dominated by the City. More plausible is that the London economy as a whole has been dogged by overaccumulation with respect to labour power, land and infrastructures, exacerbated by class struggle in the reproduction sphere (for example residents' opposition to polluting and non-confirming firms (Green, 1991: 18)). The state has then attempted to decentralize investment in general, targeting particularly those sectors (whether manufacturing or not) which would suffer the least penalty from relocation. Shifts to ROSE were easier to engineer than shifts to the development areas, with the result that overaccumulation tended to spread from London out into ROSE (Peck and Tickell, 1995). Thus regulation of London has been not so much a domination by a particular fraction of capital as a mediation of contradictions of accumulation by the state. However, the state was politically limited in its purchase over private investment, and, as we see in the next section, limited also by Britain's liberal traditions. The *effects* of this regulation have been generally negative for manufacturing accumulation within London, countering the limited forms of coherence in particular sectors.

5.9 British manufacturing decline and crisis

The present long wave of stagnation has been a period of crisis for British manufacturing, in which manufacturing in London has fully participated. The context is an international crisis of overaccumulation of capital with respect to profit (Mandel, 1978a; 1978b; Armstrong, Glyn and Harrison, 1991). British manufacturing has been *externally* impacted by this worldwide crisis through weakening of final markets and through the tendential equalization of profit rates across the international economy at lower levels than in the boom. However, because British manufacturing shares structures with the international economy, it has also actively *participated in* (and contributed to) the world crisis rather than simply being its victim (section 1.1). In particular, its profit rate has been eroded by a rising organic composition of capital (Hargreaves Heap, 1980). A decrease in the rate of exploitation was evident in the 1960s and 1970s (Glyn and Sutcliffe, 1972); as in the rest of Western Europe, and to some extent North America, the long boom strengthened workers' organization and bargaining power. When capital attempted to increase the rate of exploitation in the late 1960s in response to falling profit rates, sharp industrial conflict ensued.

British manufacturing nevertheless had important specificities (Aaronovitch and Smith, 1981; Williams *et al.*, 1983; Fine and Harris, 1985). These centrally concern the contradictory relations between the value and use value sides of the labour process and between private property and productive coordination (sections 2.3, 3.5). As pointed out by innumerable critics from the 1860s to the present, British manufacturing is generally characterized by poor investment in research and development and training, low innovation, slow productivity increase, and low profit rates compared with manufacturing in other developed countries and with other operations of British capital. The picture is uneven: armaments and pharmaceuticals – both important in London – have been more innovative and profitable, both benefiting from state purchasing. A proximate origin of manufacturing weaknesses is the lack of coordination between manufacturing firms, between them and the financial system, and between these and the state, in contrast to socialization by the banks and Länder in Germany, by the *keiretsu* and national state in Japan, and by the state in France. The British banking system has been distant from domestic industry, and dependence on the stock market has encouraged short-term profit horizons in quoted industrial firms. Productivity increase in British manufacturing may also have been inhibited by the 'stand-offish' employment relations characteristic of Britain, combining organizationally strong unions with lack of active role for them in production, in contrast to the co-determination system of postwar West Germany or the collaborationist unions in Japan after their postwar defeats. Yet, in the very long term, coordination both within capital and between capital and labour has become increasingly important as capitalism has become more technologically sophisticated, as productive investment has become larger scale and more risky, and as the division of labour has become more elaborate. The proximate causes of the relative weakness of British manufacturing thus lie both in interfirm relations and within the labour process itself.

The weak socialization of British manufacturing, in turn, can be understood as the product of Britain's particular class relations in the modern period. Since the Civil War, England has been marked by the strength of civil society and private property *vis-à-vis* the state. While this has been a thoroughly capitalist trait, and one that enabled Britain's primacy in the industrial revolution (E. Wood, 1991), it has led to weak coordination between economic actors. Political-economic individualism was reinforced by Britain's early world lead in industry and its featherbedding by protected empire markets, which reduced incentives to improve innovation and productivity raising capacity, and reinforced the rentier streak in both capital and stronger sections of labour. Thus within the characteristic capitalist tensions between individualism and socialization of firms (section 2.8) and between short-term interest and cooperation in the capital-labour relation (section 3.5), Britain has inclined towards the former. Moreover, Britain's mercantile and imperial roles gave opportunities to British capital in trade and in overseas investment such that the City of London was inclined to have a distant relationship with domestic industry (Ingham, 1984).

It is not the case, however, that British political economy simply serves the interests of financial and mercantile capital against those of industry (*pace* Anderson, 1987). International ties built up through empire (including those outside of the formal empire such as those in the Middle East) continue to provide markets for British industrial firms. Capital mobility has been used by large industrial capital in internationalizing its production, linkages and joint ventures. The cream of British manufacturing, armaments production, has been directly based on Britain's imperial role. British political economy has also involved a powerful form of class rule that has been remarkably resilient in the face of crises in the twentieth century. Capital mobility both spatially and sectorally reinforces market discipline on workers, enabling manufacturing employers to *impose* technical change (cf. section 3.2). In exchange for being allowed to pursue individual or group income maximization, and in the case of strongly organized workers, certain job demarcations, labour has wholly abandoned to capital the right to manage the labour process, product strategies, and sectoral and spatial investment policy. Compared with continental Europe, the culture of the British labour movement is economic-liberalist and depoliticized, so that capital has been able to appeal to strongly legitimated notions of 'the requirements of competitiveness' and 'market necessities'. Britain's particular political-economy, then, has *strengths* for manufacturing capital. At an abstract level, while there are tensions between rooted productive capital and mobile money capital, the two are also linked moments of capital accumulation and hence mutually constitutive (see further Chapter 13). We should therefore understand the particularity of Britain, not as an aberration from some 'normal' industrial capitalism, but as a particular form of it, involving specific reactions to its contradictions, and with specific problems *and advantages* for productive accumulation (cf. section 2.2; E. Wood, 1991).

A relevant example of these advantages is the large role of US manufacturing multinationals in Britain, particularly in the London region. United States' manufacturing capital has always preferred Britain as the site for its

European production. In 1953, 25 per cent of manufacturing employment in the south-east was in US-owned firms (Hamilton, 1991: 67); US firms pioneered Taylorist and Fordist labour processes in interwar London (Green, 1991: 31). This is partly due to the qualities of British industrial relations: not only have these in some ways resembled the liberal US model, but US management has been able to expect adaptability to radically new work practices (Dunning, 1958).

Since the late nineteenth century numerous political currents have attempted to change these class relations towards a more corporatist and productivist model (for example Hutton, 1995). These have been most strongly based in provincial manufacturing centres, perhaps because of the weak coordination of London manufacturing capital discussed above. These attempts at 'modernization' have failed. This is not only because of tensions between fractions of capital but also because of the dilemmas for capital as a whole. In particular, encouraging a more active role for labour within production risks unpredictable politicization and potential undermining of a very serviceable pattern of class power (Desai, 1996; Gough and Eisenschitz, 1996b).

5.10 Manufacturing in Britain and London in the period of study, 1976–81

From the late 1960s the combination of creeping international stagnation and its relatively weak productiveness resulted in a crisis for British manufacturing, manifested in low profit rates or losses, wage restraint, redundancies and plant closures. Between the cyclical peaks of 1968 and 1979, manufacturing output grew by 12 per cent and employment shrank by 14 per cent. The rate of return on manufacturing capital fell from an average of 9.0 per cent in 1965–73 to 4.3 per cent at the top of the cycle in 1979 (Glyn, 1989: 75). The crisis was apparent in 1972–3 in the attempt by the Conservative government to reflate industry, which resulted mainly in rampant inflation and speculative investment and in a wave of labour revolt culminating in the miners' strike and three-day week.

In 1973–4 there was an unprecedented international recession across all the major countries triggered, though not mainly caused, by OPEC's oil price rise (Mandel, 1978b). The Labour government was elected in 1974 with its most radical ever manifesto. This proposed a productivist model incorporating a stronger role for the state in industrial investment, planning agreements between state and corporations, a role for labour in firm and industry planning, and a form of nationalization of development land. Initial moves to implement this strategy were scuttled by the City and the IMF in 1975. The government then turned to a neoliberal strategy of monetary and fiscal stringency, abandoning any substantial direct industrial strategy. It won the agreement of the trade union leadership to restrain wages, formalized in the 'Social Contract'. This strategy reduced real wages, an achievement that eluded the subsequent Conservative government (Glyn, 1989). Nonetheless, the recovery from the recession was weak: from the bottom of the cycle in 1975 to its peak in 1979 real GDP increased by only 13 per cent and employment by only 1 per cent (quarter on quarter); in manufacturing the figures were 10 per cent and 1 per cent respectively; productivity increases produced jobless growth. The Social Contract was successful in containing worker militancy in manufacturing, but public sector union action against spending cuts eventually broke out in the 'winter of discontent' of 1978/9.

The negative effects for the working class of this first dose of neoliberalism, and capital's fear that Labour was still not able to tame the unions, resulted in the election of the Conservatives on a more explicit programme of neoliberalism. Neoliberalism in Britain from 1975 was of a strong variety due to the particularly low level of the rate of profit in manufacturing. It also had a deep root in traditional British political economy – the priority of private property, individual economic actors and free markets, so that 'Thatcherism' ran with the cultural grain (MacInnes, 1987). On its election, the government implemented a sharp deflation through monetary and fiscal means, resulting in the deepest recession since 1929–31. Real GDP fell by 7 per cent and employment by 8 per cent between their quarterly peaks in 1979 and their troughs in 1981. Manufacturing experienced a massive crisis, with output declining by 18 per cent and employment plummeting by 24 per cent before it bottomed out in 1984. Return on manufacturing capital, which had fallen to the perilous level of 2.8 per cent in 1975, fell back to 2.3 per cent in 1981 (*British Business*).

The dominant ideology propagated by capital and governments was of the need for discipline of labour within the work process and the employment contract, for wage restraint and for labour shedding. Parts of the trade union and Labour left, following the 1974 Labour manifesto, put forward a strategy of industrial partnership for greater innovation and productiveness with an active role for workers' organizations (Coventry Trades Council *et al.*, 1980). A particularly radical vision was developed by the stewards at Lucas Aerospace in Kingston – an expression of the craft traditions in London capital goods manufacturing (Wainwright and Elliot, 1982; Cooley, 1986). But this politics was not strong enough in any firm or industry to reverse the neoliberal attack; the historical hold of liberalism in British society continued and was deepened.

Our period of study, 1976–81, then, fell across nearly the whole of the 1975/6–1981/2 business cycle, the first full business cycle under neoliberal policy. While the recession was particularly deep, the upswing of the cycle was weak. We have seen that the upswing was weaker in manufacturing than in the economy as a whole, with scarcely an interruption to the long term decline of manufacturing employment. Moreover, the continuing (if somewhat ameliorated) adverse conditions for manufacturing in London meant that the effects of the 1975–9 international upturn were especially attenuated, with employment declining a further 9 per cent. Nevertheless, the characteristic *processes* of a business cycle upswing, including increased demand and tightening labour markets, were experienced within London manufacturing (see Appendix 1 for detail). The case study of London workplaces will contrast spatial labour process change in the two phases of the cycle.

5.11 Theoretical threads

This chapter has examined socializations of production and reproduction in London, building on Part I. It has followed a number of threads linking distinct structures:

- relations between labour processes, product activity and London markets;
- technical rents arising from these, and their impact on ground rents, wages and forms of capital;
- the dialectics of class relations in the labour process and in social life, and the worker identities these produce;
- the political regulation of manufacturing and forms of local coherence; and
- relations of labour processes to capital accumulation in long waves of development, in the present long wave of stagnation, and in waves of spatial decentralization.

These threads will be developed in more empirical detail in the remainder of the book.

Underlying the analysis of this chapter have been a number of fundamental tensions, or more precisely, contradictory unities, which we first encountered in Part I: between internationalized, mobile money capital and productive capital rooted in place; between discipline and cooperation within industrial relations; between the interests of individual firms and their coordination; and between the particular use values of production and the valorization of capital. These run through *each* of the scales with which we have been concerned – the London, British and world economies and particular sectors of them (cf. section 2.1). Thus the tension between mobility and fixity is present in British capital's relation to the world economy, in tensions between the productive efficiency and high costs of operating in London, in the very different spatial embedding of the broad sectors in London, and in the (failures of) socialization of London manufacturing. We have seen that relations *between* these spatial scales have been crucial. However, these are not simply external relations, because each scale of the economy is constructed by common social relations and internalizes the same tensions.

NOTES

1. Cohen and Zysman (1987) estimated that while officially designated manufacturing in the US accounted for around 25 per cent of employment in the 1970s, a further 25 per cent was in services directly linked to manufacturing.
2. Marshall (1987: 150, 180) argues that during the nineteenth century the City's international orientation affected manufacturing most strongly in London.
3. This account draws on Hall (1962), Martin (1966), Leigh et al (1982a), Greater London Council (1985; 1986), Buck *et al.* (1986) and Green (1991), and on the primary survey data (section 6.2).
4. Similarly, the Paris region and the Île de France have been the major single recipient of French military hardware spending. United States armaments spending has been crucial in that country's lead in electronics and software and has been central to the development of the four greatest regional agglomerations of these industries, Silicon Valley, Orange County, the Boston region, and the North Carolina triangle. These, however, differ from the British and French examples in their distance from the centre of military procurement. Reasons for this include the nature of Washington DC as a government but not an industrial centre, the greater size and regional diversity of the US economy, and a tendency to form wholly new high-technology agglomerations based on anti-unionism (Davis, 1990).

5. This has not been true in all cases, however. Craft production of steel-work, for example, has generally been single-storey, while some light mass produced goods such as electrical and electronic assembly have been carried out in flatted factories.

6. Braverman (1974) also characterized the twentieth century as a period of 'monopoly capitalism'. However, he sees this type of capitalism as leading to more rather than less direct forms of managerial control of the labour process.

7. Some authors have argued that the ability of firms to make surplus profits from product innovation and marketing makes issues of managerial control within the labour process less important than many labour process theorists suggest (Rose and Jones, 1985; Morgan and Hooper, 1987). But we see here that the former have important *impacts* on the latter.

8. Institutionalist (Freeman, Clark and Soete, 1982) and regulation theory (Aglietta, 1979) work on long waves attribute too much to technological and organizational aspects of labour processes in abstraction from value processes (for this critique of regulation theory see Clarke, 1988b; 1992; Gough, 1996a and b). I therefore do not associate waves with a particular dominant labour process. Unlike Mandel and Freeman, I do not assume that technological innovation is concentrated in particular phases of the long wave (see further section 12.4).

9. The role of the rising organic composition of capital in depressing the profit rate operates over the system within which capital is mobile enough tendentially to equalize profit rates. In the present day this is moving from the national to the world scale, and in most cases is therefore not regionally endogenous.

10. The proportional underestimate of manufacturing employment due to unregistered work has probably always been larger in London than in Britain as a whole, due to the high proportion of small firms and homeworking, particularly in the craft sectors. Over the period since the Second World War the underestimate has probably increased, due to a disproportionate decline of large factories. For example, in the early 1980s there were around 30,000 registered jobs in the London clothing industry, while union and community workers estimated that there were another 30,000 unregistered jobs (Greater London Council, 1985: 122). Thus the relative decline shown in the official statistics is probably exaggerated.

6 From Rags to Radar: A Slice of London Manufacturing

6.1 Exemplifying theory

This chapter introduces the case study by giving a theoretically informed snapshot of the panel of London manufacturing workplaces and their relations to their local and wider contexts. This adds further 'cuts' to the account of London manufacturing given in Chapter 5, and enables us to explore further the framework developed in Part I. The chapter also provides a base for the study of *change* in the labour process undertaken in Part III.

Following Chapter 3, the starting point is to categorize the panel workplaces by their dominant labour process, a novel procedure in studies of territorial economies. We shall see that this produces a very different categorization, and hence analytical starting point, from the usual product-industry divisions. I show the close mutual construction of these labour processes and the workplace's product activity (drawing particularly on sections 3.4 and 5.4). It is shown how these then underpin two aspects of capital accumulation, namely the form of the firm and the search for surplus profits (drawing on sections 5.3 and 5.5). The experiences of management in dealing with local labour power and premises are examined, showing the deep interdependencies of these with labour processes (drawing on sections 2.4 and 2.5). Finally, I look at the geography of the product-industry systems within which the workplaces are placed, the spaces of final markets, and the associated forms of competition which they face (drawing on sections 2.6, 2.7 and 5.3); we shall see that these spaces of competition are strongly related to the labour processes within London. Finally, I assess the notion that London manufacturing had declined into a 'backward' state. The chapter thus exemplifies the proposition of Part I, that the labour process should be the centre of studies of the geography of production.

6.2 The workplaces and data described

The study uses workplace data collected by the London Industry and Employment Research Group to survey change in London manufacturing and to assess local government economic policies (Leigh *et al.*, 1982a; 1982b). This data set contains rich information on labour processes and changes in them, product innovation, forms of capital, use of labour power and premises, final markets, competition, and managements' locational choices.

The data were obtained by interviews with the workplaces' general managers. The present study is therefore centred on *managers' reasons for taking initiatives in the labour process*. The absence of data from workers or their representatives inevitably produces biases, but the analysis does not exclude the motivations and actions of workers because managers' strategies take these into account; they are viewed – though not *interpreted* – through managers' eyes (P. Edwards, 1986). The outcomes were not necessarily those intended by management, in the first place because of the motivations and actions of the workforce (Friedman, 1986; 1990). Managers also could operate with inadequate theories (for example on the formation of labour power: section 6.5) or poor assessments of their situation (Rubery and Wilkinson, 1994). Strategies could also be deflected by developments outside the workplace that were not anticipated, but even where strategy and outcome diverge, the former shapes change in the workplace and deserves theorizing. Moreover, the methodology gives us a view of changes intended by management, including relocation, which were *not* carried out, and thus important insights on the barriers and contradictions they faced (Hyman, 1987). The only component of spatial change that is directly viewed in this methodology is relocation within the firm (Chapter 4; Appendix 2); but this limitation has the advantage that we have a window directly onto the link between spatial and labour process strategies.

The survey was longitudinal, with data collected by face-to-face interviews in 1979 and telephone interviews for the same workplaces in 1981. The interviews in 1979 covered the period of upswing of the business cycle 1976–9, while the interviews in 1981 covered the two-year downswing of 1980–1; the data thus give an unusually good picture of change over a business cycle.

In 1979 face-to-face interviews were carried out in 317 workplaces that had been present in 1976 and that had survived to that date. In 1981 telephone interviews were carried out with managers of 248 (97 per cent) of the survivors who had remained in situ, seven relocated workplaces and fourteen that had closed. In addition, in 1985 telephone interviews were carried out with management of 62 workplaces that had opened during the period of study; these included two overlapping sets, 47 openings and 30 relocations into the areas studied (on the terms used here see Appendix 2). The analysis in this book concerns the whole panel of 379 workplaces, which included 332 cases where production existed in 1976.[1]

Employment change in the panel varied strongly over the business cycle. In those surviving from 1976 to 1979, the initial employment total of 29,100 hardly changed; but during the downturn of 1980–1 employment declined by 14 per cent in the survivors and overall by 31 per cent including closures (Leigh et al., 1982a: 53–62). The analysis here, however, will be concerned not with these employment outcomes but with the qualitative changes that led to them.

The panel workplaces were located in five out of London's 32 boroughs, which are local government areas with a population between 150,000 and 250,000. The boroughs surveyed are located in two of London's principal manufacturing belts. Southwark, Hackney and Enfield are part of the belt stretching from the old East End (Hackney) and dock areas (Southwark) northwards up the Lea Valley to Enfield, which extends to the edge of London. Hackney and Southwark adjoin the City of London, and their industrial areas were first developed mainly during the nineteenth century; those in Enfield developed from the early twentieth century. As we have seen, this belt is strong in craft consumer goods and process plant; Enfield also had some Fordist production. The second belt surveyed was that around the Wandle river in south-west London, comprising the inner borough of Wandsworth and the outer borough of Merton. This belt was developed from the late nineteenth century, and includes particularly the mechanical and electrical engineering sectors characteristic of west London. My analysis will sometimes distinguish inner and outer London locations; the boroughs' locations will not otherwise concern us.

The workplaces were selected from fourteen Minimum List Headings (MLHs) of the 1968 Standard Industrial Classification, which were chosen as the largest product-industries in the survey areas; however, sectors with very heterogeneous products were excluded. The chosen MLHs are shown in Table 6.1. In industries where there were numerous establishments (MLHs 443, 445, 472, 489), a sample biased towards the large workplaces was used; in the other MLHs all known workplaces were approached for interview. For the purposes of analysis, two of the MLHs were combined with another because of their similarity in processes and products, giving twelve product-industries.

This set of product industries gives a good representation of all five broad sectors of London manufacturing introduced in Chapter 5. The clothing

Table 6.1 *The product-industries of the study*

MLH	Name used in this book: description
213	**Biscuits**
231	**Brewing**
272	**Pharmaceuticals**
341	**Steelwork:** Industrial plant, construction steelwork, boilers, tanks, pipes
354	**Scientific instruments:** mechanical, electrical and electronic sensing, measuring, recording, control and optical instruments and systems
365	**Consumer electronics:** TVs, radios, tape recorders, studio equipment; records and tapes
367	**Electronic capital goods:** transmitters, radar, navigation equipment, electro-medical equipment; alarms and signalling equipment
395	**Metal boxes:** cans and metal boxes
443 + 445	**Clothing:** Women's and girls' tailored outerwear; dresses, blouses, lingerie, infants' wear
472	**Furniture:** Wooden furniture and upholstery
486 + 489	**Printing:** Magazines; general typesetting, engraving, printing and book binding (excluding newspapers)
494	**Toys:** Toys, games, fancy goods and sports equipment

Note: these descriptions are abbreviated from the SIC 1968.

sector, major parts of the furniture and toy industries, and a small part of the printing sector fell within the broad sector of *craft and labour intensive consumer goods.* These were concentrated in the inner boroughs where they have a long history. In the *craft capital goods* sector we have major parts of scientific instruments and electronic capital goods, and studio equipment (within MLH 365); these were strongest in outer London, but included some longer established firms in inner London. *Jobbing craft industries* are represented by steelwork and printing, as well as by fire alarms (in MLH 367) and shop fitting (in MLH 472). Printing was concentrated in inner London so as to serve central London core businesses, while the other jobbing sectors were dispersed. *Fordist* factories were found in many of the product-industries, including intermediate and capital goods. Located mainly in outer London, they included parts of steelwork, scientific instruments, consumer electronics, furniture, and toys. Finally, *process plant* production was represented by biscuits, brewing, metal boxes and some pharmaceuticals, mainly sited in their traditional locations in inner London. The panel was thus broadly representative of London manufacturing as a whole.

6.3 Categorizing the labour process

In order to analyse the labour process dynamics of these workplaces a typology is needed. This needs to be able to encompass, albeit with the inevitable crudeness of a typology, the very wide differences in labour process we have seen within London manufacturing. To avoid excessive complexity, only the *direct labour process* is considered, thus excluding white collar work, research and development and product testing performed at the workplace.[2] The typology centres on the *form of production technology* and the *degree of skill of jobs* (section 2.3, Chapter 3). It distinguishes between broad types of production technology – tools, discrete machines (that is, machines operated by one or a small number of workers and not linked mechanically to each other), automatic flow lines, and process plant. I also distinguish between *different rates of change* in production technology, since this crucially affects rates of fixed investment, required retraining of workers, and the form of competition between firms; the labour process typology already explicitly contains dynamics. Thus, the production technologies of the 'old craft' labour process, such as simple tools, welding equipment or the sewing machine, are slowly changing in the very long term, and consequently are mostly based on old fundamental technologies. 'New craft' production technologies, such as litho printing machines or lathes, use recent fundamental technologies and related innovations. Skills are categorized in the conventional way into 'skilled' and 'semi-skilled'. Skilled jobs are also distinguished by their rate of change, linked to the rate of change of production technology. The typology encompasses the whole of direct production even when this is heterogeneous; some of the categories thus include *two different kinds of direct labour process carried out in the factory*. On this basis, the typology shown in Table 6.2 was developed; I have given the seven categories descriptive names.

As one would expect from section 3.4, these different types of labour process tend to be strongly associated with particular types of *product activity* – the range of products produced at the workplace at any one time, the rate of change of product specifications, and the length of product runs. If one distinguishes the level of skill of jobs by the complexity of each task, the variety of tasks making up a job, and the frequency of change of the task (Littler, 1979), then the latter two aspects are necessarily affected by the product regime. Old and new craft workplaces generally carried out one-off or small to medium batch production, often with substantial variety of product lines, requiring a high level of skill. Conversely, the assembly, standardized processing and Fordist workplaces carried out medium batch to mass

Table 6.2 *Typology of the direct production labour process*

Name of labour process	Job skills	Production technology
Old craft	Skilled, though sometimes each machine has skilled worker and semi-skilled assistant; 60%–100% skilled	Tools; discrete machines of slowly changing design
New craft	Skilled, although sometimes each machine has skilled worker and semi-skilled assistant; 60%–100% skilled	Discrete machines of rapidly changing design
Mixed	Skilled production of components; semi-skilled assembly; 30%–60% skilled	Discrete machines for components; tools for assembly
Assembly	Semi-skilled assembly; less than 20% skilled	Tools
Standardized processing	Semi-skilled machine minding; less than 20% skilled	Discrete machines
Fordist	Semi-skilled; less than 20% skilled	Discrete machines for components; tools and sometimes flow lines for assembly
Process plant	Proportion skilled varies	Continuous flow

production runs, and this was part of the reason for the low level of skills required. On the other hand, the high skill level in the mixed labour process and most process plant was not necessarily connected with product variety.

The categorization of workplaces by labour process type cut across their conventional categorization by product-industry, as shown in Table 6.3. While the numbers of workplaces in the different labour process types varied strongly, the numbers of workers in them were more evenly distributed since there was systematic variation of plant size by labour process type, with rising size from the left to the right of the table (see Box 6.1).

The first striking feature of Table 6.3 is that the labour processes of twelve product industries can be grasped using seven labour process categories; each labour process type is found in four or more of the twelve product industries. While the *adequacy* of the categorization can only be shown by

Table 6.3 *Labour process type by product industry*

Industry	Old craft	New craft	Mixed	Assembly	Standardized processing	Fordist	Process plant	Total
	Number of workplaces in panel in 1976							
Biscuits							1	1
Brewing							2	2
Pharmaceuticals					6		2	8
Steelwork	25		6			2		33
Scientific instruments	14	3	3	5	1	3		29
Consumer electronics	1	3	7	6	4	1		22
Electronic capital goods	1	1	9					11
Metal boxes							5	5
Clothing	70							70
Furniture	45		12		1	3		61
Printing	18	33	4	2	5			62
Toys	15		2	3	2	6		28
Total	189	40	43	16	19	15	10	332

deploying it in analysis, at this stage we can register that this method gives the potential for analysing a varied local economy, using a relatively small number of labour process categories while still reflecting important differences.

The table also shows that many, though not all, MLHs have heterogeneous labour processes. This heterogeneity arises from three different sources: the standard classification product industry is defined by a general similarity of *use* of the products, but these may be heterogeneous in their technical make up; product runs of different length can lend themselves to qualitatively different labour processes; and, in a few cases, different labour processes were in use to manufacture the same product (see Box 6.2 for details). Thus, whereas the product-industries of the standard classification are suitable for relating industries to final markets, for understanding production change they are 'chaotic conceptions': they lump together workplaces which are fundamentally different, and separate workplaces which are fundamentally similar. The analysis of this book will be based on the labour process categorization.

Box 6.1 Labour process and workplace size

Process plants have large minimum scale, and all were over 100 employees, mostly in the range of 300 to 1,000 employees. The Fordist factories, in contrast to the mixed labour process, generally needed high volumes to allow low skilled component production and automatic flow lines; all but one had over 100 employees, the largest having 1,700. Conversely, the other labour processes mostly had low minimum efficient scale. This was particularly the case in old and new craft production and in standardized processing, where a single machine could often provide a viable work unit. In much of these sectors, particularly old craft, standardized processing and assembly, there are also low barriers to entry (see section 6.5 below), tending to cause fragmentation. Plants over 100 workers were absent from standardized processing and assembly, and few among the other labour processes.

6.4 The specialization of London: second cut

We saw in Chapter 5 that the set of product industries, labour processes and product types in London distinguished it from manufacturing in the rest of the country. We can take this analysis a stage further by looking at this difference within product industries in the study panel.[3] There were in fact important spatial divisions of labour in these product industries (for detail, see Box 6.3):

- A bias in London towards *bespoke work, on site and timely production*. This arose because of the relation of London manufacturing to local final markets (section 5.3).
- A bias towards certain *specialist markets*, including fashion goods, upmarket products, traditional designs of consumer products, and specialist capital goods. In some cases this has arisen mainly because of the relation to the respective London markets, but in others because the inherited productive structure (including design capability) is geared towards these kinds of products.
- A bias towards *products of old design* for which demand is static or falling and which might therefore be called obsolescent. On the basis of section 3.5, we may hypothesize that the lack of (effective) product innovation in these workplaces was due to depletion of technologists and skilled manual labour power in London, an erosion of industrial districts through

Box 6.2 Why do the industries of the Standard Industrial Classification contain heterogeneous labour processes?

There are some *systematic* sources of difference within SIC sectors.

1. Products of different technology

- *Old/new products.* In the engineering sectors (scientific instruments, consumer electronics and electronic capital goods), the old craft establishments made products embodying old technologies. Similarly, in pharmaceuticals the two different labour processes corresponded to respectively traditional and modern drugs.
- *Capital/consumer goods.* 'Consumer electronics' actually contains studio equipment, which requires higher skilled manufacturing. Business printing tends to be more skilled than consumer printing.
- *Duplication of 'consumer software'.* A characteristic London sector, this was located in three MLHs: duplication of audio and video tapes (MLH 365), simple print duplication (MLH 489), and paper based toys (MLH 494). All these were done with using 'standardized processing', distinct from other production processes in these MLHs – showing again how the labour process categorization usefully groups similar production across product industries.

2. Different lengths of production run

- This distinguished Fordist production from other labour processes within the MLHs where it occurred. In steelwork, the mixed labour process workplaces generally produced medium batch products, the old craft ones bespoke products.
- Different labour processes could be associated with both length of run *and* old/new design. This was true in pharmaceuticals (as above), and also in furniture, where old craft methods were used for batch production of reproduction furniture and mixed and Fordist methods for long runs of modern furniture.

3. Different production methods of the same product

- *Sunk capital and technological inertia.* Where production technology is changing rapidly, it tends to be particularly uneven between firms. Thus in the printing industry, letterpress (old craft) continued to be used alongside litho (new craft, mixed or standardized processing).
- *Firm strategy.* In furniture, differences in production methods were due partly to different strategies with regard to use of advanced machinery versus use of skilled labour, producing part of the variation between old craft, mixed and Fordist production.

Box 6.3 The specificity of labour processes in London within the product-industries

Bespoke work on site, and timely production

On-site work was a bias in steelwork, furniture (shop fitting), and in electronic capital goods (alarms), producing a bias towards old craft production. Timely work was important in printing, where same-day or overnight work for central London office firms and government had particular weight, in general requiring somewhat higher skill labour processes. The London clothing industry is strongly biased towards fashion wear, where unpredictability of demand is managed by short turnaround ordering. In comparison to the labour process for non-fashion, long-run goods, London clothing production processes have a lower detailed division of labour and are more skilled. Timeliness also underlay the importance of duplication of 'consumer software' (see Box 6.2).

Specialist products

The furniture industry had an important subsector producing 'repro-duction' nineteenth-century furniture (including those much-loved heirloom pieces, the Victorian TV cabinet and telephone table). This was based on the productive structure of the old inner London industry, an industrial district of small firms using old craft methods for batch production. The engineering sectors produced a large proportion of highly specialized or bespoke goods, producing a bias to new craft and mixed labour processes; this was due to both market ties and continuity of productive structure. There were important subsectors within the clothing, furniture and printing industries producing luxury products, reinforcing old craft production; this was again derived both from London's high-income consumers and from the productive structure (cf. Scott (1998) on US cities).

Obsolescent products

In pharmaceuticals there was a high proportion of old, non-ethical medicines such as cough mixtures, producing a bias towards standar-dized processing rather than larger scale process plant. In scientific instruments, mechanical and electro-mechanical, rather than electronic,

---

instruments were prominent. The London toy industry was centred on toys made from paper, cloth and metal, and marked by an absence of electro-mechanical, let alone electronic, toys, now the mainstream of the industry. Here, and in scientific instruments, this produced a concentration on old craft rather than mixed-labour processes. All these biases can be attributed to weaknesses in the productive structure. A symptom of these weaknesses was a very low rate of workplace births in all three product-industries during 1976–81.

Old-fashioned production methods

Mainstream products were produced on a small scale by London workplaces using old-fashioned processes: in printing using letterpress, in clothing using little detailed division of labour.

underaccumulation, in some cases exacerbated by the modest aims of firm owners.

- In a few cases, the same, standardized product was produced in London as elsewhere in the country but using more *old-fashioned methods* of lower productivity. This was due to the productive structure of London being biased towards these methods.

These differences affected eight out of the twelve product-industries. We encountered London's specialism in bespoke and specialist products in Chapter 5; we can now note that this bias can run *through* conventionally defined product industries. Obsolete products and methods suggest qualitative deterioration of parts of the productive structure in London (section 5.6).

These specialisms arise in part from the specific nature of London's final markets, producing a specialization in both products and processes. Continuities in productive structure, which over time select out product types to which those structures are appropriate, have also been important. These processes taken together produced a bias towards particular types of labour process within London compared with the national product-industries: a higher weight of old and new craft and standardized processing, and less importance of assembly, Fordist and process plant production. Thus we see again, at a finer level of industrial disaggregation, how the specialization of London is shaped by dialectics of product and labour process (section 5.4).

6.5 The divided and dividing labour market

As well as being of direct interest to workers, markets in labour power in London were a major influence on labour processes. Employment relations have been differentiated by the interplay of labour processes, competitive conditions, and social life. They have been shaped by uneven accumulation between sectors of the London economy – underaccumulation in some, strongly reinforcing accumulation and overaccumulation in others. I explore here how these have created divisions in conditions of employment, unionization, and the supply of and demand for particular types of labour power – divisions which I have argued to be of crucial political importance.[4]

Mobilities versus segmentation

The principal competition for labour power faced by manufacturing capital in London was not with other manufacturers but with services. In 1976 only 21 per cent of London jobs were in manufacturing; services were also qualitatively dominant because of the strength of accumulation in the core sectors and their political dominance (section 5.7). Manufacturers competed for managerial and administrative workers with office-based services; for young working-class women with clerical jobs; for young working class men with consumer services and the informal economy; for older working-class women with public and private consumer services; and for older male manual workers with transport, utilities and the building industry. The service sector, together with London's patterns of reproduction, was also largely responsible for the specificities of the composition of the London workforce compared with the rest of the country: a high proportion of professional workers, of women in waged work, and of full-time work by women. It was services, too, which largely determined wage differentials between London and the rest of the country and thus the extent to which workers are able to recoup the higher cost of living in London. The differentials were higher for those groups for which the London economy had strong demand, namely non-manual men and women (differentials of 16 per cent and 19 per cent respectively in 1979) and manual women (13 per cent), whereas it was relatively small (6 per cent) for manual men.

Workers' long-term and long-distance mobility plays a central role in shaping the London labour market. From the 1950s to the early 1980s the number of resident waged workers in London declined by about 1 per cent a year due mainly to net emigration, matching the decline in total employment, which was powered by decline of manufacturing (Buck *et al.*, 1986).[5] As in most metropolises, there was high net immigration of young people, which increased the supply of unskilled labour to manufacturers.[6] There was net emigration of young families motivated particularly by housing, and of professional and technical workers motivated particularly by promotions; these flows tended to reduce the supply to manufacturing of skilled manual, technical and managerial labour.

The London labour market presented greater opportunities for many groups of workers than are found in smaller cities, and has a certain fluidity, of which the movement of workers between manufacturing and services is a part. But it was nevertheless *highly segmented socially, spatially and sectorally.* Firstly, the *distance of commuting* to jobs in manufacturing varied enormously with the type of worker. Managerial and technical workers might commute right across London, from ROSE into London, or across ROSE. Skilled male manual workers often commuted from outer to inner London, right across outer London, or between outer London and ROSE. Female manual workers, even the skilled, tended to commute much shorter distances and work within their local borough or adjacent ones, or were homeworkers, due to greater domestic responsibilities, lower access to cars and lower wages than men (Bashall and Smith, 1991). The high proportion of London workers who lacked formal job-related qualifications (40 per cent in the early 1980s: Buck *et al.*, 1986: 104), including a high proportion of youth, worked locally due to low wages, to unskilled jobs usually being available locally (in times of prosperity), or to employers being able easily to find local unskilled workers (when unemployment was high). Scale segmentation and social segmentation are thus inextricable: greater economic and gender power gives greater spatial mobility, and mobility in commuting and the choices it gives are a key aspect of economic and gender power (Hanson and Pratt, 1995).

From the demand side, the survey showed that manufacturing firms not only tapped into these scaled segments but often had active strategies to exploit them. Thus some firms tried to avoid recruiting workers with long commuting distances because they were not expected to stay. Some firms remained in an inner location to tap a larger pool of skilled male workers (Martin, 1966: 113). In contrast, some firms found outer London locations useful because they provided a local workforce of women or semi-skilled workers with few alternatives and hence what managers saw as greater 'loyalty'. Indeed, the pursuit of captive workforces could involve yet smaller scales, where firms located in essentially residential areas ('back street locations') where they face less competition for labour power than on the industrial estates. Some small electrical engineering firms in our panel in south-west London did this in order to use, as part timers or homeworkers, women who had acquired their skills locally in large factories before having children. Workers' daily mobility was thus integral both to employers' command of labour *and* to the very varied employment power of different groups of workers.

Different types of skill were associated with different labour market geographies – between widely applicable skills (some managers, technologists and manual workers with broad electrical or mechanical engineering competence), skills specific to product industries (the craft sectors), and workplace-specific skills. The market for widely applicable skills was diffused across the London region, though it was stronger in outer than inner London. In contrast, the agglomerations of the craft consumer goods sectors in inner north-east London and of scientific capital goods in west London attracted both employers and workers to these localities. Firms using workplace-specific skills, and those with substantial internal labour markets, such as in process plant, Fordist and large craft firms, were less spatially constrained.

The rate of turnover of workers and its relation to class power differed by extent of skill and, again, its degree of specificity. These differences were rather more complex than the conventional one between primary (stable) and secondary (unstable) labour markets. Given the difficulties in recruitment of most types of skilled worker, firms other than those in sharp decline made efforts to retain them. Sectors with workplace specific skills have tended to be the most successful in this: thus the chemical sector, including pharmaceuticals, had a low turnover of labour (Buck *et al.*, 1986). In industries with sectorally specific skills, however, workers may choose to move between firms to improve their wages or conditions during business upturns. Sectors employing mainly semi-skilled workers (assembly, standardized processing, Fordist, some process plant) tended to have a high turnover of labour. As with skilled workers, in prosperous periods workers might choose to move. But in contrast to skilled workers, high turnover also arose from management adjusting employment according to output or to get rid of less productive or cooperative workers. Many of these semi-skilled workers then acquired work records which stigmatized them and which in turn confined them to work in such sectors and to above-average rates of unemployment (Buck *et al.*, 1986).

In the 1970s, workers in manufacturing sectors in rapid decline had above-average unemployment rates, and workers who had been made redundant had longer-than-average periods of unemployment (Buck *et al.*, 1986: 105–6). But this did not produce large reserves of skilled and experienced workers for manufacturing firms, because most had the wrong sectoral skills, or moved out of manufacturing, or relocated to ROSE.

The supply of skilled manual workers was further reduced by the *organization of training*. Training in Britain has been notoriously weak compared with its rivals (section 3.7). During the period of study, training in manufacturing was organized by the Industrial Training Boards, which imposed either a training requirement or a levy on the sectors' firms. However, these obligations were not imposed on small firms, and in many London manufacturing sectors the unions were not strong enough to rectify this (the printing industry was a notable exception). Thus in the survey of the furniture sector only 50 per cent of the old craft firms, which were mostly small, carried out training, whereas 90 per cent of the mixed labour process workplaces, which were nearly all large, did so, despite the lower skill level in the latter. Moreover, low profit rates in the 1970s increased firms' propensity to solve their skilled labour power requirements by poaching. This strategy may have had particular appeal given the drain of skilled workers to other sectors and localities, which made training even less attractive.

The segmentation of the London labour market was further structured by the sphere of reproduction (section 2.4). *Housing* was particularly important. Inner London had a much higher proportion of its housing stock in public ownership and for private rental than outer London; this perpetuated a concentration of low-skilled workers in inner London. The large private rental market in inner London was associated with the high proportion of young migrants. While this geography of housing tenure is partly endogenous to housing provision, particularly the reluctance of outer boroughs to build council housing, it also reflected employment demands. Public housing and private renting have kept in inner London a workforce essential to public and consumer services, and this role has sustained this housing structure. High owner occupation in outer London emerged not only from its commuter suburbs but also from the well paid local employment in its 1930s to 1950s boom. Moreover, the inner/outer housing differences have been reinforced by skilled workers moving outwards for work reasons as well as housing ones. Thus while housing tenure produced a geographically differentiated labour force, this tenure distribution itself substantially derived from production: housing and production were strongly internally related.

All these processes of differentiation create important differences in *local labour markets* within London. First note a corollary of the discussion of scale above: sub-London labour markets matter substantially only to those workers whose commuting length confines them to this scale and to those firms that recruit within this scale. There are few areas of London where such firms and workers are the overwhelming majority. Thus it is usually misleading to speak of areas of London (boroughs, groups of boroughs) as if they were distinct production and labour markets. In the postwar period up to the early 1980s, unemployment was much higher in inner than outer London. This was due to a concentration of non-skilled workers in inner London, combined with much higher levels of unemployment for non-skilled workers wherever they are located. High inner London unemployment in the 1970s was exacerbated by the decline of non-skilled manual, especially manufacturing, employment *locally*, given that non-skilled workers do not commute across the region.[7] There was, then, a large reserve of non-skilled – but not skilled – workers in inner London.

The interrelation of reproduction and production has given rise to a differentiated geography within London of *gender divisions of waged labour*. During the 1970s the three inner boroughs of our study had local resident female workforces, which, in comparison to the national average, had high proportions of full-time waged employment, of single women, and of women who had moved into London. In contrast, in the two outer boroughs the majority of women lived in family households as full time homemakers or in part time waged work (Duncan, 1991). Manual women mostly have short commuting distances, so the supply of their labour power was different in the inner and outer boroughs. The wide availability of full-time work for manual women in London often produced difficulties for the surveyed firms in recruiting women part time, even in outer London, and some large firms laid on their own transport to ameliorate this problem. Reserves of labour power, then, were strongly structured by skill, gender, scale and location within London.

Employment and industrial relations in the panel

In order to understand the impact of these labour market conditions on the surveyed firms, we need to examine further their use of labour power. We have already seen the differentiated use of skilled and non-skilled workers between the different labour processes. There were also strongly varied *gender divisions of labour*. These were both cause and effect of different wages, conditions, and daily and weekly hours of work. The attitudes to work imputed to workers by management, definitions of skill, and its reproduction were also strongly gendered. Women were employed in three main types of labour process: in the skilled work of fabric machining in the clothing, toys and furniture sectors; in semi-skilled assembly of light components, within the

Fordist, assembly and mixed labour processes; and in some semi-skilled work in process plants. These jobs were strongly stereotyped as 'women's work'. Fabric machining has been constructed as feminine through its origin as work within the home. It is often categorized as semi-skilled because women have had less power than men to impose concepts of skill, and because learning of machining in the home has meant that firms can economize on formal training. Light assembly work was established as women's work through their use as a cheap, disciplined and numerically flexible labour force during the rapid growth of this sector in the first half of the twentieth century, with the ideological glossing of the work as requiring 'female dexterity'. These gender designations then help to naturalize and reinforce differences in wages and conditions both within workplaces (for instance between male skilled component production and female semi-skilled assembly in the mixed labour process), and between sectors of different labour process type (for example the large difference in wages of equally skilled workers in clothing and steelwork, and between semi-skilled workers in feminine assembly and masculine standardized processing).

The length of the working day that employers found it convenient to organize also had important impacts on the gender division of labour. Thus the 46-hour week typically worked in the steelworking sector, convenient for site work, excluded many women. Within semi-skilled, high capital intensity labour processes, where management wanted high daily usage of the plant, women were employed in the large process plants where management resources allowed the organization of varied shifts, but were little employed in the (usually) small standardized processing workplaces where management tended to rely on overtime worked by a male workforce. The size of the workplace thus mediated the relation between the labour process, hours worked and the gender division of labour.

Self-employment was important in our panel, but this term disguised fundamental differences, especially of gender. There was a considerable amount of 'self-employment' in smaller firms designed simply to avoid tax, usually with the support of both employer and workers with the tax effectively split between them; the short-term gain for the worker in wages had the disadvantage of loss of long term benefits and security. In the case of illegal immigrants, the arrangement was imposed on workers, who then probably took none of the tax gain. In some sectors, workers were 'self-employed' not only to avoid tax but to provide themselves with choices of hours worked and of employer. This required high levels of skill to give the worker the necessary bargaining power, and was characteristic of old craft sectors, especially steelwork and clothing. In other cases, self-employed workers worked on their own as genuine contractors; this was possible only in labour processes using tools or discrete machines, again being common in old craft production. Finally, the most numerous category of the 'self-employed' were female homeworkers. Homeworkers were most common in divisible labour processes with low capital requirements and light products; the work could be skilled, with the skills learnt either within the home or through previous factory work; they therefore occurred mainly in old craft (clothing and toys) and assembly (electrical, printing, toys). While a minority of homeworkers, particularly the most skilled, chose homework rather than factory work, the majority were forced to work at home because of responsibility for dependents, fear of racist harassment, or, in the case of some Muslim women, because of patriarchal control. Accordingly, their piece rates were low, they had to bear some of their work expenses, and their work was often irregular (Greater London Council, 1986: Ch. 17; Phizacklea and Wolkowitz, 1995). These varied forms of self-employment, with certain advantages as well as disadvantages for the worker, produce different worker *identities* from normal wage labour. But, as we have just seen, they are *constructed by* normal exploitation and capital accumulation, *pace* some postmodernist theorists (for example Gibson-Graham, 1996).

Strength of *trade union organization* was based on an interrelation of the labour process with competition in the product industry developed over long historical periods. There were two principal forms of unionism.

The first consisted of industry-specific unions in sectors where craft labour processes predominated (clothing, printing), in process plant originating in craft work (brewing), or where craft work had predominated in the past but was now mixed with less skilled processes (furniture, steelwork). One of the historical remnants of Britain's priority in the industrial revolution has been the strength of male craft unionism built up in the nineteenth century, and this tradition of unionism, remarkably durable, has been particularly important in London. The skilled nature of the work has facilitated both relative autonomy within the work process and limitation of entry, reinforced by particular definitions of skill and design of jobs, and exclusion of women to prevent ideological and economic 'dilution' (Cockburn, 1983). In London, the male sectorally specific craft unions at the time of study were still strong enough to be able to organize even in small workplaces: this was true of furniture, steelwork and, especially, printing. The unionization of skilled female workers in clothing and in craft production of toys, however, was very weak, due not only to the general barriers to women's organizing but to the fragmentation of the product-industries (section 6.8 below) and the form of competition within them (section 6.7).

The second principal form of unionism was factories where the semi-skilled workers were in a general union and the skilled workers in electrical or mechanical engineering craft unions. This pattern was formed from the end of the nineteenth century in the product industries with no *direct* craft history (see sections 5.3, 5.3). In this case we find a familiar pattern: unions were present in most of the workplaces with over 100 employees, particularly in the process plants and Fordist factories; they were usually absent in the smaller workplaces in the same product industries, particularly in assembly and standardized processing, although some of the small craft and mixed workplaces in these industries were unionized. But, even in the largest of these factories, the traditions of unionism were far from militant. The food and, especially, the electrical engineering sectors in London were stamped by their rapid growth in the interwar period, when high wages by national standards, as well as anti-union tactics by many employers, weakened unionism. Thus the most active and effective unionism in the panel was in the mostly small and medium male craft factories rather than large Fordist factories or process plants.

These product industry and labour process determinations were contradictory and developed through particular historical paths, so the form of unionism could differ strongly between workplaces that were similar in the abstract. Among the Fordist workplaces, for example, were found traditional skilled/non-skilled dual unionism, US-style management with equal status for manual and non-manual workers, profit sharing and lack of demarcations, and an anti-union firm with sweated conditions and high labour turnover. Of the two large brewing plants, with similar technology, one had strong union organization, the other paternalistic management with a weak union where working for the firm was often a family tradition. Within male-dominated old craft production there were workplaces with, variously, strong unionism, informally enforced good conditions with union rates, anti-union management of a paternalistic kind, maintenance of core and peripheral (numerically flexible) parts of the workforce sometimes aligned with ethnic differences, and finally outright sweatshops. These differences could sometimes be attributed to different final market pressures and surplus profits, but sometimes came out of conscious strategies: projects and struggle of management and labour can differentiate not only national and local industries (Friedman, 1977; Burawoy, 1985) but individual firms within them (P. Edwards, 1986; Nichols and Beynon, 1977).

Labour recruitment and labour processes

The labour market in London changed sharply between the upswing of the cycle and the recession. Unemployment of London residents fell from 5.1 per cent to 3.7 per cent between 1977 and 1979 but rose to 7.6 per cent in 1981 (*Labour Force Survey*). During the upswing, management experienced severe problems in recruiting suitable workers, though strongly differentiated by labour process. Both the origins of the problems and their impact on the firm were quite different for skilled and non-skilled workers respectively (Table 6.4), and I discuss them in turn.

Table 6.4 *Percentage of workplaces where recruitment affected output or profits during 1977–9, by labour process*

	Old craft	New craft	Mixed	Assembly	Standardized processing	Fordist	Process plant
Skilled manual	62	55	53	14	12	38	40
Non-skilled manual	4	0	9	36	15	69	20

During the upturn, managers complained of difficulties in recruiting or retaining *skilled workers* of sufficient 'quality'. The term 'quality of a worker' misleadingly implies something intrinsic to the worker, whereas in reality it is always a function of the *relation* between management and the worker. (I will nonetheless sometimes use this term for conciseness when discussing management strategies.) The incidence of such problems was partly due to the density of skilled workers in the particular labour process – high in the craft and mixed labour processes, low in standardized processing and assembly. Problems of labour recruitment also loomed larger for management in labour intensive work with slowly changing technology, and thus particularly in old craft production, because cost cutting required wage cuts and hence difficulties in recruitment (see further Chapter 9). The effect of workplace size on training has already been mentioned; this tended to worsen the problems of the craft sectors and lighten them in Fordist and process plant production. The contradiction between the interests of individual firms in skimping on training and the interest of all firms in reproducing a pool of skilled labour power was present in all labour processes but took distinct forms with skills of different generality:

• *Skills specific to one or very few local plants*, common in process plants and standardized processing. While the firm needed to carry out its own training, workers were then tied to the workplace.

- *Sector-specific skills,* in old and new craft and most of the mixed labour process factories. We have already noted the potential problems arising from the fragmented structure of these sectors and consequent high movement of workers between firms. In old craft production, the slow rate of change in the labour process tempted management to rely on the existing stock of skilled workers, often producing a disproportionate employment of older workers and crisis in the firm as they retired. In sectors such as furniture and steelwork, which had partially converted to non-craft methods, and ones where the fundamental technology had changed (letterpress to litho in printing), the stock of old craft skills was progressively depleted; the problem mainly concerned smaller firms, and the Industrial Training Boards were more interested in the requirements of the more 'modern' sector. In addition, firms using obsolete labour processes or producing in smaller than normal batches often had difficulties in recruiting suitably skilled labour. Thus both static and changing labour processes could produce difficulties. In some industrial districts elsewhere in Western Europe these kinds of problem have been mitigated by strong cooperation between firms, local state and unions (Campbell, Currie and Warner, 1989; Lorenz, 1992; Etherington, 1997). But this is alien to the individualistic business culture of Britain, and the London sectors did not have this degree of socialization (sections 5.8, 5.9).
- *Widely used skills,* such as general engineering and machine maintenance. The problems of reproduction of this section of the workforce were even greater than for industry-specific skills. These skills tended not to be the responsibility of a specific Training Board, and workers tended to be attracted out of London into the more dynamic industrial environment of southern England. Problems of recruitment were most intense in large workplaces using integrated production where interruptions of production from machine defects or setting were particularly damaging. This accounts for the otherwise surprisingly high figures for skilled labour problems in process plants and Fordist factories.

These problems of skilled labour were thus partly due to underinvestment in training due to fragmentation of industry ownership. But they were exacerbated by strong accumulation in non-manufacturing sectors in London, producing both competition for workers and high costs of reproduction, and by strong accumulation in manufacturing in ROSE.

The immediate *effects* of skills shortages were, again, strongly a function of the labour process. In labour processes heavily dependent on skilled labour (old and new craft, some mixed factories), firms often failed to recruit and thus suffered lower output. In other cases firms accepted workers with insufficient skills, leading either to lower volume productivity or, more often, to poor production quality. Low skill level also could prevent the introduction of new products, sometimes because teething problems were anticipated to be too severe. Management could react by increasing overtime for male workers (an option largely closed in the case of female workers), increasing use of contract workers, or, in a few large factories, stepping up training programmes. In Part III we shall see other more radical strategies. The outcome was often restriction of output, sometimes resulting in closure of the factory.

Managements' problems with *non-skilled labour* were quite different from those with skilled labour. Given the levels of unemployment, problems were qualitative rather than quantitative. They resulted not in restriction of output but in poor volume productivity and production quality. Managers complained that many recruits, especially young men, were innumerate and illiterate. In many cases there was a high rate of turnover due to workers choosing to leave, suggesting poor pay, conditions, interest and autonomy of the jobs (although managers blamed 'excessive' social security payments). Other managers vehemently complained that many of their non-skilled workers, particularly young workers in inner London, were lazy or indisciplined. While managers saw these as intrinsic qualities of these workers, they should be understood in relational terms as a failure of class relations within the particular firm and the wider London economy. A few, larger firms attempted to deal with these problems by having a direct relation with local schools, increasing their choice of young recruits and, possibly, improving the legitimacy of the firm's management. This policy was to become more popular in the 1980s, but had minimal impact at the time of study. One process plant firm went as far as to encourage unionization in order to reduce labour turnover. These problems meant that a strategy of deskilling (section 5.3) would produce new difficulties. Overall, for non-skilled workers there was a systematic failure to reproduce the capital-labour relation in a form adequate for accumulation, a failure spanning the work process, the employment relation, attitudes to work transmitted in social life, and students' attitudes to education. The *interrelation* of these processes made them particularly intractable for capital.[8]

The incidence of these difficulties among the different labour processes partly followed the extent of use of non-skilled labour (see Table 6.4). The form of mechanization also played a part. In standardized processing and some jobs in process plant, the machinery had very effectively subsumed the skills of the worker and was relatively insensitive to workers' skill or commitment. In contrast, the simple production technologies used in assembly workplaces and in the assembly stage of Fordism were more sensitive to the workers' attentiveness. In the case of Fordist production, poor work or sabotage could also disrupt the flow of the line. These relations between machinery and human initiative are reflected in the greater problems registered by management in assembly than in standardized processing, and the particularly severe problems in Fordist factories.

The labour process, then, was central in shaping managements' problems in the labour market. This could produce sharp differences within product industries. In furniture, for example, in the old craft firms the predominant effects of labour recruitment difficulties were restriction of output and low product quality and innovation, whereas in the mixed and Fordist factories the main effect was low volume productivity.

In the view of managers, their problems were due to labour markets and popular cultures which were wholly *external* to their own actions and even those of capital across their sector. But we have seen that, while the problems were partly a function of national structures of training and of competition from service sectors, they were partly endogenous to the sectors and firms themselves. In the case of skilled workers, they were strongly constructed by the poor coordination of firms within or across product-industries. In the case of non-skilled workers, the wages, conditions and forms of control exercised by firms contributed directly to their own problems, and in aggregate contributed to a culture among non-skilled workers problematic for capital. Labour processes and the reproduction of labour power are indeed, as I argued in Chapter 2, internally related.

6.6 Work and buildings

The role of buildings in academic discussion of industrial change is a curious one. On the one hand, industrial studies and labour process theory have had little interest in the topic; it is as if work took place on a featureless, infinite plane (but see Pratt, 1994). On the other hand, urban economics and urban planning have tended to attribute extraordinary importance to buildings in the generation of local economic change. Neoclassical urban economics is focused almost entirely on the markets in land and premises. The bedrock of regional and local economic policy until the 1980s was the provision of new premises, upgrading of the old, and improvements to the physical environment, and this has also been a constant preoccupation of 'urban regeneration' policy. The most thorough argument for the importance of buildings in spatial industrial change has been the work of Fothergill, Gudgin and collaborators (1982; 1988).

The concept of the labour process as a unified, albeit internally differentiated, structure, provides a way through this theoretical dichotomy. Premises form an integral part of the means of production and of the labour process as a whole; but the stock and reproduction of premises can be in tension with production (section 2.5). A priori this is likely to be the case in London given the high price of land, the high average age of the built environment, and, since the Second World War, the shortage of green field sites (section 5.7).

The *quantity* of industrial space available in London, combined with a general form of change in manufacturing labour processes, has forced some employment out of the city (for detailed argument on this issue see Box 6.4). Manufacturing tends to increase its 'space intensity' – floor space per employee – over time, mainly as a result of mechanization. For given competitiveness and given total manufacturing floor space, this would have accounted for approximately half of London's manufacturing employment loss in 1966–81. This process is complicated by two factors. Firstly, not all labour processes behave in the same way. Where space is at a premium, labour processes of low or slowly growing space intensity tend to fare better and be selected out; this appears to have happened in London. Secondly, a physical squeeze of manufacturing activity is mediated by ability to pay ground rent. The quantity of industrial space in London decreased in 1966–81, and this was principally due to the locationally associated surplus profits to be made in manufacturing being less than those in service sectors. The squeeze on manufacturing employment by the premises market was thus not only a question of use value (technically determined space intensity) but of exchange value.

The *quality* of premises was potentially a problem for firms partly because of the inherently long turnover time of premises and disparity between their development and that of other aspects of the labour processes. For the surveyed workplaces the majority of premises in inner London had been built before the First World War, and in outer London before the Second World War, and most were multistorey. But uneven profitability was, again, also a problem. Some surveyed firms were inhibited from moving to better premises by their cost, and this problem was partly due to the high average level of rent in London. Moreover, firms may fail to upgrade their premises, whether owned or rented, just as they may fail to upgrade their machinery. In

Box 6.4 'Constrained location' in the metropolis?

Fothergill and Gudgin have argued that the central reason for the differential rates of change of manufacturing employment in the 1960s and 1970s between conurbations, large cities, towns and rural areas in Britain was the lack of land for expansion in the larger settlements coupled with rising use of land per employee, leading to 'constrained location' on cramped sites. London experienced the largest contraction in manufacturing employment of all cities due to having the strongest development pressures and the earliest and most rigorously enforced green belt. In changing the geography of industry, premises have been far more important than, for example, capital-labour relations (Fothergill and Gudgin, 1985). The labour process is taken into account here, but in one dimension, the relation between mechanization and space used.

Firms in London have undoubtedly experienced restriction of growth from their *existing* site (for example McIntosh and Keddie, 1979). But Fothergill and Gudgin's thesis that manufacturing is hampered by an *aggregate* lack of space can be, at best, only part of the picture. During 1966–81 London manufacturing employment declined by 50 per cent. If the quantity of industrial floor space had remained constant, and if floor space per employee had increased at the average rate for British manufacturing, then employment would have declined by 25 per cent (Buck *et al.*, 1986: 49); thus only half of the decline can be accounted for by the simplest version of the Fothergill and Gudgin model. However, in large settlements, and London in particular, space pressures are likely to select out labour processes that are space intensive so that these become more important over time, mitigating the effects on total employment. Thus London manufacturing has been strong in craft sectors, which generally have high space intensity. Martin (1966: Ch. 10) argued that manufacturing sectors declined or grew in London during the 1950s according to their space intensity. Moreover, where production has remained on a craft basis rather than converting to Fordist or mass-production forms, the rate of *increase* of floor space per head is likely to be low. Decrease in space intensity can therefore account for less than half of the decline of London manufacturing employment.

Total industrial floor space was, in fact, not static but rather declined by 25 per cent during 1966–81 (with land in industrial use declining by 10 per cent) (Buck *et al.*, 1986: 42–9). One might pursue the constrained location model by arguing that this space was withdrawn from industrial use by other activities in London, and that the consequent lack of space forced out manufacturing. During this period there was an increase in warehousing floor space roughly equal to the decline in industrial space, so one could have forced out the other. The high price of industrial space in London – rents in our panel were 25 to 50 per cent above those in most other urban locations in Britain – would then reflect this absolute shortage of space, and be the mechanism by which manufacturing was evicted from London.[9] But this fits uneasily with the fact that vacant industrial land in London was increasing over this period (Buck *et al.*, 1986: 42). Moreover, the origins of London rents are more complicated than the constrained location model allows. High industrial rents partly reflect surplus profits associated with London location (section 5.5; Harvey, 1982). To the extent that they reflect speculative pressure for conversion to other uses, they depend on the *profitability* of those uses. A squeeze on manufacturing from the premises market therefore involves the *relation between* the location related profitability of (sections of) manufacturing and that of (sections of) services. Manufacturing was not simply physically restricted but subjected to a profitability squeeze.[10]

the survey there were in fact substantial problems experienced with the quality of premises: during 1976–9 17 per cent had their output or profits substantially affected, with a similar figure in 1980–1; as we shall see in Part III, these affected the investment and relocation strategies of firms. However, these difficulties varied sharply with labour process, because of the very different *stringency and specialization* of the demands they make on premises. This had a dynamic aspect: in labour processes with changing production methods there was a greater possibility of a mismatch, while this was rare in old craft and in assembly (for details see Box 6.5). Problems with premises thus arose partly from differential rhythms of investment in the built environment and particular labour processes, mediating technical differences, and partly from sectoral unevennesses in profitability. Value and use value are again intertwined in time and space.

The quality of premises was not simply an external constraint. We have seen that it was substantially constructed by manufacturing itself, both as a stock in the long term and as individual premises in the short term. Indeed, the stock used by each of the labour process groups discussed in Box 6.5 was largely conditioned by the spending and requirements of firms in that particular group. Inadequacies in the stock of premises are then as much a product as a cause of poor accumulation. This point is reinforced by considering the behaviour of our sample firms. First, few firms that sought to

Box 6.5 Problems with the quality and appropriateness of premises, by labour process type

'Problems' here are constraints on output or profits.

1. Indifference to quality and type of premises

The lowest requirements were of old craft sectors, and the assembly of non-delicate goods (printing, toys). Batch production with low mechanization could be accommodated in multistorey blocks with poor layout; steelwork, with its greater weight and bulk, could be accommodated in crude ground-floor accommodation such as railway arches; in neither case was cleanliness important. Firms in these categories were generally in the oldest and cheapest accommodation. The endemic difficulties of the old craft firms in recruiting skilled labour did, however, sometimes mean that poor-quality working environments exacerbated these difficulties. Buyers could also be put off (showing that buyers, too, may believe that the built environment is either a determinant or a symptom of production quality). Despite being in the poorest accommodation, these firms experienced only half of the panel average for problems with premises quality (8 per cent).

2. Multistorey premises, but clean and with specialist forms of space

This group included new craft and standardized processing; non-bulky production by the mixed labour process (electronics, printing, toys); and assembly of delicate products (electronics). Multistorey premises were possible here, though sometimes with productivity penalties, but machine maintenance and production quality required them to be dust free. Electronics firms needed laboratory space, and, because of the more complex technical nature of these labour processes, more office space was usually required than for old craft production. This generally meant post-Second World War or heavily modernized premises. This group of workplaces had around the average rate of problems for the panel (18 per cent).

box continues

Box 6.5 – *continued*

---

3. Single storey premises, with good layout and goods access

These were required by Fordist production, and by production of bulky products by the mixed labour process (furniture, steelwork). These workplaces had a high rate of problems because premises were difficult to modify to required standards, and cost could be high because of the extensive use of land.

4. Process plant

In this case the plant itself, and any building associated with it, was purpose built. This labour process was therefore affected by the land market but not the market in premises. (Workplace-specific plant is associated with the workplace-specific skilled labour needed to operate it: section 6.5.) These workplaces also experienced a high rate of qualitative problems with their site. The integrated nature of the plant makes modifications difficult. Moreover, fixed-capital intensity, generally higher in process plant than in the other labour processes, meant that firms were unwilling to abandon sites; problems could therefore build up over a long period. The fictitious capital aspect of the labour process here affects its use value.

---

improve the quality of their premises by moving were frustrated by inability to find suitable premises in London (see section 7.9 and Appendix 3). Secondly, only six relocations were made out of London with the aim of improving premises, and in most of these there were additional reasons for relocation. Thirdly, the proportion of workplaces experiencing problems with the quality of their premises did not fall between 1979 and 1981, despite around 20 per cent of industrial space in London becoming vacant during that period. All these suggest that the problems with premises quality were essentially due to firms' lack of investment in their premises or inability to pay higher rent. The problematic 'vintage' and condition of industrial property in London should thus not be seen as a constraint exogenous to manufacturing.

Problems of both quantity and quality of premises, then, were substantially constructed by the dynamics of manufacturing itself, albeit with external impacts from service sectors. This is similar to the argument of the previous section about managements' problems of labour power. Both these arguments show the relevance of an internal relations approach. By contrast, managers tend to see these problems as given externally to both firm and sector, because their control of the sector and local production as a whole is limited: epistemological differences are bound up with forms of control.

A final point concerns the asset value of premises. Rents have been analysed here as a cost, but for owner-occupier firms property was an asset and inflation of its value a benefit. Relocation decisions were sometimes strongly affected by this. For example, some firms postponed relocation in the recession because of the low value they would receive for their land and premises. The logics of productive efficiency and of fictitious capital here diverge; but the latter is no less intrinsic to capital accumulation than the former.

6.7 Competition and profitability

The London sectors were embedded in the world economy through two market systems, namely their competitors in the product-industry and their final markets, each with its particular geography. Earlier discussion cautions against seeing these systems as purely external to local production, as they are commonly pictured: we need to examine the *dialectics* between London industries and these larger scale systems (sections 2.6, 2.7, 5.4).

Consider *the intensity of competition* faced by a London sector.[11] The limited territory of the final market constrains the demand into which the sector can tap. The geography of the product-industry is important in defining the qualitative form of competition dominant in the industry, and thus the likely effects of the strategies that the London sector might be able to deploy. The latter are constructed out of the labour process and product innovation structures already considered. Together these construct both the intensity of competition and its type, and prospects for output growth of the London sector. The twist is that the geographies of both the final market and product-industry into which the London sector is inserted are themselves dependent on London's production capacities.

These relations are shown in Box 6.6, and organized according to a five-fold typology. *Group 1* was composed of sectors with strong potential for reaping technical and design rents. These product activities were built on labour processes of generally high skill in groups (i), (ii) and (v) of our 'broad sectors' (section 5.3). Though an important part of their customers were located in London, product differentiation and innovation enabled the sectors to sell into world markets; they had correspondingly strong growth

Box 6.6 Competition and growth potential of London sectors associated with the geographies of final markets and product industries

Competition from outside London	Final market area	Product-industry area
1. Competition through value productivity with potentially large markets		
Upmarket and specialist old craft (clothing, toys, furniture)	London, world	Developed countries
Scientific capital goods	London, world	W. Europe, N. America
High-value-added process plant (ethical drugs)	World	Developed countries
2. No competition but market limited		
Jobbing old and new craft sectors	London region	London region
Downmarket fashion clothing	London region	London
3. Markets protected by product design but stagnant		
Some process plant and standardized processing (patent medicines, biscuits)	Britain	Britain
4. Moderate cost competition		
Bulky products from process plant (beer, metal boxes)	London region, Britain	London region, Britain
Craft or craft originated production but long runs of standardized products (printing, steelwork)	Britain	Britain
5. Severe cost and quality competition		
Old craft production: – standardized clothing	London, Britain	Third World
– toys, reproduction furniture	Britain	Third World
Mixed, assembly and Fordist production of consumer goods: – modern furniture	Britain	W. and E. Europe
– electrical/electronic consumer goods, elaborate toys	Britain	Japan, other developed countries

potential. These sectors were found predominantly in the developed countries since these have the supporting scientific and technical infrastructures and designer, technologist and buyer milieux. Labour process competition was based on skilled labour, sometimes advanced machinery, and the ability to deploy these in product change. *Group 2* was made up of sectors where timeliness or on-site work restricted production for the London region to workplaces within the region. To the extent that the time and space of the labour process itself were involved, the production process again tended to be skilled, governing the form of competition within London. Outside competition was largely blocked, but by the same token output was limited.

Group 3 produced slowly changing products with relatively low skill processes. The products were designed to meet national tastes and did not sell well in foreign markets; demand tended to be in decline due to cultural internationalizaton, but by the same token overseas producers had little interest in these products. The pressure was then to cut unit costs in order to maintain sales. *Group 4* was made up of sectors which faced cost competition from the rest of Britain. For bulky products of process plant, transport costs prevented overseas competition and mitigated interregional competition. Craft traditions in production, timeliness and on-site work restricted overseas competition in some long-run standardized products. These products were not strongly differentiated in design, and consequently faced cost competition in which the London sector could be disadvantaged.

Group 5 consisted of consumer goods where product differentiation is weak, coming out of London's specialism in producing for popular consumer markets. These face intense competition partly because of the London sectors' failure to develop innovative or well designed products; given its traditions, this is something which British manufacturing finds more difficult in mass markets than in niche and luxury products (section 5.9). Thus the cases of obsolescent products (section 6.4, iii) are within this group and Group 3. This limited final markets to London or Britain, and also made the sectors vulnerable to competition from overseas. Competition in the labour process was of two types. *Old craft* and *assembly* production can be relatively easily replicated in Third World countries given their labour intensity, slowly changing skills and low minimum efficient scale; these therefore faced intense cost competition, somewhat mitigated by London's quicker response to demand. *Fordist and mixed* labour process production, on the other hand, had a higher capital intensity, used fast changing machinery, and required high level skills in (at least) machine setting and maintenance, so that the product-industries were located principally in developed countries. Competition proceeded through relative surplus value extraction as well as integration of product design into production, but there were developed countries which had better capabilities in these respects than Britain. Thus both sections of this group faced intense overseas competition.

Surplus profit rates: second cut

These five groups, then, exemplified the dialectics of the structures of local production with the competitive system of the product industry. Because of the varied competitive pressure on them, the groups tended to have different long-term rates of profit, from strong profitability in Group 1 to low in Group 5.[12] In sections 5.3 and 5.4 I examined the origin of different profit rates in the local structures of production; the argument here extends the analysis by incorporating the effects of the product-industry and the final markets, not simply as additional variables but in *interrelation* to the production structures.

These long term profit rates were key to the durability of the respective sectors in London. In particular, they affected the ability to afford London premises and attract the required labour power. Thus Fordist workplaces, falling within Group 5, were under intense pressure to hold down wages, and this partly accounted for their great difficulties in recruiting suitable labour (Table 6.5). We have seen that there were severe difficulties in recruiting skilled labour within the old craft sectors – in 62 per cent of workplaces in 1976–9. This figure too was influenced by the profit rate. For old craft workplaces in steelwork and printing, predominantly in Groups 2 and 4, there were difficulties in 52 per cent of cases; in contrast, for those in clothing and toys, predominantly in Group 5, the figure was 70 per cent. The least difficulties amongst craft sectors were experienced by manufacturing opticians, where prices were set at a comfortable level through the influence of NHS procurement. Thus profit rates react back onto the firm's relation to labour and premises markets.

These interrelations of local productive structures with markets under-pinned the labour process changes made by firms which we examine in Part III and the geography of competition faced by workers which is discussed in Chapter 13.

6.8 Forms of capital

Finally, we can consider the types of firm or 'forms of capital' in the sample: their ownership, size, sectoral and spatial spread, and the organization and culture of management. We have seen some of the variety of forms of capital in London manufacturing in Chapter 5. Here I shall again seek to show the strong internal relations of the form of capital with the labour process.

The direct labour process affects the fixed capital intensity and minimum efficient scale of workplaces (section 6.3), and hence the form of capital. Thus labour processes involving large scale integration, namely Fordist factories and process plants, were owned by national or transnational firms. In the other labour processes machines can be used discretely, and fixed capital requirements depended on the varied size of the workplace; fixed capital per worker was highest in new craft, standardized processing and mixed labour processes, lowest in old craft and assembly. In consequence, some of the larger new craft and mixed workplaces were owned by multisite or transnational firms; most of the rest of the panel was made up of single site firms, the majority of which were owner-managed.

Both the type of owners setting up new firms, and the possibilities for workers to become entrepreneurs, were a function of the labour process (sections 4.4, 5.3). In old and new craft and mixed labour processes, the skilled labour process makes knowledge of it an important asset for owners; this is not a question simply of technical knowledge but of sufficient experience to manage task distribution and control of workers. In contrast, in the less skilled standardized processing and assembly sectors production knowledge is relatively unimportant. Thus data from the firm births show that whereas entrepreneurs in the former group were overwhelmingly former skilled manual workers, those in the latter group were from technical or managerial backgrounds, typically from other industries. These backgrounds could lead to firm weaknesses. In the high skill sectors, managers often lacked financial and marketing skills. In the low skill sectors managers lacked the technical knowledge to move into higher value added production.

Experience as a direct worker was an advantage in the high skill labour processes, but not always sufficient. Where product innovation rather than adaption was important, owners generally needed formal technical training; hence worker entrepreneurialism was common in furniture, printing and some types of steelwork but much less so in the engineering sectors (see further Chapter 8). Gender was also crucial. The transition to entrepreneur is much easier for men than women because of capital needed, ease of obtaining credit, daily time and mobility needed for setting up a small firm, and the exclusion of women from the sector's public culture. Thus in the London clothing industry, where the majority of skilled manual workers were women, there were very few female owners but many male entrepreneurs who had worked as cutters or machinists. The 'blurring' of roles between owner and worker in craft firms (section 5.3) was thus strongly gendered.

The form of capital, then, is strongly structured by the labour process, product activity, and class and gender relations; it should not be considered simply as an additional 'factor'.

6.9 Was London manufacturing 'backward'?

When a local manufacturing economy with a long history has declined over a long period, as London's has, it is tempting to attribute this to a structural backwardness, to old-fashioned processes and products, and to an old vintage of fixed capital. A consideration of this issue can highlight some connections, which I have made in this part of the book.

The backwardness of particular structures of London manufacturing needs to be understood and assessed relationally. The *labour processes* of London are biased towards ones which have a long history (craft, assembly) and which have slowly changing technology (old craft, assembly). However, this in itself does not imply backwardness: these labour processes may be the most appropriate for a strong form of competition in the given products (for example in Groups 1 and 2, section 6.7). Only in a few cases were production methods clearly old fashioned for the given product (section 6.4). The importance of high skill production would be a sign of backwardness only if one wrongly assumed some secular trend toward deskilling (section 3.2). However, such production forms do present *potential* problems of subordination of labour (section 3.5), which are investigated in Part III.

Product innovation capacity had in a substantial minority of cases resulted in obsolescent products (section 6.4, iii). A larger problem was products of a design that limited their market to Britain, or which were poor in relation to overseas competition in both design and cost (Groups 3 and 5). A large section of London manufacturing was tied to London markets, signalling limitation of growth but not backwardness. Thus *the geographies of final markets and of competitor product industries*, though in many cases problematic, were not an autonomous source of problems but arose from the production structures. As to the *form of capital*, we have seen that the numerous owner managers often had one-sided competencies, which could harm efficiency; in Part III we shall see further restrictions they put on growth.

The supplies of *labour power and premises* in London offered *potential* problems of high cost, lack of political control, and domination by non-manufacturing activities; manufacturing in a metropolis to this extent threatens backwardness. We have seen that these problems were indeed severe in many sectors. They varied sharply between the different labour processes, although none escaped them entirely. They were exacerbated by low long-term profit rates, particularly in Group 5. Manufacturing as a whole suffered from its weak *political position* within London, and sectors from lack of *political-economic coherence*. When taken together with the weak structures of British manufacturing, these constituted important weaknesses. They inhibited product innovation and coordinated reproduction of skilled labour power, and they underlay the failure to address the cultural-economic reproduction of non-skilled labour.

These various problems were responsible for the cases of chronic lack of renewal of fixed capital and products. The largest problems were relational, so it is better to speak of weaknesses in accumulation strategies and in socialization rather than 'backwardness' with its implication of weakness in particular factors. Labour processes and product capacities of workplaces played central roles in causing competitive weakness. But locally effective structures at the London scale were also important: the reproduction sphere and the built environment, the coordination of sectors, and uneven and combined development of the city's economy as a whole. Moreover, these produced weakness only in relation to the larger scale product-industries and markets in which they inserted themselves. Again, it is the mutual relations of the structures which are crucial.

Notes

1. The construction of the panel of firms present in 1976 is detailed in Leigh *et al.* (1982a: 10–16). The sample frame for the panel of openings consisted of all openings in the sectors.
2. Links to these activities are however considered in Chapter 8.
3. Evidence on this point comes from secondary sources on the product industries and from the survey; see Leigh *et al.* (1982b).
4. As well as survey data, this subsection uses Leigh *et al.* (1982a), Buck *et al.* (1986), and Greater London Council (1986).
5. Buck *et al.* (1986: Ch. 5) argue that population decline is due to housing provision, not employment opportunities. This implausibly simple argument ignores important differences between segments of employment, of labour power and of housing.
6. I use 'unskilled' as distinct from semi-skilled, and 'non-skilled' as distinct from skilled.

7. Buck *et al.* (1986) wrongly argue that inner London public housing played a role in unemployment only in stigmatizing its residents in the eyes of employers. They also wrongly dismiss the role of declining manufacturing employment in inner London by taking insufficient account of social and spatial segmentation.

8. In the 1980s and 1900s, an enormous social engineering programme was developed to address this problem, encompassing school-business links, the national school curriculum, welfare-to-work policies, and community employment and 'enterprise' initiatives.

9. Buck *et al.* (1986: 43) argue that for rents to play such a role the London differential would have to be increasing over time. In fact, a substantial but static differential is sufficient. These authors' view of the Fothergill and Gudgin thesis is unclear: they first criticize it (43), then apparently adopt it (48–50, 58).

10. Fothergill and Gudgin's approach is within a productivist-Keynesian tradition that focuses on quantities and proportions of factors of production while playing down their price (value) relations (Cole, Cameron and Edwards, 1983).

11. Evidence from the survey and secondary sources is presented in Leigh *et al.* (1982b); see also Greater London Council (1985).

12. Evidence on these differences in profit rate comes from qualitative data from managers, and from workplaces' stability. Quantitative data on profit rates was less useful due to lack of workplace data in multisite firms and the 'creative accounting' practised by most small firms.

PART III
CHANGES OF THE LABOUR PROCESS
IN SPACE AND THEIR RHYTHMS

INTRODUCTION TO PART III

How is labour process change created by management and workers out of the ensemble of structures so far considered? How is location used in these changes? How are they inflected by the business cycle and other rhythms of accumulation? In this part of the book these questions are explored by analysing labour process change in the surveyed workplaces during the business cycle 1976–81. The analysis has a number of dimensions:

- Following Chapter 3, these changes are divided into three groups according to their broad *aim*: to increase productivity of labour, to improve the product, or to cut unit costs; these are considered respectively in the next three chapters. In each case I shall consider the different *means* used to pursue the aim, which may be either alternatives or complementary to each other. The way in which class relations both condition and are altered by these changes will be explored.
- Many forms of change of the labour process may be carried out in either of two modes, in situ or through changing location. The inertia of the workplace and its relations to the locality may cause management to make changes in situ, or these changes may be facilitated by locating in a different locality or by the act of movement itself (section 4.4). For each type of labour process change I therefore investigate the non-spatial and spatial modes of carrying it through, looking at what they have in common and what is distinct, and how use of one spatial mode may result from a blocking of the other.
- Some forms of change varied strongly over the business cycle, being applied differently in the upswing and downswing. I investigate how labour process dynamics are implicated in this rhythm of accumulation.

My interest in this study is in *qualitative* labour process change. All workplaces made at least one significant qualitative change over the study period, and most made several. I abstract from changes in product-industry demand, and therefore do not investigate changes in the output or size of workplaces as such. However, we have seen that the size of output of a workplace may be bound up with qualitative aspects, associated with reinforcing accumulation, underaccumulation and overaccumulation within it (section 4.3). I shall therefore discuss quantitative changes, both in situ and in relocations, to the extent that they were intertwined with qualitative change.

The findings of this part of the book are thematized, summarized and further theorized in Part IV.

'Relocations'

The notion of 'relocation' needs to be made somewhat more precise than hitherto; the distinctions made below are tabulated in Appendix 2. Firstly, we are concerned here with 'relocations' within a firm, rather than 'spatial shifts' effected by differential growth, openings and closures of workplaces in different localities (section 4.4). There is a grey area between these, however, namely shifts of production between sites in *multisite firms*, possibly involving closures and openings. Our interest is in investment and the labour process, so I shall count such shifts within multisite firms as 'relocations' where they involved investment decisions, and exclude them if they were merely output shifts.

Secondly, many relocations in the panel were motivated in part by increase or decrease in *floor space required* within the firm; these are discussed where they have qualitative implications. Floor space may alter not only because of output change but also because change in the labour process may alter the ratio of floor space to output; I discuss such relocations in section 7.10. I shall refer to 'expansionary' and 'contractionary relocations' according to the change in floor space involved. The geography of these expansionary and contractionary relocations, the role of multisite firms, and their entwining with quality issues, are set out in Appendix 3.

Finally, relocations were sometimes motivated by the workplace's distance from its *final markets*. I shall discuss these where the broad labour process was involved, that is, liaison with clients over design and on-site work (section 5.2). Relocations related to transport cost do not concern us here.

Quantitative data and underlying processes

I shall propose explanations of the different forms of labour process change based on the theory presented in Part I and the view of London manufacturing presented in Part II. The observed labour process changes and their use of location are determined by complex interrelations of different structures: the initial labour process, product activity, their use of labour power and premises, the form of capital, sectoral competitive pressures, the potential of relocation, and the business cycle. For the workplaces carrying out each type of spatial labour process change, the respective roles of these different structures, and their articulation, were teased out.

Because of these multiple causes, and because a particular causal process could have contradictory effects, the pattern of a particular form of labour process change empirically associated with a particular explanatory process should not be taken as *direct evidence* of the role of that process (section 1.6). I shall nevertheless present such correlations, using them as *illustrations* of the differences which *may* arise from particular processes. Particularly important will be variations of spatial labour process change with the initial labour process and with the business cycle, though associations with other processes will also be presented. We shall therefore be examining the *tendencies* or *potential* of each causative structure to change the labour process.

Most of the patterns that I present are of the number of workplaces where particular forms of labour process change occurred during the study period or sub-periods of it, as a function of the explanatory processes. If the study period were too long these frequencies would be trivial, because every workplace would be likely to experience that form of change. This study period, however, was short enough that these frequencies are revealing of difference.

7 STRUGGLES OVER INCREASING PRODUCTIVITY

7.1 To stay or go? Location and raising productivity

A central aim of capitalist firms is to increase the volume of production of given products produced by each worker. As we saw in Chapter 3, there are many ways of doing this, each with its own potential and problems. In this chapter I examine three broad ways of increasing volume productivity, which differ in their relation to accumulation and to class struggle: improved machinery, changes in the use of premises, and intensification of work. Each of these could be carried out either in situ or as part of relocation; I discuss these in respectively sections A and B of the chapter. Productivity increases in situ involved the use of qualitatively different machinery, reorganization of the layout of production, intensification of the labour of the existing workforce, and change in the composition of the workforce in order to intensify work. Productivity increases associated with relocation involved consolidation of production onto superior plant, relocation to improve premises quality, relocation to different sized premises associated with higher productivity processes, and relocation to intensify work. The correspondences between these different means of raising productivity are shown in Table 7.1. Each of the different aspects of the labour process – technology, tasks, control of workers, and the employment relation – is addressed by both spatial and non-spatial measures. We shall see that the different means of raising productivity may be either alternatives or complementary to each other.

Increases in productivity were of unambiguous benefit to the employer, but for the workplace's labour force were more contradictory. They could benefit the labour force by increasing competitiveness of the workplace and thus securing jobs (though at the expense of workers elsewhere), but if this did not result in substantial increase in sales and output the productivity rise would mean lost jobs. The means used varied in their impact on labour.

Table 7.1 *Different means of raising volume productivity*

	In situ (section A)	With relocation (section B)
Machinery and plant	New machinery	Consolidation onto superior machinery
Premises	Change in layout of factory	Improved quality of premises
		New premises to accommodate new labour processes
Intensification	Intensification with existing workforce	Intensification by switching the workforce and labour market
	Intensification by changing the workforce	

Intensification of work was directly at workers' expense. Change in the composition of the workforce transferred jobs from one group to another, with corresponding gainers and losers. New machinery could enable either better or worse quality tasks and jobs. The measures discussed in this chapter thus had varied implications for industrial conflict and for divisions within the workforce.

Section A: Change in situ

7.2 Changing mechanization

Investment in new machinery could be directed either at expansion of capacity with more-or-less the same technology, 'extensive investment', or at installing different machinery which would enable higher labour productivity, 'intensive investment'. The survey data enabled these different aims to be distinguished (sometimes with fuzzy boundaries), and here I consider the intensive component of fixed investment.

The incidence of intensive investment by labour process type and by sub-period is shown in Table 7.2. A striking feature of the table is that the rate of intensive investment was maintained and even increased in the recession 1980–1 compared with the upswing of 1977–9 (noting that these were periods of two and three years respectively). Despite falling domestic demand, squeezed exports due to the rise in sterling, sharply increased interest rates

Table 7.2 *Workplaces in which intensive investment took place, by labour process and sub-period*

	Old craft	New craft	Mixed	Assembly	Standardized processing	Fordist	Process plant	Total
Percentage of workplaces that survived to the end of each period								
1977–9	19	67	40	12	42	60	70	38
1980–1	19	48	28	0	62	50	57	32

and depressed profits, firms continued to invest to increase productivity in order to attempt to survive the increased competitive pressures. Moreover, this was so in nearly all the labour process categories.

The second striking feature of Table 7.2 is the sharp differences between categories of labour process. These were due to a minor extent to the different profitability and growth prospects of these categories (section 6.7), tending to depress the rate of investment in old craft and Fordist production and increase it in new craft and standardized processing. But the major reason for the differences was the labour process itself (for detail see Box 7.1). Those labour processes with generally slow changing production technology had the lowest rate of intensive investment. Intensive investment was low not only in the pure assembly workplaces but in the assembly stage of the mixed and Fordist labour processes. Due to the higher production volumes in Fordism, however, assembly could sometimes be substantially mechanized, producing a higher investment rate in Fordist than mixed workplaces. It is interesting that the investment rate was as high in new craft as in Fordism and process plant: skilled production using discrete machines can be just as dynamic technologically as the stereotypical forms of mass production.

We can obtain another view of this pattern by examining *spending* on intensive investment. In order to make meaningful comparisons of investment spending between labour processes, I compare them within particular product-industries.[1] Table 7.3 shows investment rates in scientific instruments and consumer electronics, which both contained a variety of labour processes (Table 6.3). On this measure too, we see that the rate of investment per employee was maintained during the recession. Moreover, the variation in the value of spending on intensive investment between labour process types follows closely its frequency for the whole panel (Table 7.2): the quantitative funding requirements for intensive investment parallel the qualitative possibilities for its use.

These findings have interesting implications for the relation between labour process types and product-industries discussed in the previous chapter

Box 7.1 Intensive investment and productivity increases in different labour processes

Old craft

Slow changes in production technology, by definition, and hence in productivity. Large increases in productivity only in particular, small parts of the overall production process, for example automatic pocket-stitching machines in clothing.

Assembly, including in the mixed and Fordist labour processes

Most cases resembled old craft production. However, the detailed division of labour and deskilled tasks lend themselves to automation where large volume production can cover the capital costs. This was carried out in some Fordist factories, and productivity increases were then enormous: volume productivity rose by a factor of 2.5 in one TV factory.

New craft and standardized processing

The highest productivity gains were achieved in these labour processes. Improvements in one generation of machines, particularly via microprocessor based controls and mechanisms, could be dramatic: new machines in one record duplicating firm increased volume productivity by 60 per cent; computerized typesetting increased it by 100 per cent, while laser scanners used in printing-plate making increased it by a factor of ten.

Component production in mixed and Fordist labour processes

Some similarities to the previous group, but generally smaller productivity increases. This was probably because the processes were more specialized, so that the machines were produced in small numbers or were bespoke, and thus tended to be less sophisticated. Hence the degree of specialization of machines affected the rate of change of productivity.

Process plant

Improvements to the plant could be made frequently, but because of the already high capital intensity these tended to shed little labour. This can be seen in national statistics for three product industries dominated by process plant, namely biscuits, brewing and pharmaceuticals; in 1970–9 these achieved increases in real gross value added per employee of respectively 7 per cent, 13 per cent and 14 per cent compared to an average for manufacturing as a whole of 27 per cent.

Table 7.3 *Average intensive investment per employee per annum, by labour process and sub-period, for scientific instruments (MLH 354) and consumer electronics (MLH 365)*

		Investment (£ p.a.)					
		Old craft	New craft	Mixed	Assembly	Standardized processing	Fordist
MLH 354	1977–9	110	160	380	50	235	315
	1980–1	85	210	420	80	130	380
MLH 365	1977–9	0	380	410	30	–	1,300
	1980–1	0	140	240	0	–	n.k.

Note: MLH 354 here excludes manufacturing opticians, and MLH 365 excludes duplication of tapes and records.

(section 6.3). Firstly, we see that within product industries of standard definition, fixed intensive investment rates may vary enormously between labour processes. Aggregate figures for investment in the industry hide this variety; and differences in investment rates between regions are likely to be due in part to geographical differences in the labour process composition of the industry (section 6.4). Secondly, the two product industries had similar basic technologies and similar batch sizes in corresponding labour process groups (given that 'consumer electronics' was in reality mainly capital goods). Table 7.3 shows that there was remarkable similarity in the rates of intensive investment within each labour process category *between* the two MLHs, despite the substantial difference in product types. Both these points suggest the logical coherence of the labour process categories and the incoherence of the product industry categories.

The survey gives us rough indications of the extent of *increases in volume productivity* achieved with new production technologies.[2] The extent of productivity increases varied sharply with labour process type (Box 7.1). It was generally least in old craft and assembly, greatest in new craft, standardized processing and Fordism, and intermediate in the mixed labour process and process plant. These differences were partly due to different rates of technological change within each stage of production, partly to the *number* of stages in which change was substantial. Productivity rises thus largely followed the incidence of intensive investment made with this aim, with the exception of process plant where fixed investments in an already highly mechanized process could give rather limited returns. By-and-large, then, our measures of the *means*, intensive investment, give an indication of the intended *outcome*, productivity increase. We can conclude that the labour process classification gives us a better guide than a product industry one to the possibilities of intensive investment and its effects.

7.3 New machines and new skills

What was the causative role of, and effects on, skill of these investments? We have seen that the effects of capitalist mechanization on skill levels are mediated by varied and contrary processes (section 3.2). In the carrying out of *individual tasks*, change in machines may either raise skill requirements, due to greater sophistication of the process, or deskill, with benefits to capital in the employment relation; I shall term these *absolute* changes in skill. But increases in productivity in one section of the labour process can change the weight of skilled and non-skilled work *in the workplace or the sector as a whole*, even if the skill level of each task remains the same. Thus increased productivity of non-skilled work, using the relative ease of automating highly divided non-skilled tasks, may raise the weight of skilled jobs in the total workforce; while increased productivity in skilled work, perhaps prompted by the costs and difficulties of recruiting skilled labour, may cause a decline in the average skill of the workforce. I shall call these *relative* changes in skill.

Qualitative change in machinery and plant in the surveyed workplaces had varied impacts on skill, with upskilling and downskilling occurring, each through both absolute and relative change (Box 7.2). The underlying processes suggested above had different purchase in the various labour processes. Part of these differences arose from different labour market pressures. We saw in section 6.5 that the craft firms had particularly acute problems with skilled labour power, whereas these were less where skills were more specific to workplace, particularly in process plant. The changes in skill appear to have responded to this difference. In *old craft* production there were some moves to deskill tasks, but because of slow technical change these had only a small impact on overall demand for skilled labour. In *new craft* workplaces, however, there was substantial deskilling, both absolute and relative, which labour was unable to prevent despite relatively strong unionization. In contrast, in *process plant* and *standardized processing* the trend was always towards upskilling, again through both relative and absolute change; upskilling took place in 70 per cent of the former labour process and 16 per cent of the latter – a higher rate of change of skill than in other labour process categories. These results suggest that management's strategies

---

Box 7.2 Changes in skills resulting from productivity increasing machinery, by labour process

Absolute change of skill in particular tasks

Deskilling
Old craft, new craft, mixed, Fordist. Further mechanization. Numerically controlled and computer numerically controlled machines in component production in electronics and furniture.
Old craft. Automation of bookbinding.

Upskilling
Standardized processing, process plant. Further mechanization or automation in pharmaceuticals, metal boxes, tape and record duplication, and in screen printing.
New craft. Higher volume litho printing.
Increase in skilled maintenance jobs for the above.

Relative changes in the skill composition of the workplace labour force

Deskilling by higher productivity in some skilled jobs
New craft. Computerized typesetting and printing plate making.
Automated testing equipment in electronic industries.

Upskilling by higher productivity in some non-skilled jobs
Standardized processing. Automatic tape duplication; mechanized print finishing.
Mixed and Fordist labour processes. Automated assembly in electronics and steelwork.

---

towards machinery and skills were strongly a function of local labour market conditions.

In the heterogeneous labour processes, *mixed* and *Fordist*, there were contrary tendencies: in assembly a relative upskilling through automation and a (limited) absolute upskilling of tasks, but deskilling of tasks in component production. These again went with the grain of the labour market. The result was that in terms of both skill and capital intensity there was convergence between component production and assembly. This had the potential to erode the sharp differences in status between workers in the two sections. However, these very pre-existing differences affected the way in which restructuring took place. In the electronics sectors, semi-skilled female assembly workers lost their jobs through automation while men filled the new high skill maintenance jobs; but men followed the deskilled component production jobs. Thus the gendering of skill had considerable continuity but also significant change.

The great heterogeneity of labour processes in London manufacturing therefore gave rise to very different trajectories in skills (cf. Gallie, 1991). Although there was absolute upskilling in some labour processes, most saw absolute or relative deskilling, and relative upskilling did not provide more skilled jobs. Resistance to deskilling was relevant mainly to the craft sectors. The immediate problems for workers were also different in absolute and relative skill changes respectively. Labour is likely to resist absolute decreases of skill because of the job quality of the workers concerned. In contrast, relative changes in skill, whether upwards or downwards, are likely to be resisted because of the job losses consequent on the productivity gains. These differences make a collective labour politics of skill difficult. I return to this problem in Chapter 13.

7.4 Changing things around: the micro-geography of production

The layout of stages of production within the factory, although regarded as a key aspect of the labour process by industrial systems designers, rarely makes an appearance in academic industrial studies (an exception is Massey and Meegan (1982)). Layout could have important effects on productivity, whether in factories with automatic transport between stages or, as was far more common in the survey, without. Layout changes sometimes required substantial building work, but in other cases could be carried out with little cost. As we shall see, this aspect has an interesting relationship to machine investment and to the choice between spatial and non-spatial strategies.

The incidence of this type of change was largely a function of the volume and degree of standardization of production. Thus over the study period only 6 per cent of workplaces in old craft made layout changes whereas 17 per cent did so across the other labour processes. Layout change could be either complementary to re-equipment or an alternative. In some cases re-equipment required a change in layout; this was particularly the case in the highly integrated process plants, which had a 30 per cent incidence of layout change. In other cases re-equipment was simply the occasion for changes in layout. On the other hand, layout reorganization could be an *alternative* to machine investment, used by management when the latter was technically infeasible; thus there was a high incidence (24 per cent) of layout change in assembly.

There was also a financial reason why layout change could be an alternative to machine investment. The incidence of layout change per year was more than three times as high during the recession as in the upswing; reorganization could offer a low cost route to increased productivity at a time when retained profits were low and investment risky. This aspect of labour process change suggests a wider point: the choice of alternative means towards a particular aim could concern either the use values of different labour processes or the exchange values of the associated investments.

7.5 Intensification of work

The power of machinery to increase productivity has by no means made intensification of work obsolete, not only because of technical barriers but also because of managerial control and finance (section 3.2). Indeed, intensification played a major role in the panel.[3] Its use was strongly cyclical: it occurred six times more often during the recession than in the upswing, in 35 per cent and 6 per cent of workplaces respectively. Managers' accounts indicate that this was partly because of a greater *need* to make productivity improvements in order to survive. While managers always have an interest in principle in increasing productivity by all possible means, recessions tend to make them try harder and steel their resolve. More importantly, intensification took advantage of the sharp change in labour markets and bargaining power of workers produced by the recession (section 6.5). It was not so much that the recession weakened formal union power, because in our panel this had not been exerted to prevent intensification in the earlier period, with the exception of the larger printing factories. Rather, intensification used the fear of redundancy: in half of the cases of intensification in 1980-1 managers mentioned this as an enabling factor. The fear was either of outright closure of the factory, or where job cuts were being made, of the individual worker being selected as less productive (see section 7.6 below). Moreover, the abrupt change in labour market conditions meant that managers in most cases no longer had to worry that intensification would cause them to lose skilled workers or exacerbate high turnover of non-skilled workers. The recession therefore had a particular importance in *London* manufacturing, given the specific difficulties in recruitment and retention of workers that firms had experienced in 1977-9. The recession was therefore successful in disciplining workers – an aim of the government's deliberate deepening of it (section 5.10). This therapeutic effect of the business cycle for capital is examined further in Chapter 12.

In the recession, then, intensification was as common as investment in new machinery. We saw in section 3.2 that intensification may be an *alternative* to mechanization, due to technical features of the labour process, relations to labour power, or firm finances. Alternatively, mechanization and intensification *may proceed hand in hand*, the latter either an achievement or a precondition of the former. Both these relations were found in panel workplaces. Consider the incidence of intensification by labour process type (Table 7.4, row 1). We have seen that the labour processes with slow changing or simple production technology had low rates of machine investment, and intensification could here be an alternative to re-equipment; this was the case in old craft and assembly. The higher rate of intensification in assembly than old craft may have reflected the greater ease of speeding up in Taylorist semi-skilled work than in craft production with its weaker subsumption of labour to management. However, the incidence of intensification was actually larger in the labour processes with faster changing technologies, where intensification and mechanization were often complementary. Thus paradoxically those labour processes where management most *needed* intensification to raise productivity – old craft and assembly – had a smaller rate of intensification than those where mechanization could be used.[4] This highlights again the specific problems for capital in labour processes where change in process technology is slow.

The labour processes also differed in the *form* of intensification and the *means* by which it was carried out. The most common form of intensification was increase in the speed of carrying out given tasks. It could also consist of increasing task flexibility, that is, blurring the technical division of labour and increasing the number of tasks carried out by each worker. These dif-

Table 7.4 *Incidence of intensification of work with the existing labour force*

	Old craft	New craft	Mixed	Assembly	Standardized processing	Fordist	Process plant
Total, as percentage of survivors to 1981	34	55	52	46	38	40	43
Via compulsion, number	16	9	7	2	3	2	3
Via supervision or incentive, number	25	5	5	0	2	1	0

ferent forms could depend on the labour process. Thus in process plant, the speed of operation tends to be set by the plant technology, and intensification took the form of supervising more parts of the plant. In contrast, with the discrete machines used in standardized processing, the number of operators tended to be fixed and intensification proceeded through speed-up in the pace of the machines.

The *means* used to speed up work also varied between labour processes, depending on the ease of measurement or mechanical regulation of output, and on the degree of autonomy of workers (Table 7.4, rows 2 and 3). In large volume production with a fine technical division of labour it is relatively easy for management to measure the pace of work by individual workers or small groups of them. This is particularly the case in machine production, where the machine can monitor productivity, but also in assembly. The intensity of work can then be increased directly by management setting new norms, particularly when workers fear losing their jobs and know that their individual productivity can be measured. In these cases, management tended to say that the intensity of work had been increased 'by cuts in the workforce' or 'by workers' fear of redundancy' – as if these *automatically* increased the speed of work. Management regarded as unproblematic, and thus took for granted, the direct means by which intensification took place.

By contrast, in the less standardized production found in old craft and some new craft and mixed workplaces, speed of work of individual workers was more difficult to measure because the technical division of labour is more complex and more fluid. Moreover, in these labour processes the quality of production was also problematic (see Chapter 8), so that a simple imposition of speed-up could result in deteriorating quality, whether through the deliberate action of workers or not. Thus in these labour processes management tended to make more use of methods that could motivate workers: increasing the element of payment-by-results in the wage, or increasing direct supervision of the labour process. The latter allowed management to understand the labour process better and find ways of increasing productivity, while ensuring that production quality was not compromised. Increased supervision was thus used particularly frequently in the old craft factories, with their complex and varied tasks. The fear of individual or collective redundancy was still used, particularly in product industries like clothing that faced very strong competitive pressures, but tended to be combined with increased supervision. These differences in the means of intensification between labour processes have some correspondence to Friedman's ideal-type distinction between direct control and responsible autonomy (section 2.5).

It was also in (male) craft sectors that trade unions were strongest, and it was in them that management had the only significant organized resistance to intensification. Only in the printing industry did any managers (five out of 65) consider that the unions had set limits to the intensity of work through negotiations on employment levels and demarcation of tasks. In three printing firms and one brewery the unions had slowed down the introduction of new process technology by bargaining over employment levels, hours of work, and pay increases to reflect increased productivity. For the most part, then, it was not formal union organization that posed the crucial barriers to re-equipment or intensification (cf. section 6.5).

We have seen, then, that in contrast to the case with re-equipment, there was a fairly even incidence of intensification across the different labour processes. But this hid important differences in whether intensification was an alternative or complementary to investment in machinery. Moreover, there were sharp differences in the form of intensification and the type of control through which it was carried through, so that workers' experience of intensification varied with the labour process.

7.6 Intensification by changing the workforce

Management can intensify work by changing the workforce. Formally, this strengthens managerial control through using the employment relation (section 2.3). Such change is effected most radically by relocation to a different labour market (section 7.11 below), but, though the constraints are greater, it may also be done in situ. Management was inhibited from using this tactic in the upswing by both the relatively high use of skilled labour in London manufacturing and by the tightness of much of the labour market. Nevertheless, it was a significant strategy.

Change in the labour market over the business cycle was again crucial. In the upswing, as we have seen (section 6.5), management experienced both shortages of skilled labour and high turnover of non-skilled labour, resulting in an unsatisfactory, and in some cases deteriorating, 'quality' of the workforce – in other words, disintensification. In some cases, such as old craft workplaces in furniture, firms had to modify their labour process to decrease its skill and thus fit the available workforce. This trend was reversed in the recession, when management was able to change the composition of the workforce through various means:

- Higher unemployment enabled *changes in recruitment practices.* The minority of firms that continued to recruit in 1980–1 were able to be much more selective. Firms were able to recruit skilled workers with higher levels of skill. They were also able to use segments of the labour force that had been in short supply in the upswing, especially older women (section 6.5). Thus some firms switched from employing school leavers to employing older women with whom a more productive employment relation could be formed. Others switched from part time to full time women, who were expected to be more productive by virtue of achieving more experience on the job. Note that, in this latter case, pace and skill of work were in conflict with the convenience for the employer of part-time workers: numerical flexibility can conflict with the rate of exploitation and task flexibility.
- In the large unionized factories redundancies were made according to 'last in, first out'. In the others management was able to make *selective redundancies* according to who was considered least productive.
- Turnover of labour slowed down, especially among non-skilled workers. In consequence, productivity increased through *greater experience in the job.*

Since both skilled and non-skilled workers were involved, this means of increasing the intensity of work was used fairly equally across all labour processes.

Paradoxically, in some labour processes the recession produced a tendency towards *disintensification* arising from the quality of labour power. Some firms had a permanent regime of *managed* high turnover of labour, in which workers who turned out to be most productive were retained through individual higher wages or other favourable conditions, whereas others left spontaneously or were encouraged to leave. This strategy was most characteristic of non-skilled production, insensitive to production quality, found within standardized processing and assembly. This suggests that the high voluntary turnover of labour that exists in many parts of the London economy, in services as well as manufacturing, may sometimes be useful rather than a problem to management. This method of improving quality of labour power was dependent on the business cycle: it functioned best with the high voluntary turnover of the upswing, and management complained that it was snarled up by the sharp drop in turnover in the recession.

The labour process literature has tended to neglect the connection between the intensity of work and the segment of the labour force used. We see here that management strategies on labour force segment, and their use of the business cycle, may have important impacts on the work process. This represents an important aspect of the competition between workers for employment.

7.7 Productivity and divisions

The three means of increasing volume productivity in situ that we have considered – re-equipment, reorganization of layout, and intensification with or without change in the labour force – were used very differently in the different labour processes. The means were to some extent alternatives, but were sometimes complementary or necessary conditions for each other. Aside from re-equipment, the means were strongly cyclical, either for financial reasons or because of changes in the labour market.

These processes could produce large differences within a product-industry in the politics of raising productivity. The furniture industry during the upswing of the cycle is a case in point (Leigh *et al.*, 1982b). We can here regard it as made up of two subsectors: old craft production within small and medium firms centred in Hackney, producing mostly reproduction antique furniture and upholstery, and mixed or Fordist production of modern furniture in larger factories in the Lea Valley in Enfield. Both subsectors faced intense pressure of cost competition, mitigated by product quality only in a small part of the craft sector (section 4.7). In the old craft subsector, the incidence of fixed investment was less than in modern furniture and its impact less. Moreover, intensification was carried out principally in the modern subsector, often accompanying re-equipment. It was achieved partly through greater supervision, but also through payment-by-results schemes and imposition of norms that would have been very difficult to administer in the craft subsector due not only to the labour process but also to lack of managerial resources. There was a trend towards deskilling in both parts of the industry, but for very different reasons. In the craft subsector, the proportion of skilled workers fell substantially because of inability to recruit them. This arose from inadequate training in the industry as a whole, a particularly low rate of training in the small craft firms, and lower rates of pay and poorer conditions of work in the craft sector, in part resulting from its slower long-term rate of productivity increase; the difficulty of holding skilled workers, and the competition between craft and modern sectors for them, then tended to worsen training in a vicious circle. In the modern sector, by contrast, deskilling arose from the introduction of new machinery (occurring in a quarter of the factories), and was associated with productivity increases.

In each dimension, then, the old craft firms had greater difficulties in increasing productivity than the mixed and Fordist workplaces. The result was an increase in productivity in real value terms of 8 per cent in the modern furniture subsector but a decrease of 10 per cent in old craft production over the period, or approximately +23 per cent and +5 per cent, respectively in volume terms.[5] There were very different pressures on the workforces of the two subsectors. The jobs of workers in the modern firms, unlike those in craft production, were threatened by productivity increases. They also had to contend with greater pressures towards intensification and deskilling, compensated somewhat by better wages and conditions than the craft sector. Both subsectors faced job losses through failing competitiveness (Best, 1990). Problems of the craft subsector, centred on the failure of reproduction of the labour force, originated in the lack of coordination within the sector and were correspondingly difficult for workers to confront. Differences in the means of increasing productivity, closely connected with reproduction of labour power and forms of control, can thus produce deep divides among workers even within a local product-industry, and require different trade union tactics.

Section B: Change through relocation

Changes in machinery, in premises and in the intensity of work were made not only through change in situ but also through relocation (Table 7.1). The different spatial form involved different relations to investment and rhythms of accumulation, and different types of industrial conflict: the geographical means of change made a political difference.

7.8 Consolidation onto more advanced plant

There were few relocations carried out with the principal aim of installing new plant. However, when capacity or floor space was being cut in multisite firms (Appendix 3), the average quality of plant was often improved by consolidation onto the most productive site. Capacity at the different sites had typically been installed at different times, so the differences in technology could be large. Of the sixteen 'contractionary relocations' between existing sites, the quality of already installed machinery was a criterion for site selection in eleven cases. Thus the overall quality of machinery in the firm (and sector) was improved not only by new investment, principally in situ, but through devalorization and associated relocation.

The importance of the quality of plant at different sites as a criterion in reorganization depended on the labour process. Significant differences were more likely in *capital intensive* labour processes, while *rapidly changing* labour processes were more likely to have machinery of significantly different vintages. This is reflected in the labour processes represented (Table 7.5); consequently the sites concerned were generally large. Thus these relocations were powered by relative surplus value extraction and the pace of change associated with it. The relocations were both a result of change in the labour process and a means by which it was (destructively) effected.

The geography of this type of relocation was a function of the history of investment within the firm or its antecedents. Rationalization was sometimes between London sites. In others, a factory outside London had more modern equipment since it had been set up in order to decentralize from London and restructure (rather than merely to serve a regional market). Sometimes the London factory had the most advanced equipment. In labour processes with a rapid rate of technological change, periodic re-equipment is usually essential if a workplace is to survive at all, and so long-established London sites could have up-to-date equipment (cf. sections 6.9, 7.2). In capital intensive production, the London site tended to have a strong inertia, leading to reinforcing accumulation at the site (section 4.3). There was thus often a 'leap-frogging' of technology between sites, and this could result in relocations into London as well as out of it.

Table 7.5 *Relocations between existing sites where machine quality was important, by labour process*

Old craft	New craft	Mixed	Assembly	Standardize processing	Fordist	Process plant	Total
0	2	1	0	1	5	2	11

7.9 Changes in site number and size due to dynamic labour processes

It is usually assumed that expansions and contractions of sites are due to changes in output, but they can originate in a quite different source, namely changes in the labour process and in labour productivity and their associated changes in floor space use. This is an important way in which spatial reorganization of production can arise from labour process change.

This is the kind of process highlighted by Fothergill and Gudgin, who emphasize *increases* in floor space use per employee (section 6.6). The trend in floor space use in a particular product-industry is the result of a complex set of processes: change in the volume of output per machine, in machines per unit of floor space, in unit cost and price of products, and hence, given demand elasticities, in value and volume of output; these can produce *reductions* as well as increases in floor space. The consequent changes in floor space can be accommodated in various ways including through relocations. In the panel there were in fact a roughly equal number of expansionary and contractionary relocations, twelve and nine respectively, originating in this way. These again mostly involved large workplaces.

As one would expect, these relocations occurred predominantly in labour processes with rapidly changing production technology. While the contributing processes were complex, the expansionary relocations were generally marked by increases in space used per machine and often substantial change of layout for more efficient flow (cf. section 7.4). Most took the form of openings of new sites (Appendix 3).

The contractionary relocations, on the other hand, involved large increases in the volume productivity of a typical machine, so that a given, or increased, output volume could be accommodated by much less plant. They thus involved some of the largest productivity increases in new craft, standardized processing, the mixed-labour process and process plant and in the automation of assembly (see Box 7.1). The contraction in the use of space in these cases was thus not a contraction of production but the opposite. Investment in these new labour processes could take place in situ, but the large productivity increases involved tended to shake up the spatial division of labour. Most of these relocations were of the type discussed in the previous section, with consolidation of investment and production onto the technically more advanced site; a new round of investment could be easier at such sites – a form of reinforcing accumulation. Thus, for example, an old brewing plant was closed while the firm continued investment at a newer plant in ROSE.

Rapid increases in volume productivity resulted not only in investment in situ and contractionary relocations but also in closures. Thus in the printing industry, developments in new craft labour processes gave large productivity increases in typesetting and in the overnight ('City') printing subsector. Competitive investment then resulted in overaccumulation: excess capacity, intense competition, price cutting, and eventual firm deaths and site closures as well as contractionary relocations (Leigh *et al.*, 1982b: III). This is a good example of the variety of spatial forms that a given labour process change can take. It also shows that evolution in the physical form of capacity resulting from labour process change does not necessarily take place through smooth adjustment but through the switchbacks of under- and overaccumulation (section 4.3; see further Chapter 11).

7.10 Relocation to improve the quality of premises

We saw in section 6.6 that the type or condition of premises could substantially reduce productivity. Action taken to rectify this most often took the form of investment in situ rather than relocation, reinforcing the argument in section 6.6 about the importance of firms' own investments in reproducing the stock of premises. Nevertheless, relocation was also used to address this problem. We have seen that the stringency of firms' premises requirements and the likelihood that pressures would arise from labour process change were strongly a function of the labour process (Box 6.4). Table 7.6 shows that the rate of relocation to improve the quality of premises closely followed these differences. These differences were amplified by the fact that the more demanding labour processes were also the ones where the form of fixed capital (plant plus premises) was particularly difficult to modify in situ. As with improvements in machinery (section 7.8), some of these relocations were to existing sites within the firm, and similarly motivated by the quality of fixed capital, in this case premises; this was so of a third of relocations in groups 2 and 3 and all of those in group 4.

The rate of relocation and their destinations partly reflected the adequacy of premises available on the market in London. None of the firms in group 1 reported difficulties in finding better premises, while a few in the other groups did; all the relocations in group 1 were to London, whereas a third of

Table 7.6 *Relocation to improve quality of premises, by type of labour process*

Labour process grouping (from Box 6.5)	Relocations as % of 1976 workplaces
1. Old craft, assembly of non-delicate products	2.6
2. New craft, standardized processing, light mixed labour process, assembly of delicate products	14
3. Fordist, heavy mixed labour process	12
4. Process plant	20

those in the other groups were out of London. Thus both the rate and the geography of these relocations were conditioned by the labour process, suggesting one reason for differential rates of decentralization from London by labour process (section 5.6).

Firms could, then, improve their premises either through building work in situ (section 6.6) or through relocation. Labour process pressures underlay both of these spatial means. Thus in scientific instruments and consumer electronics, which had relatively stringent premises requirements, 22 per cent of firms carried out improvements in situ and 8 per cent relocated to improve premises quality, while in steelwork and clothing, which had low requirements in this respect, these figures were respectively 9 per cent and 1 per cent. The alternative means were, then, governed in a similar way by the labour process.[6]

It is interesting to compare the three forms of relocation so far considered with the findings of Massey and Meegan (1982). Firstly, each form of relocation considered here was associated with improvements in fixed capital, and thus tended to be more important the faster the technical change. This fits with the finding of Massey and Meegan that product-industries dominated by rapid technical change are particularly prone to rapid shifts in spatial distribution. Secondly, in the relocations in the present study labour process change was often effected through consolidation of capacity. Massey and Meegan treated such consolidation as one of their major forms of production change, 'rationalization'; but they treated it essentially as quantitative adjustment, albeit arising from overaccumulation sometimes reinforced by prior productivity increases. The present study shows that such 'rationalization' can be associated with substantial qualitative change in the labour process, a conclusion which will be reinforced when we consider product activity in Chapter 8.

7.11 Intensification through relocating to a new workforce

We have seen that management sought to intensify work both through measures of control inside the workplace and through tapping into different segments of the local labour market. However, the former measures often came up against the 'quality' of the labour force, whereas the latter changes were generally only possible during the recession. A further alternative was to relocate: there were thirteen cases where relocation had the sole or partial motive of change in the characteristics of the workforce, varying in distance from a kilometre or two to moves to Scotland. However, many managers who would have liked to have relocated for this reason did not, and these failed relocations are illuminating.

A striking aspect of these relocations was that they nearly all took place during the upswing of the business cycle, that is, the opposite timing to the changes to the workforce made in situ. The main reason for this was that managers' difficulties in labour supply were greatest during this period due to the tightness of the labour market; and although labour markets at possible destinations might also be relatively tight, there were significant differences between localities. The spatial and non-spatial methods of intensifying work were therefore applied in different phases of the business cycle.

Relocation out of London for craft skill – and the reverse

As with changes of labour force in situ, relocations were concerned with the quality of both skilled and non-skilled workers, but they were concentrated in labour processes reliant on sectorally-specific skilled labour, namely old and new craft and the mixed labour process. Here, managers' view was not that London lacked high level skills but rather that the overall supply of reasonably skilled labour was inadequate (sections 5.8, 6.5), forcing firms to accept workers with either poor skills or 'poor discipline'. Given the substantial responsible autonomy in these labour processes, these were severe problems. The destinations for these relocations depended on managers' views of labour markets within London and nationally. These were often conflicting and, particularly in the case of small and single site firms, based on rather weak anecdotal evidence. However, fairly clear pictures of the intranational geography of sectoral labour markets emerges from the interviews. As we have seen, the parts of the product-industries located in London were biased towards old and new craft labour processes and strong use of skilled labour (sections 5.3, 6.4). The use and reproduction of skilled labour outside London, however, varied between the three 'broad sectors' of craft production. In craft consumer goods, supply of skilled labour outside London was weak; in the jobbing sectors, it was reasonably strong, and considerably cheaper than in London, whereas in the science-based craft sectors skilled labour was more plentiful in ROSE than in London (see Box 7.3). Accordingly, relocation out of London to improve skilled labour quality was a promising strategy in the jobbing and science-based sectors, but more problematic in craft consumer goods production unless accompanied by deskilling. Indeed, some managers in clothing and furniture said that they knew of firms in their industries that had moved out of London to ease labour shortages but found them worse in their new locations. These varied pressures and possibilities are reflected in the fact that relocations out of London to improve skills quality took place in electrical engineering (to ROSE) and in printing, but none were carried out in the consumer goods industries.

Only five firms, however, carried out such relocations from London; many others considered doing so but remained in situ or, as we see shortly, relocated within London. This small number reflects two particular constraints, which are not additional factors but are integral to craft production. The first was the importance of *holding on to the existing workforce*. A new workforce would have less experience in the particular labour processes used, their quality would be hard to gauge in advance and, in the case of small firms, it would not be known if they would get on with the owner manager. Craft skilled labour was thus not merely sectorally specific but often, in effect, firm specific or indeed individual: labour power was often quite concrete rather than abstract. For management, then, obtaining an adequate supply of skilled labour was highly contradictory: on the one hand the importance of skill and its imperfect subsumption within the craft labour processes made relocations to areas of better supply attractive, while on the other the same features tied firms to their existing workforces. A second conservative force was *the ties to the final market* of many craft firms. We have seen that ties to technologists, designers, clients, buyers and wholesalers and fast turnaround and on-site work have been integral to the craft sectors and have shaped their labour processes, so that these ties should be regarded as internally related to the craft labour process rather than as a separate factor.[7]

These conservative forces greatly reduced relocations out of London, and thus exacerbated problems of supply of sectorally specific skilled labour. Indeed, these forces could result in relocations *into* London: this took place in two multisite craft firms in order to reinforce investment in highly skilled and experienced workforces, in spite of older building and plant and higher costs – strong examples of reinforcing accumulation.

Gendered relocation within London for craft labour

We have seen that skilled labour power has uneven distribution within London and non-isotropic commuting patterns, both strongly gendered (section 6.5). There were four relocations to take account of this geography, but again the retention of the existing workforce often prevented such

Box 7.3 Regional geographies of sectorally specific skilled labour

Labour-intensive consumer goods (clothing, furniture, and sewing and wooodworking skills used in toy production)

Until the Second World War these industries were concentrated in London and other large cities (and in the case of furniture in High Wycombe). Taylorization, however, enabled and encouraged decentralization, producing important differences in the characteristic levels of skill between the cities and elsewhere. Though its reproduction was poor, London still contained a unique pool of skilled labour in these industries. Thus outside London, already skilled labour could be difficult to obtain, but there was a better supply of young trainees and of semi-skilled workers, and skilled workers were easier to hold. London had advantages for firms willing to pay a premium for high levels of skill. The wage differential of London was somewhat lower than in the jobbing sectors because of weaker unionization, because there was less demand outside London attracting skilled workers to decentralize, and because such relocation would anyway generally be difficult for women workers. The comparative labour market advantages therefore depended on the strategy of the firm towards investment in training, skilling in the labour process, and wages. Again, the geography of labour markets needs to be understood in relation to labour process strategies (section 2.4).

Science-based craft industries (particularly electrical and electronic capital goods)

The substantial shift of this sector to southern England, and the *relatively* successful reproduction of skilled labour within it (section 5.6), meant that the supply of sectorally specific skilled labour was considered to be better in the Sun Belt than in London.

Jobbing sectors (most printing, much steelwork)

Although London has particularly high-level skills in these sectors, high-skill labour processes are used in most regions, since firms able to supply bespoke and complex work need to be close to their customers. Large workplaces and firms outside London meant reasonable levels of training. London's wage differential for this type of worker was high, due to high surplus profits in some London factories, strong print unions, and long commuting distances for men which required compensation. Labour supply considerations thus gave both a strong incentive for relocation and strong possibilities to do it successfully.

moves. For skilled *women* workers, short maximum commuting distances and the history of spatially uneven development of the sectors within London meant that effective supply of skilled workers could vary strongly over a kilometre or two. This was particularly the case in outer London, due to inferior public transport and thinner and more uneven distribution of production. Thus relocations with positive effects on the quality of labour power could be undertaken over short distances. By the same token, however, even short distance relocations threatened to lose part of the existing workforce. Thus the limited mobility of skilled women workers was contradictory for the employers: though it could create captive labour forces, it also made employers dependent on relatively small pools of labour and particular workers; and while short-distance relocations could make a difference, they had correspondingly large risks.

The geography of skilled *male* workers was different because they had longer commuting distances, mostly by car, and mostly lived in outer London or ROSE. Relocations to improve the quality of these workers were accordingly from inner to outer London. Moreover, such relocations did not threaten to lose so many of the existing workforce as was the case with women workers because much of the prior commuting was long distance and often would be shortened by the relocation. Whereas Martin (1966: 113) found that in the early 1960s firms sometimes remained in inner London because there they could tap the largest pool of skilled male workers, including those coming from outer London, this pattern seemed to have changed by the late 1970s due to the shift from public to private transport.

These locally effective structures concerning female skilled workers, and even those governing male workers, show that major parts of the London labour market remain strongly spatially segmented and uneven (Greater London Council, 1986: Ch. 17; section 6.5). The argument, based on neo-classical theory, that commuting patterns in London adjust to neutralize the effects of local residential concentrations of particular types of labour power (for example Metcalf and Richardson, 1976; Evans and Eversley, 1980) ignores both constraints on daily mobility and the internal relations of labour power and production. Relocation within London could therefore aim to exploit this spatial unevenness.

Discipline, semi-skilled workers and unknown geography

We have seen that management often complained of low productivity arising from the indiscipline, lack of basic skills and high turnover of non-skilled workers. Relocations to rectify these problems were, however, made difficult by the possibilities of knowing the geography of these employment relations. It was widely believed by managers that non-skilled workers, especially the young, were of poorer quality in London, or in inner London, than elsewhere, but this view was based on little evidence. The problem was not measured by bodies responsible for labour markets, unlike problems of gross supply such as occurred with skilled labour. But it went deeper than this: problems of 'discipline' were directly a function of the *relation between* the worker and management, although management tended to reify this by seeing the problems as intrinsic to the worker. Thus consistent information on the geography of this characteristic does not exist. Keynesian location theory rightly emphasizes the role of limited knowledge in location decisions (Dicken and Lloyd, 1990: 272–84); but because it does not see the elements of the economy as internally related it can miss the *inherent* indeterminacy of those elements.

The majority of semi-skilled workers in the panel were employed in the mixed and Fordist labour processes; these were further inhibited from relocating to improve labour supply by high sunk fixed capital (and in the mixed labour process case by their use of skilled workers). Overall, there were thus only two relocations to improve the quality of semi-skilled labour, both in labour intensive assembly. Both of these were out of London, and in multisite firms where management was better able to judge labour power in other locations. We see here, once more, that firms' relation to labour markets cannot be understood as an external market relation, as in neoclassical theory and, in more sophisticated form, in institutionalist labour market theories, but is rather a moment of internally related production and reproduction practices.

7.12 Relocations to discipline workers

One of the aims of the relocations just considered was to increase managerial control. Other relocations had this as a specific aim, intended particularly to deal with workers' collective resistance to labour process change. In these it was the *process* of relocation or the threat of it that enabled intensification.

In the upswing of the cycle, when the unions were in their best bargaining position, they were strongly restrained by the collaboration of the union leaderships with the Labour government in the Social Contract (section 5.10), while in the recession there was minimal resistance to either wage restraint or job loss in the panel workplaces. Thus employers did not face a *systematic* problem of collective resistance by labour. Recall that unionism was strongest in the male craft sectors and in deskilled production directly derived from it, whereas large Fordist factories and non-craft-based process plants were formally organized but non-militant (section 6.5). The case of the four Fordist electronics factories in the panel is striking. All four were subjected to major restructuring during the period: a massive intensification of work and halving of the workforce; a transfer of a large proportion of production to another plant; a relocation within London and reorganization of tasks; and automation of assembly which cut jobs by half. All of these were carried through with the cooperation of the unions. The same was true in the large plants in the toy sector, where there was a major transfer to another plant and in the recession two closures.

Nevertheless, the unions did constrain management in significant ways, and management in some cases used, or attempted to use, relocation to deal with this. Since during the recession management was able to intensify work in situ, this form of relocation, like relocations to new labour markets, was used predominantly in the upswing.

The process of relocation can be used to weaken worker resistance in four distinct, though sometimes overlapping, modes:

(a) Relocation to a *locality or region* where the relevant union, or unions in general, are weakly organized or relatively passive (Ross, 1983; Harrison and Bluestone, 1988). This is closely allied to relocations to new labour markets considered in the previous section.

(b) Relocation to a *new plant with a 'green' workforce* – one not previously employed by the firm or even in the industry – can give management greater leeway in organizing and reorganizing the labour process. In contrast to (a), it is not so much the characteristics of the new workers that is important as their *newness* in itself (Gordon, 1984; Massey and Meegan, 1978). Thus the relocation may be a short-distance one; this was the case in the celebrated move of News International's London newspapers from Fleet Street to Wapping in 1986, when a completely new workforce with new working agreements and a different union was installed using a move of only a mile.

(c) Relocations can be made from strongly to weakly organized *existing plants with the firm.* These are most easily made within firms with 'cloned' plants producing similar products (Massey, 1984).

(d) Alternatively, the relocation may be made *with the existing workers,* but the shift to a new plant is used by management as an occasion for work reorganization.

All of these types of relocation were encountered in the panel; but they were rather complex and 'impure', and demonstrate some of the difficulties for management in carrying this strategy through. They confirm the differences in union strength between sectors described above. There were four such relocations out of London, all from large establishments in craft sectors – brewing, furniture and printing. The favoured sites were not new, but they had all been opened within the previous seven years whereas the London sites were long established; union organization at the receiving sites was decisively weaker. Indeed, it is likely that at the time when these sites were opened their locations (three in ROSE, one in Scotland) were chosen because of the weaker organization of the relevant union in those districts. Moreover, the new investment at the favoured sites employed workforces new to the firms; these relocations therefore combined types (a), (b) and (c). The firms concerned were small to medium sized: it is not only large firms, as in Massey's example of cloned sites, which can play off sites against each other.

The lack of relocation to completely new sites during the period of study may have been due to the fact that, precisely in the sectors (craft) and in the period (the upswing) where it would have benefited management, labour recruitment and training would have been difficult. It may also have been due to successful resistance by the unions to such relocation. The largest printing firm in the study attempted to weaken resistance to restructuring by relocating within London (type (b)), but the unions were able to compel management to staff the new site with the firm's existing workers: not all companies have the financial and political resources of News International for defeating unions in short distance moves. In contrast, in the successful relocations the substantial distances between the London site and the site of expansion may have been significant in preventing workers from following the work.

This kind of relocation could be used as a threat without necessarily carrying it through. One printing firm successfully used the threat to relocate part of production to a somewhat more weakly organized site (also in London) to force the unions to accept new working practices on a new press in situ; this kind of tactic was common in the London printing industry around this time (Greater London Council, 1985). In this example, as in the relocations actually carried out, the unions' weakness was partly in the *spatial unevenness* of organization and partly in the lack of collaboration *between* union shops at the different sites; in the printing unions spatial unevenness was less than in most unions, but collaboration between sites could be weak.[8] Thus the relocations or threats of them exploited specifically *spatial* weaknesses of the unions in their command of *both* places and distance. Harvey

(1989: Ch. 14) has argued that labour tends to be stronger when organizing in place than in controlling flows of money, productive and commodity capital over distances ('space'); but we see here that *unevenness* in organization *in place* is one of the bases for labour's weakness in dealing with such flows.

Not every relocation to weaken workers' organization was away from London. There was a large relocation, again within a multisite firm, from a plant in the north of England to the London factory, due to the London workforce being seen by management as less militant (type (c) above). Not coincidentally, this was not in craft production but in Fordism. Fordism in the development areas of Britain has a different tradition to London: its strongest period of growth was in the post-war boom, and these economic circumstances, together with the union traditions of these regions, tended to produce somewhat more oppositional unionism than was typical of Fordism in London. This example shows both that the labour process can make a difference (here between craft and Fordist unionism in London) *and* that this is always melded with locally specific histories (here between London and the developing areas). It also shows how opposite geographical patterns – relocation out of and into London respectively – can be motivated by the same aim.

In other cases, firms tried to use relocation, largely with the existing workforce, to ease reorganization (type (d)). Management in a large Fordist plant that moved within London considered that the relocation had helped change labour processes by creating expectation and acceptance of change. A large printing workplace attempted (but did not eventually carry out) a move within London aimed at pushing through new working arrangements. This points to the importance of continuity in place for union organization. Union organization is built up cumulatively over time within particular sites, organized around very particular micro-geographies and temporalities of machines, shops, shifts and workers' place in them. In relocating, management is using *distance*, rather than the existing properties of the new *place*, to weaken this spatially embedded organization; thus even short distances may be sufficient (see further section 9.7).

Finally, the *absence* of relocation can be due to management's wish to combat union control. One printing firm decided not to merge two acquired sites, despite potential economies of scale, in order to prevent unionization of the one spreading to the unorganized workforce of the other. There were other cases where unionization had taken place before the period of study in the wake of a merger of sites or of firms. Hence relocation, where it was part of consolidation of capacity or centralization of ownership, could be to the advantage of labour rather than capital.

We have seen, then, that relocation in a number of different modes was carried out or threatened in order to weaken union influence, although the unions were sometimes able to block this tactic. Not surprisingly, this action was most common in those labour processes and product industries where unions were not only present but most active. It was also overwhelmingly used by multisite firms, relocating incrementally between existing sites; these firms had direct knowledge of workers' organization in different localities, and the existing production reduced problems of skilled labour recruitment and relocation costs. Geography, then, was here used directly in class struggle, albeit with many constraints.

7.13 Conclusions: locations and times of increasing productivity

The activity of raising productivity is thus highly differentiated by labour process, by its spatiality and by its timing. Improvements to fixed capital were most commonly carried out in situ, but could also use spatial consolidation and moves to better premises and require relocation to adjust floor space to changing labour processes. Intensification could be carried out as an alternative to mechanization *or* to complement it.

Intensification could be imposed on a given workforce or through the act of relocation to a new site or workforce. But change in the qualities of the workforce, either in situ or through relocation, was also important. These qualities were not only, or mainly, a question of union politics but one of skill, of cooperativeness, of stability over time (and hence experience on the job), and of willingness to work particular hours. This shows that intensification can proceed through the use of different social and spatial segments of labour power, that is, through the interrelation of production and reproduction of labour, something neglected in labour process theory.

Whereas intensification in situ was used mainly during the recession, it was carried out through relocation mainly in the upswing. While improvements to fixed capital were made in situ in both phases of the cycle, relocation was used during the recession. Forms of labour process change are thus strongly structured by the business cycle, as we explore further in Chapter 12.

We have seen that the form of capital could also be significant. In particular, multisite firms had greater capacity to carry out some forms of relocation using their *existing* sites. They could reshuffle their portfolios of fixed assets, hedge their bets by using London and out-of-London sites for distinct purposes, use (threatened) relocations to discipline workers, and exploit their superior knowledge of different locations. All of these are forms of reinforcing accumulation within the firm (section 4.3).

Finally, the mix of these various ways of increasing productivity was dependent on the labour process: this both shaped the pressures on management and conditioned the means of action. This dependence is explored further in Chapter 10.

NOTES

1. We should expect the labour process categories as wholes to be internally varied in the *cost* of investment per head because of the heterogeneity of technologies for different products. For example, within the new craft sector the value of investment per employee may be quite different in printing and in scientific instruments even though the *qualitative* use and impact of forms of investment may be similar. Accordingly I here use comparisons of labour processes within particular product industries, and exclude products that are radically different from the rest of the product-industry.

2. Note that productivity measured in money terms (value added per head) increased much less fast than volume productivity because the *generalization* of a new technology lowers the socially necessary labour time and thus final prices.

3. 'Intensification' refers here to initiatives taken by management with this aim. These may or may not have been successful (section 6.2). The degree of success was not measured because (i) it was often accompanied by machine change, and (ii) in the recession there was large fall in intensity of work due to overcapacity.

4. The study by Massey and Meegan (1982) has often been misread as arguing that product-industries pursue strategies based on either intensification or mechanization. In fact, they show that, although one of these forms of labour process change may be dominant in an industry, they are often combined.

5. Unit price changes during the period for the respective products of the two subsectors were similar, around −15 per cent in real terms.

6. Requirements regarding the quality of premises were a constraint on *all* relocations. This constraint, too, varied with labour process. For example, workplaces in group 1 were less inhibited in moving than those in

other labour process types by considerations of premises quality, one reason for a high rate of relocation in this group.

7. These contradictions of location were less acute for firms with sites both in London and outside it. These could maintain their existing workforce in London while taking advantage of easier labour markets elsewhere. They could maintain final market and design ties in London linked into direct production, while expanding production elsewhere.

8. The London print unions did, however, ensure that work contracted out from unionized workplaces went only to other unionized firms.

8 THE PRODUCT MATTERS

8.1 Products, production and labour

The quality and design of the product may be as important to a firm's profit as volume productivity. Ensuring adequate quality of manufacture and the ability to put product changes into production are therefore central to designing and reshaping labour processes (section 3.4). But these aims may require different – even opposite – work relations from those required to maximize volume productivity: whether in the design of machinery, control of labour, or the employment relation, quantity may conflict with quality. Industrial relations and the connections between production and locality are about products as well as productivity.

I consider the issue of production quality first, as it is closely – though problematically – connected to the changes in productivity discussed in the previous chapter. Design as a labour process, its social divisions of labour, and different strategies of product change are then considered. I investigate the changes in labour processes made to meet these product strategies, the constraints of the labour process encountered, and the ways in which relocation was used to avoid these constraints. All this then gives us a further cut on the dialectics of product and labour process change. Finally, we look at how radical technical change in intermediate products can result in restructuring of the production chain and its geography. In this chapter changes in situ and through relocation are considered together.

8.2 Improving the quality of production

Ensuring the quality of production was, overall, a major preoccupation of management, but its significance varied between sectors. In consumer goods, quality of production was important in upmarket goods, but often neglected in downmarket lines. In contrast, in capital and intermediate goods supplied to firms, quality was always important because knowledge and scrutiny of the product by the user was greater than in consumer goods. In jobbing firms, quality of production was a key aspect of competition, because these firms lacked proprietary products that could give them an edge, and because the timeliness and appropriateness of the fitting on site were crucial. Thus the major division was between consumer and producer goods, that is, the class of the customer. As in increasing volume productivity, firms in the panel took measures to improve quality of production within each aspect of the labour process, namely, equipment, control and employment relations, which we consider in turn.

Re-equipment

Mechanization has the potential to overcome human shortcomings of judgement, dexterity and concentration but its application with this aim was easier in some labour processes than others. In processes that were already substantially mechanized, machine changes could often improve production quality at the same time as increasing productivity. This was particularly the case in long run, standardized products, where the complications of product variation did not have to be taken into account. Thus automated electronic assembly was considered more reliable than manual assembly, automated welding more reliable than manual, and automated tape duplication better quality than the semi-automated process it replaced. Re-equipment that improved production quality was consequently introduced most often in labour processes with high mechanization and long runs: standardized processing, Fordist and process plant. Moreover, in these cases the large production volumes could more safely amortize the costs of the new equipment. It was also in these labour processes that improvements to premises in situ or through relocation, and changes in the layout of production, could most easily be used to improve production quality (sections 7.4, 7.10).

Whereas in these cases increased productivity and improved quality went together, in new craft sectors the opposite was often the case: changes in production technology that increased productivity often compromised the quality of the varied and changing products. The transition from letterpress to litho printing, and from hot metal compositing to photosetting and computer-aided page make-up were widely considered to have had this drawback.

These differences are reflected in the incidence of investment in

Table 8.1 *Investment in new machinery to obtain better production quality, by labour process*

Percentage of 1976 workplaces						
Old craft	New craft	Mixed	Assembly	Standardized processing	Fordist	Process plant
7	5	5	6	16	20	20

machinery aimed, at least partly, at better production quality, shown in Table 8.1. Just as with mechanization aimed at increasing productivity, the *effect* of these investments tended to be greatest in the labour processes where they were most common. In the craft, mixed and assembly labour processes, machines improving production quality were typically introduced only in particular stages of production or the testing stage, whereas in the others they could affect the majority of production.

Improved control of the work process

This method of improving quality of production was most used precisely in those labour processes where mechanization could not be: in old craft and assembly, and to some extent new craft. Increased supervision could make a large difference to production quality here because of the complexity and variability of tasks and because of the often uneven levels of skill. In the case of small firms, this could require the owner-manager to devote more time to supervision of work.

As we saw in section 7.5, in these labour processes closer supervision was also an important means of increasing productivity. In some cases improved production quality and increasing productivity were pursued in tandem, in others they were alternatives because speed-up would damage production quality. Indeed, in some cases management actually *slowed down* the pace of work in order to improve production quality. Again, this could be particularly beneficial in the least mechanized labour processes: volume norms in semi-skilled assembly within a large electronics factory were reduced with this aim.

The use of homeworkers within old craft and assembly posed a sharp trade off for management between cost and quality. This is nothing new: problems of quality control were a major reason for the transition from putting out to factory work in early industrialization. In our study, homeworkers were sometimes used in preference to 'indoor' workers because of their high levels of skill and consequent good quality of production; this was so with some upmarket clothing producers who used experienced workers who had retired from the factory. But by far the most common reason for using homeworkers was their cost: exploiting their lack of access to factory jobs, employers could pay homeworkers lower piece rates than indoor workers and avoid accommodation costs (section 6.5; see further section 9.2). This could, however, result in lower production quality. Homework has a low degree of mechanization that, as we have just seen, makes production quality more difficult to ensure. Homeworking exacerbates this problem through lack of supervision. This contradiction tended to be most acute in the more skilled work (old craft rather than assembly) and where there was large variety and changeability in product design (again, mostly in old craft). The lack of opportunities for training of homeworkers compounded these problems: homeworkers who had never done factory work tended to have lower skill levels. Moreover, in using homeworkers firms did not directly control the carrying out of work and its timely completion, and to ensure completion had to rely on the threat of cutting off future work. There was thus a contradiction between numerical flexibility and wage cutting on the one hand and value productivity on the other. This is reflected in the frequent changes in tactics by firms regarding homeworkers: of the 66 clothing firms that used homeworkers, eight reduced their use very substantially (and two increased it) at some time during the study period for reasons of production quality or turnaround time.

Thus the least mechanized labour processes had the greatest problems of control affecting *both* productivity and quality. Management in these labour processes also had the greatest dilemmas of *trade-offs* between volume productivity and cost on the one hand and production quality on the other.

Change in the workforce

Changes in the composition of the workforce in situ or through relocation aimed at productivity increases (sections 7.6, 7.11) usually also improved production quality: better skills, lower turnover and greater commitment tended to serve both aims. While changes in the workforce were made in all labour processes, the impact on production quality was most significant in the least mechanized. *This* means of improving quality, then, had the advantage for management that it did not conflict with volume productivity.

Taken together, these measures to improve production quality were a major aspect of labour process change. The means by which management pursued this aim depended on the degree of automation, batch size and degree of variety of the product, and the supply of appropriate labour power. Improvements in both production quality *and* productivity could be obtained by machinery for long-run standardized production, employment of better quality labour power, and sometimes increased supervision. But management often had to choose between volume productivity and quality of production when mechanizing short-run varied production and when using home-workers. Labour process analysis needs to take account of these com-plementarities or conflicts between productivity and production quality.

8.3 Design work, technical rents and the division of labour

We now turn to the relation between the labour process and the specification of products. The activity of product design is a labour process in itself, 'design labour'. Its central problem is one of valorization: in both scientific and artistic design it is impossible to know in advance the usefulness of the products developed. A second problem is one of ownership: since design ideas are embodied in the designers themselves, who are free labourers and potential entrepreneurs, firms can have difficulty in retaining control of the product of design work. A third problem, or set of problems, is similar to that of the direct manufacturing labour process: recruitment of suitable labour power, and control by management of a labour process in which there is always a high degree of responsible autonomy (Massey, Quintas and Wield, 1992: 92–101).

Partly because of these problems, many firms do not develop their own products, or do so only in interaction with other actors. For analysing the panel it is useful to distinguish three kinds of design labour and the social division of labour within it:

- *proprietary products* (ostensibly) unique to the firm;
- *commissioned products*, where the design is given to the firm by a contractor for batch or long run production;
- *bespoke design* of a product which is unique, though it is usually a modified version of either a proprietary or standard product; the design is devel-oped by the firm, sometimes in collaboration with the client or their designers.

There was variation within each of these categories and fuzzy boundaries between them. Proprietary products could be the product of major research and development work, or serious evaluation of consumer demand and

Table 8.2 *Design labour by broad sector*

Sector	Proprietary	Commissioned	Bespoke
Craft consumer goods	Most furniture, toys, few clothing	'Cut, make and trim' clothing firms	Few furniture, printing
Scientific craft goods	Some	Some components, instruments	Some
Craft jobbing	–	–	All; product difference = process difference
Fordist	All	–	–
Process plant	Most	Some metal boxes, pharmaceuticals	–

fashion; alternatively, they could be trivial variation in a design for a table or a blouse, or simply copied from another firm. In some commissioned products, especially components, the producing firm could contribute ideas towards the design or modify it somewhat for production reasons. Bespoke design could involve very substantial *ad hoc* design work, or trivial variation on a standard theme. But much bespoke 'design' is a question of quality of production: in jobbing work, particularly, the variation of the bespoke product is the *same thing* as the variation in the production process. The incidence of the different types of design labour within the broad sectors is shown in Table 8.2.

The inter firm division of labour in design was due not only to its financial risks and the difficulties of managing design labour but also to the learning that collaboration could enable. We have seen the particular importance of this within London manufacturing (section 5.2). It takes place both 'horizontally' as flows of knowledge between firms in the development of proprietary products, and 'vertically' in exchanges between firms in commissioned products and between firm and clients in bespoke design. Thus design is socialized in ways which cut across private appropriation. These relations need to be conceived fundamentally as *labour* – both design labour and the work involved in organizing collaboration. This is missed in the traditional notion of 'ties to markets'. Similarly, transaction cost theory (Williamson, 1975; Scott, 1988) sees the labour of coordination in purely negative terms as cost and misses its nature as value creation.

Design work, while in many ways problematic, was nevertheless important in giving the firm a competitive edge. Conversely, where design and product differentiation were weak – in trivial proprietary design, in commissioned products, and in bespoke production of little distinction – there was a tendency to overaccumulation and acute cost competition, whether at the London or wider spatial scales, particularly in labour processes with low barriers to entry (cf. sections 5.3, 5.9, 6.7). However, increasing product innovation raised difficulties of the relation between product change and the direct labour process, to which we now turn.

8.4 Changes in products and the expansion of capital

Change in products manufactured took three forms: change in design of products, diversification of product range, and vertical integration:

- Change in the design of existing types of product

Despite the importance of product innovation in the contemporary economy, its incidence in the panel was extremely uneven. In craft capital goods firms it varied from the sporadic, with products unchanged in essentials for ten to 20 years, to continuous innovation. In many consumer goods firms, products remained unchanged over many years (for instance in beer, biscuits, non-ethnical medicines, reproduction furniture and toys); in others, design work was perfunctory (in clothing, modern furniture and toys). The technically simple form of the products in craft and labour intensive production of consumer goods made it easy for firms to copy designs. In contrast, some large Fordist factories and process plants made products developed by substantial research and development units within the firm.

A particular type of product change was movement from simple, cheap, large batch products to complex, expensive, smaller batch products or vice versa. In consumer goods, these are respectively moves upmarket and downmarket. Changes in incomes during the study period – stagnation or fall of lower incomes, increase in higher incomes – encouraged either cheapening of consumer goods or shift towards more expensive ones; both directions of change were found in the panel, though neither conferred automatic success. In machine goods and jobbing sectors, some firms repositioned themselves towards specialist niches at low volumes, while others on the contrary simplified and cheapened the product to widen the market.

- Diversification

Diversification of the product range was seen by many firms as the primary means by which they could expand, rather than by winning greater market share in existing products. Diversification could occur in all three types of design work: increase in the number of proprietary goods; taking commissioned work in a wider variety of products; or carrying out bespoke work of more varied types or with more diverse customers. Diversification could be aimed at exploiting economies of scope, but the motivation generally appeared to be expansion of output and valorized capital. In the case of niche capital goods, firms often had a very large share of the national or even world market, and so diversification was the only way to grow. But in many other cases diversification was seen as a way of sidestepping design or production competition in the existing products. Very few firms moved in the opposite direction, towards greater specialization in products.

• Vertical integration

Some firms invested in capacity to produce more stages of the existing products in-house, with few doing the reverse. Again, this was usually aimed not at efficiencies and cost reduction but at expansion of productive capital and output. Thus the panel firms were far from exemplifying what is often claimed to be a feature of the present epoch of industrial organization, namely increasing product specialization and outsourcing of heterogeneous stages of production. Advocates of the latter model might see this as a sign of the backwardness of London manufacturing (cf. section 6.9). A more plausible interpretation is that product specialization and outsourcing is always in tension with the pressure for firms to expand their capital. Considerations of productive efficiency may *conflict* with those of capital accumulation (Gough, 1996a).

Each of these forms of product change accelerated in the recession. This was particularly true of diversification of products or stages of production, which were seen as the quickest way of countering sales decline. However, the products were mostly only weakly innovative; a frequent result was crowding of the market.

We see, then, that the incidence of product change cannot be reduced to production efficiency and changes in consumer taste, as it tends to be in much contemporary work on industrial organization (cf. section 3.4). Product change was also powered by the firm's capital growth and by the rhythms of capital accumulation expressed in the business cycle.

8.5 How product change alters the labour process

These product changes had implications for the direct labour process. Moves

Table 8.3 *Re-equipment to change products, by labour process*

Percentage of 1979 workplaces						
Old craft	New craft	Mixed	Assembly	Standardized processing	Fordist	Process plant
7	3	4	3	3	20	29

upmarket often meant a shift towards more skilled or craft-type labour processes, while conversely moves downmarket implied a shift towards assembly, standardized processing or Fordist operations. Diversification in conditions where total output and employment were stagnant – and thus particularly in the recession – tended to require an increase in the number of tasks performed by each worker, increasing skill requirements and reducing economies of scale (for the case of furniture, see Leigh *et al.*, 1982b). Indeed, diversification reflected a low emphasis among managers on economies of scale (section 9.6 below).

The extent to which *re-equipment* was needed for redesign or diversification was strongly dependent on the type of labour process (Table 8.3). Re-equipment tended to be needed most often in Fordism and process plant. In Fordist production, component producing machinery in particular was often dedicated. In the case of process plant, a substantially new product normally required radical modifications or an entirely new plant. In both cases, diversification often meant setting up an extra line, thus requiring extra floor space or land and contributing to the long-term increase in land use (section 6.6). In contrast, craft production had great product flexibility. Product change could sometimes require additional special machines, but the core production technology would remain the same. Thus product design could be changed without great organizational or financial difficulties. Assembly was the most product-flexible labour process of all: product change needed only minor retraining of the workforce.

Standardized processing was a more complex case. The product-flexibility of the machinery tended to be inversely related to its sophistication, and hence ranged from technologies resembling old craft or assembly to ones resembling Fordist component production or process plant. Thus secondary pharmaceutical production was product-flexible, while most forms of duplication (tapes, records, print) were not. However, in the latter case, the informational content of the product could easily be changed without altering its physical form: firms could switch from, say, classical to pop music tapes without having to re-equip. This example suggests a wider point: if the informational content of products is increasing (Lash and Urry, 1994), and if this is distinct from the physical form of the product, then much product change can be accomplished with little change in the labour process.

8.6 How the labour process shapes product change

It is not simply that a given product strategy can require changes in the direct labour process: the latter can constrain and condition the former. In other words, product strategies are shaped not only by pressures of product competition (sections 8.3 and 8.4) but also by the given labour process.

Firstly, the product-flexibility of *production equipment* influenced product strategies. New craft and mixed-labour process firms in capital goods tended to centre their strategies on innovative products, which they were able to introduce with relatively weak constraints from their machinery. For the same reason, old craft consumer goods firms in furniture and clothing were able to switch or diversify frequently between quite different types of product (for example, between tables, chairs and bookcases; between dresses and blouses); thus in 1976–9 a quarter of these firms diversified substantially.

However, the ability to change products was also constrained by availability of *skilled labour power*. This constraint was strongest in exactly those labour processes in which machinery was most flexible, namely the craft sectors. Thus problems of supply of skilled labour made furniture and clothing firms hesitate to change products; when they did so, productivity often fell, at least temporarily. This compelled some firms in clothing and toys to position themselves downmarket. One case of new craft production suggests the pressures within this labour process. A scientific instruments firm redesigned its product from a specialist instrument produced in small batches to a general-use instrument produced in large batches in order to use a smaller number of skilled workers whom it found hard to recruit. Supply of design workers could also be a constraint: while supply of consumer goods designers did not appear as a problem, firms in scientific capital goods often had great difficulty in recruiting designers (section 6.5). The latter problem was essentially limited to small firms: large firms had most of their research and development work located separately from their direct production, and, having more capital for this long-turnover investment, were able to afford better wages.

These constraints are summarized in Table 8.4. The differences between the labour process types arise from their contradictory logics. The product-flexibility of the machinery in group A requires skilled workers for its

Table 8.4 *Constraints of the labour process on product change, by labour process*

	Group A: old and new craft, mixed labour process	Group B: assembly, standardized processing	Group C: Fordist, process plant
Production equipment	no	no	yes
Skilled labour supply	yes	no	no

operation, with the problems of reproduction of labour power and sub-ordination of labour that this implies. In group C in contrast, labour problems are minimized by more elaborate mechanization and automation, but this then inhibits the introduction of new products. These are problems, then, both of the technical nature of processes and products but also of the tension between responsible autonomy and direct control of labour, which thus affects not only productivity but also product change. The paradox is that while the use of skilled labour power in group A and investment in machinery in group C are problematic for capital they are also the potential basis for earning product (technical, design, quality) rents: these are hard to generate in group B. Note that narratives of Fordism and flexible specialization as stable forms dominating historical periods occlude these contradictions of product-production links and the latter's variety (cf. sections 3.4, 3.6).

8.7 Relocation to facilitate change in products

Product change, then, could both elicit change in the labour process and be constrained and shaped by it. Relocation arose from both these circum-stances: it was a way of implementing labour process change to facilitate product change, while side-stepping constraints embodied in the existing labour process. This was done in two ways, the first mostly within single-site firms, the second in multisite firms.

• Relocation to new sites for skilled labour power

Relocations of craft and mixed labour process production to improve supply of skilled labour were sometimes carried out not only to increase productivity (section 7.11) but in order that new products could be introduced more easily. Such relocations in craft production of scientific goods, most often to the Sun Belt, sometimes had the additional aim of obtaining better supply of technologists for product development; indeed, in moves made by two small firms this was the sole motive.

- Relocation to alter the specialization of sites

Within multisite firms, management sometimes moved product lines so as to alter the degree of specialization of sites and hence productive efficiency. The contradictory considerations involved are suggested by the fact that changes were made both to decrease and to increase specialization:

(a) Shifts in investment between sites sometimes favoured those with the *most diversified* product range, on the grounds that the existing productive capacity made it easier to introduce further new products or modifications to them. This potential was particularly important in those labour processes, groups A and C in Table 8.4, where production constraints on product change were the greatest. Thus there were relocations in an old craft firm and a medium-batch mixed labour process firm motivated by the diversity and high level of *skills* in the targeted factories; and relocations were made in a Fordist firm and a large-batch mixed labour process firm motivated by the diversity of the product-inflexible *machinery* at the receiving site. As with relocations between existing sites motivated by productivity (section 7.8), the London sites were sometimes the superior ones in these respects, as reinforcing accumulation over a long period had laid down a rich mix of products; thus two of these relocations were into London, two out of London.

(b) On the other hand, relocations were sometimes made in order to *increase the specialization* of sites: production of products or components of particular type was concentrated at specialist sites. The constraints of the existing labour processes were accepted, and the particular capacities of existing factories more effectively exploited. Again, these relocations took place in the most constrained labour processes, and both into and out of London: two in Fordist production aiming to use dedicated machinery more fully, two in new craft and the mixed labour process to better exploit particular labour skills. Thus although the overwhelming tendency *for firms* was towards diversification of product range (section 8.4), some firms specialized their *factories*; the former was motivated by capital accumulation, the latter by productive efficiency.

Thus a given aim, to better match productive capacity to products, could result in two quite opposite tactics and relocation behaviour – either a widening of sites' product diversity and exploitation of economies of scope, or a sharpening of sites' specialism. It is interesting to note that while recent management and academic literature has stressed the advantages of product specialization, diversified factories may provide greater product flexibility and was as important a tactic in the panel.

***

The discussion of the last three sections gives us *a third cut on the dialectic of products and labour processes.* We have seen this connection in the abstract (section 3.4) and its operation in the long-term evolution of sectors (sections 5.4, 6.4). Here, we find this structural logic expressed in the medium-term development of firms and workplaces. A given *product strategy* may elicit changes in the labour process either in situ or through relocation (section 8.5 and this section), so that the product is the guiding thread. Alternatively, the *labour process* may be the constant which circumscribes product strategies (section 8.6). Tactics on the degree of specialization of sites also reflect different emphases: diversification accommodates the labour process to product change, while specialization restricts products in order to improve productivity (as well as to facilitate small product changes). Which constraint is seen as the dominant one by the firm can thus have major effects on its evolution both in situ and through relocation.

8.8 Major technical change in products and the social division of labour

A common type of change in the design of a product is change in the technology of a component or in a particular stage of production. This can both alter the labour process within the firm and change the social division of labour between the firm and its suppliers. These changes can be *major* ones, in the senses both of a discontinuous technical change and in having impacts on a wide range of sectors (Freeman, Clark and Soete, 1982). The electrical/electronic industry has experienced many such changes over its history; during the period of study, major changes in component technology were being implemented: from wired to printed circuit boards, and from separate components to integrated circuits. It is characteristic of such major changes in *products* that they also involve large changes in *labour process.* Technical development is addressed not only to the new product in itself but its method of production; thus the widening use of printed circuits and integrated circuits has been powered by innovation in production technique as much as product design (cf. Walker, 1989a). In consequence, the production requirements of such new components are typically quite different to those they replace; both the geography of their production and the firms involved tend to shift, so that we can talk of the creation of a new 'sector'.

This was indeed the case with the increasing use of printed and integrated circuits by the panel firms: wiring of components performed within the firm was simplified by the printed circuits which were produced sometimes in-house, sometimes outsourced, while wiring and assembly were replaced by integrated circuits which were always outsourced. Much production was thus shifted to other parts of Britain or other developed countries. The new components allowed a reduction in assembly work, both directly and because in some cases simplification facilitated automated assembly. Thus both the labour process and the social division of labour changed rapidly. This occurred most often in faster changing labour process groups, and in those which already had the most elaborated technical and social division of labour: Fordist and process plant production rather than new craft and standardized processing.[1]

We have seen that the surveyed firms, for reasons of accumulation, generally attempted to increase the stages of production that they carried out. But changes in components forced them, on the contrary, to increase their outsourcing. The requirements of the labour processes in the new components were too exacting to allow modification of the workplace to produce them, going much further than the constraints discussed in section 8.5. Decline in value added and employment in local sectors can sometimes be the result of this sort of change in major components. At a larger scale, Lappe (1988) reported projections that 30 per cent of job loss in German engineering in the 1980s and 1990s would come from change in product design, higher than the proportion due to automation.

This discussion shows that in analysing the labour process one cannot confine one's attention to the (existing) technical division of labour within each workplace, as has generally been the practice in labour process theory. The tendency towards increasing 'roundaboutness' of production (Sayer and Walker, 1992) means that the technical and the social division of labour are often changed simultaneously. This gives a further twist to the dialectics of product and labour process. Radical innovation in intermediate goods, components and materials occurs, powered in part by innovation in their processes of production. This alters the use value of final products, requiring change in *their* labour processes and geographies of production.

8.9 Conclusions: products, labour processes and space

The product, then, is of crucial importance to understanding labour processes both concretely and in the abstract. Varied aspects of the product are important here – the quality of production, rents earned on qualities of the product, changes in product use values, the range of products produced, and changes in intermediate products. The reverse is also the case: product innovation, range, and quality, and the associated marketing strategies, are strongly founded in the labour process. Marxist writing on industry, following Marxist value theory, has tended to abstract from the use value of products. But we have seen that the latter arise not simply from contingent technical change and shifts in consumer demand but from production. Product innovation is in a large part process innovation; direct labour processes constrain product change; and competitive pressures arising in the labour process may be mitigated by product strategies. Similarly, product rents are earned not only through investment in design labour but also by the often difficult reshaping of labour processes to make new products. In short, product and process change are strongly internally related.

Pressures for productivity increase, better production quality and product innovation respectively can sometimes be met by the same measures, but at other times conflict. Moreover, the ability to address each of these three requirements varies with the type of labour process. Paradoxically, both those labour processes in which labour is most strongly subsumed *and* those in which workers have the greatest responsible autonomy pose difficulties for product innovation.

As with increasing productivity, product strategies have important spatial and temporal aspects. Product change was accelerated in the recession as a response to increased competitive pressure. The stepping up of some forms of labour process change during the recession to increase productivity was reinforced by product aims. Blockages in labour process change in situ required for either production quality or product change could sometimes be met by relocation. Relocations, then, can have product as well as process aims – to the extent that the two are separable.

NOTE

1. Old and new craft sectors and standardized processing can nevertheless be substantially affected by change in *materials* technology, an often overlooked branch of technological innovation. Thus steelwork firms in the panel were affected by new welding materials, and the furniture industry since the Second World War has been profoundly altered by laminates and coatings.

9 THE COSTS OF CUTTING COSTS

9.1 Cost cutting and its causes

The principal means of cutting unit costs are through increases in productivity via combinations of mechanization and intensification (Chapter 7). But we saw in section 3.3 that there are other, 'pure' methods of reducing costs within the labour process: cutting wages of existing workers, using a new workforce with lower wages, increasing the total weekly hours worked, and altering the scale of the workplace. This chapter discusses these measures in turn. We shall see that cost cutting was often highly contradictory for capital.

Both the motives and the opportunities for cost cutting were variable. Pressure was stronger in product-industries where average profit rates were low and where competition proceeded strongly through price (section 6.7). The business cycle also made a difference, as the recession intensified pressure to cut costs. However, the feasibility of cost cutting was sharply dependent on the labour process. As with the measures considered in the previous two chapters, management could seek to cut costs both through measures in situ and through using relocation.

Many cost-cutting measures redistributed income and benefits from labour to capital. But, as we shall see, they spilled out beyond the employment relation into other aspects of the labour process. In particular, changes in the size of the factory, both upward and downward, involved not merely unit costs but all aspects of the capital-labour relation, and are thus relevant to management aims discussed throughout this part of the book. Scale change is therefore discussed at the end of this chapter.

9.2 Redistributing income: wage cuts in situ during the recession

The sharp recession in 1979–81 gave firms an incentive to cut wages and, in changing labour market conditions, a means to do so. Inflation remained high in the recession (partly due to increases in value added tax), totalling 30 per cent over the two years. Firms were therefore able to carry out real wage cuts even when they 'gave' nominal wage increases. Average hourly manual wages in London increased by 26 per cent for men and 19 per cent for women in the two years to April 1982, effecting substantial cuts in real wages.

But there were constraints, and possible penalties, in cutting wages, which were unevenly distributed by labour process. The pattern of wage cutting was therefore uneven and, because of the contradictions of such cuts, a matter for conscious tactics of management. We have seen that in the upswing firms experienced shortages and high turnover of sectorally skilled labour, general engineering skills, and cooperative semi-skilled workers (section 6.5). These pushed up wage levels, though to a degree dependent on surplus profits in the product industry. The recession caused a sharp change in all labour market segments, but the different pressures present in the upswing did not disappear. Thus cuts to both wages and employment were differentiated by degree of skill, competition within the product-industry, and strategy of individual firms towards labour:

* Degree of skill

The wages of skilled jobs were generally cut less than those of non-skilled ones; in many cases different wage changes were given to the two groups within the same workplace. This was also apparent in sectoral differences: within process plant, for instance, wage rises were lower in the less-skilled metal boxes sector than in brewing and in pharmaceuticals. This difference reflected the fact that firms now had such a large reserve army of non-skilled labour that they could be selective without paying a premium, whereas, on the other hand, managers still had anxieties about retaining skilled workers, sometimes even when they were reducing their numbers.

The continuing constraint of skilled labour is reflected in the fact that in the recession many firms held on to more skilled workers than were needed to meet their output. In some cases this was to retain workers with very particular skills or long experience, especially in the craft sectors. In others it was because of fears of difficulties in recruitment in the subsequent upturn, given the severe difficulties many had experienced in 1976–9. In addition, in larger, well unionized factories, workers were sometimes able to work more slowly in order to avoid redundancy ('soldiering'). These processes tended to reduce productivity and inflate the total wage bill. This effect was less significant than the intensification of work that management was able to impose in the recession (Chapter 7), but it does nonetheless point to the continuing difference in management tactics towards respectively skilled and non-skilled workers even during the recession.

On the other hand, some firms were able to retain male skilled workers in the recession by cutting overtime, although this was not straightforward. Long overtime hours for male skilled workers were common in expansionary times, with the effect of integrating these workers more closely into the firms; if this was the norm, cutting overtime was tantamount to a basic wage cut and led to conflict.

- Cost competition in the product-industry

The interplay of labour process and product-industry system in generating different forms of competition (sections 2.6, 6.7) was also important. Sectors which were under the least pressure of cost competition granted larger nominal wage rises. Broadly, those competing primarily on quality or against other London firms (Groups 1 and 2 in Box 6.6) paid nominal wage rises of 15 per cent to 30 per cent over the two years 1979–81, whereas those that competed on price *and* faced national or international competition (Groups 4 and 5) gave rises over the wider range 0 per cent to 30 per cent.[1] Thus firms under less competitive pressure did not necessarily force down real wages to the maximum, presumably in order to retain cooperative workers and to mitigate the reduced cooperation which wage cuts tend to elicit.

- Firms' profitability and skills strategies

Wage cuts also varied with the profitability of the particular firm. This dispersion was strongest among small, non-unionized firms, which were better able to link wages to profits. Small firms in trouble during the recession generally paid nominal wage rises of only 0 per cent to 10 per cent. The contradictions for management that this involved are indicated by the pattern in craft sectors facing intense cost competition, those in Group 5, in which the weakest firms carried out large real wage cuts, whereas others maintained or even increased real wages in order to retain or improve their skilled labour force.

Wage cuts could also have negative long-term consequences for capital, most evident in the sectors under greatest cost-competitive pressure, Group 5. In the craft sectors the large cuts in real wages during the recession stored up trouble for later. Thus in the slow upturn in the clothing industry in 1982–6 the shortages of skilled labour experienced in 1976–9 reappeared with renewed intensity, so much so that there were steep wage rises for well-skilled machinists in 1984–6. In the mixed, assembly and Fordist labour process subsectors, the further sharp deterioration of wages of non-skilled workers relative to London norms would exacerbate the existing problems of their reproduction as effective wage labour (section 6.5; Greater London Council, 1986). Moreover, the ability to protect profits by sharply cutting wages removed the pressure from these firms to improve processes and product design; this is a characteristic path through which British manufacturing weakness has been reproduced (section 5.9). Wage cutting, then, could have penalties for capital.

The *differences* in treatment of different segments of the workforce, by skill and by profitability of sector and firm, adumbrated a pattern of widening wage inequalities that was to become increasingly pronounced (and denounced) in the 1980s and 1990s. These differences had the value for capital of increasing political divisions within labour. Specifically, they widened the status distinctions, always so important in London, between white collar technicians, male skilled workers and other manual workers, and they made more direct the dependence of workers on the profitability of their employer. Subsequent government policies sought to deepen exactly these divisions.

We can draw two conclusions. Firstly, London manufacturing firms used the new labour market conditions of the recession to carry out real wage cuts. These benefited capital not only in cost savings but also in the deepening of long-standing divisions within labour. This harsh and direct method of increasing the rate of exploitation is, then, not a relic of the nineteenth century: contrary to social democratic hopes, it is not ruled out by either the 'needs' of labour processes nor the long-term balance of class power in modern capitalism. But, secondly, these cuts may have costs for capital. They are constrained by the use of skilled labour power and the element of responsible autonomy within the labour process, affecting productivity and quality. They tend to cut against relative surplus value strategies. Again, value processes can conflict with productive efficiency.

9.3 Wage cutting by changing the workforce

Just as with intensification (Chapter 7), wage cutting can be pursued not only with the existing (type of) workers but also through shifts to different segments of the workforce. Since the 1970s British capital has increased the employment of women, youth, part timers, short-term contract and 'self-employed' workers as means of cost cutting. However, some accounts of this trend have been exaggerated, and it has largely taken place through changes in the weight of sectors in the economy rather than changes in employment practices *within* sectors (Pollert, 1988). The panel firms did undertake some changes of this kind, but these were limited because of the pressure to maintain continuity of experience of individual workers and continuity of work culture in employment of particular groups.

There were a few cases of firms employing semi-skilled labour reducing wages and add-on costs by shifting from older women to young workers and from full-time to part-time women. The most significant change was shifts from indoor workers to homeworkers. Of the 66 clothing firms employing some homeworkers in 1976, thirteen increased their use to cut wages, particularly during the recession; a few others made this shift in order to obtain a better supply of labour at the piece rate offered. The salience of this particular labour segment change arose from the fact that homeworking is *structurally different* from factory work. The payment differential between indoor and homeworkers was probably the largest between any substitutable segments of the London workforce, due to the qualitatively different constraints on homeworkers. The shift to homeworking was also sometimes a geographical shift. While most of the commissioning factories were in inner London, many of the homeworkers were in outer London or ROSE, since these women had fewer opportunities for local factory employment; a few firms even used homeworkers from the Asian communities in the Midlands where piece rates were significantly lower than in London. This decentralization could give rise to problems of turnaround times, but employers were able to exploit non-local workforces without moving the factory; the geography of homeworking is not only about the different *places* of home and factory but also uses the potential *distances* between them. A shift to homeworkers, then, provided the greatest cost savings to employers, but only a minority of labour processes could be relocated in this way (section 6.5).

Cutting wages through change in workforce segment was, then, very limited in extent. It was also contradictory in its results. The cheaper workers generally had lower productivity and production quality than those they replaced. Again, it was craft production in which this tension was most acute. Indeed, we have seen that employers made changes in workforce composition in exactly the opposite direction – from youth to older women, from part-time to full-time women, from homeworkers to indoor workers – in order to improve quality of production (section 8.2). Thus in the clothing industry there were overall nearly as many shifts towards as away from indoor working.

Table 9.1 *Relocation to cheapen wages, by labour process*

	Number of workplaces						
	Old craft	New craft	Mixed	Assembly	Standardized processing	Fordist	Process plant
Relocations	6	2	2	2	0	1	0
Total workplaces	189	40	43	16	19	15	10

9.4 Relocation to cheaper labour

The problems that firms experienced in cutting wages in situ might be expected to have resulted in relocation. But the number of workplaces relocating to cheaper labour was small – only thirteen, all out of London. There was a large overlap between this set of firms and the ten firms that relocated out of London to reduce their premises costs, suggesting that these firms faced intense pressure to reduce costs by all means possible. And indeed, all thirteen firms were producing long-run, standardized goods within product industries facing strong cost competition, in Groups 4 and 5 of Box 6.6.

Table 9.1 shows the labour processes of these relocating firms. The absence of the most capital intensive labour processes, standardized processing and process plant, is not surprising, because these are under the least pressure to reduce wage costs. Craft firms were prominent. We saw in section 7.11 that supply of skilled labour power in steelwork, printing and electrical engineering was better in some other areas of Britain than in London, and relocations were made not only to obtain better quality labour but also to reduce wages.

There were differences among these relocations in their incidence over the cycle. Managers' intentions about future relocation were more influenced by concerns about cost during the recession in 1981 than they were at the end of the upswing in 1979. In the case of less skilled production, the relocations to reduce wages were clustered in the recession. However, the relocations to cheapen *skilled* labour took place overwhelmingly in the upswing. In this period the skilled labour market ruled out reductions in wages in situ: thus relocation was used when in situ action was blocked. The decisive cost pressures could thus come *either* from final markets *or* from labour power.

These relocations show, then, that the cost disadvantages of London can be large enough to cause relocations away from it. However, this strategy was only undertaken when cost-competitive pressures were extreme, and was evidently only open to firms that were not dependent on specialist skills and that had weak product ties to London. Neoclassical and Ricardian location theory suggest that firms are constantly on the move in pursuit of cheaper workers; but we have seen that this depends on the labour process, on competitive pressures arising from the interrelation of labour process geography and the industry system, and on the phase of the business cycle.

9.5 Working for the machine: longer hours and overhead costs

Another way of reducing unit costs through changes in the employment relation is to use fixed capacity for longer periods each day or week. In contemporary capitalism, capacity is depreciated, and its costs per unit time reckoned, not mainly by its physical wearing out, but rather by the time elapsed since its installation. This is obviously true of rented premises and machinery. But it is also true of owned means of production, since these are technically depreciated, which takes place at its own pace (Harvey, 1982). Unit costs can therefore be lowered by increasing the output realized from machinery and buildings during their period of hire or before they become obsolete. This can be done by increased overtime working or by adding shifts, given that extending the length of the standard day is politically difficult.[2] During the twentieth century, the costs of machinery per unit time have tended to rise relative to variable costs, at least in the production of given products, due both to increasing sophistication of machinery and to a shortening technical depreciation time (Mandel, 1978a). This may also be one reason why the standard working week reduced very little during the twentieth century, and is one of the main reasons that shift work has become increasingly common.

Possibilities for cutting unit costs by lengthening working hours, however, depend on the labour process. As we have seen, the annual investment in machinery per employee of the different labour process groups varies within a range of an order of magnitude (section 7.2). It is therefore not surprising to find that shift work was the rule in process plant, common in Fordism, standardized processing and capital intensive new craft printing, and virtually absent in the other labour process. Lengthening of hours during the study period was also most marked in these labour processes: there were nine cases of extension of hours of use of machinery in process plant, standardized processing and printing. Lengthening of hours took the form of introduction of extra shifts, increase in systematic overtime, and even lengthening of shifts. Most of these took place in the recession, because this increased the need for unit cost cutting, and there were fewer problems in recruitment to the new shifts. The number of cases in the expansionary phase of the cycle would doubtless have been greater had there not been such difficulties in labour recruitment during that time. The timing of this tactic was thus a product of both final market and labour market pressures. It gave the paradoxical result of firms increasing their employment and output capacity just when demand was weakening (Robinson and Eatwell, 1973).

Capital intensive workplaces were not the only ones where this tactic was used, however: it was also found in labour intensive factories where cost competition in the product-industry was intense, particularly the clothing sector (Box 6.6, Group 5). Like all London producers, these faced substantial fixed costs for their premises, even though their machinery was cheap. Margins on output were very small, and thus small changes in unit costs could make a large proportional difference to profit rate. Moreover, these firms were often competing with others using homeworkers, which thus avoided most of the fixed costs of the factory based enterprises. Indeed, the effect was to move the indoor workforce towards the varied and long shifts worked by homeworkers.

Thus, again, cost-cutting measures are constructed by the internal relations of labour process, labour market and value processes in the product-industry. While firms' motives were quantitative ones, there were qualitative consequences for workers. For most people the hours required are anti-social. Where shifts are rotated in order to staff the least popular ones, there are damaging psychological and physiological effects. The extension of shift work can therefore be regarded as a form of intensification of work for the worker even if the output per hour worked is not increased. Moreover, shift work makes effective union organization more difficult. Thus, while this change does not fall within traditional definitions of absolute surplus value, it has similar negative effects on workers.

Finally, we turn to upward and downward changes in the size of the workplace, which aimed not only to reduce unit costs but also to increase managerial control.

9.6 Increasing the scale of the workplace

Increasing the scale of the workplace may reduce unit costs in a number of ways: enabling more powerful machinery to be used; allowing a finer technical division of labour; enabling tasks for underoccupied workers to be found more easily, thus lowering 'porosity'; and expanding output relative to fixed overhead costs such as indirect labour or premises. These are forms of reinforcing accumulation within the workplace.

During the cyclical upswing, there was considerable investment to increase capacity in situ; but in only eight cases was this directed, even partly, to lowering unit costs rather than simply expanding output and the mass of profit. It is likely that increasing scale economies were realized more frequently than this, but they may have been too incremental for management to notice, or have been an unintended benefit of output expansion. The potential for these gains was strongly varied by labour process. In the furniture sector, productivity increased with workplace output throughout the sector, but more strongly in the mixed and Fordist labour processes than in old craft. Scale economies in direct production proper, as opposed to those in the use of overheads, were largest in process plant.

In contrast, multisite firms had substantial success in achieving scale economies through *merger of sites*. Such mergers could increase the scale of production very substantially in the short term, so that the unit cost reductions were perceptible by management and the subject of conscious action. It is significant that Massey and Meegan's (1979) study, in which economies of scale play a major role, was concerned with the merger of firms and rationalization of sites. In the present study we have already seen examples of such action, in the four cases of multisite firms increasing the product specialization of sites (section 8.7), thus increasing the scale of production of particular types of product. There were a further 20 cases of site reorganization where one motive was an increase in production scale, some following mergers. In around half of the site mergers, the economies of scale were in direct production rather than indirect overheads; these were all in high-volume, capital-intensive production of standardized products and involved both larger scale plant and more intense use of labour power. However, consolidation was not necessarily onto the largest plant but the most efficient.

The total number of firms adopting measures for economies of scale was modest, but the workplaces involved were generally large. Once again, multisite firms were able to deploy strategies unavailable to single-site enterprises. Relocation was a more powerful means of achieving the given aim (economies of scale) than change in situ: it was more frequently used, and the economies of scale achieved were more strongly based in direct production. While, as one might expect, some scale economies were achieved during the upturn, they were achieved almost as often during the recession using contractionary relocations.

9.7 Limiting the scale of production

More common than pursuit of economies of scale were strategies of *limiting the scale of production* for reasons related to the labour process; this was done by 66 firms. Smaller workplaces were thought to have potential benefits for both control and employment relations. They could thus not only help to ensure wage restraint but also productivity and production quality.

The most common reason for limiting workplace size was *management control within production*. Supervision was thought to deteriorate as size increased, even when the number of supervisors was increased proportionally. Several managers said that the 'family atmosphere' would be lost if they expanded significantly. Both these difficulties would damage productivity and, especially, quality of production. The size of workplace at which these effects were thought to set in varied enormously between managers even within the same labour process and product industry. In the new craft section of the printing industry, for example, the limit for a 'family atmosphere' was placed variously at between 20 and 300 employees. Evidently, the style of management and history of industrial relations in the firm could strongly affect the relation between size and control. There are determinate scaled processes here, but, as so often in geography, their concrete manifestations are quantitatively variable.

Connected but distinct was management's limitation of workplace size in order to limit the *formal organization and rights of the workforce and the impact of these on the employment relation*. We have seen that smaller firms were better able to adjust wages to profits in the recession (section 9.2). In better times, some firms abstained from recruiting in order not to set a new wage level within the firm. Others kept their employment level below the threshold of 20 employees at which workers' legal protections increased. In the male craft sectors, with their relatively strong unionization, management sometimes limited employment in order to weaken unionization. Thus in the printing and furniture industries, some firms restricted their employment to a level – generally below 50 workers – at which they hoped to avoid unionization altogether. In printing, the strength and militancy of the chapels (workplace union branches) tended to increase with size, and some employers therefore limited employment to 50 to 200 workers. Limiting unionization was aimed at better control of both work and employment relations.

We have seen in Chapters 7 and 8 that the problems of control of the work process were broadest and most acute firstly in the most skilled and variable work (the craft sectors and mixed labour process) and secondly in the least mechanized work (old craft and assembly). The problems of self-motivation –

Table 9.2 *Limitation of workplace size without relocation, by labour process type*

Percentage of 1979 workplaces						
Old craft	New craft	Mixed	Assembly	Standardized processing	Fordist	Process plant
24	23	14	12	11	0	10

implied by the notion of 'family atmosphere' – were largest in these cases. The incidence of limitation in workplace size by labour process, shown in Table 9.2, reflects these problems of control, together with the threats posed by strong unionism. One can see this variation by labour process within particular product-industries: for example in the furniture sector 22 per cent of the old craft workplaces were limited in size, but only one of the sixteen mixed or Fordist factories.

The limitation of workplace size could also involve *relocation*. We have seen in section 7.12 that some multisite firms relocated production towards existing sites with weaker union organization. Other firms carried out relocations with the particular aim of limiting site employment: six firms with expanding output opened a new site in order not to increase the size of their existing one(s), while another firm went further and split production between two sites within London with the partial aim of making them more 'manageable'. The difficulties of management control in craft sectors, and the role of the skilled male unions within them, show themselves again here: these relocations were made in three old craft and four new craft firms; three of these were in the printing industry, and the split into two sites was carried out in the largest printing workplace which employed 650 people. The fragmentation of production within the craft sectors, then, was not only a product of relative ease of entry (sections 5.3, 6.8) but was also due to management strategies for limiting workplace size in order better to control labour. The social division of labour within industries is a matter of politics as well as of productive efficiency (Gough and Eisenschitz, 1997).

This strategy, then, was aimed at avoiding overaccumulation within the workplace that would strengthen labour. It probably had little impact on total output and employment within the London sectors, but it did tend to fragment both production and ownership, and substantially strengthened the hand of management against labour.

Within particular product-industries, management sometimes has the notion of 'the ideal size of plant' – a frequent topic of discussion in trade magazines. However, as the case of 'family atmosphere' in the printing industry suggests, there can be no industry-wide or timeless figure for this size. It will depend on the state of industrial relations in the firm, locality and country, and on the firm's strategies of work control.

Management's limitation of workplace size is an example of what Neil Smith (1993) has termed 'the politics of scale', in which the scale at which an activity is carried out is such as to produce particular relations of power (see also Jonas, 1994). We have seen that the scale *of the London economy* can present particular problems for employers in managing labour (sections 5.8, 6.5). Employers may counter these problems through a strategy of scaling down workplaces.

Relation with the form of capital: the satisficing owner-manager

The form of firm ownership and management also played a role in the limitation of workplace size: owner-managers were particularly prone to limit the size of the workplace. The behavioural literature understands this limitation as arising from intrinsic characteristics of the owner, who chooses to make a target income rather than maximize profits – 'satisficing'. However, limitation is also constructed by *relations within production* – the difficulties of control and employment of labour just discussed, and the control of management itself.

A significant minority of owner-managers were unwilling to take on (additional) partners or to employ managers. This was a matter of not diluting the earnings of the firm, or not diluting the control of the owner and a wish to avoid conflicts with partners. As a result, managerial resources were limited, exacerbating problems of control. The size of workplace was often limited to that which could be directly supervised by the owner-manager(s) given the particular labour process. Sometimes owner-managers would have problems in devoting sufficient time to recruitment, particularly where labour turnover was high, and limited size for that reason. In other cases owner-managers did not trust their ability adequately to supervise certain indirect labour and had a policy of carrying it out themselves. For example, some owner-managers of engineering background would not trust anyone else to carry out product design work, whereas others would not delegate any work involving liaison with customers. In a further twist, some owners would not take on partners or managers because they did not trust others to manage sensitive aspects of the labour process. Thus control of labour was an important contributor to satisficing.

These processes were compounded by the low rates of profit in many – though not all – of the sectors where owner-managers were common, because both these traits arise from low barriers to entry (section 6.7). This made owners more unwilling to dilute earnings by sharing them, and made substantial expansion of the firm objectively difficult. Limitation of size was, then, compounded by the competitive dynamics of product-industries, based in their turn partly on the labour process.

Thus, as with entrepreneurship (section 6.8), the behaviour of owner-managers is not simply a matter of intrinsic individual attributes but rather is based on *social relations and accumulation dynamics*. The form of capital is not another factor to be *added*, but rather is internally related to the labour process and valorization.

9.8 Conclusions: the costs of cutting costs

Cost cutting, then, was a substantial preoccupation of London manufacturing firms in the study period. Wage cutting was significant. Adjustments to the scale of the workplace were also important – a process that needs to be given greater prominence in analysing the use of space by labour processes. Consequently, the role of relocation in cost cutting was not simply in moves to lower cost locations, the form privileged in location theory: relocation could also cut costs through reorganization of sites within the firm in order to change their scale, whether to increase it or decrease it. In these cases, again in contrast to the usual assumption, the sites' location was less important than their scale.

Cost cutting was determined in a complex way by the cyclical variation of markets. It was most common in the recession because final market pressures were largest then and because rising unemployment enabled wage cutting. But cost pressures from the labour market were strongest in the upswing, resulting in some relocations out of London in this period. Cost reductions through scale economies were achieved in both periods of the cycle, though in different spatial modes.

There were systematic barriers to cost cutting, however, and the possibilities for it were strongly varied by labour process. Reduction of wages tended to conflict with retaining high quality and experienced workers, and thus with increasing volume and value productivity. In high skill workplaces, management sought wage cutting most strongly during the upswing, yet this required relocation. Relocations from London for most firms would involve weakening product ties. These contradictions of wage cutting are an instance of the conflict between the partial interests of capital – in redistributing income from workers to employers, and its universal interests – in augmenting the skill and experience of labour power (section 3.5). These problems also meant that, within absolute surplus value extraction in its widest sense – changes in the labour process at the direct expense of workers – intensification was more significant than wage cutting.

Changes of scale of the workplace, while they could significantly reduce costs and the manageability of the labour process, also faced barriers. To achieve significant scale economies large increases in scale were needed, generally requiring relocations. Maintaining or creating smaller workplaces lost potential scale economies, and in single site firms it limited accumulation.

Because of all these difficulties of cost cutting, in most cases it required a strong impetus from cost competition or wage pressures. Contrary to neoclassical theory, firms do not seek out cost reductions constantly and above all else.

NOTES

1. Money wage rises tended to be on the larger side in large multisite firms with national wage bargaining, in process plant sectors particularly (cf. section 5.5).
2. In the 1980s and 1990s such lengthening was, however, sometimes achieved by capital through moves to individual contracts and contracting out.

PART IV

THE LABOUR PROCESS, CAPITAL

ACCUMULATION AND BEYOND

INTRODUCTION TO PART IV

In Part III we examined a variety of forms of labour process change with three broad aims – increasing productivity, improving products, and cutting costs. I now use these findings to discuss the interrelations of the labour process, industrial relations, capital accumulation, location and the business cycle at a more abstract level. In doing so, the most salient patterns detailed in the preceding three chapters will be summarized.

The first three chapters focus on the causative role in labour process change of three groups of structures which have been central to the analysis. Chapter 10 focuses on the initial labour process and on the product activity, use of labour power and occupation of premises associated with it. Chapter 11 is concerned with the relation of labour process change to the accumulation of productive capital and the socialization of production at different spatial scales – workplaces, firms, sectors and the London economy as a whole. Chapter 12 examines the role of the business cycle.

The three chapters give particular windows onto the space and time of the labour process. Chapter 10 examines the contrasts and links between in situ change and change through relocation, showing how these were responses to the same pressures in the labour process. Chapter 11 focuses on contrasted rhythms of accumulation, their varied spatial scales, and their impact on workplaces and localities. Chapter 12 looks at the phases of the business cycle and how these modulated the use of location. Thus both Chapters 11 and 12 are concerned with capital accumulation in time and space and its relation to the labour process.

Each of these three chapters draws out implications for workers' collective politics. These are drawn together and developed in the final chapter, which examines how capitalist accumulation, labour processes and their geography oppress and divide workers, and how a politics of and for labour could overcome these.

10 CHANGING LABOUR PROCESSES AND CHANGING PLACE

10.1 The labour process and location

Two central aspects of the analysis in Part III were the difference made by the initial labour process, and the alternative between change in situ and through relocation. This chapter draws together the findings on these two themes. It asks, firstly, how the *different types of labour process* differ in their characteristic forms of change. Secondly, it investigates how management decides between *spatial and non-spatial modes* of changing the labour process. These two issues are not, of course, independent of each other: the initial labour process affects not only the types of production changes sought by management and workers but also the potential for management to use in situ change and relocation respectively. The issues are therefore intertwined in this chapter.

The broad types of logical relation between relocation and labour process change found in the study are first discussed. I then examine the choice between in situ change and relocation for carrying out particular types of production change, and give a first cut explanation of the pattern found (sections 10.2, 10.3). The chapter then focuses on the difference that the type of labour process makes to production and locational change. The study has shown that different labour processes reacted in quite different ways to the common conditions of the London and wider economies during the period of study. Managements' aims were implemented through varied means and differentiated resort to in situ change and relocation. The incidence, forms and geography of relocation and the immediate goals it served thus differed strongly between labour processes. I discuss the notion of dynamic tendencies of labour processes abstracted from other structures. These dynamics are explored by analysing the role of particular dimensions of the labour process in shaping its change both in situ and through relocation. A further cut on the locational decision is presented by examining the influence on relocation of the initial labour process. Finally, the central role of class struggle in labour process change is drawn out.

10.2 Labour process change and relocation

A premise of this study is that labour process change and relocation within firms are closely connected to each other (Chapter 4). Having looked at many examples in Part III, we can now examine the logical status of this relation more deeply, and thus contribute to the wider debate on the relation between society and space (Gregory and Urry, 1985; Gough, 1991; *Political Geography*, special issue 16 (2), 1997). To what extent was spatial change a *result* of essentially non-spatial labour process change and capital accumulation? Conversely, to what extent was relocation *constitutive of, or integral to,* change in the labour process?

Following Chapter 4, we may distinguish three types of impulse to relocate arising from different scales of the economy, namely the firm itself, localities, and product-industries. These involve different relations between geography and economy:

(i) Relocation to change resources and relations inside the firm

Some relocations involved internal restructuring of the firm's resources and relations. Production was relocated between sites on the basis of their productivity, diversity of products or specialization, and to achieve economies of scale (sections 7.8, 8.7, 9.6). Relocations were carried out to limit the size of workplaces in order to sustain management control (section 9.7). In these cases, the relocation itself more-or-less *directly achieved* the change in the labour process. The relation was even more direct in the cases where relocation was made (or threatened) in order to discipline the workforce (section 7.12). Here, it is the *process* of relocation itself that effects the change in production relations: *distance* obstructs workers' organization. In all these cases, then, the relocation was *directly constitutive of* the labour process change.

(ii) Relocation to access the resources of other local economies

Relocations to other localities to change qualities of the labour force enabled improved productivity, production quality and product innovation (sections 7.11, 8.2, 8.7). With more difficulty, they could cheapen labour power without productivity penalties (section 9.4). Moves between localities could allow improvements in premises with impacts on productivity and production quality (section 7.10). Here relocation does not directly effect labour process change but rather (it is hoped) provides the *means* for it.

(iii) Relocations associated with labour process change across a product-industry

We have seen that some relocations were associated with labour process change across the product industry: rapid technical change resulting in the scrapping of capacity; change in production leading to change in floor space per unit of output; and radical innovation in components resulting in a redrawing of the spatial division of labour (sections 7.8, 7.9, 8.8). Reorganization of capacity was the result not only of changes in the labour process but also of the relation between aggregate capacity in the industry and externally given demand. Relocations by firms to expand or contract capacity and reorganize product lines were then in the first place an *effect of* the industry-wide labour process change. However, the relocations also played an active role in *stabilizing* the labour process change by bringing the use values of production more closely into line with its valorization.

These are the *proximate* causes and purposes of the relocations. But they are premised on patterns of spatial uneven development of labour processes between sites of the firm and between local economies, built up over long periods (section 2.8). Space is therefore also active in the form of historically accumulated spatial-economic patterns.

The relations between relocation in the firm and labour process change are thus complex: relocation (i) can be *integral to and directly achieve* the labour process change, (ii) may provide *a means or basis* for it, or (iii) can be largely *an effect of it* while *reinforcing it*. In all these cases relocations were underpinned by *spatial histories* of the labour process. This complexity arises from the internal relations approach used here. In this approach, causal connections can be self-contained and hermetic, as in the direct relation between relocation and labour process change in relocations of mode (i). However, causality and mutual determination can also spill outwards and involve other structures and systems – in this case local economies and product-industries; the logical connections are then more mediated. The internal relations approach, then, leads to varied and layered relations between economy and space.[1]

10.3 The choice between in situ change and relocation: patterns and first cut explanation

There are, then, deep reasons for labour process change to be accomplished through relocation. The choices made by management between in situ change and relocation that we encountered in Part III reflect the key role that workplace location can play in altering the social relations of production and material use values. Thus any analysis of labour process change needs to take account of the ways in which management uses space to its advantage. The corollary is that any analysis of workplace (re)location needs to be grounded in the labour process and its tensions.

The spatial form of labour process change was, however, dependent on the particular type of change being undertaken (Table 10.1). Certain types of labour process change were more often carried out in situ than through relocation: improving the quality of premises and machinery, increasing the intensity and quality of work through increased management control, and extending working hours. This was so because in these cases the barriers to in situ change were relatively small for most labour processes and product industries; for example, collective opposition by workers to intensification of work and changes in working hours was generally weak. But in other types of labour process change such barriers were more substantial, and management resorted to relocation. Thus due to the tightness of some parts of the London labour market, relocation was used to a similar extent as action in situ to make changes in the labour force. The same was true of improvements in capacity for product innovation, where the requirements of both skilled labour power and of machinery were exacting and would either be difficult (labour power) or expensive (machinery) to change in situ. In achieving economies of scale, consolidation using relocation was the major means available, since the increases in scale generally had to be very substantial to have significant effect. Relocation was also the main path to cheapening wages, given the conditions of the London market and the pressures to maintain quality of labour power.

One may therefore understand some of the broad differences in spatial behaviour of different forms of labour process change in terms of the conditions in the locally effective structures of the London economy, and of the use by firms of their accumulated resources. However, we know from Part III that the choice between action in situ and relocation varied strongly with the initial labour process; for example, whereas intensification of work in situ was possible in the majority of cases (Table 10.1), in some craft or formerly craft sectors it met significant resistance, so that relocation was an important tactic

Table 10.1 *Balance between in situ action and relocation in different types of labour process change*

	In situ action	Relocation
To raise productivity and product quality:		
– Premises quality	more	less
– Machine quality	more	less
– Floor space increase/decrease	no	yes
– Management control	more	less
– Change in labour force		
skilled	yes	yes
non-skilled	yes	yes
Product diversification or specialization:		
– Machinery requirement	yes	yes
– Labour requirement	yes	yes
Cheaper labour	less	more
Extension of working hours	yes	no
Economies of scale	less	more
Diseconomies of scale	yes	yes

(sections 7.11, 7.12). We therefore now need to consider how the initial labour process shaped both the forms of labour process change and their use of space. Before undertaking this discussion, however, some consideration is needed of the form of abstraction to be deployed.

10.4 Do labour processes have intrinsic dynamics?

Do particular types of labour process have specific intrinsic dynamics? Some writing on the labour process implies that they do: skilled labour processes have a tendency to be deskilled; Fordist labour processes have difficulties of coordination, line balance and worker resistance and hence a tendency to be vertically disintegrated; production of high fixed capital intensity has a tendency to overaccumulation. This runs the risk of assuming, in a positivist fashion, a direct relation between (abstract) cause and (concrete) outcome. In contrast, our theoretical starting point was that the potential of labour processes is always more or less strongly mediated by other structures, and that this potential may anyway be contradictory. We have seen many examples of these complexities in Part III.

We should therefore seek the role of the initial labour process in constructing production change in dynamic *tendencies* or *potentials*. The detailed analysis of labour process change in Part III enables us to tease these out. This analysed the combined effects of a set of relevant structures, but for each type of change sought the role of the initial labour process (see introduction to Part III). The 'labour process' here was not narrowly circumscribed: both the labour process typology and the forms of 'labour process change' considered encompassed product activity and the labour power and premises used by the firm; these are included in the 'labour process dynamics' discussed below. The analysis in Part III was also able to distinguish the *blocking* as well as promotion of change, and sometimes found that a given labour process had dynamics towards *contrary* types of change. These too are included in the 'tendencies of the labour process', which will be synthesized and compared below. The realization of these tendencies is, of course, always dependent on other structures, on context. But they give a suggestive starting point for analysing production change in other industries, places and times from those of the study.

In analysing the panel I have often conceived of the actions of management and workers as being either 'constrained' or 'enabled' by the labour process or aspects of it. This is a useful way of linking a structure to conscious decisions because it is the way actors tend to think about their potential actions. Important constraints for both management and labour were the resources and actions of the other – strongly differentiated by labour process (P. Edwards, 1986). Difficulty in changing a particular 'constraining' aspect of the labour process could lead management to put more emphasis on another 'enabling' aspect. Often these were completely intertwined, so that the pressures of labour process were strictly contradictory.

With these clarifications, I now synthesize the dynamic tendencies of different labour processes.

10.5 The dynamic tendencies of the labour process

The labour process is a unity, but an internally differentiated and complex one (sections 2.3, 3.2–3.5): in what way, then, should one specify it in order to grasp its dynamic tendencies? The analysis so far has proceeded in terms of mutually exclusive types of labour process. But, rather than contrast the dynamics of these, I shall approach the question more analytically by unpicking the typology into some distinct *dimensions of the labour process* and

Table 10.2 *Typology of the labour process by dimensions*

	Old craft	New craft	Mixed	Ass'bly	Stand. proc'g	Fordist	Process plant
Capital intensity/ mechanization	low	med./ high	med.	low	med./ high	med./ high	high
Rate of change of process technology	low	high	med.	low	med./ high	med./ high	low/ med.
Product-flexibility of equipment	high	high	med.	high	varied	low	low
Degree of continuous flow	low	low	med./ high	high	low	high	high
Use of skilled labour power	high	high	med.	low	low	low	varied
Trade union militancy	varied	varied	varied	low	low	low	varied

presenting the tendencies of those dimensions. In the study the most significant dimensions have been:

(1) the degree of mechanization and fixed-capital intensity;
(2) the rate of change of production technology;
(3) the degree of product variety;
(4) the regularity of flow between stages of production;
(5) the extent of use of skilled labour; and
(6) the strength of unionization and worker militancy.

Table 10.2 maps these dimensions onto the usual typology of the labour process. The differences between the rows of this table show that although the dimensions *construct* each other (section 2.3) they are nevertheless *distinct*.

What, then, are the dynamic tendencies of the labour process associated with these dimensions, both in situ and through relocation? I shall highlight not only the dynamics of the labour process but its blockages, and not only management's characteristic projects but labour's potential for resistance.

(1) The degree of mechanization and fixed-capital intensity

This dimension has a use value aspect, mechanization, and a value aspect, capital intensity, each of which produced particular tendencies.

Mechanization provided a means for capital both to appropriate the power of labour and to control labour. Capital intensity affected firms' sensitivity to the technical depreciation time of equipment, to its utilization, and to wage rates. As we go towards either end of this dimension we therefore tend to find particular kinds of labour process dynamics.

A *high degree of mechanization* produced a tendency to relocate in order to improve the quality of machinery or premises. This was partly because these labour processes were sensitive to the quality of fixed capital (the use value aspect), and partly because relocation of output to existing sites could better valorize the large capital sunk in machinery and premises (the value aspect). A contradictory pressure, however, was that a high degree of mechanization inhibited relocation by making it more difficult to find appropriate premises. High capital intensity produced pressure towards a lengthening of weekly hours worked in order more rapidly to valorize the fixed capital.

Conversely, *a low degree of mechanization* produced quite different pressures. Since labour tended to be less well subsumed to capital, there was a somewhat higher use by management of increased control over the work process and of change in the workforce aimed at improving the quality of production. The problems of exerting such control could lead to owner-managers limiting the size of their workplace, or to multisite firms relocating production in order to strengthen managerial control.

The *value aspect* of mechanization was also directly relevant here. Firms carrying out labour intensive production were more inclined to use relocation in order to lower wage costs, though where skilled labour power was used this could be difficult (see dimension 5 below). Labour-intensive production can often, although not always, be carried out with reasonable efficiency on a small scale. In some cases this made homeworking possible, which could be used to cut costs or to ease labour recruitment at low wages. However, this could exacerbate the already severe problem of subsumption of labour, resulting in low production quality. Thus labour-intensive production resulted in contradictory pressures: it led to pressure to lower labour costs, but these could then exacerbate control problems arising from the weak subsumption of labour.

(2) The rate of change of process technology

Where *production technology was changing rapidly*, management was able to use it to raise productivity and sometimes also to improve the quality of production. This could be implemented by fixed investment in situ or, as in (1), by relocation of production to more advanced sites within the firm. Thus relocation between sites to improve the quality of plant can be associated either with a high degree of mechanization or with rapid change in it. Rapid improvement of plant often also required improvements to premises or changes in the layout of production which, again, could be carried out in situ or through relocation. Fast changing process technology also had a value effect: when generalized across a product-industry, it can exacerbate over-accumulation of fixed capacity. It also often alters the space intensity of production, requiring adjustments in aggregate floor space. Through both these mechanisms, it tends to produce reorganization of the industry's capacity, realized partly through relocation within firms.

Conversely, *where production technology was changing slowly* and relative surplus value was blocked, management had greater resort to intensification of work. Intensification could be carried out in situ, although in the case study this relied on recessionary labour market conditions. Alternatively, it could be pursued through relocation, either to enable access to different labour power or to discipline the existing workforce.

(3) The degree of product variety

Consider those workplaces that had *a small range of relatively slowly changing or standardized products.* Due to the ease of monitoring of volume productivity, this attribute helped management to intensify work through direct control. This was true *a fortiori* in standardized production using substantially mechanized labour processes with dedicated equipment, where the pacing of machines could be used. The dedicated nature of the machinery also meant that the quality of production tended to be strongly dependent on the equipment rather than on operator skill; accordingly, production quality could often be improved through re-equipment. Thus the standardization of the product, and the high degree of subsumption of the worker which this facilitated, allowed management to use particular paths both to increase volume productivity and to improve production quality. The lack of variety of the product also made it easier to pursue cost cutting through economies of scale, achieved particularly through relocations.

These advantages of product standardization came at a price, since the labour process could inhibit product diversification or modification. Where production was substantially mechanized with dedicated equipment this could be the main blockage. In less mechanized labour processes, workforce skills were the main blockage to product change. Alteration in products could then require change in workers' skills or in mechanization. In multisite firms this could be pursued through diversification or specialization of sites via relocation of products, on the basis of the capacities of the existing fixed capital or labour forces. In other cases planned product changes were abandoned due to their equipment or labour power requirements.

(4) The regularity of flow between stages of production

In this study flow lines had rather limited importance. Labour processes involving continuous flow between numerous stages of production, whether or not automated, tended to have more stringent premises requirements, including one-storey operation, and these requirements could change sharply with reorganization of the work process or its stages. Thus changes in premises could be important, and these were achieved overwhelmingly through relocation. Efficiency could also be improved by changes to the layout of production, which was generally achieved in situ. It was these simple material features of the labour process that were important in our case, rather than the much-studied problems of line balance or the use of automatic flow lines to enforce speed-up. Because of longstanding lack of worker militancy in those labour processes most dependent on continuous flow, and because of labour market conditions, the classic conflicts around (automatic) flow line production were weak. (This illustrates sharply the importance of the interrelations of elements in realizing the tendencies of labour processes: section 10.4.) In all labour processes, however, orderly and regular flows between stages were sometimes seen by management as both a sign of, and pressure towards, orderly and regular work.[2]

(5) The extent of use of skilled labour

The skill level of tasks and jobs crucially affected both the employment relation and management control of the work process. Thus labour processes with *a high proportion of skilled labour* put a number of constraints on capital. Shortages of suitable labour power could prevent intensification and wage cutting, as well as constraining output. Where intensification was achieved, it was pursued through incentives rather than direct compulsion. Improvements to the *quality* of production tended to be pursued through greater supervision rather than through change in machinery or in personnel. The opportunities for intensification offered by the recession took the form of greater selectivity in recruitment rather than direct speed-up. This benefit of the recession to capital tended to be offset by the inclination to retain skilled workers for continuity of experience and to avoid future recruitment difficulties, and by the difficulty for management in preventing skilled workers from slowing their work.

Firms employing a high proportion of skilled labour power also tended to have particular relocation behaviour. They tended to relocate to different labour markets in order to improve skill levels or to ameliorate recruitment difficulties. They sometimes carried out relocations to existing plants with an accumulated skilled workforce in order to diversify or specialize the product range. However, the desire to keep existing skilled and experienced workers acted to inhibit relocation. Finally, the problems for owner-managers in controlling the work process were particularly acute in the case of skilled production; this factor, as well as labour intensity (dimension 1), could incline such firms to limit the size of the workplace.

Production centred on *non-skilled labour* had converse properties. Intensification of work through direct compulsion was facilitated by tasks of low skill (in addition to low product variety, dimension 3). The recession gave different opportunities to management from the skilled labour case. The wages of non-skilled workers could be cut. The opportunities for intensification took a particular form, namely a lower turnover of workers. Relocation to different labour markets was less constrained than with skilled labour power. It tended to be aimed at reducing wages or at finding a more disciplined workforce, although the geography of the latter was moot.

(6) The strength of unionization and worker militancy

The evolution of the labour process was affected not so much by high union membership as such as by traditions of strong bargaining. These were found principally in male craft or formerly craft sectors. Union pressure was exerted at the workplace level rather than through national or district bargaining, in keeping with the shop-based traditions of craft unionism. In some of these workplaces, the unions were successful in improving the terms under which new technology would be introduced and in limiting intensification of work. However, the effect of overt conflict on wages was small. An important countervailing strategy of management was to limit the size of the workplace in the hope that this would lessen militancy; this was pursued particularly by (emergent) multisite firms, using relocation between sites. Relocation as a

Table 10.3 *Types of labour process change in situ and through relocation, or their blockage, versus the attributes of the labour process favouring them*

Labour process dynamics	Attributes of labour process
Use of fixed capital to raise productivity	
– better machinery or premises via relocation	Highly mechanized
– better machinery, premises or layout in situ or through relocation	Fast changing process technology
– better premises via relocation	Flow line
– better layout in situ	Flow line
Rationalization of capacity due to overaccumulation or change in floor space intensity	Fast changing process technology
Intensification via management control	
– via incentives in situ	High skill
– via compulsion and direct control in situ	Slowly changing process technology; low skill; standardized products
– via disciplinary relocations or threat of them	Militant workforce
[Resistance to intensification and disintensification in recession]	[High skill; militant workforce]
Intensification via change in the workforce	
– via selection in situ in the recession	Slowly changing process technology; high skill
– via lower turnover of labour in situ in the recession	Low skill
– via relocation to a different labour market for	Slowly changing process technology
stronger discipline	Low skill
better skill	High skill

table continues

224

Table 10.3 – *continued*

Labour process dynamics	Attributes of labour process
Improved quality of production	
– via machinery, premises or layout in situ or through relocation	Fast changing technology; standardized products
– via supervision in situ	Labour intensive; high skill; product-flexible machinery
– via change in workforce in situ decreased use homeworkers	Labour intensive Labour intensive
Product change	
– via re-equipment in situ or through relocation	Product inflexible equipment
– via reorganization and retraining in situ	Product-flexible equipment
– via relocation of output to skilled workforce	High skilled
[Product change inhibited by:	
– labour power	[High skill
– equipment]	Product-inflexible equipment]
[Relocation inhibited by loss of skilled workers and experience]	[High skill]
Economies of scale through relocation	Standardized products
[Size of workforce inhibits]/Size workplaces restricted or reduced in situ or through relocation	Slowly changing process technology; high skill; labour intensive; militant workforce
Longer weekly hours	Fixed-capital intensive
Relative wage reductions	
– with same workers	Low skill
– increase homeworkers	Labour intensive
– relocation to different labour market	Labour intensive; low skill
[Wage reductions inhibited in situ]	[High skill]

Workers' initiatives and other blockages to management's aims are shown in square brackets process was also used to attempt to weaken collective organization, though with the attendant problem of losing skilled workers.

Each dimension thus provides certain *potentials* for labour process change and certain *blockages* to it. These tendencies are summarized in Table 10.3, which is arranged by the types of change considered in Part III.

This analysis of the dynamic tendencies of dimensions of the labour process is necessarily schematic, but it suggests the variety of dynamic tendencies of different labour processes – in the aims that management tends to pursue, the tactics or mechanisms used to pursue those aims, the use or not of relocation, and the type of conflicts with labour that arise. Difficulty with, or blocking of, some mechanisms tends to make management pursue its aims through others.

10.6 Relocation pressures, second cut: different labour processes

We saw earlier (section 10.3) that different types of labour process change make differential use of in situ action and relocation, depending on conditions in local labour and premises markets and the use by firms of their accumulated resources. We can now see that the choice of the spatial mode for carrying through particular types of change is strongly conditioned by the initial labour process. An implication is that, in a given local economy, some labour processes face a greater *variety* of pressures to relocate, whereas others experience more blockages to relocation.

This point can be seen by returning to our basic typology of labour processes. For these, Table 10.4 summarizes the broad forms of labour process change that give rise to pressures around relocation, derived partly from Tables 10.2 and 10.3.[3] The labour processes experiencing the greatest variety of tensions around relocation were the new craft and mixed labour processes. Management here had to deal with pressures arising from rapidly changing process technologies (and hence issues connected with machinery, premises, layout and floor space), difficulties in the employment relation and the control of skilled workers, and in some cases militant unionism. Other types of labour process could experience strong relocation pressures, but on narrower fronts. Thus, in old craft production, relocation pressures were acute but focused on the employment and control of skilled labour. In contrast, in the Fordist and process plant cases, relocation pressures were concentrated around issues of fixed capital.

The fewest types of locational pressure were experienced in assembly and standardized processing. There were no major problems of skilled labour,

Table 10.4 *Relocation tensions by type of labour process*

Type of labour process change	Type of labour process						
	Old craft	New craft	Mixed	Assembly	Stand. proc'g	Fordist	Process plant
Premises quality*		+	+	#	+	+	+
Machine quality		+	+		+	++	+
Floor space increase	#	#	#			#	
Floor space decrease		#	#		#	#	#
Control of work process*		#	#				#
Change in workforce:							
– skilled*	+	+					
– non-skilled	+			+			
Change in products:							
– machinery			+			++	
– labour power	+	+	+				
Economies of scale			+			+	+
Diseconomies of scale	+	+					
Cheaper labour power	#	#	#	+		+	

Key: Strength of tendency: + medium; ++ strong
variation within the labour process category
* pressures to both relocation and stasis

and the production technology was either simple (assembly) or small scale, discrete machines (standardized processing). In addition, most of the labour processes could experience pressures to relocate in order to cheapen labour power; the main exceptions were strongly capital-intensive process plant and standardized processing.

It is interesting that the pattern of overt class conflict was the opposite of that found in the popular narrative of Fordism and post-Fordism (section 3.6). Conflict was relatively muted in Fordist and assembly workplaces, contrary to the usual tale of a specific crisis of *Fordist* industrial relations in the 1970s. On the other hand, conflicts over skills, hiring and location were pronounced in the craft sectors, most overtly in the male-dominated ones. This contrasts with the stereotypical view of craft industrial districts as reproducing cooperative industrial relations. These differences are understandable if the labour process is seen in its historical evolution in place, and in particular is related to the local reproduction of labour power (Part II). This cautions against reading off industrial politics from the labour process without mediations.

The numbers of different forms of pressure around relocation do not determine the frequency of relocation in an unmediated way; but they do indicate the complexity of the issue of location for management and its strong dependence on the labour process. By the same token, workers' experiences associated with relocation, and the disruption of work and social ties they involve, are strongly conditioned by the labour process.

10.7 Labour process change and class relations

Our starting point for considering labour processes and their dynamics was to note that they are both material processes and social relations, both 'technical' and 'political' (sections 2.3, 3.5, 3.6). I end this chapter by returning to this key issue. To what extent were the dynamics analysed in the study determined technically and to what extent by capitalist social relations? What is the relation between the material particularities of labour processes and the social relations that affect them all? This theme will be central to considering socialist strategy in Chapter 13.

Each of the six dimensions of the labour process analysed in section 10.5 has a directly material aspect. This is obvious for the dimensions of mechanization, technical change in processes, product diversity and flow lines, but it is also true of workers' skill and workers' organization, to the extent that these capacities are partly material and because they are embodied in people whose actions are materially constrained. The dynamics associated with each dimension rest on this materiality.

They also, crucially, involve the relations between capital and labour and the relations among workers. These relations are crystallized in the dimension of *union militancy*, but this is only their most overt expression. The dynamics associated with the use of *skilled work processes*, for example, depended on the influence that possession of skill gave to workers in the detailed implementation of tasks, on management's wish to retain their accumulated experience, and on the difficulties and risks of recruiting new workers. Indeed, worker militancy in London manufacturing largely grew out of these forms of influence, reinforced by male craft pride and the mutual respect of workers based on it.

The dynamics associated with *mechanization* were equally political. Mechanization can provide a basis for managerial control over both speed of work and production quality. The subsumption of labour is also affected by the *rate of change* of mechanization. Rapidly changing production technology sometimes follows from, and frequently elicits, conflict over the autonomy of workers within the work process; it requires, or enables, not only job shedding but reorganization of capacity and sites and hence of labour; it tends to disorganize the workforce (although it frequently disorganizes management too). Moreover, mechanization involved class conflict not only in the material organization of the labour process but also in its valorization. The fixed-capital intensity of the labour process influenced the sensitivity to wage rates and the weekly hours of work needed to valorize it. The rate of technical change affected tendencies to overaccumulation and consequent attacks on labour.

Similarly, the dynamics associated with the *product variety* of the labour process were a political matter. Limited product variety and variability, particularly with the use of dedicated machinery, tended to facilitate managerial control. However, this limited the technical rents obtainable and thus the ability of management to construct cooperative relations with labour through wage concessions. Firms' decisions on changes to product mix involved issues of skill, management control, initiative and discipline, and these were further affected by the technical rents that could be reaped.

Against overly political or discursive readings of the labour process, then, (spatial) production dynamics were shaped by its material and technical nature, by its particular use values (on discursive readings see Smith and Thompson, 1999). But against currently influential accounts which focus on institutional regulation serving a productive logic, labour process change was also marked by specifically capitalist relations between management and workers and among the labour force. Though these relations were always conflictual, and the balance of power could shift, they were set within the logics of capital accumulation. Firms not only had the power to shape investment and the labour process but also to deploy them in space in ways that *reproduced* their power over workers. Conflict did not escape from the power of capital over labour. These were, then, not merely advanced industrial labour processes but *capitalist* labour processes. How they might become something else is discussed in Chapter 13.

NOTES

1. Massey and Meegan (1982: 147–8) make a distinction between 'spatial' and 'non-spatial' processes which is starker than that used here, perhaps because they were rightly concerned to combat conflation of spatial difference with spatial process in earlier geographical literature. They

treat 'internal' attributes of workplaces and firms as non-spatial. But these are constructed by, and thus internalize, spatial mobilities and uneven development. See further Gough (1991).

2. Chris Jones, National Union of Tailor and Garment Workers, personal communication.

3. This table does not give the *frequencies of occurence* of relocation but rather a qualitative picture of relocation pressures. This is because here (a) I am concerned with both pressures towards relocation and blockages of it; (b) I am abstracting from causal processes other than the labour process; and (c) a particular relocation often had a variety of labour process aims.

11 RHYTHMS OF CAPITAL, THE LABOUR PROCESS AND SCALE

11.1 Varied rhythms and varied scales of accumulation

Labour process change is always also capital accumulation. Workers are always subject to the acceleration and braking, the booms and slumps of investment, and their 'fictitious' and distorted reflection in assets values. Capitalist accumulation involves both long cumulative build-ups and sharp switches and destruction. These capitalist switchbacks can be experienced within individual workplaces but also across local, national and international economies. We saw many examples of these problems in Parts II and III, and this chapter synthesizes and develops them.

In discussing accumulation dynamics, I have used the terms 'reinforcing accumulation', 'overaccumulation' and 'underaccumulation' to denote how economic structures and actors are brought together in ways that promote respectively sustained growth, self-destroying growth and cumulative decline (sections 2.8, 4.3). The concept of overaccumulation has a venerable history in Marxist economics. The notions of reinforcing and underaccumulation have roots in Keynesian theory, but are developed here within a Marxist understanding of capital accumulation. Sections 11.2–11.4 discuss these three modes of accumulation in turn. They are not, however, separate in their operation: a particular phenomenon often combines them. For example, skills shortages typically combine overaccumulation in production with underaccumulation in training and reproduction of labour power. This chapter examines several such dialectics.

There are other forms of interplay between the three accumulation rhythms. A particular workplace can be pulled in different directions – both economic and spatial – by different modes of accumulation. This leads to dilemmas, varied and contrary behaviours, and sometimes 'structured paralysis', which I discuss in section 11.5. Furthermore, scrapping and devalorization are the condition for profitable accumulation elsewhere or in the future; section 11.6 focuses on this dialectic.

All these rhythms of accumulation operate at *each* spatial scale. In parts II and III we have seen examples of their operation within not only workplaces but also the firm, the London sector, the London economy as a whole, and across product industries. In this chapter I show the similarities, resonances and interactions between accumulation at these different spatial scales.

The time scales of accumulation are equally varied, from structures built up over decades to the sharp turns of the business cycle. The accumulation of capacities over the long term involves socializations of production that link different social actors and different aspects of production, and articulate production with reproduction of labour power, each at varied spatial scales. This chapter thus relates short-term change in workplace labour processes to longer term and spatially wider accumulation rhythms – emphasizing once again the interplay of temporal and spatial dimensions. In particular, the chapter shows how these rhythms construct management's decisions to remain in situ or to relocate.

Accumulation and the labour process comprise both use values – machines, premises, labour power and product designs, and exchange values – retained profits, asset values, investment money. This chapter brings out the interplay of these two sides of accumulation, their reinforcements and divergences. The discussion emphasizes the extent to which the rhythms of accumulation are specifically capitalist in nature, with implications for political strategy.

All these themes are continued in the discussion of the business cycle and long waves in the next chapter.

11.2 Reinforcing accumulation

In Parts II and III we encountered a variety of forms of reinforcing accumulation. What were the principal structures and scales in which it appeared, and how did these affect workplace location?

Firstly, reinforcing accumulation took place in the stocks and reproduction of labour power in London or, more precisely, in the nexus of production and labour power. While management experienced many problems around skilled labour, the stocks of both industry-specific and wider skills were large in absolute terms, and contained sections of workers with particularly deep skills. This inclined firms to relocate locally in order to retain skilled workers, at a neighbourhood level for women workers, at the London level for men.

Table 11.1 *Geography of relocations by type of labour process change*

	Number of relocations		
	Within London	Out of London	Into London
Machine quality	3	6	2
Premises quality	18	6	
Floor space increase	12		
Floor space decrease	3	3	3
Improved management control	1	4	1
Change in labour force for productivity:			
– skilled	4	5	2
– non-skilled		2	
Product change:			
– to skilled labour		5	
– to diversify the site		2	2
– to specialize the site		3	1
Economies of scale	13	8	3
Reduce scale of site	5	2	
Cheaper labour		13	
Cheaper premises	1	9	

The stock of skilled labour power could even result in relocations into London (Table 11.1). Similarly, the stock of premises in London was often suitable for production needs: all relocations to increase floor space were made within London, despite the lack of green-field sites; even relocations to improve the *quality* of premises were, in their majority, made within London. In this moment, production itself *creates* appropriate 'factors of production'. Spatial inertia, then, arises not only from fixed capital but from these locally effective structures reaching into local economy and society.

Reinforcing accumulation also took place within workplaces. Labour process change was often most easily carried either in situ or through relocation to an existing site within the firm. The accumulated skills and experience of the workforce could be attractive compared with a green workforce at a green-field site; workers' knowledge and tacit skills can be strongly cumulative within the factory (Polanyi, 1967; Perulli, 1993; section 7.11). Established industrial relations practices could be more attractive to management than developing them from scratch, and this could sometimes make London sites more attractive to management than factories elsewhere (section 7.12). Machinery suitable for diverse products or which could be the basis for particular specializations could provide the means for new product strategies (section 8.6).

The financial aspect of existing sites could also give rise to reinforcing accumulation. Significant economies of scale were usually achieved through consolidation of *existing* production (section 9.5). The lengthening of the weekly hours of factory operation was motivated by the fixed pace of technical and hence financial depreciation of the plant – reinforcing accumulation driven by fictitious capital (section 9.4).

Not only the accumulated knowledge of workers but that of management inclined firms to reinvest at existing sites; in multisite firms this experience could make relocation to existing sites more attractive than setting up new ones (sections 7.8). Articulating technologies, tasks, employment relations and forms of control is necessarily a largely empirical process, requiring continuous trial and adjustment. Making changes in one of these aspects can produce unforseen consequences; a new site is even more hazardous. Thus we have seen management's difficulty in predicting how relocation to a new labour market would affect the qualities-in-use of a new semi-skilled labour force (section 7.11). This element of uncertainty, however, varies strongly with the type of labour process change. To take two extreme examples, the effects of updating machinery within standardized processing are more predictable than changing the workforce within old craft production. Note that the type of uncertainty here is not that privileged in conventional economic discourse, unknowable future technologies and hard-to-predict changes in markets, but rather involves the uncertainty inherent in the conflictual relations between management and labour. This is concrete and tacit rather than abstract and codifiable knowledge, and it is centrally a knowledge of people and social relations rather than of things.

All these reasons for continuity impacted differently on different types of labour process change. This was manifested in the relocations in particular: the more difficult types of labour process change tended to use relocations to existing sites rather than new ones, drawing on existing fixed investment and continuities in management of labour. 'Difficult' here included increasing the skills of the workforce, increasing management control, and changing the product mix, all of which could be conflictual.

The importance of reinforcing accumulation in part explains the geographical pattern of relocations. The relocations into London had a variety of motives (Table 11.1), but they were all to existing sites within the firm rather than openings. It was the advantages of continuity that were able to induce relocation into the city.

Reinforcing accumulation could link heterogeneous production dynamics in different historical periods. For example, some relocations were made to sites in ROSE in order to build on their stock of machinery or experienced labour force, but the original investment in ROSE may have been made because of the freer availability of skilled labour there. Thus the advantages of a site at one time may be the basis for exploitation of *different* advantages at a later time. Reinforcing accumulation means that the maps of 'locational advantages' at different times bleed into one another.

11.3 Overaccumulation

Accumulation, nevertheless, is contradictory, and we have seen many cases where reinforcing accumulation turned to overaccumulation. Overaccumulation often manifested itself in disproportionality between production and labour power, production and effective demand, or between sectors. It originated in the lack of coordination of economic actors within capitalism. It tended to result in blocking of investment in existing sites and in relocation from them.

The most obvious form of overaccumulation was pressure on *costs* of labour power and premises. These were set principally by the London economy as a whole and only secondarily by manufacturing sectors, and to this extent represented unevenness in profit rates between manufacturing and the rest of the local economy (sections 5.2, 5.6, 6.5, 6.6). This produced a significant number of relocations out of London to cheapen labour and premises, and shifts to cheaper sections of labour within London. But note the limits of this purely quantitative form of overaccumulation. The importance of costs to the firm depended on both the form and intensity of competition in the product-industry (section 6.7). In many of the craft sectors it was offset by rents reaped from the productive contacts of a London location; it was in less skilled, more standardized forms of production that costs led to relocation. Thus costs due to overaccumulation had differentiated impact.

A more important form of overaccumulation was inadequate reproduction of skilled labour power. This was manifested in shortages leading to restriction of output and unsatisfactory quality; it exacerbated management's difficulties in controlling skilled workers who anyway tended to have a substantial degree of responsible autonomy. These difficulties in turn led to relocations both within and out of London (sections 7.11, 8.7). Moreover, they meant that particular, problematic methods were often needed to intensify the labour of these workers (section 7.5). These problems arose from overaccumulation in production relative to the reproduction of skilled labour power. The latter was inadequate due to lack of investment in training, and to wages and conditions that were often inferior to those in accessible jobs outside manufacturing, that is, to *under*accumulation in the reproduction of labour power. However, the exodus of workers from manufacturing was also due to strong accumulation in ROSE and in non-manufacturing activities in London, and was exacerbated by workers moving out of London because of its high cost of living (section 6.5). Management's problems with skills thus arise from *combinations* of overaccumulation and underaccumulation, causing disproportionality both between sectors and between production and reproduction.

Another manifestation of overaccumulation was the degree of control exercised by the male craft or formerly craft unions. Overall, this was a smaller problem for management than the reproduction of skilled labour, and was limited to particular product industries (printing and, more weakly, furniture and brewing). Even in these sectors, it was not a chronic problem nor a problem for all firms: management most often took action against the unions when substantial restructuring was to be done. Nevertheless, limitations in workplace size and relocations were made or threatened in order to weaken union influence (sections 7.12, 9.7). The latter was built partly on the chronic shortages of skilled labour just discussed, which gave workers bargaining power both in the employment relation and in the control of work. It was also due to the accumulated experience of workers in dealing with management within the particular sectoral labour processes, and also in dealing with the social division of labour and form of capital within the industries, for example in the printing unions' control over outsourcing. This experience was accumulated by individual workers within particular workplaces. But it was also based on a collective experience, which was remembered and handed down between generations over the very long histories of these sectors in London, partly through the formal union policies and procedures, partly through initiation of new workers into industry culture, partly within families given the strength of father-to-son recruitment in these sectors. This union organization was thus an aspect of overaccumulation, a contradiction for management of strong long-term accumulation in these sectors (Lembcke, 1993; section 4.4). The continuity of experience of industrial relations in local sectors and workplaces is then contradictory: the experience of management helps it to control labour process change, but the experience of workers – which perhaps has greater historical continuity – is a basis for resistance.

The time and place of overaccumulation in cities

It is interesting to compare overaccumulation in London during the study period and the relocations it produced with the study by Massey and Meegan (1978; 1979) of the geography of labour process change in British manufacturing in 1966–72. They found that the major labour-related motive for relocations out of the conurbations was to employ less-organized workers or to weaken trade union organization by the act of relocation. We have seen that this played a significant but relatively small role in relocations from London in the present study. The major problem for management was not workers' collective organization but the reproduction of skilled and, to a lesser extent, non-skilled, labour power. Like union organization, this tended to increase wages and could make management's control of the work process more difficult. However, these were effects of the *individual* bargaining power of workers, and the underlying processes giving rise to them were distinct from (although they sometimes supported) strong union organization. This difference in the findings of the two studies can be explained by their differences of time, place and firm selection. Massey and Meegan were looking at large national firms with formal union organization, whereas in the present study unionization was limited and, in the large firms, non-militant (section 6.5). The London labour market also differed from that of other British conurbations in that competition from non-manufacturing sectors was stronger and living costs higher. Labour markets were generally tighter in the 1960s than in the late 1970s, but reductions in training programmes in the 1970s tended to worsen the supply of skilled labour. The changed political situation was also important. The 1964–70 Labour government saw a rising level of union militancy, leading to a crisis of capitalist control during the Heath government. In contrast, by the late 1970s the unions had been weakened by the sharp recession of 1974–5 and, especially, by their successful incorporation in austerity through the Social Contract.

This comparison of the two studies serves to emphasize that dynamic tendencies of labour processes take specific forms in particular times and places (section 10.4). The task of analysis is to unearth *abstract* rather than *general* processes, but studies of particular spatial and historical circumstances do tend to produce particular theoretical emphases. The work of Massey and Meegan (1978; 1979; 1982; Massey, 1984), which has been enormously influential, emphasized those problems in the capital-labour relation that arise from the collective organization of labour, but they had little to say about problems arising from overaccumulation with respect to labour power and its effects in the reproduction sphere, which are central to the present study. Correspondingly, the role of space in the capital-labour relation in Massey and Meegan's work was centred on capital's *exploitation* of the *distance* between localities and sites to weaken collective organization. They showed that spatially uneven development can be useful to capital in providing differentiated labour forces which can be played off against each other, and which are inhibited from uniting by distance. In contrast, in this study I have focused on the construction of capital-labour relations in *place*, and on the ways in which uneven development between localities can result in over-accumulation and hence *difficulties* for capital. This connects to a further difference. Massey and Meegan were concerned with conflicts between capital and labour, and also between different sections of these. These are important in the present study, but I have also emphasized contradictions in structures and contradictions in the interests of *each* class. The disruptions of the reproduction of labour power in London are produced by just such contradictions, encapsulated in the broad concept of overaccumulation.

11.4 Underaccumulation

Underinvestment in a workplace or local sector eventually leads to its decline. Such competitive failure is often attributed, whether by firms, academics or policy makers, to aspects or factors of production essentially *external* to the firm or industry. This enables firms to justify help or concessions from other economic actors said to be responsible (banks, retailers, government, and so on), academics to study a limited set of variables, and policy makers to formulate limited and hence 'realistic' policies.

But we have seen that blockages to accumulation often arose from *within* workplaces and sectors and from the *internally related* elements of local economies. This was particularly the case with managements' 'labour problems'. As we saw in the previous section, their problems with skilled labour arose substantially from low wages and lack of training. This was especially severe in sectors faced with strong cost competition, leading to vicious circles of underinvestment and falling competitiveness. With regard to non-skilled labour, firms' problems with 'lack of discipline', basic skills and high turnover were not merely an external imposition on manufacturing but were in a large measure due to its internal dynamics. At the aggregate level, the decline of employment opportunities for non-skilled workers in the 1970s, and for young men in particular the erosion of the apprenticeship system, made discipline and basic skills appear irrelevant to many young people; this may explain why managers tended to date the deterioration of the quality of non-skilled labour power to the 1970s. At the workplace level, the wages, interest of the job, and prospects for training and movement to higher status jobs were generally poor, reproducing a high turnover of labour. Thus the negative effects of non-skilled workers on accumulation were substantially due to underaccumulation within London manufacturing itself (though combined with accumulation in other sectors in London, especially the informal economy: sectoral uneven development again).

Similarly, we have seen that problems with the quality of premises, though often pictured as the product of an external market, were largely produced by inadequate investment by the user firms themselves (section 6.6). Generalized underinvestment was sometimes proximately caused by the form of capital. The modest ambitions of self-limiting firms, arising from problems in labour management, could restrict not only the quantity but the quality of investment (section 9.7).[1] These various forms of underaccumulation tended to result either in stagnation or decline in situ or, where they could be afforded, in relocations to exploit premises and labour power built up by other firms. Thus labour process change both in situ and through relocation could be powered by downward spirals of underaccumulation, in which deterioration of the forces of production led to low profitability leading to further deterioration.

11.5 Contradictory spatial accumulation and structured paralysis

It is a commonplace of location theory that heterogeneous processes determining the location of a workplace may conflict with each other, so that the firm has to choose which processes are the most important for it. What is not generally recognized is that a given process influencing location may produce *contradictory* pressures towards both stasis and relocation. These can arise from the process operating in the mode of reinforcing accumulation, tending to lead to stasis, and in the mode of overaccumulation or underaccumulation, leading to relocation pressures. We have seen an example of this kind of contradiction in this chapter: long continuity at a site can produce both reinforcing accumulation through management's practical knowledge of production, and overaccumulation through workers' knowledge of how to deal with management.

A further case in point is the role of industry-specific skilled labour (sections 7.11, 8.7). The sensitivity of the firm to the degree of skill, experience and commitment of the workforce, together with inadequate supplies of skilled labour power, often inclined firms to remain in their existing location, or to make moves only within the commuting distance of the relevant workers, so as to retain existing workers or at least remain within a known market for skilled labour – a mode of reinforcing accumulation. But this spatial conservatism exacerbated local skills shortages, that is, the underlying problem of overaccumulation. Moreover, the same considerations could lead to relocation to other labour markets where supply was thought to be better. These contrary pressures were both strongest during the expansionary period of the cycle. The contradiction here is a form of the tension between management's dependence on particular workers and the tendency of capital to render labour abstract, between durable ties and commensuration through mobility (sections 3.2, 3.5). The result was that different, even opposite, spatial behaviour could be produced by the same underlying process.

The management strategy of relocation to weaken trade union organization similarly had its spatial contradictions (section 7.12). Management could use relocations away from well-organized sites, but such relocations could sometimes lead to the spread of union organization to previously unorganized factories within the firm. Even the quality of premises could produce contradictory pressures (section 7.10). The labour processes that had the most stringent and fastest changing requirements (those other than craft and light assembly) were the most likely to fail to invest adequately in their existing premises, and thus had the greatest incentive to relocate for this reason, yet they had the greatest difficulty in finding suitable premises on the market. Thus for them there was a tension between reinforcing accumulation through in situ investment and underaccumulation through disinvestment in situ and the use of relocation.

These tensions not only resulted in varied tactics but also meant that any line of action was unsatisfactory. They could also produce chronic indecision and failure to act *either* in situ *or* through relocation – a structured paralysis. The many changes of spatial strategy revealed by the management interviews owed much to this sort of contradiction.

11.6 Accumulation and devalorization: the creative destruction of value

In any industrial economy, technological and organizational innovation in the labour process causes changes in the spatial division of labour, and hence scrapping of capacity and changes in employment at particular sites. But these capacity cuts are organized in specific ways by *capitalist* industrialism:

they are enmeshed with private ownership of the productive assets and with value processes. The 'universal' process of selective closure of capacity is given 'partial' forms by the accumulation *of capital* (cf. section 3.5).

In this study the clearest examples of scrapping of capacity were in sectors with rapid technical change, resulting in devalorization of fixed capital. New process technologies that enabled large leaps in productivity tended (subject to elasticities of demand) to greatly reduce the volume of plant and number of workers necessary in that product line (section 7.2). New process technologies could also require a contraction of floor space given over to the product and a potential devalorization of premises (section 7.9). Major technical change simultaneously in components and their method of manufacture could result in scrapping of capacity (section 8.8). All relocations, for whatever motive, by definition involved some scrapping, even if the vacated site was re-used for manufacturing.

How 'partial' were these processes? In some cases scrapping removed fixed capital that had lower productivity or inferior product capabilities; this was usually the case in contractionary relocations within multisite firms (section 7.8). To this extent the process had a 'universal' justification. But there were also specifically capitalist mechanisms in operation. Firstly, cuts were often the culmination of overaccumulation in fixed capital, powered by the characteristically capitalist lack of coordination of investment by individual firms. This was most strongly the case in labour processes with rapid technical change. Secondly, the capacity which was cut was not always decisively technically inferior; indeed, in some cases it was recently installed (section 7.9; cf. Massey and Meegan, 1982: Ch. 5). Overaccumulation resulted in sharp price reduction, which tested the financial resources of the firm rather than the efficiency of the workplace. Decisions on scrapping of particular capacity depended on the (variable and somewhat arbitrary) profit targets of the firm. For example, overaccumulation in overnight printing resulted in the exit of some firms from this sector, although this was not technically required nor necessarily efficient. Thirdly, the cuts were often the counterpart of new investment but, in the absence of sectoral planning, the sites and locations of the two were in general different. This undermined continuity of employment for some workers, and cut off possibilities for reinforcing accumulation. Fourthly, we have seen that many relocations were aimed at shifting industrial relations to the benefit of the employer; the associated scrapping essentially served class power. The patterns of capacity cuts were thus partly formed by specifically capitalist processes.

However the need for cuts developed, and however they were allocated, reduction in capacity then served to reduce competition faced by surviving capacity and thus to enhance its valorization. A given mass of profit will realize an adequate *rate* of profit only if the aggregate value of the assets on which it is calculated is restricted. 'Creative destruction' is thus not simply a matter of technical obsolescence but a writing down of asset values as a continuous counterpart to investment and growth of assets.[2]

Devalorization was not, then, only the result of underaccumulation and competitive failure, as it is portrayed in both neoclassical and Keynesian-productivist theory. It was also a result of overaccumulation, and a necessary condition for new reinforcing accumulation. Change in labour processes, then, proceeds through the accumulation of value as productive capital on the one hand and its devalorization on the other. This dark side of accumulation gives specifically capitalist social and geographical forms to labour process change.[3]

11.7 Conclusion: the labour process, class control and socialist politics

In this chapter we have examined how the labour process is enmeshed with capital accumulation and the socialization of production at a variety of spatial scales. Much analysis of the labour process focuses on short-term change on the shop floor and in the personnel office, but the labour process needs to be placed within wider and longer dynamics of accumulation. These involve the creation, reproduction and destruction of relatively durable structures rooted in places: not only machinery, plant and buildings, but labour power, ways of doing things, accumulated knowledge, and durable cultures of industrial relations. It is the mutual construction of these elements – the socialization of production – that is important, whether it be the dependency of an employer on particular workers, or the reproduction of labour power through interaction between production and social life within a locality. These dynamics always involve both the moment of use values – the construction of the forces of production, and the moment of abstract value – the realization of profit and the accumulation of money capital and asset values. The two moments express each other but also often collide.

The dynamics of reinforcing, overaccumulation and underaccumulation occur within each *spatial scale* in structurally similar ways; we have here considered the workplace, the locality and product industries. The rhythms of accumulation at the different scales may be congruent with and reinforce each other, as, for example, when a firm's investment in training is matched by that of other firms in the local sector. The dynamics at different scales may also flow in different directions: reinforcing accumulation in a strongly competitive workplace, for instance, may be undermined by over-accumulation in the local sector as a whole. The articulation of scales of accumulation is thus crucial.[4]

The theoretical move from the short-term practices in the factory to these wider dynamics has important implications for socialist politics. Work narrowly focused on the labour process has been politically important in showing the way in which apparently neutral technologies and organizations of work are actually constructed by antagonistic relations between employers and workers (section 2.3, Chapter 3). This points towards workers' control of technology, tasks and employment conditions within the workplace. However, the wider focus of this chapter shows that, for change within the factory to be effective, it would have to be articulated with democratic control at larger spatial scales and over long time periods: syndicalist communism or worker-owned cooperatives would be insufficient. It would be necessary to supersede the fetishistic logics of capital accumulation that we have examined. Planning would be needed to address the long-term accumulation of skills, knowledge and product and process technologies and the relations between production and the reproduction of labour power within territories. These strategic considerations are developed further in Chapter 13.

NOTES

1. The *quantitative* restriction of investment in these firms may not have harmed the London sector as a whole: high rates of entry into these sectors meant that capturable demand was probably captured.
2. Marx (1976 ed.); Mandel (1968). Harvey (1982; 1985b) has explored this dialectic in the combined and uneven development of territorial economies.
3. The role of contraction of capacity and of devalorization was neglected in economic geography until the work of Massey and Meegan (1978; 1979), and is still neglected in much work since (for example Walker and Storper (1981), Dicken and Lloyd (1990) and Scott (1998)). During the postwar boom the location of new and relocated investment *appeared* as more important than that of scrapped capacity, and a period of stagnation has naturally led to greater interest. But in reality devalorization was a central moment of accumulation during the boom (Glyn and Sutcliffe, 1972; Mandel, 1978a; Aglietta, 1979).

4. *The firm* is another important scale of capital accumulation and socialization. Accumulation at this scale, too, is internally related to the labour
process and its change, as we saw at various points in Parts II and III. The
firm-labour process relation runs through the history of London manufacturing given in sections 5.3 and 5.4. In the panel, changes in the
division of labour between firms, and hence the constitution of each,
were dependent on the labour process and its changes (sections 6.8, 8.8,
9.4). The size of the firm was constructed by management in ways that
partly depended on control of labour (section 7.11, 9.3, 9.7). Management's ability to modify the labour process and product mix was
enhanced by having several sites (sections 7.11, 7.12, 8.7, 9.4), as were
the possibilities for consolidation and economies of scale (section 7.8,
7.9, 9.6). The need for capital growth (as distinct from competitiveness)
could determine firms' product strategy (section 8.4) while, conversely,
lack of money capital could severely limit production (section 9.7). The
book's analysis, then, suggests that the labour process and the form of
the firm (including its geography) construct each other over time. This
differs from two, contrasted, views which have been influential in economic geography. On the one hand are those for whom the form and
geography of the firm and the division of labour between them are
essentially a by-product of labour processes and product activities,
including their knowledge aspects (Storper and Walker, 1989; Walker,
1989b; Sayer, 1995). On the other hand are those who attribute very
significant causal powers to the form and geography of the firm which
are substantially independent of generalized labour processes. These
include systems theories (Taylor, 1994; Taylor and Conti, 1997; section
2.1) and some institutionalist work on transnationals (Dicken, 1992).
Much work in the new regional geography correctly sees a *mutual* construction of forms of capital and interfirm divisions of labour on the one
hand and labour processes and product activity on the other. However,
the one-sided focus of this literature on use values of production (section 3.6) misses the tensions within firms between productive efficiency
and valorization imperatives (Gough, 1996a).

12 WORKING ON THE ROLLER-COASTER: THE BUSINESS CYCLE AND SPACE

12.1 The cyclical time and shifting spaces of work

In the previous chapter we examined some general rhythms of accumulation and their entanglement with the labour process. These can have very varied time spans, but the study has shown a particularly important rhythm with a distinct (though not invariant) period, namely the business cycle. We have seen that labour process change differed sharply between the expansionary and contractionary phases of the cycle. The aims of management's initiatives, the mechanisms used, and the use of space all varied over the cycle. In this chapter I focus on this axis of change. Like the previous chapter, it is concerned with economic time and its relations with space.

Over the whole long wave of stagnation from the late 1960s to the present, the business cycle has had major economic and political impacts. The period has been marked by international recessions in 1973–5, 1979–82, 1989–92, with another ominously gathering pace in late 2002. These have been far deeper and more internationally coincident than in the previous long wave of expansion (albeit that the upswings in the 1980s and the 1990s were long by historical standards). The scrapping of perfectly useful assets, the dispersal of groups of previously collaborating workers, the wayward chains of knock-on effects, and the creation of mass unemployment expose the irrationality of capital and are potentially a source of radicalization. But the threat of redundancy and the closer tie of jobs to firm profit tend to defuse politicization (Clarke, 2001); this is largely what has occurred in the developed countries in the last two recessions. The recessions have then laid the basis for renewed accumulation, although this has remained subject to a long-term crisis of accumulation (Moseley, 1999). A close examination of the impact of business cycles on workplace labour process change is thus of great importance for developing labour's strategies.

There has been little systematic research on the business cycle and labour process change. Studies have been made of the impact of the business cycle on particular aspects of production such as fixed capital investment, innovation and layoffs; but labour process theorists, concerned with the whole range of forms of labour process change and their mutual relations, have given little attention to the cycle. Theories of the long waves, including Marshall's (1987) consideration of the regional scale, cannot simply be transferred to the business cycle: the former concern fundamental shifts in dominant technologies, sectors and forms of surplus profit and in institutionalized forms of class struggle (section 5.4); transformations over five to ten years cannot go so deep. A fortiori, geographical aspects of the business cycle/labour process relation have not been theorized.[1] Harvey has analysed relations between conjunctural crises of varied duration and spatial shifts of capital, centring on investment in fixed capital, the built environment and infrastructures (1982: 236–7, 390–412, 424–31), but he has not investigated the relation of these to labour process change. Marshall's and Harvey's work does, however, suggest that vital relations exist between temporal crisis tendencies of accumulation, spatial flows of capital, and class relations within production.

There are a priori reasons for thinking that the business cycle has systematic impacts on labour process change. We may distinguish three aspects of the cycle, those in profitability, output and labour markets. The cycle in profitability can affect the ability of firms to fund changes to production. It can also affect the pressures on them to increase productivity, change products or to cut costs. The cycle in effective demand, and hence output, can affect those aspects of the labour process associated with workplace scale, and characteristics of production associated with the opening, closure and rationalization of workplaces. The cycle in the market in labour power can be expected to impact on terms of employment, firms' use of labour power and the balance of power within the work process. Each of these pressures on the labour process involves workplace location decisions. Moreover, there are likely to be strong interactions between the cycle's operation at different scales from the workplace up to the international level. A systematic consideration of the links between the business cycle, labour process change, workplace location and scale is therefore in order.

In this chapter I develop a theoretical framework for considering these relations, using the patterns found in the case study as working material. I first present an aspatial model of the business cycle; this is far from a complete theory of the cycle, but brings out the aspects most relevant to labour process change. I argue that the cycle is an expression of contradictions which have been central to the discussion thus far, so that this 'axis' of analysis is not separate from the issues already considered. This model is then developed to take account of scale, and thus enable workplace-level cycles to be theorized. The patterns of labour process change over the cycle in the case study are summarized, and the model of the business cycle is used to suggest explanations for these. The aim is the same as in the previous two chapters, that is, to investigate potentials or tendencies of the cyclical dynamics of the labour process, which may or may not be realized in concrete cases. I then focus on how contradictions are manifested in the patterns of change over the cycle, and how these appear from the viewpoint of management. The final section reflects on the varied temporalities, periods and rhythms that have been involved in this study, bringing together ideas from this and the previous chapter. I argue that all of these are expressions of the interwoven tensions of capitalist accumulation and labour processes, which have implications for socialist strategy.

12.2 The business cycle

The business cycle has existed since the dawn of industrial capitalism, although its form has varied between different periods (Mandel, 1978a: Ch. 14). The ceaseless and ubiquitous repetition of this form of instability suggests that it is related to the element of the capitalist economy that is inherently both the most dynamic and the most unstable, namely *accumulation of productive capital* (Marx, 1976 ed.). It is inherently dynamic in the sense that capital as a whole cannot expand except through this path. It is inherently unstable in that it embodies two contradictions. Firstly, because productive investment is made by many capitals without (substantial) coordination, there is a chronic tendency for aggregate capacity in each product industry to expand beyond what the market will bear. Secondly, the expansion of productive capital proceeds through exploiting workers; but it tends to outstrip supply of socially and geographically suitable labour power and thus to shift the balance of class power. For both these reasons, productive capital has a chronic tendency to *overaccumulation*, leading subsequently to reduced pace of investment and devaluing of capacity (cf. Harvey, 1982: 190–203, 222–3). The cycle is *manifested* in employment levels, output, demand, prices, interest rates, and so on; but none of these has an inherent dynamic that could *generate* cycles in such a systematic way. Productive accumulation is, then, the kernel of the cycle. The model of the cycle used in this chapter focuses on this aspect, and, as we shall see, this links directly to the labour process.

Let us first examine the basic propagation of the cycle in a closed economy (Weisskopf, 1979; Hahnel and Sherman, 1982; Mandel, 1968; 1978a; 1978b). An upturn in productive investment eventually runs into either excess capacity relative to demand or to supply of labour power or both. The first of these is partly caused by the lead time of fixed investments: in the time between their ordering and their coming on line an unpredictable amount of other capacity has also done so (Mandel, 1978b: 178–9). Increasing capacity puts downward pressure on profit rates, as a result either of excessive competition and weakening prices, or of rising wages, rigidities in labour markets and increased worker militancy. Weakening profits and emerging excess capacity then cause cuts in fixed investment, and reduction in the valuation of businesses. Employment and working capital utilization begin to fall. Declining consumer spending and spending on fixed capital cause falling demand, which exacerbates overcapacity and cumulatively causes further contraction of investment, employment and demand. The upturn comes through the recuperative effects of the downturn: scrapping brings capacity into line with demand; decline of employment creates a reserve army, helps to hold down wages, and strengthens 'management's right to manage'. Profit per employee rises, and the devaluation of fictitious capital benefits the profit rate on capital. This provides a stimulus to investment, and the cycle starts again.[2]

The cycle is thus an expression of fundamental contradictions of capitalist economies: that productive accumulation increases the capital with a claim on surplus value; that it proceeds through exploiting labour power, but thereby tends to exhaust its supply; that surplus value is realized only through effective demand, yet declining profitability leads to declining demand via workers' and firms' expenditures (Marx, 1976; Harvey, 1982). These result in the paradoxical temporality of the cycle, in which good times produce the bad and devalorization is necessary for accumulation (cf. section 11.6).

This abstract model of the cycle can be elaborated and made more historically concrete (Mandel, 1978a: Ch. 14; Marshall, 1987: 92–8). In particular, the state may respond to, and thereby re-express, contradictions of the cycle. Institutionalized industrial bargaining and state regulation of labour markets tend to reduce, though not eliminate, the variation of wages, employment and transfer incomes over the cycle (Burawoy, 1985). While it sustains demand, the failure of incomes to adjust exacerbates problems of profitability. State monetary intervention may alter the interest rate cycle (Harvey, 1982: 300–5, 324–7), as when the state forces up interest rates prematurely in order to damp down an upturn; state fiscal policy may act either to counter or to deepen the cycle (Mandel, 1978a: 442–56). Thus in our case study the government in 1979–80 forced up interest rates and increased taxation, greatly deepening the downturn. While dressed in a rhetoric of 'taming inflation', the motive was to discipline labour and shake out capital, that is, to reinforce the recuperative mechanisms of the cycle.

It is not only aggregate investment that fluctuates over the cycle but also its aims and intensity. Here we find a paradox: there are motives for *intensive* investment in both the upturn *and* the downturn of the cycle. In the first part of the upturn, good current profitability encourages both extensive investment, replacing capacity lost in the previous downturn and responding to expanding demand, and intensive investment aimed at strengthening the firm's competitive position, including not only fixed investment but spending on research and development, product innovation and training. Investment in the upswing is powered firstly by good profitability, which favours the transfer of money capital into productive capital ($M \rightarrow P$), and secondly by the relation between capacity and demand. As the upswing continues, the role of demand in stimulating investment becomes relatively more important, that of profitability less. Rising demand encourages extensive investment. In the downswing, declining profitability and then falling demand reverse these mechanisms, but the competitive pressure on firms is accentuated as they attempt to escape devaluation or even bankruptcy. This produces an *increased* pressure to make defensive intensive investments (Itoh and Lepavitsas, 1998).[3] As a result, we can expect extensive investment to be concentrated in the upswing, whereas intensive investment *per worker* to occur more evenly over the cycle.[4]

This cyclical relation between intensive and extensive investment is again based on contradictions: between the financial and productive aspects of capital, and between capital as a whole and individual capitals. On the one hand, during the downswing money capital as a source for productive investment, and realized profit as a stimulus to invest, lead to decline of productive investment, and this is reinforced by the devalorization of fictitious capital. On the other hand, the competition between firms based on production in its use value aspect, as technical efficiency, creates pressure for innovation and renewal in the downswing as much as, or more than, in the upswing. These contradictions have a geographical aspect. During the downswing the financial aspect inclines capital to geographical and sectoral mobility, whereas the use values of production incline it to geographical fixity.

The business cycle, then, is an expression of a number of fundamental contradictions of capital. These include ones which have been important throughout the book – between production and labour power, productive efficiency and value, total capital and many capitals. The cycle thus provides us with another window onto these contradictions and their expression in the labour process.

12.3 The business cycle, scale and the workplace

This model of the cycle strictly applies only to a closed – that is, global – economy. But we are concerned here with change in workplaces set within local economies. How, then, can the cycle at these smaller scales be conceptualized?

The most obvious connection between the larger and smaller scales is an *external* one: cycles in global, national and local economies impinge on the workplace as exogenous influences. These influences operate through the cycles in output and demand, profit rates, and labour markets (Figure 12.1). The workplace's output is influenced by the cyclical balance between aggregate capacity and aggregate demand in its industry. The cyclical average rate of profit in the large territorial economies impinges on that in the workplace via its effect on investment flows within those territories. The average profit rate of the particular industry impinges on that of the factory via competition in the final market. Labour markets and industrial relations at the local and national scales impinge on employment relations and managerial control within the workplace. All of these external influences on the workplace are, however, mediated by its competitiveness. Through these influences, then, we expect the workplace to experience pressures derived from the cycles in its industry and in territorial economies of varying scales.

The cycle in the workplace is not, however, a purely external imposition. The contradictory processes that generate the cycle are *internal* to firms and workplaces, which thus *actively participate* in the cycle (sections 2.1 and 4.3; Chapter 11). Thus the tendency towards overcapacity relative to demand during the upswing is generated by the impulsion *within* each workplace to expand capacity. A period of expansion of *workplace* output and of good enterprise profitability strengthens the confidence and bargaining ability of the labour force, and can thus undermine profitability and accumulation within that enterprise. Cuts in *workplace* output and, *a fortiori*, cuts in capacity tend to discipline the workforce even if the local economy is buoyant. Thus workplaces and firms are not the 'innocent victims' of the cycle. Rather, they contain within them the social relations that underlie cyclical behaviour (Figure 12.1). This will be important when we consider the contradictory

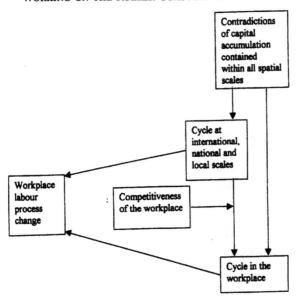

Figure 12.1 *Cyclical determinants of workplace production change.*

pressures on firms which lead to the cyclical and spatial patterns of their labour process change. (A similar argument can show how the cycle is generated partly internally within *local economies.*)

How does this cycle at the workplace level affect labour process change within it? In introducing this chapter, I suggested that labour processes are proximately affected by three cyclical variables: workplace or firm profitability; workplace output; and workplace industrial relations combined with local and wider labour markets. In the next section I investigate the impact of these three variables on labour process change in the sample firms. The analysis is concerned with the aggregated panel of workplaces; I abstract from differences in the competitiveness of workplaces and from the particularities of individual product-industries, focusing on the broad trend of profit rate, output and labour markets across London manufacturing.

12.4 The business cycle and labour process change: evidence and explanation

The cyclical patterns of labour process change that we encountered in Part III are brought together and summarized in Table 12.1 for in situ change and Table 12.2 for relocations. We can use the model outlined in the previous

Table 12.1 *Cyclical behaviour of selected forms of labour process change in situ*

	Workplaces in which change made, as percentage of those at the end of each period	
	Upswing, 1977–9	Downswing, 1980–1
New machinery for higher labour productivity	38	32
New machinery to enable product change or improve production quality	7.3	10
Improved layout of production	11	26
Intensification through change in managerial control on the shop floor	6.3	35
Intensification through lower turnover or change in the 'quality' of workers	0	4.7
Limitation of workplace size to retain manageability	19	1.2
Expansion for economies of scale	2.5	0.4
Changing hours of work to increase capacity utilization	0.6	3.9

Note that the upswing is three years, the downswing two years.

section to understand these patterns by looking in turn at the effects of the cycles of profitability, output, capital-labour relations, and of combinations of these.

(i) The cycle in workplace profitability

I have suggested that, in response to cyclical profitability pressures, intensive investment may hold up more strongly in the downturn than extensive investment (section 12.2). The pattern of intensive investment in situ in the study illustrates some effects of this process (Table 12.1). The rate of investment in machinery to increase productivity was only slightly lower in the downswing than the expansionary period.[5] This effect is particularly sharp for investment in improved layout and for fixed investment to enable change in products; both of these took place at a *higher* rate in the downswing than the upswing. This could be because these investments were more modest in scale than re-equipment for productivity; accordingly, they were less constrained by considerations of funding, and reacted more strongly to

Table 12.2 *Cyclical behaviour of forms of labour process change through relocation*

	Workplaces in which change made, as percentage of those at the end of each period	
	Upswing, 1977–9	Downswing, 1980–1
New machinery for higher productivity, change in products or improved production quality	1.9	9.4
Better premises quality for the same aims	12	12
Floor space increase due to labour process change	7.3	5.5
Floor space decrease due to labour process change	0.9	8.2
Intensified management control of work	3.2	2.0
Improvement in supply of labour power		
skilled	9.5	1.2
non-skilled	1.3	1.2
Product change through–		
better skilled labour	2.2	0
diversification of sites	1.9	2.3
specialization of sites	1.9	2.0
Cheaper labour power		
skilled	6.6	0.8
non-skilled	2.2	3.1
Achievement of economies of scale	3.8	11

management's perception of the need to improve competitiveness. In addition, investment for product change was regarded by some firms as the key to improved competitiveness, and was thus prioritized in the recession (section 8.4). Thus the contrast between the type of investment undertaken in the two phases of the cycle is partly one between extensive and intensive investment, but also between expensive and cheaper forms of investment.

(ii) The cycles in workplace profitability and output combined

The surprisingly strong rate of fixed capital investment during the recession is found also in investment associated with relocation. Table 12.2 shows this cyclical pattern in the relocations associated with various types of change in fixed capital. Improvement in machine quality and pursuit of economies of scale were both strongly concentrated in the recessionary period. Relocations to improve the quality of premises and to diversify or specialize the product range at sites occurred in both phases of the cycle but were stronger in the recession.

However, this pattern was not due solely to the increased pressures of competition in the recession: many of the relocations involving fixed capital investment carried out in the recession were aimed also at reorganizing production between sites while cutting overall capacity, and thus reflected the cycle in output as well as profitability. Nevertheless, these were not purely quantitative 'rationalizations' but were rather used to make improvements in productivity, products or quality of production, using economies of scale or improvement in machinery, premises or change in sites' product mix (section 11.6). The labour process changes were achieved partly through selection of the most suitable sites for concentration of production. They often also involved new fixed investment; but as this was modest in scope it could be accommodated to the funding constraints of the recession. The cyclical pattern of these relocations, then, reflects the same contradictory pressures of the cycle of profitability which constructed fixed investment in situ (point (i) above), combined with the cuts in output during the downswing.

A slightly different articulation of profitability and output underlay the cyclical patterns of relocations associated with changes in floor space that arose from labour process change in the product industry (Table 12.2). The rate of relocations associated with increased floor space was maintained in the recession, whereas that associated with decreased space accelerated. The former pattern suggests that, although output was weakening, competitive pressures caused firms to expand their floor space per employee in order to increase efficiency. The acceleration of floor space cuts during the recession was not simply a result of output cuts: in these product industries, investment in new techniques during the expansionary period would have reduced space requirements. It is therefore likely that it took the spur of intensified competition to get the firm to relocate and reduce its use of space. Note that, again, all relocations to adjust floor space involved some new investment, which was carried out despite the deteriorating profit conditions.

(iii) The cycle in workplace output alone

The direction of output change could affect the balance of power between management and labour and their respective strategies in situ (Table 12.1). The expansionary phase led some managers to limit the size of the workplace with a view to better control. In the recession, workers, particularly skilled workers and those with greater bargaining power, sometimes reduced the intensity of their work in order to adjust it to the available output. On the other hand, management could use reduction in workplace output to make redundancies in a selective way, thus increasing the average skill or cooperativeness of the workforce.

Not surprisingly, pursuit of economies of scale through organic growth in situ was concentrated in the expansionary phase of the cycle, in contrast to the discontinuous changes of scale achieved through relocation and consolidation in the recession.

(iv) The cycles in profitability, industrial relations and labour markets combined

We have just seen that industrial relations in the workplace were affected by the cycle of output but they were also strongly constructed by the cycles in local labour markets and in workplace profitability. These impinged on management's control of both the volume and quality of work and on management's ability to influence wage levels. These were, however, constructed by complex interactions between workplace, local and national scales of these cycles; a rather more extended discussion is therefore needed at this point. I examine industrial relations during the expansionary and contractionary phases of the cycle in turn.

During *the expansionary phase of the cycle*, the markets for skilled labour in London were very tight. Many firms consequently experienced difficulties in recruitment and retention of workers, wage inflation, the quality of skills, and the volume and quality of work done. The principal means through which management dealt with these problems was *relocation* to different labour markets – for male workers out of London, for female workers within London. Conversely, in the recession these labour market conditions changed sharply, and management was able to re-establish its control of labour in situ. Thus improvement in the 'quality' of skilled workers, recruiting skilled labour suitable for producing new products, and holding down of their wages were achieved during the expansionary period overwhelmingly through relocation, whereas relocations for these motives were rare in the recession (Table 12.2). Moreover, relocations aimed at strengthening management control, particularly over strongly organized workers, were as common in the expansionary as contractionary phase of the cycle.

In contrast, *in the recession* management was better able to pursue its interests in situ in both the control and employment aspects of the labour process (Table 12.1). In general, this was done by using *both* (a) the changed conditions in local labour markets *and* (b) the threat posed by reduced profitability of the workplace. The cycles at the scales of workplace and locality were both relevant.

The dialectic of industrial relations in workplace and locality respectively could, however, take different forms, depending on the workplace's employment regime:

(a) *The rise in unemployment in local labour markets* had least effect on those workplaces where turnover of labour was low and which were not pro- posing, or plausibly threatening, to make redundancies; the employ- ment relation in these cases prevented management from using the 'therapeutic' mechanisms of the recession to shift the balance of power. However, in workplaces where a high turnover of labour was normal (either through workers leaving voluntarily or through deliberate firm policy), the recession offered management the ability to replace workers with others, to reduce voluntary turnover and to find workers willing to work different hours. These changes were more difficult to realize, even during the recession, in workplaces where labour turnover was usually low, since they would then involve making compulsory redundancies.

(b) On the other hand, *a substantial reduction in workplace profitability* could be used to threaten compulsory redundancies even in workplaces that had previously had a low rate of labour turnover. But which 'profit- ability' is relevant here? If workers had reliable knowledge of the prof- itability of their workplace, then this would be the relevant measure. However, this is seldom the case: the factory's profitability is generally known only through the claims of management, who in their dealings with labour (though usually not with other capitals) have an interest in presenting a bleak picture. The reference point for workers is thus more likely to be the profitability of parts of the local economy and of their product industry, as deduced from closures. The effect of profitability on shifting bargaining power between capital and labour is thus strong but mediated by imperfect knowledge, itself structured by firms' power. Knowledge at different scales – workplace, firm, locality, nation – may be mingled here. Redundancy arising from reduced profitability can be a threat even where workers have a good chance of immediate re- employment, because they may have valued social ties in the factory or may have workplace-specific status. But high unemployment in local labour markets reinforces the threat of redundancy because of the fear of not finding another job at equivalent or better conditions.

The slackening of the labour market in the recession, then, had differentiated effects depending on patterns of profitability, workplace regimes of labour turnover, and the unemployment rates of the relevant groups of workers.

These workplace and local shifts in power towards management were reinforced by *national* political-ideological processes, further complicating the scalar politics of the cycle. The actions of the Labour government against labour in 1977–9 disorganized union politics, given the institutional link between the party and the unions. The election of the Conservative government in 1979 on an explicit platform of taming labour weakened the bargaining position of workers. The unexpected sharpness of the recession caught labour off-guard, and failures to oppose redundancies acted cumulatively to produce a defeatist mood. This shift in workers' consciousness (mediated, of course, by sectoral, local and firm traditions) affected how they reacted to the pressures of changing profitability and labour markets. The shift in mood was contested; but the evolving national political situation strengthened the arguments of those in the unions who wanted to accommodate to the 'dictates' of profitability and labour markets. A national politics of crisis was thus a further moment in the impact of the cycle in London workplaces.

Through these interweaving pressures, management was able to impose a variety of changes on labour in situ that had been difficult to implement during the expansionary period except through relocation. Using the labour market directly, the average intensity and quality of work of, particularly, non-skilled workers was increased through decreasing voluntary turnover and through replacing workers who left with higher quality ones ('intensification through the employment relation' in Table 12.1). Using the threat of redundancies and locally higher unemployment, management could impose intensification through tighter control on the factory floor of both skilled and non-skilled workers. They were also able to impose wage cuts, particularly for non-skilled workers (85 percent of all sample workplaces in 1979–81). Changes in shifts in order to increase weekly hours worked could be carried out either by recruitment of different workers or through changing the shifts of existing workers. The therapeutic aspect of the business cycle for management's relation to labour during the recession thus reduced the need for relocation. This process in the abstract worked itself out through significantly different mechanisms depending on the type of employment relation, the segment of the labour force and the profitability of the workplace.

We can thus theorize the variation in the main types of labour process change over the business cycle using a model of the cycle within which the proximate variables are, firstly, the profitability, output and industrial relations of the workplace, and secondly, conditions in local and national labour markets and their political mediations. The proximate pressures came from the cycle at a *combination* of scales.

In this section I have traced the causality from the cycle to workplace labour process change. But notice that the workplace labour process changes in each phase also *constructed* the cycle by affecting investment rates and by actively changing capital-labour relations. This reinforces the argument made in section 12.3, that the cycle does not merely impinge on the social relations of workplaces but is constructed by them.

12.5 Cyclical switches in the causes and spatial forms of labour process change

The analysis so far has focused on the effects of phases of the cycle on the labour process. But we can turn the results around to track the vicissitudes of particular types of labour process change over the cycle (Table 12.3). We then find that both their causes and their spatial forms can switch between phases of the cycle.

First, even where the incidence of a particular form of spatial labour process change was fairly even between the two phases of the cycle, *the causes in the different phases could be significantly different*. For example, improvement to machinery in situ and relocation to improve premises both had a fairly even incidence between the two phases of the cycle (rows 1 and 2 of Table 12.3). However, the causes were contrasted. In the expansionary phase investments were powered by availability of funds, the promise of good returns and the expectation of reasonable demand. In the recession they were carried out not merely despite falling profitability and output but precisely in order to improve competitiveness in the face of these. Thus changed – in fact reversed – conditions can produce broadly the same outcome, contrary to empiricist assumptions of a one-to-one correspondence between effect and cause (cf. section 10.4).

The second notable pattern is that for some forms of labour process change there was *a switch in the spatial mode* of carrying out the change between the phases of the cycle. Profitability, labour market conditions and

Table 12.3 *The spatial and temporal incidence of selected types of labour process change*

Type of labour process change	Phase of the cycle	
	Upswing	Downswing
Better machinery to improve productivity and production quality	in situ	in situ and relocation
Better quality premises	relocation	relocation
Economies of scale	in situ	relocation
Improved quality skilled workers	relocation	in situ
Increased managerial control (directly within the work process rather than through the employment relation)	relocation	in situ
Relative wage reduction	relocation	in situ

Note: To heighten the contrasts discussed, if a spatial form of change took place mainly in one phase of the cycle it is shown here only in that phase.

the trajectory of output could favour one mode over the other. Whereas economies of scale and improvement of machine quality (rows 1 and 3 of Table 12.3) were achieved in situ during the upswing, in the recession they could be pursued in multisite firms through reorganization of sites, and declining profitability and output reinforced the latter solution. Some of the forms of change in capital-labour relations, which during the upswing were achieved mainly through relocation, in the downswing could be carried out in situ (rows 4–6). Whereas the expansionary period forced management to make these changes using distance and the difference between places, the favourable time of the recession enabled management to use existing place.

In section 10.2 we discussed firms' choice between using existing spaces (the existing workplace and local economy), using new ones (other local economies), or using the act of relocation itself to pursue changes in the labour process. We now see that these choices may vary strongly over the business cycle. The *time* of the cycle can make a sharp difference to firms' use of *space*. If relocations are regarded as a 'spatial fix' (to use Harvey's term) to managements' problems in the labour process, then the need and opportunities to use such fixes are a function of the rhythms of capital accumulation.

12.6 The cycle as contradiction

I have argued that the business cycle is an expression of a number of characteristic contradictions of capital operating at different spatial scales. It is these contradictions that underlie the combined spatial and temporal variations analysed here – the changes in labour process initiatives over the cycle and the variation in their use of space. Let us focus on this theoretical thread.

The role of contradiction can be traced in particular labour process changes. For example, the different purposes of fixed investment between the phases of the cycle, with intensive investment holding up more strongly in the recession, was underpinned by the restriction of funding in the recession combined with increased need to improve competitiveness. In other words, the switch in the purposes of fixed investment expressed a *contradiction* between pressures of funding and pressures of productive competition, both underpinned by the cycle in profitability. The same pressures can be seen in the greater role in the recession of relocations to improve fixed capital, which reflected the therapeutic role for capital of scrapping together with the intensified compulsion to increase competitiveness. To take another example, the switch in the spatiality of initiatives in industrial relations, from changes through relocation during the upswing to initiatives in situ in the downswing, rested on the contradictory relation between accumulation and supply of labour power (section 12.2) combined with the pressures and opportunities presented by spatial uneven development.

Thus the restless shifts in the temporal-spatial behaviour of the labour process and the switches in spatial modes are not merely a reflection of contingent changes in external conditions nor of *sui generis* changes in management strategies. Rather, they are the expression of contradictions that are intrinsic to the capitalist labour process. Moreover, these are internal to workplaces as well as to larger scale economies.

We can see this point in another fashion by taking the viewpoint of management. Each phase of the cycle presented both benefits and disadvantages to firms in their relation to labour, in their competition with other firms, and in the possibilities for accumulation (Table 12.4). The expansionary phase, despite offering obvious benefits to firms, nevertheless contained developing problems in the balance of power against labour. The contractionary phase imposed sharper competitive pressures and dangers on firms, but it also had the benefits of shifting the balance of power against labour, and of reducing the capacity that had a claim on aggregate profits. Each phase of the cycle, then, was contradictory for management.

In consequence, *within each phase* management made some changes to the labour process taking advantage of favourable conditions, and made other changes under duress. Some of these are shown in Table 12.4, with greatly simplified effects of the cycle. If we shift perspective and travel *through* the

Table 12.4 *Benefits and problems for management and resulting labour process change in the two phases of the business cycle*

	Phase of the cycle	
	Upswing	**Downswing**
Benefits to capital	High profits fund investment and lead to investment optimism → *Improved machine quality and economies of scale in situ* Expanding output → *Economies of scale in situ*	Scrapping of capacity reduces competition → *Contractionary relocations improve machine quality and economies of scale* Increased local unemployment → *Greater selectivity and lower turnover of labour* Low profitability threatens redundancies and higher unemployment closes alternative options for workers → *Intensification via control in situ*
Problems for capital	Labour markets create skills shortages and wage inflation → *Relocations to less tight labour markets to improve supply and cost of skilled workers* Increased output and profits strengthen labour's bargaining power → *Relocations to weaken strong union organization* Increased output → *Need of some managements to limit workplace size by in situ restriction or partial relocation*	Lower profits stimulate competitive strategies → *Better machine quality and layout in situ for productivity, products and production quality* → *Relocation to improve premises quality* → *Relocations to cheaper markets for non-skilled labour*

Key: Aspects of the cycle and their benefits or disadvantages are in ordinary type.
→ *Resulting labour process changes are below, in italics.*
Note: the effects of the cycle have been greatly simplified here: see section 12.4 for details.

cycle, then aspects of accumulation that were problematic for management become positive and vice versa. These reversals can result in switches in how particular types of labour process change are carried out. Thus the changes in labour process behaviour over the cycle discussed in the previous section are constructed by changing pressures on management, which express the underlying contradictions of accumulation.

12.7 The business cycle, space and the labour process: some conclusions

We can draw a number of general conclusions from this discussion. First, labour process change, both in situ and through relocation, is strongly dependent on the phase of the business cycle in which it is undertaken. The cycle is experienced by both management and workers as offering temporally limited opportunities and constraints on labour process change. Studies of the labour process therefore need to take account of the cycle.

Secondly, I have theorized these opportunities and constraints in terms of three aspects of the cycle – variation in rate of profit, in output and in industrial relations, which proximately shape labour process change. Workplace-level labour process change is influenced simultaneously by these variables *at different spatial scales* (Figure 12.1). For example, the labour market and industrial relations nationally, locally *and* within the workplace itself all impinge directly on the preparedness of workers in that particular workplace to press for their interests. The influence of the business cycle on labour change, then, needs to relate cycles at varied spatial scales. Thus geography as scale adds something to our understanding of the cycle.

Thirdly, the managements' choices between change in situ or through relocation are dependent on the business cycle. For a given form of labour process change, the choice of spatial mode can vary between a period of expansion and one of contraction. Taking all types of labour process change together, this may mean that, for a given initial labour process, relocation is more common in a particular phase of the cycle. Thus studies of workplace (re)location need to take account of the mutual construction of the business cycle and labour process change.

Finally, this analysis opens itself to conscious action through emphasizing not merely conflict between management and workers but the contradictory qualities of both labour processes and accumulation paths (cf. section 2.2).

The business cycle is understood as an expression of contradictions between the tendency of capital to expand itself and limitations in both labour power and effective demand. Cyclical labour process change is then constructed both by *conflicts* between management and workers and by the response of each to the *dilemmas* they face.

12.8 Accumulation rhythms: why time matters to space

A popular idea in recent theoretical geography is that, with postmodernity, 'space has become more important than time' (Harvey, 1989; Soja, 1989). In one interpretation, this means that long-term historical change, and even medium-term social reform, are not popular preoccupations, whereas it is the differences between places that seem to express both possibilities and fears. It is certainly true that notions of radical economic and social alternatives have been widely discredited since the 1970s – not, I would argue, because of a new epoch of postmodernity but because of the success of the neoliberal and globalizing offensive of capital in closing off politics and collective choice. Indeed, it was in the period of this study that this denial of alternatives was put into play in Britain through the world recession of 1973–5, the subsequent austerity measures of the Labour government, and the all-out offensive of Thatcher's recession in 1980–1. This shift underpinned a cautious and defensive stance of workers in London manufacturing. This period was also one of deepened uneven development within Britain between regions, localities and neighbourhoods. In widely disseminated discourses, life chances were seen as being increasingly bound up with *place*. Those with the means had greater reason to change places – from north to south, from city to rural suburbia, or into gentrified metropolitan spaces – rather than hope for improvement in situ, let alone radical reform. To this extent one can agree that space gained importance beside time.

There are, however, many senses in which social time remains relevant. I have emphasized certain 'times' of crucial importance to workers but which have of late been neglected in locality studies and labour process research. In this chapter we have seen how the time of the *business cycle* shapes both labour process change and patterns of relocation. Chapter 11 argued that labour process change in space is shaped by rhythms of *overaccumulation, reinforcing accumulation and underaccumulation,* and by *devalorization* as a counterpart to accumulation. These patterns of accumulation are not necessarily cyclical and have varied time frames. Like the business cycle, they are internal to the dynamics of both workplaces and local economies and they profoundly affect spatial uneven development of the labour process. The study has also been placed within a *long wave* of low profitability and intensified competition, taking particular form in Britain and London (section 5.9). We have seen, too, that the nature of manufacturing in London has been shaped historically, albeit in paradoxical ways, by long waves of the national economy (section 5.6).

Two observations follow. First, *the structurings of time by rhythms of accumulation had vital implications for spaces of production.* Each of the accumulation rhythms had ramifications in spatial movement and spatially uneven development. Cumulative buildup and unravelling of productive forces and relations – the imprint of histories at varied scales – were crucial. It makes no sense here to counterpose space to time: both the nature of places and the flows between them are shaped by dynamics which have their own proper rhythms. If economics needs to better acknowledge *spatially* uneven development, the latter cannot be understood outside of the *temporally* uneven development of capital.

Secondly, the dynamics of the labour process in the workplaces studied were constructed by an *overlaying and melding of these accumulation rhythms.* The time of workplace labour processes is complex but not arbitrary: it has the grain and structure of these rhythms.

The accumulation rhythms of different types and time spans have their own specific features, but in this chapter and the previous one we have encountered underlying processes and contradictions that they have in common. I now draw these together. This enables us to appreciate *the structural similarity of the accumulation rhythms at different temporal and spatial scales.* We can view these most easily by looking first at those processes within each of the accumulation rhythms that tend to produce strong accumulation, then at those processes that tend to disrupt it.

(i) Strong accumulation

As always, strong accumulation has both a use value and a value aspect. In our examples of accumulation rhythms, the common use value aspect is the *effective socialization of production.* Accumulation proceeds strongly on the basis of quantitative and qualitative harmony between labour power, production, infrastructures and interlinked sectors, and harmony in capital-labour relations and wider industrial politics. Upward long waves of accumulation, for example, may involve particular 'social structures of accumulation' that achieve partial matches of some of these elements (Bowles, Gordon and

Weisskopf, 1986; sections 5.6, 5.8). 'Reinforcing accumulation' too, whether in localities, firms or workplaces, involves effective articulation of these elements, even though this may not be embodied in any wider and more durable social structure of accumulation. Even the short timespan of the upswings of some business cycles can involve particular articulations of labour power, production, infrastructures, and so on: for example, the upswing of the world economy from 1982–9 was partly powered by the revolution in electronic infrastructures and qualitatively widened application of ICT (Castells, 1996), and also by the boom of the financial sector, itself underpinned by rearticulations of production, profit, distribution of income and spending. Thus the socialization of production plays a central role in each of these accumulation rhythms, despite the different scales and temporalities.

In each case socialization provides a partial answer to the problem of articulating economic elements that are not only the responsibility of diverse actors but also have different rhythms of production, obsolescence and depreciation. Reinforcing accumulation in a local economy, for example, coordinates the times of basic education and particular training, the time of use of particular production technologies, the time of relevant communication infrastructures, and so on. Thus our accumulation rhythms articulate in complex ways the rhythms of production-depreciation of each economic element.

The coordination of these elements would be problematic in any industrial society, but in capitalism it is enmeshed with problems of valorization of capital. Strong profitability within the accumulation rhythms involves not only effective socialization but also the maintenance of *favourable value ratios* entering into the rate of profit, and means for depreciating capital in ways that sustain accumulation. Thus long upward waves are based on previous destruction of capital, lowering the organic composition of capital, and a consequent high rate of profit, sustained by continuous rapid depreciation of productive capital (Mandel, 1978a; Aglietta, 1979). Reinforcing accumulation within the workplace depends on favourable ratios of wages and final prices, of effective demand and value of sectoral capacity, and so on (sections 2.6, 5.5, 6.5). Moreover, the pace of accumulation is woven together with the pace of devalorization of capacity. We have seen how strong investment in capacity of higher productivity, in production of lower space requirements, or in radical product change requires devalorization of *other* capacity if the investment is to be profitable (section 11.6). These linked movements of investment and scrapping can take place across an industry or within the same firm or even workplace. Finally, we have seen in this chapter how the upswing of the business cycle requires favourable ratios between values of productive assets, wages and demand.

Bringing all these points together, we see that strong capital accumulation is fragile because the articulation of the various economic elements has to be positive *simultaneously* at the level of use values and exchange values.

(ii) Disrupted accumulation

Each of our accumulation rhythms contains forms of disruption. These can arise within socialization or valorization, or from their divergence. Within the *socialization of production*, quantitative and qualitative disjunctions can appear between labour power, production, infrastructures and interdependent product-industries, and political conflicts erupt (Eisenschitz and Gough, 1996). Sectional interests intervene: individual capitals pursue their paths without (sufficient) regard to their effect on others, and cooperation between capital and labour dissolves. Thus the present long wave of stagnation emerged from a period of heightened industrial conflict and of 'urban' conflicts around the articulation of production and reproduction (Bonefeld, 1993; Gough, 2002). Decline of local economies can be caused by conflict between heterogeneous sections of capital (section 2.8). Overaccumulation often takes the form of disproportionalities between production and the supply of labour power, or between production and infrastructures, whereas underaccumulation feeds off vicious circles of disproportionalities between these elements (sections 11.2 and 11.4). Even business cycle recessions, whose path of descent is usually rather rapid, can be reinforced by disruptions of supplier chains by scrapping, or, as in 1973–5, by class struggle that disrupts long-established patterns of industrial relations. Disruptions of socialization can thus affect each one of the accumulation rhythms.

These are entangled with their *value form*. The present long wave of stagnation originated in part in wages rising as fast as productivity (Glyn and Sutcliffe, 1972), in part in a rising organic composition of capital (Hargreaves Heap, 1980), in part in fiscal crisis (O'Connor, 1973), all arising paradoxically from the strong socialization and accumulation of the long boom. Overaccumulation in the London economy has at various times taken the form of rapid rises in wages and in prices of services and land, and London manufacturing has been damaged by contradictions of value relations for metropolitan capital as a whole (section 5.7). Overaccumulation in some of our panel workplaces arose from resistance to intensification and commensuration of labour by well-organized workers, again on the basis of previously strong accumulation in the site. Similarly, the business cycle falters because of an increasingly unfavourable relation between asset values, wages and demand, whereas the downswing is powered by devalorization of assets and cuts in value of investment. Thus across these accumulation rhythms of different scale and temporality we find the same value contradictions of capital: between strong accumulation and the value and price of labour power; between depressing wages and maintaining consumer demand; between unbridled productive accumulation and limited demand; between the ability of some sectors to extract rents and the maintenance of average profits in other sectors. The breakdowns of socialization both cause and are caused by these contradictions of valorization.

We can conclude, then, that accumulation rhythms are generated by socialization, value proportions, and their contradictions. Just as these manifest themselves at different *spatial scales*, so their generative structures are manifested in rhythms of different *temporal scales*. There are differences between the various accumulation rhythms, but they share their source in characteristically capitalist features of accumulation and the labour process.

The disruptions of labour processes caused by these accumulation rhythms are a major problem for labour and resident populations, no less than the problems of spatial uneven development with which they are so closely bound. Ameliorating these disruptions is in part a technical task, requiring better information on rhythms of investment in the various elements of the economy, but the foregoing analysis shows that it is far more than this. Combating the various forms of temporal uneven development means facing up to the disparity between the dynamics and interests of individual capitals on the one hand and the requirements of effective socialization on the other. Forms of socialization serving popular needs would require coordination of investment within product-industries. They would require new criteria for the relation between profit and investment, whether at workplace or larger scales, something which would negate capitalist rules of valorization and devalorization. They would require planning of average wages, linked to planning of final demand. All these imply an overriding of the rights of private capital by democratic planning.

We therefore have a further cut on the relation between labour process and capital accumulation. Workers' politics needs to address the terrain of the labour process in a narrow sense, but it has also to consider how economic coordination can overcome the characteristically capitalist forms of temporally uneven accumulation – a socialist rather than a syndicalist project. This forms the subject of the final chapter.

NOTES

1. Marshall (1987: 92–100), following Mandel and Itoh, discusses the *changing form* of the business cycle between different epochs of capitalism, but not the forms of labour process transformation within those cycles. Clark, Gertler and Whiteman (1986: 107–24) discuss the relation of the business cycle in particular territorial economies to the employment of individual workers, but without relating this to the labour process as a whole. Two other key texts in radical quantitative economic geography, Sheppard and Barnes (1990) and Webber and Rigby (1996), do not discuss the business cycle.

2. This account uses certain elements of Mandel's theory of the cycle (1968; 1978a; 1978b). Mandel emphasizes the interlocking of the dynamics of production and realization. Thus the limitation of demand is crucial to ending the upswing, in particular because the rate of exploitation increases over the whole upswing due to increase in relative surplus value, depressing consumer demand relative to the increasing capacity in Department II (1978a: 439; 1978b: 165–9, 179–80). His model also includes an overshoot of fixed investment with respect to demand at the top of the upswing (1978b: 178–9). However, Mandel also argues that the organic composition of capital rises substantially during the upswing as a result of technical change, rather than of overshoot, and that this depresses the profit rate. This appears to be contradicted by the evidence for the US economy since the Second World War presented by Weisskopf (1979); Hahnel and Sherman's (1982) figures do show a rising ratio of fixed capital to output in the upturn, but they doubt these figures' significance.

3. Mensch (1979) has made a similar, though controversial, argument for the *long* wave: that technical innovation is strongest in the downward wave due to increased competitive pressures.

4. Here I abstract from the shaping of the investment rate by the rate of interest and the dynamics of money capital; see Itoh and Lepavitsas (1998).

5. The relationship of funding to investment was also dependent on the form of the firm and its relation with external sources of finance. I do not analyse this aspect here.

13 DIFFERENCE, FRAGMENTATION AND THE ASSOCIATED PRODUCERS

13.1 Divisions and socialist strategy

I started this book with the offensive of capital against labour under the banner of neoliberalism. This offensive has had considerable success in depoliticizing the economy, weakening the trade unions, imposing managerial discipline and eliciting more active cooperation from labour within the work process – Britain being a particular success story for capital in these respects. But capital has not always succeeded in imposing fragmentation and individualization. There has been much resistance to new working practices (Martinez Lucio and Stewart, 1997), and in the late 1990s in many Western European countries there were large scale actions against austerity. Collective action for labour's interests is thus by no means dead. This intensifying conflict makes consideration of strategy all the more urgent. This chapter considers the implications for socialist strategy of the book's analysis.

I shall consider labour strategies in more detail than is common in academic writing. Partly this is to counter the reticence of the left, following the 'death of socialism', on useful strategies for workers' struggle. But it is also because concepts are only valid to the extent that they lend themselves to practice; examination of practical socialist measures therefore throws further light on the concepts so far developed. For example, my characterization of forms of the labour process, investment, competition and so on as *capitalist* rests partly on an implicit comparison with earlier modes of production but also, of more practical relevance, comparison with a practicable socialist economy (Sayer, 1995: 36–7).

I have stressed the intertwining of labour process and capital accumulation in constructing class relations (Spencer, 2000). The immediate objects of workers' struggles span them: within the labour process workers address issues of task definition, of quality of work, its organization and intensity, and of wages and conditions of employment; and whereas accumulation in its fetishistic forms often eludes workers' demands, its results in the quantity of jobs and in wages are commonly the subject of struggle. In this chapter I shall examine the challenges posed to labour in both these aspects, and their problematic and controversial relation.

We have seen at many points the tension between disciplinary and coop- erative capital-labour relations. Radical industrial studies, including those of geographers, have tended to focus on one or the other side of this relation. In the 1970s, influenced by the sharp struggles at the onset of the wave of stagnation, researchers tended to focus on direct conflict between the classes and the use of space (distance) by capital to impose control over workforces. From the early 1980s, the offensive of capital and the downturn in union struggles led to increasing interest in the actuality and potential of colla- borative industrial relations, particularly through productivist arrangements that appeared to offer advantages to labour, such as flexible specialization, industrial districts and 'learning regions'. Both these literatures are one sided, the first in neglecting the pressures on workers to collaborate with their employers, the second in underestimating the sources of disruption of productivist collaboration by accumulation and within the labour process itself (section 3.6). In this chapter I shall be concerned with the contradictory relation between discipline and cooperation – their mutual construction, the tensions between them and thus within each. For those of us who see struggle against capital as necessary and progressive, it is particularly important not to underestimate the pressures towards adaption to capital's demands.

Crucial moments in constructing capital-labour relations are the divisions, differences and outright competition between workers. At the most abstract level, capitalism does not constitute workers as collective members of a class but as *individuals*, as sellers of labour power in competition with others. It is true that the conditions of wage labour provide many reasons for collective action by workers; but these are always in tension with individualism and division. The processes discussed in this book are at the heart of how com- petition or cooperation between workers develops. Competition and flows of capital between sites and territories, mediated by particular types of firm, pit groups of workers against others. Differences in labour processes create differences in experience, resources and identities among workers, which can be a barrier to collaboration. The temporal rhythms of accumulation can foster either division or cooperation. Thus relations between workers in different workplaces and localities are constructed by both the labour process and accumulation dynamics. The 'vertical' relations between capital and labour cannot be separated from the 'horizontal' relations between workers and between capitals (Gough and Eisenschitz, 1997).

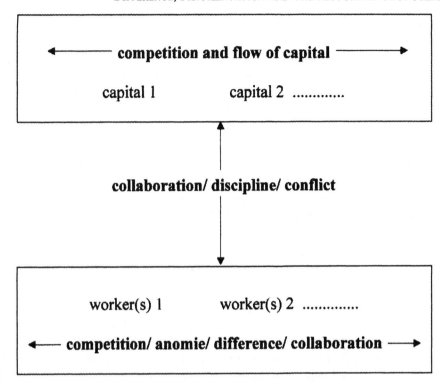

Figure 13.1 *The subject of this chapter.*

Divisions and differences among workers are important from a moral and cultural point of view. But they are also crucial to their ability to take on capital, because workers' influence on firms, and *a fortiori* their ability to supersede capital, are dependent on collective action. We therefore need to pay particular attention to the sources of division. In this chapter I shall be concerned with how labour processes and accumulation dynamics *simultaneously* construct both vertical and horizontal class relations (Figure 13.1).

I begin by developing an abstract theorization of competition and collaboration between workers in space and its implications for labour strategies. I then examine the divisions created by capitalist labour processes and how these might be combated. Interclass and intraclass relations are constructed through accumulation within different scales and sites. I consider two of these, of different types, and how socialist policy might address them: product-industries and the metropolis. Finally, I discuss how struggle within capitalism and construction of a socialist economy can create practices and cultures of collectivity.

13.2 Relations between workers, relations between the classes

The impulses to competition or to collaboration between workers, and to their cooperation or conflict with capital, need to be theoretically constructed at successive levels of abstraction (Gough, 1992; 2001). In their most abstract form, capitalist social relations construct workers as competitors in the sale of their labour power. The (tendential) separation of workers from the means of production makes them dependent, not merely on capital but on strong profitability and accumulation to provide the best possible conditions of employment. More concretely, each worker has an interest in strong accumulation within a particular part of global capital – their existing workplace if they have one, and in other workplaces, sectors and territories to which they may have access in the short or long term (Cressey and MacInnes, 1980; Hudson and Sadler, 1986; Terry, 1989). The interests of the worker are thus tied to successful competition by these sections of capital against their rivals, and to maintaining or enhancing flows of capital into those sites. The *access* of workers to job possibilities depends on their skill, the social and economic resources they have for changing their skills and for promoting themselves in other jobs, and on their daily and long-term geographical mobility. These characteristics are constructed not only by production but by the reproduction sphere and are strongly gendered. We thus have linked systems of competition-mobility in capital and in labour respectively: competition between workers is dependent on competition of firms and capital flows between them, mediated by workers' ability to move between types and sites of production. The less mobile the worker or group of workers, the greater the pressure to collaborate with the capitals actually or potentially employing them.

However, capital expands only by exploiting workers. Indeed, the competition between firms that draws workers behind them *also* proceeds through exploiting them. This lays the basis for antagonisms between capital and labour.

These contradictory pressures towards and against collaboration with management are played out and given more concrete form within the labour process. Pressures to collaborate may be institutionalized by a cooperative regime, with its implications for worker autonomy, skill and security of employment, while workers' resistance may be stimulated by a more disciplinary workplace regime (section 3.5). These workplace regimes link to the local socialization of production (section 2.8). A commitment by capital to spatial stability, to investment in situ and loyalty to the locality, can reinforce the commitment of workers to local capital and its competitiveness.

The pressures on workers towards collaboration can be expressed in support for local investment and boosterism and in support for competition against other areas (Gough and Eisenschitz, 1996a). Conversely, capital whose strategy is one of mobility between sites, sectors or territories tends to elicit antagonism from labour and may stimulate collective action.[1]

These geographical labour process regimes nevertheless have their own contradictions. Collaborative regimes in workplaces and localities can be disrupted by overaccumulation at different scales with respect to the supply of labour power or to demand (sections 2.8, 11.3). Labour's willing cooperation with management can become more demanding and conflictual. Management may then attack even skilled and privileged sections of labour, and capital may become more mobile. Conversely, the antagonism of workers to disciplinary employers or those offering low skill or low security jobs may give way to forced cooperation in the face of threatened relocations of production and redundancies. The hermeneutics of the strategies and attitudes of capital and labour is complex and can have paradoxical outcomes (Burawoy, 1979; Kelly, 1985; P. Edwards, 1986). The point here is that, whereas impulses to collaboration *or* antagonism arise from the nature of capitalist social relations in the abstract, they are developed by the nature of the labour process, its local socialization, and its geographical mobility (Moran, 1998).

The disempowerment of workers, then, arises fundamentally from their mutual competition underpinned by the competition of capital and its flows in space. The insecurity of workers may be mitigated by strategies of capital that emphasize investment in situ, relative surplus value, and by active collaboration between management and labour; but this strategy is always unevenly applied and can unravel. Increasing workers' control over the economy therefore requires their control over flows of investment in space and the competition between workplaces. This argument will be elaborated further below.

13.3 Differences and cooperation between workers

Within this framework, what is the significance of *differences* in the labour processes in which workers find themselves? Workers are divided by differences in wages, security, skill and status associated with the interplay of labour process difference on the one hand and differences in social life on the other (section 2.4); I shall term these 'work identities'. Differences in work identities separate workers in different workplaces, as in the typology used in this book, but also frequently divide the workforce within workplaces.

How do these divisions affect competition and collaboration between workers, and how should the labour movement react to these differences? Schematically, one may distinguish four aspects of these divisions, with distinct political implications:

- Difference in job quality

A loose but useful distinction made in everyday discourse is between 'better' and 'worse' jobs in the dimensions of wages, security and conditions of employment, control and autonomy, and skill. These differences are seldom compensation for differences in effort or unpleasantness of work, and in this sense are unjust. Perception of this injustice can stimulate workers in worse jobs to fight for better conditions and may prompt solidarity from others.[2]

- Difference in ability to fight capital

The ability of workers to confront capital is reduced by lack of security of employment, by low skill, and by low autonomy, which can be opposed for this reason.

- Lack of recognition of other workers' situation

Varied labour processes mean that workers' daily concerns differ. This leads to lack of recognition of the problems facing other workers. This division is compounded if the workers are from different social groups, because then the more privileged may regard others' problems in work as appropriate to their social status.

These three types of clevage among workers thus affect, in contradictory ways, workers' recognition of common interests and their ability and willingness to undertake collective action with those in different labour processes. They can incline workers to compete in attracting investment to *their* type of work and to be indifferent to others. But unlike the competition for jobs considered earlier, these differences do not themselves constitute conflicts of *interest*. This is because work identities, though hierarchically differentiated, do not form systems of exploitation and do not give workers access to work or income other than in relation to capital. Competition between workers is tied to capital's competition and flows of capital; differences in work identities can *exacerbate* this competition by weakening collective action, but they are not its origin.

- Socially exclusionary agreements supported by workers

There is, however, another type of difference in work identity which *does* create a difference of interest between workers. Groups of workers, in competing for jobs, sometimes form agreements with employers or the state to give themselves priority in recruitment or preference in layoffs. These agreements, which may be explicit or covert, often use social identities as their exclusionary principle, particularly gender, ethnicity, age or citizenship. The advantaged workers sometimes use arbitrary definitions of skill to create obstacles to entry into 'their' jobs. These work identities thus construct *direct* oppression and antagonisms between workers (Gough, 2001).

We may, then, understand competition and collaboration between workers in terms of the competition of capital and workers' access to employment by productive capital, mediated by differences in work identities. Ending the fragmentation and disempowerment of labour therefore means both gaining control over investment flows *and* confronting oppression and difference within the labour process. I first examine the latter issue, and then look at how different forms of competition and flows of capital might be tamed.

13.4 Struggle against capital, struggle against difference

Exploitation justifies and can elicit struggles by workers across various aspects of the labour process. This is particularly pressing for those in the worst jobs; any evening-up of conditions that is achieved then also has the benefit of lessening differences in work identities and so strengthening the potential for collaboration.[3] I therefore examine here *both* the kinds of demands that might be made on the labour process *and* how the differences between workers such as we saw in the study might be addressed. The dialectics of struggle for common aims and struggle against inequality are by no means straightforward. Moreover, we shall see in subsequent sections that these demands require actions that go beyond the labour process itself.

It is useful to consider first durable regimes of the labour process, and then its dynamics – though of course the former are cumulatively constructed by the latter.

Durable aspects of the labour process and differences in them

The study panel contained differences of labour process and associated differences in job quality of long duration, institutionalized in distinctive cultures of capital-labour relations (section 5.3; Chapter 6). In what ways should labour attempt to combat such differences? A first point is that the job quality dimensions of wages, security, skill and autonomy, though interconnected, cannot be reduced to each other (section 2.3): skilled clothing workers were low paid, skilled steelworkers could be casualized, and low skill process plant workers had secure employment. Each dimension therefore needs specific attention.

Struggles to increase *wage rates* in general are justified by exploitation, but there is a particular need to increase low wages. These are found especially in non-skilled work (or work deemed to be such), and in those labour processes where increased productivity through mechanization is technically difficult and where employers have compensated for this by low wages, as in much of old craft production. The *employment contracts* in the jobbing industries and sweated sectors of the study indicate the importance of security and of guaranteed hours at predictable times of the day, week and year.

The labour processes were sharply differentiated in the predominant *gender, ethnicity and age* of their workers, compounded by combinations of these (cf. Mann, 2000). It is a question not only of opening up better quality jobs to oppressed groups but of improving the jobs presently taken by those groups. These divisions are both a cause and effect of disadvantage in the reproduction sphere (sections 2.4, 5.3, 6.5), and thus need to be addressed across production *and* reproduction (Barrett, 1988).

The issues of *skill and autonomy within the work process* are more controversial. These issues were central to Braverman's work and to the early labour process literature, but their significance has been the subject of much debate. The defence or extension of skill and autonomy can certainly have benefits for workers both individual and collective. Worker's satisfaction in their jobs is often enhanced by higher skill and greater responsibility, bringing greater interest, variety, choices and sense of achievement. They give workers greater leverage in bargaining with management (but see Steiger, 1999).[4] Ideologically they can unmask the process of creating surplus value in showing that it is the worker, not capital, that is the creative force (Burawoy, 1985: 50). These considerations justify pushing for upskilling and greater autonomy through the design of processes (machines and tasks) and of the detailed division of labour (Rosenbrock, 1977; Noble, 1979; Cooley, 1986), particularly in types of labour process such as assembly and standardized processing. Differences in skill, mediated by gender, have certainly been an important political division in London. In the late nineteenth century the 'new unionism' had to develop independently of the long-standing male craft unions, which had failed to organize unskilled and women workers and indeed had been at pains to exclude them from their ranks; these divisions have continued to weaken the union movement in London in the twentieth century (Cockburn, 1983; Green, 1991).

Skill and autonomy have their limitations. As the male craft sectors in London show, they can be the basis for a conservative culture in which the status of workers, their involvement in day-to-day decisions on production and products, and the potential for becoming an entrepreneur head off any more radical ambitions (section 5.3). This is not to say that skill and autonomy are undesirable but that their radical potential needs taking forward on other fronts. One such front is the erosion of the *division between mental and manual labour* (Radice, 2001). Indeed, Armstrong (1988) has argued that Braverman's argument was not essentially for an upskilling and diversification of *manual* tasks, a return to an idealized craft past, but rather for workers to appropriate the tasks of *conception and planning* monopolized by management. Burawoy (1985: 54) has argued that a merging of mental and manual labour is compatible with capitalism, implicitly restricting 'mental' tasks to decisions narrowly concerning the labour process. However, a consistent appropriation of the mental work of management by workers would move into decisions on investment and finance, which *does* have an anti-capitalist dynamic. Burawoy's view is too static: a struggle to appropriate areas of managerial authority can potentially raise issues about wider forms of control, and it is an inherently *collective* form of 'upskilling'. Capital – British capital especially – can be extraordinarily reluctant to involve workers even in quite minor issues for fear of unleashing precisely this dynamic (Wainwright and Elliot, 1982).[5]

Different experiences of labour process change

It is not only labour process regimes that create radically different experiences among workers but also their forms of change, as we saw in Part III. Workers are sharply divided by the types of (spatial) measure which management tends to attempt. Consider for example *mechanization*. In the first place, the possibilities for pushing for upskilling when production processes were being modified, or the need to resist deskilling, are very unevenly distributed (section 5.3). Secondly, the problem of job loss through radical change in production technology, whether in situ or through consolidation onto advanced plant (sections 7.2, 7.8), poses the need for retraining and local investment in sectors with growing employment. However, workers in sectors where this is not a significant problem, such as old craft, tend to experience other severe pressures precisely because radical increases in productivity through mechanization are blocked.

In contrast, the study suggests that, in a long wave of stagnation, *intensification* may be widely experienced across diverse labour processes (section

7.5). It may occur not only in sectors that are labour-intensive or with slowly changing production technology but also as an accompaniment to technical change. This gives the potential for common cause in resisting intensification. However, although intensification may be widely experienced, the *means* which management uses to impose it vary sharply between workplaces with different degrees of mechanization, between skilled and unskilled workers, with existing workers or by replacing them, or by using the process of relocation (Chapter 7); building common resistance to intensification would have to take account of such differences. In the period of writing, there is an urgent need for such resistance. Methods of intensification pioneered in manufacturing have been applied to diverse service sectors (Nichols, 2001). Research has exposed the ill effects of over-intense work, but in official union (let alone parliamentary) politics the issue hardly surfaces.

The experience of *wage change* in the case study varied strongly between different labour processes and product industries. In particular, in the recession there was a marked division in wage changes between skilled and non-skilled – a gap that has continued to widen in the last 20 years. Unlike issues around mechanization and skill, wage change does not present difficulties of recognition between different groups of workers – it is a common currency of industrial relations. Between industries where national bargaining exists, a common wage demand (percentage increase, or more radically an absolute increase) is feasible and desirable, although it would have to confront not only parochialism and status divisions between skilled and non-skilled but also the different cost pressures on product-industries, rendered ideologically as 'what the market can bear' (sections 6.7, 9.2). Common wage rises do not in themselves confront the ways in which management can cut wages through relocation (section 9.3). This is often thought to be a problem mainly for non-skilled workers; but where there are chronic skills shortages and problems in the reproduction sphere, as in the case study, relocation may be used primarily to cut *skilled* wages. This can be headed off partly through national wage rates for given job types (with allowance for locally differentiated living costs). Attempts to reduce wage differentials need to consider geographical uneven development.

Cohen (1987) has argued that workers' collective struggles are, and should be, focused on questions of wages, intensity of work and job security; the concern of labour process theorists with *skill and autonomy within work* is a diversion. But, as I have argued, issues of skill and autonomy are important to individual workers, and they impact on job security and the capacity for collective organization, as the study showed repeatedly. Analytically, Cohen argues that the notion of 'control' in the labour process literature is vague and insubstantial and avoids the real issue of exploitation. She thus sets up two distinct structures, firstly the labour process, understood as material processes of production (particular use values), and secondly accumulation of value and exploitation (quantitative value), and then portrays the latter as the exclusive concern of capital and the proper terrain of socialist politics. Cohen's argument avoids addressing the internal relations between labour process and accumulation by a one-sided focus on the latter. Rather, the labour process needs to be conceived as a *contradictory unity* of use value and exchange value. Thus the 'control' issues around skill and autonomy are central to capital's labour process strategies (relative versus absolute surplus value, quality versus cost competition, and so on), impinge directly on the power relations in production, and hence impact precisely on the quantitative rate of exploitation.

Cohen's argument that workers' collective struggles are not actually focused on skill and autonomy is largely – although not completely – true, but this often reflects difficulties in organizing a collective response around these issues rather than their lack of importance. It is hard to oppose small inroads into skill or autonomy even though they may be cumulative, and divisions of labour make it difficult for workers to formulate demands around production technologies (Hales, 1980; Cooley, 1986). Moreover, building collective politics across workplaces and sectors around this aspect of the labour process is particularly hard: skill and autonomy within work involve so many subtleties and particularities that it is difficult for workers to recognize them in labour processes other than their own.

The problems of Cohen's dichotomy are evident also when we consider the problems for workers posed by the business cycle, particularly *recessions*. To workers these threaten job losses and wage cuts, fitting Cohen's criterion of an important issue. Moreover, the cycle affects all sectors and labour processes, giving the potential for common struggle. But there are problems. Recessions appear as wayward fluctuations of markets beyond anyone's control, naturalized as 'burst bubbles' or, as a Labor finance minister of Australia notoriously put it, 'the recession we had to have'. This market fetishism disguises the origin of recessions in specifically capitalist accumulation dynamics (Chapter 12), and makes struggle against them more difficult. For this reason, the left tends to emphasize the waste of material use values – means of production and individual and collective skills and knowledge – which recessions involve. However, we saw in Part III that the cycle impacts very differently on different labour processes precisely with respect to these use values. Managements' responses to the cycle depended sharply on degree and type of skill, product activity, form of mechanization and so on, leading to very different forms of attack on labour, including location strategies, during the recession. Thus common struggle against the irrationality of the business cycle needs to take account of the material particularity of labour processes.

The discussion of this section suggests that the problem of non-recognition varies in important ways between different dimensions of the labour process: some are more common currency than others. Wage levels and, especially, wage rises, because of their purely quantitative nature, are the easiest issue to recognize, which helps in constructing common collective action. Workers' problems with insecure employment vary strongly across the economy, but it is in varying degrees a *concern* of most workers, and its variations are relatively easily understood. We have seen that opposing intensification can have broad resonance, at least in certain periods. More heterogeneous are workers' experiences of the connection between technological change in processes and quantity of jobs within their workplace or sector, because rapid change can either *shed* jobs through rising productivity or *increase* them through their association with new products or through greater competitiveness of the particular capital; hence building common politics on process technology is difficult. Difficulties in constructing broad collective action around a dimension of the labour process are thus not only a function of its importance to workers but also of its variation and the ease of recognizing other workers' situation.

Despite these difficulties, it is possible both to address exploitation within the labour process in its varied dimensions and simultaneously to *combat differences* in this exploitation between groups of workers and hence to mitigate the political divides within labour. These measures not only conflict with firms' right to manage the labour process in a narrow sense, but also often impinge negatively on the competitiveness of particular sections of capital; indeed, the wider the unity achieved by labour, the greater the impact on accumulation. Successful challenges by labour would therefore often be met by disinvestment. Accordingly, we need to consider how to address the interrelation of labour processes and investment. I now consider this question within two sites, product industries and the metropolitan economy.

13.5 Competition within the product-industry and beyond

As we begun to explore in section 13.2, competition *between* workers is integral to capital's domination of labour *within* each workplace and locality. The competition between workers, the pressures on them, and their resources for struggle are therefore constructed not only by the labour processes but also by the form and geography of competition between firms within the product industry. In particular, territorial competition between workers derives from territorial competition between capitals. This competition is partly constructed by the nature of the industry's customers and (geographical) relations to them. For workers to cooperate across the industry means confronting the competition of capital within it, and thus points towards the democratic planning of investment.

Competition proceeds through the varied labour process strategies used within industries (sections 2.6, 6.7). These varied strategies then create particular types of division among the industry's workers. We saw in section 13.2 that cooperation between capital and labour *within workplaces* varies with the labour process strategy of management – its use of skill, stability of employment, quality of production and rootedness in the locality. The *distribution* of such strategies *across the product industry* can affect the kinds of mutual collaboration which workers need to, and are able to, construct. Thus we saw that cost-cutting pressures on London workers varied sharply depending on the geographies of product industry systems and the labour process strategies used within them (section 6.7, Box 6.5). Within an industry dominated by absolute surplus value strategies, labour in each locality is under pressure to accept intensification and hold down or reduce wages in competition whose terms tend to be set by the cheapest locations. This type of workers' competition is well recognized in the literature on globalization as 'the flight to the bottom' (Ross, 1983; Peck, 1996: Ch. 8). Divisions are often exacerbated by the perception of better-paid workers in long-standing locations of the industry that they are being undermined by the preparedness of workers elsewhere to 'accept' lower wages and higher work intensity. Collaboration between workers in the industry thus needs to address such differences in work intensity and in wages, pointing ultimately towards their *planning* across the industry.

We may contrast this with product industries where relative surplus value strategies and quality competition predominate. The problems of this form of competition are much less recognized than those of 'the flight to the bottom'. After all, competition here proceeds through combinations of innovation, investment in advanced processes, interfirm cooperation, and skilled labour power; who can be against these? But these structures are developed in highly uneven ways across the product-industry, with strong tendencies to overaccumulation and underaccumulation (Chapter 11; Sayer and Morgan, 1988; Gough, 1996b; Eisenschitz and Gough 1996; Lovering, 1999). On the one hand traditional centres of the industry can be undermined by new ones; on the other, many localities that might benefit from entering such industries typically find it hard to build up the minimum efficient scale and experience. It is therefore not enough for workers to push for high value-added strategies within their locality or nation, as in neo-Keynesian perspectives: there is again a need for forms of planning of investment that can counter the tendencies to local overaccumulation and underaccumulation.

Further twists to these processes are given by the forms of demand within the product industry; this is well illustrated by the London case (sections 2.7, 5.3–5.7). We have seen how a combination of particular organization of production with particular structures of demand gave rise to high technical and design rents within certain London manufacturing sectors. In some cases a part of these rents has been passed on to workers in high wages or good employment conditions (sections 5.3, 9.2). While these are positive in themselves, their geographical uneven development has sometimes led to London workers seeing themselves as superior to others, a tendency that is reinforced by craft labour process and by gender. This has perhaps been true, in particular ways, of workers in national newspapers, in craft luxury consumer goods production, and in armaments. An 'aristocratic' culture may be supported not only by high rents but by qualities of the industry's clients. Workers in luxury goods production may identify with the taste and culture of the upper class clients for whom they produce bespoke goods. In two small luxury furniture firms that were substantially run by their workers, I was told with pride of the British and Middle Eastern royalty for whom they had produced bespoke work. Similarly, workers in armaments production may support the military and imperialist activities of the British state on which this industry is founded (section 5.3; Lovering, 1991). In general, then, workers' loyalties are mediated by the politics of consumption of the industry's products.

The final process affecting workers' collaboration is the most purely quantitative and most general. The chronic tendency towards over-accumulation of productive capital within industries (section 11.3) threatens scrapping of capacity and redundancy of workers, or measures to cut wage costs and intensify work. This is the case not only in industries dominated by absolute surplus value strategies but also in ones where quality competition predominates. To tame these divisive pressures would require planning of investment across the product industry, in the modes considered in the conclusion to Chapter 12. The projected volume of capacity in the industry would be planned to meet projected demand, hence reducing the danger of overcapacity and premature scrapping.

Workers' competition is constructed not only by flows of capital within product industries but also by flows *between* them. In any industrial economy, employment in some sectors declines as a result of increasing productivity and shifts in demand, whereas product innovation creates sectors of growing employment. Capitalism organizes these shifts and the relationship between the respective workers in specific ways. The workers employed by the sunrise industries typically differ socially and/or geographically from those in the declining sectors. Workers losing their jobs in declining manufacturing industries in London have seen new manufacturing jobs appear elsewhere (for example in ROSE), new manufacturing sectors employing workers from different social groups (sections 5.3, 5.6, 6.5), or growing service sectors employing people of different age, ethnicity and qualifications. Workers in sectors of employment decline thus come under particularly sharp pressures to accede to their employers' demands, whereas workers in the sunrise sectors have to construct collective organization without continuity with well-established organization in the sunset sectors (Lembcke, 1993). Workers are thus weakened at both ends of these capital flows. To confront these divisions requires full employment, retraining programmes of a depth that few capitalist societies have achieved, and planning of the geography of investment in both declining and growing sectors. If workers need to shift their politics to the geographical scales on which capital operates (Therborn, 1983; Harvey, 2000), this means winning control over investment flows both within and between sectors.

This discussion suggests a political implication concerning some of the distinctions that have been central to this book. The contrasts between responsible autonomy and direct control, between relative and absolute surplus value, between value and volume productivity, between strong and weak socialization, and between rooted and mobile productive capital are the basis for a variety of social democratic strategies that propose to promote the former and supersede the latter (on recent formulations see Zuege, 1999). Within capitalism these contrasts are contradictory unities, however, whose positive poles cannot be detached from the negative. Local regimes built around the positive moments are always threatened by unplanned investment flows. Thus proposals such as Thompson's (1990) to move from defensive resistance within the labour process towards its radical transformation need also to move towards the democratic planning of investment. The contrasts in capitalist production strategies do indicate that progressive alternatives are possible, but only through addressing both the labour process *and* control of investment flows.

13.6 The big smoke: workers' struggles and divisions in a metropolis

> The hundreds of thousands of all classes and all ranks crowding past each other, are they not all human beings with the same qualities and powers, and with the same interest in being happy? And have they not, in the end, to seek happiness in the same way, by the same means? And still they crowd by one another as though they had nothing in common . . . And, however much one may be aware that this isolation of the individual, this narrow self-seeking is the fundamental principle of our society every-where, it is nowhere so shamelessly barefaced, so self-conscious as just here in the crowding of the great city. (Friedrich Engels, *Condition of the Working Class in 1844*)

Industrial relations within a metropolis present a paradox: the very features that might strengthen the hand of workers compared with those in smaller towns also tend to divide them. While Engels pointed to the individualism of great cities, it was also he and Marx who argued that the concentration of workers into large factories and large towns gave the basis for collective organization. On this basis one would suppose that metropolitan workers would create particularly strong organization: because of their ability to immobilize a large value of capital, because the density of workers would facilitate both practical organization and the spread of militancy, and because of the possibilities for solidarity from numerous workers close by.

Indeed, qualitative features of metropolitan economies reinforce these quantative ones. Key infrastructural sectors such as finance, national gov-ernment and national transport hubs are typically located in metropolises. The complex linkages between sectors typical of metropolitan economies (section 5.3) enable action in one sector to impact on others. Industrial districts are common in such economies, due to the importance of jobbing, fashion and high-technology industries; and although these usually involve a large proportion of small firms, strong interfirm linkages and sectors' spatial concentration give unions potential leverage. The substantial technical, design and locational rents reaped by many metropolitan industries often stimulate collective action by those industries' workers in order to claim their share. Finally, the reproduction sphere in metropolises tends to be strongly politicized by high land prices and the difficulties of managing its hetero-geneities, and this often stimulates class struggle around that sphere.

But working-class struggle also faces particular barriers in the metropolis. The first returns us to the starting point of this chapter: the ownership and disposal of labour power by *individuals*. The metropolis provides an exceptional density of avenues for individual advancement, or at least the promise of it; this weakens the appeal of collective action, and tends to create an individualist employment culture. The possibilities for advancement are partly a function of the large number of firms within most sectors, promising job improvement through transfer to another firm, and of the variety of alternative sectors offering better average conditions. The importance of product rents in the metropolitan economy creates large *unevenness* in firm profits, which often (though not necessarily) filters down to large inequalities in wages and conditions (section 5.3); workers can often improve their employment by moving to a firm or a sector that is currently doing well. The metropolitan economy also has an exceptional depth of job hierarchy, due to the importance of technical, professional and design jobs and of medium and upper command functions; these offer career advancement either within or between sectors. Such upward mobility is achieved through a great variety of types of personal promotion: demonstrated existing skills, retraining, personal contacts through work or social life, sycophancy. Finally, the metropolis offers particularly good opportunities for escaping from wage labour into entrepreneurship (section 6.8).

To be sure, these possibilities for individual advancement are unevenly distributed, being stronger for the better educated, the already skilled, men and people of the dominant ethnicity. These differences arise not only from the jobs that employers offer to different groups but also from differences in the reproduction sphere and the consequently varied resources that individuals possess for pursuing new job opportunities. Owner occupiers in London, for example, have the resources to move from inner to outer London or ROSE to advance their careers, while public housing tenants generally do not. The metropolis holds out to all the promise of personal advancement while at the same time deepening social divisions. Paradoxically, the possibilities for personal advancement tend to most weaken the collective organization of those groups that have the strongest economic bargaining power.

It is not only divisions between individuals but also those between workers in different sectors which inhibit collective action. It is not merely that metropolitan economies contain many sectors, but also that there is often a *structured* diversity of labour processes and product markets. Thus we have seen in the case of London that its metropolitan character has *generated* sharply distinguished types of manufacturing: science-based, fashion-based, jobbing, luxury, raw materials processing, and mass market consumer goods. These involve contrasted labour processes and varied abilities to reap rents, and hence provide jobs sharply differentiated by skill, autonomy, security and wages. As I argued in section 13.4, such differences make the recognition of common interests more difficult and deepen anomie. This problem is reinforced by capital's use of different social groups in these different types of job, including by exploiting the typically large ethnic divisions of metropolises.

Over the long run these divisions tend to weaken the development of collective organization and politics. But politics is an active element here: good strategies can enable the deep divisions of metropolitan workforces to be confronted. Metropolitan diversity may then become a *strength* for the workers' movement: the spatial proximity, personal ties and possibilities of recognition between socially diverse workers in diverse jobs may enable those divisions to be overcome in a way that would be difficult if the respective groups of workers were spatially dispersed. The dispute at the Grunwick factory in 1976–7, for example, was carried out by workers who might have been expected to have little power: they worked in standardized processing, and the majority were Asian women. Their militant approach to the dispute, however, won active support from workers in different social groups and different types of job (Levidow, 1981). This was helped by the location of Grunwick in London, and it contributed to an awareness of sweatshop production and its use of oppressed groups which would have been more difficult to generate in a smaller urban area. Thus the positive potential of the metropolis for workers' organization may be realized, but this is dependent on political strategy.

The nature of labour politics within metropolises is, of course, not constructed hermetically within manufacturing but, to an increasing degree over the last century, also within 'services'. The abstract concepts I have deployed in this study, including those of the labour process, product activity, product industry systems and rents, are fully applicable to services (Sayer and Walker, 1992: Ch. 2). Indeed, at a medium level of abstraction some of the key divisions amongst manufacturing workers in this study can be discerned also in metropolitan services. One finds the divisions between old craft (traditional professions, most management jobs, personal services), new craft (software writers, skilled manipulators of digital information, technologists, computer based designers), standardized processing (routine clerical and back office work, some jobs in distribution) and, with a certain stretching of the category, assembly (most jobs in retail and standardized consumer services). As in manufacturing, one can distinguish sectors that reap technical rents from sales in national and international markets (finance and business services), those reaping locational rents from local customers (some personal services and standardized consumer services), and those that have to accept an average rate of profit. Labour has variable ability to extract a share of such rents, with the extraordinary salaries of finance market dealers on the one extreme and the low wages of hotel workers on the other (Sassen, 1991). The arguments I have made for labour politics in metropolitan manufacturing thus apply, *mutatis mutandis*, to services. The greatest difference between services and manufacturing in this context lies not in the nature of markets, the product or labour processes but rather in the high proportion of metropolitan consumer services in public ownership; these tend to have high union density and, to a degree mediated by state policies, a certain militancy. They are regarded as *essential* services, so collective action within them can both suffer and benefit from the relation of their workers to their client populations; here again, the nature of the 'product' is of key importance.

Home and work

The study points to a further specifically metropolitan influence on workplace politics, namely the spatial relation between home and waged work. Since in contemporary cities decisions about this relationship are taken overwhelmingly by individuals or nuclear families, not by or for collectives of workers, this is another aspect of the individual sale of labour power. The qualitative diversity of employment opportunities and individuals' use of them discussed above tend to lead to journeys to work being longer the larger the city region; this generates greater social differentiation of residential areas, which in turn reinforces long journeys to work. As a result, the occupations significantly represented in each residential area of a metropolis tend to be more diverse than in smaller cities and towns. These processes increase anomie in employment relations; the skilled printers and engineers employed in London live in areas of the outer suburbs and the Home Counties with stockbrokers and accountants rather than their professional peers as neighbours. This reduces the mutual reinforcement, which occurs most clearly in company towns and one-industry settlements, between collectivity of workers within the workplace and social ties within neighbourhoods (for example Hayter and Harvey, 1993).

However, there are other possibilities. The size of the metropolitan population and the variety of its environments allows the formation of some neighbourhoods characterized, in part, by work identities as well as income: the concentration of new craft workers in the media, arts and design in inner north-east London is an example. These neighbourhoods form from a wish to participate in a common culture derived from work, and they facilitate networking and, potentially, collective organization. Other concentrations of workers with similar identities arise from the relatively short commuting distances of many women and low paid workers (sections 6.5, 7.11). The metropolitan economy tends to contain many substantial localized industrial districts, so these commuting patterns create neighbourhoods where similarities of work resonate in local social relationships, and where most of the workers in a given workplace live close to each other; classic cases are the former concentration of process plant and dock workers in residential districts of east London, and of clothing industry workers in north-east London. The implications for collective organization are contradictory. On the one hand this spatial pattern reflects less choice of job for the *individual* worker, which tends to undermine both individual and collective bargaining power. On the other hand, work solidarity may be reinforced by concrete social ties and mutual knowledge and recognition within the residential area. Thus the clothing firms of north-east London have a local labour force whose bargaining power is restricted simultaneously by the nexus of geography, skills, gender and ethnicity. However, the Turkish clothing workers have used spatial concentration and national political traditions (a strong Communist Party) to build effective union organization in the industry; and spatial concentration has made possible the neighbourhood-based organization of clothing homeworkers (Greater London Council, 1985: Ch. 17; Phizacklea and Wolkowitz, 1995). The geography of waged work-home links within the metropolitan economy thus has varied and contrary results.

Products and clients

A final specificity of metropolitan labour relations arises from the nature of the goods and services being produced and the class purposes and class supports of these markets. I have already suggested that in some types of product industry, wherever located, workers may develop an 'aristocratic' attitude and an identification with the employer on the basis of the rents reaped by the product and the status or political standing of the consumers (section 13.5). Sectors of this type exist in many types of locality, but they are particularly common in metropolises. Command functions and high-level business services, which reap high rents, are concentrated in these cities. Metropolises have concentrations of high-income residents and business visitors and thus of manufacturing and service workers producing luxuries (Leyshon and Thrift, 1996: Ch. 4). They are centres of scientific commissioning and military procurement. Each of these tends to produce a *distinct* 'labour aristocracy'.

A specifically metropolitan labour politics is created not merely by the *serial aggregation* of this type of industry but also by the *core processes* that underlie it. The metropolis is the organizing centre of the bourgeoisie, of the appropriation, distribution and redistribution of surplus profits, of the expenditure of these surpluses in luxury consumption and through the state. The metropolis would not exist without these class processes, and the metropolis as a whole is stamped by them (section 5.2). This has its counterpart in popular ideologies. In the most commonly presented images of these cities, and much of the daily experience of living in them, the working class, and particularly the organized working class, is marginalized. For most people in Britain, and for most Londoners themselves, London is not an industrial city, despite being the largest single concentration of manufacturing in the country. Nor is it seen as a centre of union militancy – with the partial exception, too obvious to miss, of those communications workers who can paralyse national and international flows. Much of the working-class culture of London looks (up) towards the bourgeoisie: the Roman Road, running through the old East End, is lined with shops selling (discounted or fake) Sloane Street high fashion. Collectivist cultures of labour in London have had to contend with this cultural dominance of the ruling class. Even in the heyday of socialist culture in the East End, the labour movement was strongly split between male craft workers, with their potential access to rents derived from the core, and the largely non-skilled workers of the new unions. The labour movement cannot change the core class nature of the metropolis this side of socialism, but building labour solidarity in metropolises would benefit from recognition of these ideological pulls.[6]

13.7 Conclusions: fragmentation, difference and socialism

In seeking to construct collectivity and solidarity, we have to be aware of the sources of fragmentation and anomie. Workers confront capital in the first place as individuals. This is not simply a 'structural' feature of capitalism in a static sense but something that is continuously reproduced by its dynamics. The flow of capital between sectors and places, which appears as the competition between capitals, pulls workers in its wake, forcing them to compete and pressuring them to pursue purely individual advancement. The many contradictions of the capitalist labour process, as well as technical differences, produce multiple differences in work relations and conditions, and pull groups of workers towards different forms of collaboration and conflict with their employers. These differences also involve distinct work identities that produce anomie and barriers to recognition. These impulsions to individualism are reinforced by both fragmentation and difference within the reproduction sphere, within which production itself is a creative moment. Contemporary neoliberalism bases itself on these individualizing processes.

A generalized culture of individual advancement conflicts with human needs, however. It is not only inegalitarian but unjust in that most of its benefits accrue to the already privileged. It is a short-sighted and often illusory path even for them: good conditions in one aspect of jobs often go together with poor conditions in others (sections 2.3, 13.4), and the flow and competition of capital ensure that those good conditions are always vulnerable to disruption and reversal.

To develop a politics of solidarity means, then, to confront difference in labour processes, in jobs and in work identities – to confront difference as it is produced by both capital and workers themselves. The theoretical and political task is to take difference seriously without reifying it, to avoid giving it a false fixity and inevitability. Mainstream sociology treats difference within classes in a descriptive and static way, as different class locations in an essentially unproblematized hierarchy. 'Poststructuralist marxism' (Resnick and Wolff, 1987; Gibson-Graham, 1996) arrives at substantially the same end point. Class positions are 'overdetermined' by differences in labour process technologies, skills, forms of enterprise ownership and access to knowledge, and by social differences partly formed by structures outside production (such as gender, ethnicity, socially defined age); each of these generative structures is substantially distinct. There is therefore a whole range of work identities and labour process and enterprise strategies from which to choose; each of these is weakly interrelated with the others, and each is substantially non-contradictory. The fundamental theoretical strategy of poststructuralist marxism of substituting overdetermination for contradiction allows difference to be generated but as a set of discrete, weakly-related forms. Struggle and choice are then necessarily external to the theory, and accordingly appear in a voluntarist and individualist form: workers should choose the better forms of work, and if enough of us do so then the economy as a whole will be transformed.

As Wood (1986; 1995) has argued in her critique of these ideas, class and difference within class should be understood not as heterogeneous locations but as *moments of contradictory processes*. Differences in work and work identities are, to be sure, constructed by the complex interplay of distinct social structures and by differences in the use values of technologies, but these social structures are strongly internally related (Chapter 2). Moreover, as we have seen at many points, difference often arises from the development of contradictions *within* these structures, so that the forms of difference are inherently unstable and contestable. This approach allows the theoretical and practical recognition of unity of position and of interests within the working class while at the same time recognizing the materiality and the force of difference. As against postmodern celebrations of difference, it sees the divisions within the working class considered in this book as negative in themselves and as barriers to collaboration, but also as contestable.[7]

Developing solidarity, however, means not only struggle within the labour process and against its differences, but also measures to control and plan competition between enterprises and flows of capital. This is denied by those left programmes, increasingly influential in recent years, which seek to pursue benefits for labour narrowly within direct production and within the individual enterprise. Supporters of flexible specialization and strongly integrated regional economies in essence see a strategy of 'strong competition' (Storper and Walker, 1989) *in the labour process* as substantially overcoming the waywardness and vicissitudes of money capital and capital flows. Skilled, autonomous, well-paid and secure jobs can then be achieved through action within the sphere of the labour process, including knowledge relations and interfirm collaborations (Best, 1990; Scott, 1998; Cooke and Morgan, 1998; section 3.6). Similarly, supporters of cooperatives within capitalism (Hodgson, 1984) and, more ambitiously, of a market socialism based on cooperatives (Nove, 1983; Sayer, 1995; Cohen and Rogers, 1995), picture workers designing high quality jobs for themselves through their formal control *of the labour process*. In 'strong competition' the antagonisms between labour and capital are overcome, and workers' interests realized to the maximum degree technically possible, through productive collaboration, realizing the universal side of capital; in an economy of cooperatives, the same aims are achieved more directly through ending the role of capitalists. These arrangements make it possible formally to undertake the kinds of progressive changes to the labour process discussed in section 13.4.

But the competition between workers in workplaces linked only (or mainly) through the market would create an individualistic and parochial culture and make it unlikely that greater equality and cooperation would be sought, let alone achieved. Moreover, neither productivist capitalism nor market socialism contains serious mechanisms for dealing with the issues considered in section 13.5: spatially and temporally uneven development, tendencies to overaccumulation and devalorization, and downward spirals of competition. Workers would still be faced with undermining by production elsewhere; with sudden development of overcapacity; with pressures to cut wages, intensify work and to make hours more 'flexible'; with disinvestment or withdrawal of new investment; and with finding new jobs in economies that have no substantial mechanisms for planning full employment. These conditions inevitably react back onto the labour process itself: flexible specialist or cooperative-enterprise economies cannot systematically sustain high skill, autonomous, well paid and secure jobs over time and space, even though they may create them locally and for certain periods.

This problematic relation of labour processes to capital flows has an important ideological aspect. The productivist and market socialist strategies, including in their green versions (for example Lipietz, 1992), can be radical in their proposals for the material aspects of the labour process and for the development of technologies, but they concede freedom to money capital and regulation by the valorization of capital. This is a serious ideological concession, particularly in an era dominated by neoliberalism. During the long boom a – possibly *the* – dominant form of legitimation was technological rationality: both the basic structures of the economy and its concrete paths of development were portrayed as based on technological imperatives and as in turn developing technology in the most beneficial way (Habermas, 1976). With neoliberalism the dominant form of legitimation has shifted to the imperatives of 'the market': while local outcomes may be unpleasant, they are required by competition in production and the freedom of flow of money capital; work and production may seem irrational when viewed locally, but the cohesion and integration of the world market ensures a higher rationality. This neoliberal ideology has no need to claim that either the experience of work or the development of technologies is attractive to those immediately involved; anxiety and stress in waged work and tyrannous developments of technology can be dismissed as the inevitable price of 'competitiveness'. The abstraction of market rationality has replaced the assertion of the concrete benefits of technological advance. The demise of technological optimism as a dominant ideology does make it easier for the left to present a critique of material aspects of the labour process and of technology. But this radicalism is inadequate and evasive unless it opposes the ideology of determination by 'the market', that is, the right of capital to make investment choices.

This discussion points to the need for *planning of the flows of investment within and between industries*. This is necessary to address the competition between workers and the reproduction of differences in quality of jobs, in particular to overcome the weaknesses of productivist and market socialist strategies on these issues. An approach to socialist planning that avoids some of the contradictions of the (former) non-capitalist countries[8] has begun to be developed by Devine (1988) and Adaman and Devine (1997) (see also Itoh, 1995). This model needs further elaboration, but it is sufficient for the present argument. Socialist planning would focus not on the planning of prices or interenterprise trading, nor on extending the non-marketed sector (*pace* Mandel, 1986), but on *the planning of investment*. Planning, on the basis of the public ownership of the major means of production and investment money, is carried out through negotiation and conflict between democratic bodies representing workers and citizens of different types and at different spatial scales. Aggregate investment would be planned to meet targets of income growth and working-hour reductions with a constraint of full employment, taking into account trends in the relation of investment to productivity and demand for wage jobs. In this way overaccumulation, long waves and the business cycle at large scales could be minimized. Sectoral distribution of investment, and major shifts in investment within sectors, would be planned to meet projected capacity and demand trends, as well as broad social and ecological objectives. Spatial distribution of investment would be negotiated by territorially representative bodies so as to mitigate geographical uneven development. Control over many of the details of the labour process and innovation would remain at the workplace level, and certain forms of regulated competition between them would be possible. In consequence, contrary to the critique of socialism by Hayek and the Austrian school, the planning processes require knowledge only of broad economic aggregates and not of details of enterprise labour processes and products. The feasibility of this model indicates that the problems of accumulation, uneven development and competition discussed in this part of the book are not problems of industrial societies as such but of *capitalist* societies.

By mitigating the pressures of investment flows, devalorization and competition, such an economy would enable many of the issues of quality of work with which I have been concerned to be addressed in quite new ways. Contrary to the implication of Cohen's argument (section 13.4), workers' control over the quantitative aspects of the economy should and can be directed to issues of the quality of work. Competition within a sector, particularly major expansions and contractions of capacity, would be mediated by the sector planning body, and wages and conditions of work negotiated at a sector-wide level. This would allow real debate and advance in questions of skilling, variety of work, the autonomy of individual workers and of work groups, and the wider mental/manual division of labour, without these being undermined by excessive or short-term pressures of competition, even though productivity and profitability are still important targets. The planning body for a sector can consider major innovations in processes, including those associated with new products (Chapter 9), and the main directions in which they are to be developed. These possibilities indicate a problem with the conceptual divisions made by Burawoy (1985): in seeking to distinguish the labour process from 'the politics of production', the 'relations in production' from the relations of production, he implies that difference and choice in the labour process is substantially detached from the basic social relations of the economy. The argument here indicates, on the contrary, that socialist relations of ownership, investment planning and workers' collective organization could make a *deep and systematic* difference to the evolution of labour processes.

I have argued that labour processes and the associated formation of labourers impinge strongly onto workers' empowerment and hence their influence over the macro economy (section 13.4). We now see that the reverse is also the case – workers' control over the macro economy can change the labour process in progressive ways. My central argument, that labour processes and the organization of investment within capitalism are strongly internally related, thus has important implications for the potential of a *socialist* economy.

The taming (although not supersession) of value in this model of socialism would also enable issues of social reproduction and consumption to be addressed in new ways (Gough and Eisenschitz, 1997). Different consumer and welfare services can be coordinated socially and geographically in ways which are very difficult, both politically and in accounting terms, when they are in disparate ownership. This enables, for example, women's oppression within reproduction work to be addressed far more effectively than it can be under capitalism, complementing measures against gender difference in production (Hayden, 1980). Pressure and initiative from women's organizations would then be on a much more favourable terrain than within capitalism. The structure of consumption and effective demand would also change. The distribution of incomes earned in production would be far narrower. Consumption patterns would alter with changed notions of gender and of status in work. Qualitative aspects of consumption could also be directly addressed via production, for example in decisions over major types of product and in the planning of infrastructures.

All these fields of planning have implications for the metropolis. The erosion of the mental/manual division of labour and new relations between production and the management of investment funds would fundamentally alter the spatial division of labour within which the metropolis is privileged, revolutionizing its 'core'. Given that the metropolis is presently the centre of luxury and business people's consumption, the structure of locally satisfied demand would be radically altered by the changed distribution of income, the withering away of the category of business people, changed notions of status, and an ending of the metropolis as the locale of cohesion of the ruling class. The characteristically deep problems of reproduction and the built environment in the metropolis (sections 6.5, 6.6) could be tackled in new ways. Each of these changes would have major impacts on manufacturing sectors (cf. Chapter 5) and on consumer services. The category of 'metropolis' would be put into question not so much in its size as in its social specificity.

I have approached socialism as those social relations of production that could effectively sustain collaboration, solidarity and the overcoming of oppressive difference between workers. This could be accused of putting the cart before the horse: does not the fragmentation and disempowerment of workers under capitalism – especially under neoliberalism – make the *achievement* of such an economy impossible (Giddens, 1998)? This is to look at the problem statically. Conflict between workers' short term, 'realistic' projects of competing with each other and the long-term and difficult project of collaboration is mediated by practice and political creativity. Collective organization is built up through struggle against capital, which can also simultaneously be a struggle against the divisions reproduced by capitalism (sections 13.4 and 13.5). Moreover, there is not a simple determinism between these divisions and people's consciousness. E. P. Thompson (1968) has described how the English working class in the first half of the nineteenth century achieved a substantial degree of political unity despite the enormous – indeed growing – differences in labour processes, product industry dynamics and competitive conditions. Thompson argued that this unity was underpinned by a sense of cataclysm arising from the industrial revolution, which was shared by otherwise diverse sections of the class (see further E. Wood, 1995). It is not utopian to suppose that the labour movement could develop a similar shared opposition to the contemporary cataclysm of neoliberalism, and behind that of capitalist relations of production as such; the international conferences and discussions organized by the Zapitistas are an indication of the potential. Capitalist social relations are embodied in abstract value, in quantity; while this can reify and mystify these social relations, it also gives them a ubiquitous resonance. Resistance can proceed – and is currently proceeding in many places – against both the fetishistic logic of capital accumulation and markets *and* the particularities of the labour process. A project of broad collective struggles can have an optimism justified by the common structures spanning the diverse experiences of workers, but also needs a sober attention to divisions and difference. Beyond that, constructing a socialist economy would mean not only being able to meet workers' and citizens' individual needs more adequately but would enable us to deepen and widen a culture of solidarity initially created in struggles against capital.

NOTES

1. Capital does not, then, always threaten labour with geographical mobility, as in Burawoy's (1985) notion of 'hegemonic despotism'. Spatial stability and stable and cooperative industrial relations linked to relative surplus value strategies is a more promising strategy for much of capital (Gough, 1996c). The form of capital expresses and mediates these spatial-production relations: see Chapter 11, note 4.

2. Some might add that the worse jobs involve 'super-exploitation' and that the resultant super-profits accruing to the employer are unjust. But in a Marxist rather than Ricardian framework, worse jobs do not necessarily mean higher profits; in fact, generally the contrary is the case (sections 3.2, 3.3; Jenkins, 1984).

3. Opposition to difference does not mean that better-off sections of workers should restrain their demands on capital, as sections of the left have sometimes argued, for example in the 'feminist incomes policy' proposed by the Communist Party of Great Britain in the 1980s. This is because it is capital and not the better-off workers who exploit the worse-off (section 13.2). Passivity of workers with greater bargaining power discourages and materially weakens the organization of those with less leverage. Moreover, even better-off workers are exploited.

4. Lembcke's (1993) argument, following Therborn, that middle-class people derive their bargaining power from skill and autonomy within the labour process whereas manual workers rely on collective organization is schematic, misrepresents the contemporary situation of both groups, and misses the many cases of *interplay* of these forms of power.

5. An aspect of the mental/manual division of labour largely neglected in radical industrial studies is that between members and officers within trade unions. Often-undemocratic procedures, coupled with the lack of time of members for union matters, restrict the use of unions for radical

change. This important issue, however, goes beyond the scope of the present study.

6. It is interesting to note the relation of my argument here to notions of 'the urban' in classical sociology. Wirth (1938) argued that key elements of urbanism, which are particularly pronounced in metropolises, are (i) social diversity, leading to anomie; (ii) density of population, which the individual deals with by social withdrawal; and (iii) the possibilities for escaping one's past and for social mobility. Point (iii) is paralleled by my argument on individual employment mobility. Point (i) has some parallels in the argument that diversity of labour processes and labour power inhibits solidarity, though I stress that this process can be contested by popular organization. Point (ii) goes in the opposite direction to my argument.

7. On negative and positive social difference, see Hartsock (1987) and Harvey (1996: Ch. 12).

8. There is no space here to discuss the extent of, and reasons for, the economic failures of the non-capitalist countries. But their economic and political evolution was massively damaged by their initially backward level and by severe external pressures on them, both economic and military. The model argued for here differs from them particularly in their form of political rule (bureaucratic dictatorships) and in some of their economic planning mechanisms (central planning of enterprise inputs and outputs and of prices; non-marketed benefits tying workers to the enterprise).

APPENDIX 1
THE BUSINESS CYCLE IN
LONDON MANUFACTURING IN
THE PERIOD OF STUDY

Each business cycle has a differentiated impact on different sectors and different territories. The cycle is propagated in each unit of the economy (sector, territory) partly through cyclical pressures acting on it from *outside* (that is, from larger scale units), and partly through internal contradictions of accumulation *within* the unit (see section 12.3). The effects of the cycle in a unit are also mediated by its long term growth rate and competitiveness. In units where accumulation is relatively weak in the long term, upturns will tend to produce modest increases in output and, because of productivity increases, small or even negative employment rises, while downturns tend to produce big cuts in output and employment.

These considerations are relevant to the form of the cycle over 1975/6–1981/2 within which our case study is set: within the British economy manufacturing was a low growth sector, and within UK manufacturing London was a low growth locality for reasons explored in Chapters 5 and 6. Thus the downturn in 1979–81 impacted much more severely on manufacturing than the rest of the UK economy (Table A.1), though it was scarcely more severe in London manufacturing than in the rest of the UK (Table A.2). The upturn of 1975–9 produced only a weak increase in UK real manufacturing output (Tables A.1 and A.2), and, year on year, no increase in output in London in the estimated figure shown in Table A.2. (Note that adjustment of nominal output for inflation was problematic throughout the period because of its very high level and its variation between different economic categories.) Between the years 1975 and 1979 manufacturing employment declined in both the UK and London due to productivity increases (Table A.2).

Given this weak upturn in output and employment terms, in what sense was there a cycle in London manufacturing during the study period? Firstly, there were clearly sharp *changes* in growth rate of both output and employment between the downturn of 1973–5, the upturn of 1975–9 and the downturn of 1979–81 (Table A.2). Data from the survey (section 6.2) also show that profitability, a key outcome as well as cause of the cycle, was higher in 1977–9 than in 1980–1 (Leigh *et al.*, 1982a and b). London manufacturing

Table A.1 *Cyclical changes in real GDP and employment, UK, 1973–81*

	Changes between peak and trough quarters, % (number of quarters of the up- or downswing)		
	Downswing, 1973–5 approx	Upswing, 1975–9 approx	Downswing, 1979–81 approx
Whole economy			
Real GDP	−4.2	+13.0	−6.7
Employment	−1.2	+1.2	−7.6
Manufacturing			
Real GDP	−9.7	+9.5	−17.7
	(8Q)	(15Q)	(7Q)
Employment	−7.8	+1.1	−24.7
	(9Q)	(4Q)	(26Q)

Source: *Department of Employment Gazette*

Table A.2 *Cyclical change in employment and output in UK and London manufacturing, 1973–81*

	Change between year-averages, %		
	1973–5	1975–9	1979–81
Britain			
Employment	−4.3	−4.6	−13.6
Real GDP	−8.1	+4.6	−14.1
London			
Employment	−9.4	−8.7	−15.0
Real GDP, estimated*	−13.0	0.0	−15.4

* GDP estimated from employment using productivity change in UK manufacturing for the corresponding years.
Source: Britain: *Department of Employment Gazette*. London employment: *Annual Abstract of Greater London Statistics 1973–75*; *Regional Statistics 1977*; *Department of Employment Gazette 1980–2*; 1979 employment calculated from data for Southeast region and 3-year trend in London/Southeast ratio. UK productivity change calculated from employment and real GDP indices in *Department of Employment Gazette*.

thus experienced a cycle in its simplest definition, as an alternation of periods of weaker and stronger accumulation.

But, more fundamentally, London manufacturing was affected by the *processes* which power the business cycle. In particular, during the upswing of 1975–9 it experienced and participated in processes characteristic of a cyclical upturn. Data exist on two such processes, demand and labour markets.

• Demand

Demand is not a cause of the cycle in a closed economy, but in economic units smaller than the global economy it may be an important external driver (see sections 12.2 and 12.3). London manufacturers sold into, variously, international, national and London markets (sections 5.3 and 6.7). These all experienced substantial upturns in 1975–9. For example, between the years 1975 and 1979 there was a increase in UK consumption of manufactures in real terms of 6.4 per cent (*Annual Abstract of Statistics* production and trade tables and 'output of manufactured products' price index). Factories in London took advantage of these expanding markets. The survey shows that workplaces surviving the period 1976–9 perceived strengthening demand and increased their output substantially: their aggregate increase in real output was, for example, 10 per cent in furniture, 28 per cent in steel work, 13 per cent in printing, and approximately 20 per cent in metal cans, 18 per cent in electronic capital goods, and 20 per cent in pharmaceuticals (Leigh *et al.*, 1982b). In some of these industries the increase in the *volume* of output was larger than these figures, reflecting weakening relative prices. These gains in output were offset by high rates of workplace closure (Leigh *et al.*, 1982a: 53–4; Greater London Council 1980; section 6.2).

• Markets in labour power

Labour markets are central to the generation of cycles both within economic units (here, London manufacturing) and through external influence on them (from the London and wider British economies) (sections 12.2 and 12.3). The immediately relevant labour market here is that for manual and technical workers in London as a whole, since the manufacturing workforce was not sealed off from the rest of the economy (section 6.5). The 1973–5/6 recession raised registered unemployment sharply, from 44,000 in December 1973 to 149,000 in June 1976. But the labour market tightened during 1976–9. Unemployment of London residents fell from 5.1 per cent to 3.7 per cent between 1977 and 1979 (*Labour Force Survey*). Estimated vacancies rose sharply over most of the period, starting in first quarter 1976 at 65,000 and rising to 180,000 in first quarter 1979 (Greater London Council, 1980). Workplaces in the survey reported tight labour markets in 1976–9, especially for skilled labour (section 6.5). The labour market conditions in 1976–9 were thus those characteristic of the mature phase of an upturn. Interestingly, unemployment was lower and labour markets tighter in London than in the UK as a whole during the whole period (Greater London Council, 1980); indeed, this was a factor in the relative decline of London manufacturing (section 6.5). In this sense the upturn of the cycle was more serious for firms in London than the rest of the UK, despite the fact that the upturn had a smaller *effect* on output and employment in London. This emphasizes the importance of distinguishing between causes and effects of the cycle.

Processes characteristic of cyclical upturns were, then, at work in London manufacturing in 1975/6–9. Because of long-term weak accumulation in British manufacturing, and because of some locally-specific adverse conditions in London (particularly in markets in labour power and land), these processes produced weak outcomes in terms of aggregate output and employment, though there were output increases in many surviving workplaces. These adverse conditions did not, however, remove the *processes* generating the upturn; and it is these processes, rather than their output and employment outcomes, with which we shall be concerned in this book. The study of London manufacturing workplaces in 1976–81 can thus throw light on the relation of business cycles to labour process change, despite the specificities of this economic unit in this period.

APPENDIX 2
SOME TROUBLESOME TERMS
IN SPATIAL ECONOMIC
CHANGE

Components of change

Floor space change

Increase	Decrease
Opening = production of qualitatively new type at the site, which is either	**Closure** = end of production of distinct type at the site, which is either
– a firm **birth**;	– a firm **death**
– opening of production of a new type in a multisite firm;	– closure of all production of distinct type in a multisite firm
– **relocation** to the site	– **relocation** away from the site
Expansion in situ	**Contraction in situ**

Change in spatial distributions

Change in the distribution of a given type of production may take place through:

– relocation within firms, and
– **spatial shifts** which are
    – differential expansions and contractions of workplaces; and
    – differential rates of openings and closures.

Relocation within the firm

Relocation within the firm, or **relocation** for short, is either:

– a **move** = closure at one site and opening at another, in either a single-site or a multisite firm, or
– **other types of relocation** within a multisite firm created by the re-allocation of investment between sites, which are either
    – an opening with contraction elsewhere;
    – a closure with expansion elsewhere; or
    – contraction and expansion at different sites.

Relocations may be **expansionary** or **contractionary** or neither, depending on the change in floor space in the given type of production within the firm.

APPENDIX 3
RELOCATION AND CHANGE IN
FLOOR SPACE

The motives for change in floor space, and the geographical pattern of relocation within firms which resulted, are shown in the table below.

The importance of multisite firms in contractionary relocations is due to their 'rationalizing' their existing sites, whereas single-site firms tended to contract in situ until they died rather than moving. The difference between relocations within London and out of it was partly due to this: multisite firms were more likely than single-plant firms to relocate between London and other parts of Britain, and hence contractionary relocations were more likely than expansionary ones to involve sites outside London.

The motives of the expansionary and contractionary relocations respectively were also important. Considerations other than premises size played a role in only a minority of expansionary relocations. Their locations were then predominantly in London, because the qualities of the stock of premises on the market in London were on the whole acceptable (section 4.6). Firms were usually able to move locally, within the borough or to an adjacent one: this was so in 43 of the 51 cases. In contrast, considerations other than premises size played a *major* role in contractionary relocations. Qualitative differences between sites therefore came into play, leading to more relocations between London and ex-London sites.

Table A.3 *Relocations associated with floor space change: motives and spatial form*

| | Change in floor space | | |
	Expansion	Contraction	All
Change in output	45	10	55
Change in floor space/output ratio due to labour process change	12	9	21
Total	57	19	76
To existing sites in multisite firms	4	16	20
Within or into London	51	9	60
Out of London	6	10	16

BIBLIOGRAPHY

Aaronovitch, S. and Smith, R. (1981) *The Political Economy of British Capitalism*, Maidenhead: McGraw-Hill.

Adaman, F. and Devine, P. (1997) On the economic theory of socialism, *New Left Review* 221, 54–80.

Aglietta, M. (1979) *A Theory of Capitalist Regulation*, London: New Left Books.

Allen, J., Massey, D. and Cochrane, A. (1997) *Rethinking the Region*, London: Routledge.

Amin, A. and Robins, K. (1990) The re-emergence of regions? the mythical geography of flexible accumulation, *Environment and Planning D: Society and Space* 8, 7–34.

Amin, A. and Thrift, N. (1995) Institutional issues for the European regions: from markets and plans to socioeconomics and powers of association, *Economy and Society* 24, 1, 41–66.

Anderson, P. (1964) Origins of the present crisis, *New Left Review* 23, 26–53.

Anderson, P. (1987) The figures of descent, *New Left Review* 161, 20–77.

Andreff, V. (1984) The international centralisation of capital and the reordering of world capitalism, *Capital and Class* 22, 58–80.

Armstrong, P. (1988) Labour and monopoly capital, in Hyman, R. and Streeck, W. (eds) *New Technology and Industrial Relations*, Oxford: Blackwell.

Armstrong, P., Glyn, A. and Harrison, J. (1991) *Capitalism since 1945*, Oxford: Blackwell.

Atkins, P. (1990) The spatial configuration of class solidarity in London's West End 1792–1939, in Roger, R. (ed.) *Urban History Yearbook* 17, Leicester: Leicester University Press.

Bagguley, P., Mark-Lawson, J., Shapiro, D., Urry, J., Walby, S. and Warde, A. (1990) *Restructuring: Place, Class and Gender*, London: Sage.

Ball, M. (1988) *Rebuilding Construction*, London: Routledge.

Baran, P. and Sweezy, P. (1968) *Monopoly Capital*, Harmondsworth: Penguin.

Barrett, M. (1988) *Women's Oppression Today*, London: Verso.

Bashall, R. and Smith, G. (1991) Jam today: London's transport in crisis, in Thornley, A. (ed.) *The Crisis of London*, London: Routledge.

Benders, T. (1995) Output characteristics as input in the skilling debate, *Work, Employment and Society* 9, 2, 329–42.

Berberoglu, B. (ed.) (1993) *The Labour Process and Control of Labour*, Westport, CT: Praeger.

Berger, S. and Piore, M. (1980) *Dualism and Discontinuity in Industrial Societies*, Cambridge: Cambridge University Press.

Best, M. (1990) *The New Competition*, Cambridge: Polity Press.

Beynon, H. *et al.* (1989) 'It's all falling apart here': coming to terms with the future in Teesside, in Cooke.

Bird, J., Curtis, B., Putnam, T., Robertson, G. and Tickner, L. (eds) *Mapping the Futures: Local Cultures, Global Change*, London: Routledge.

Blyton, P., Hassard, J., Hill, S. and Starkey, K. (1989) *Time, Work and Organisation*, London: Routledge.

Bonefeld, W. (1993) *The Recomposition of the British State during the 1980s*, London: Dartmouth.

Bonefeld, W. and Holloway, J. (eds) (1991) *Post-Fordism and Social Form*, London: Macmillan.

Bowles, S., Gordon, D. and Weisskopf, T. (1986) Power and profits: the social structure of accumulation and the profitability of the postwar US economy, *Review Radical Political Economy* 18, 132–67.

Braverman, H. (1974) *Labour and Monopoly Capitalism*, New York: Monthly Review Press.

Brusco, S. (1982) The Emilian model: productive decentralisation and social integration, *Cambridge Journal of Economics* 6, 167–84.

Bryan, R. (1985) Monopoly in the Marxist method, *Capital and Class* 26, 72–92.

Buck, N., Gordon, I., Young, K. (1986) *The London Employment Problem*, Oxford: Oxford University Press.

Budd, L. and Whimster, S. (1992) *Global Finance and Urban Living*, London: Routledge.

Burawoy, M. (1979) *Manufacturing Consent*, Chicago: University of Chicago Press.

—(1985) *The Politics of Production*, London: Verso.

Camagni, R. (1991) *Innovation Networks, Spatial Perspectives*, London: Belhaven-Pinter.

Campbell, A., Currie, W. and Warner, M. (1989) Innovation, skills and training: micro-electronics and manpower in the UK and West Germany, in Hirst and Zeitlin.

Castells, M. (1977) *The Urban Question*, London: Edward Arnold.

—(1996) *The Rise of the Network Society*, Oxford: Blackwell.

Clark, G., Gertler, M. and Whiteman, J. (1986) *Regional Dynamics*, Boston: Allen & Unwin.

Clark, G., McKay, J., Missen, G. and Webber, M. (1992) Objections to economic restructuring and strategies of coercion: an analytical evaluation of policies and practices in Australia and the United States, *Economic Geography* 68, 43–59.

Clarke, S. (1988a) *Keynesianism, Monetarism and the Crisis of the State*, Aldershot: Elgar.

—(1988b) Overaccumulation, class struggle and the regulation approach, *Capital and Class* 36, 59–92.

—(1992) What in the F - -'s name is Fordism?, in Gilbert, N., Burrows, R. and Pollert, A. (eds) *Fordism and Flexibility*, Basingstoke: Macmillan.

Cockburn, C. (1983) *Brothers*, London: Pluto.

—(1985) *Machinery of Dominance*, London: Pluto.

Cohen, J. and Rogers, J. (eds) (1995) *Associations and Democracy*, London: Verso.

Cohen, S. (1987) A labour process to nowhere? *New Left Review* 165, 35–51.

Cohen, S. and Zysman, J. (1987) *Manufacturing Matters*, New York: Basic Books.

Cole, K., Cameron, J. and Edwards, C. (1983) *Why Economists Disagree*, London: Longman.

Conference of Socialist Economists (ed.) (1976) *The Labour Process and Class Strategies*, London: CSE.

Cooke, P. (ed.) (1989) *Localities*, London: Unwin Hyman.

Cooley, M. (1986) Socially useful design, in Roy, R. and Wield, D. *Product Design and Technological Innovation*, Milton Keynes: Open University Press.

Coventry, Liverpool, Newcastle and Tyneside Trade Councils (1980) *State Intervention in Industry: A Workers' Enquiry* Newcastle upon Tyne: Newcastle Trades Council.

Cox, K. (ed.) (1997) *Spaces of Globalization*, New York: Guilford Press.

—(1998) Spaces of dependence, spaces of engagement and the politics of scale; or, looking for local politics, *Political Geography* 17, 1, 1–24.

Cox, K. and Mair, A. (1988) Locality and community in the politics of local economic development, *Annals of the Association of American Geographers* 78, 307–25.

—(1991) From localised social structures to localities as agents, *Environment and Planning A* 23, 2, 197–213.

Cressey, P. and MacInnes, J. (1980) Voting for Ford, *Capital and Class* 11, 5–33.

Davis, M. (1990) *City of Quartz*, London: Verso.

Dear, M. and Scott, A. (eds) (1981) *Urbanisation and Urban Planning in Capitalist Society*, London: Methuen.

Desai, M. (1996) Debating the British disease: the centrality of profit, *New Political Economy* 1, 1, 79–93.

Dennis, R. (1978) The decline of manufacturing employment in Greater London 1966–74, *Urban Studies* 15, 1, 63–73.

Devine, P. (1988) *Democracy and Economic Planning*, Boulder: Westview Press.

Dicken, P. (1992) *Global Shift*, London: Paul Chapman, 2nd ed.

Dicken, P. and Lloyd, P. (1990) *Location in Space*, New York: HarperCollins, 3rd ed.

Duncan, S. (1991) Gender divisions of labour, in Hoggart and Green.

Dunning, J. (1958) *American Investment in British Manufacturing Industry*, London: Allen & Unwin.

Edel, M. (1981) Capitalism, accumulation and the explanation of urban phenomena, in Dear and Scott.

Edwards, P. (1986) *Conflict at Work*, Oxford: Blackwell.

Edwards, P. and Elger, T. (eds) (1999) *The Global Economy, National States, and the Regulation of Labour*, London: Continuum.

Edwards, P. and Scullion, H. (1982) *The Social Organisation of Industrial Conflict*, Oxford: Blackwell.

Edwards, R. (1979) *Contested Terrain*, New York: Basic Books.

Eisenschitz, A. and Gough, J. (1993) *The Politics of Local Economic Policy*, Basingstoke: Macmillan.

—(1996) The contradictions of neo-Keynesian local economic strategy, *Review of International Political Economy* 3, 3, 434–58.

—(1998) Theorising the state in local economic governance, *Regional Studies* 32, 8, 759–68.

Eldrige, J., Cressey, P. and MacInnes, J. (1991) *Industrial Sociology and Economic Crisis*, Haywards Heath: Harvester Wheatsheaf.

Elger, T. (1991) Technical innovation and work reorganisation in British manufacturing in the 1980s: continuity, intensification or transformation? *Work, Employment and Society* 4, 67–101.

Etherington, D. (1997) Trade unions and local economic development: lessons from Denmark, *Local Economy* 12, 3, 267–74.

Evans, A. and Eversley, D. (1980) *The Inner City*, London: Heinemann.

Fagan, R. (1990) Elder IXL Ltd: finance capital and the geography of corporate restructuring, *Environment and Planning A* 22, 647–66.

—(1991) Industrial policy and the macroeconomic environment, *Australian Geographer* 22, 102–5.

Fainstein, S., Gordon, I. and Harloe, M. (1992) *Divided Cities*, Oxford: Blackwell.

Fine, B. and Harris, L. (1985) *Peculiarities of the British Economy*, London: Lawrence & Wishart.

Fothergill, S. and Gudgin, G. (1979) Regional employment change: a subregional explanation *Progress in Planning* 12, 3, 155–219.

—(1982) *Unequal Growth*, London: Heinemann.

—(1985) Ideology and methods in industrial location research, in Massey, D. and Meegan, R. (eds) *Politics and Method*, London: Methuen.

Fothergill, S., Gudgin, G., Kitson, M. and Monk, S. (1988) The deindustrialisation of the city, in Massey and Allen.

Freeman, C., Clark, M. and Soete, L. (1982) *Unemployment and Technical Innovation*, London: Pinter.

Friedman, A. (1977) *Industry and Labour*, Basingstoke: Macmillan.

—(1986) Developing the managerial strategies approach to the labour process, *Capital and Class* 30, 97–124.

—(1990) Managerial strategies, activities, techniques and technology: towards a complex theory of the labour process, in Knights and Willmott, 177–208.

Friend, A. and Metcalf, A. (1981) *Slump City*, London: Pluto.

Frobel, F., Heinrichs, J. and Kreye, O. (1980) *The New International Division of Labour*, Cambridge: Cambridge University Press.

Gallie, D. (1991) Patterns of skill change: upskilling, deskilling or the polarisation of skills? *Work, Employment and Society* 5, 3, 319–51.

Garofoli, G. (1991) The Italian model of spatial development in the 1970s and 1980s, in Benko, G. and Dunford, M. (eds) *Industrial Change and Regional Development*, London: Belhaven Press.

Gartman, D. (1983) Structuralist Marxism and the labour process: where have the dialectics gone? *Theory and Society* 12, 659–69.

Geras, N. (1998) *The Contract of Mutual Indifference*, London: Verso.

Gertler, M. (1997) The invention of regional culture, in Lee and Wills.

Gibson-Graham, J.K. (1996) *The End of Capitalism (As We Know It)* Cambridge, MA: Blackwell.

Giddens, A. (1998) *The Third Way*, Cambridge: Polity Press.

Glyn, A. (1989) The macro-anatomy of the Thatcher years, in Green, F. (ed.) *The Restructuring of the UK Economy*, Hemel Hempstead: Harvester Wheatsheaf.

Glyn, A. and Sutcliffe, B. (1972) *British Capitalism, Workers and the Profit Squeeze*, Harmondsworth: Penguin.

Gordon, D. (1980) Stages of accumulation and long economic cycles, in Hopkins, T. and Wallerstein, I. (eds) *Processes of the World-System*, Sage: Beverley Hills.

— (1984) Capitalist development and the history of American cities, in Tabb, W. and Sawers, L. (eds) *Marxism and the Metropolis*, 2nd edn, New York: Oxford University Press.

— (1988) The global economy: new edifice or crumbling foundations? *New Left Review* 168, 24–64.

Gordon, D., Edwards, R. and Reich, M. (1982) *Segmented Work, Divided Workers*, Cambridge: Cambridge University Press.

Gorz, A. (ed.) (1978) *The Division of Labour*, Hassocks: Harvester Press.

Gough, J. (1986) Industrial policy and socialist strategy: restructuring and the unity of the working class, *Capital and Class* 29, 58–82.

— (1991) Structure, system and contradiction in the capitalist space economy, *Environment and Planning D: Society and Space* 9, 433–49.

— (1992) Workers' competition, class relations and space, *Environment and Planning D: Society and Space* 10, 265–86.

— (1996a) Not flexible accumulation: contradictions of value in contemporary economic geography, Part 1: Workplace and inter-firm relations, *Environment and Planning A* 28, 2063–79.

— (1996b) Not flexible accumulation: contradictions of value in contemporary economic geography, Part 2: Regional regimes, national regulation and political strategy, *Environment and Planning A* 28, 2179–200.

— (1996c) Neoliberalism and localism: comments on Peck and Tickell, *Area* 28, 3, 392–8.

— (2001) Workers' strategies to secure jobs, their uses of scale, and competing notions of justice, Institute of British Geographers Economic Geography Research Group Working Paper.

— (2002) Neoliberalism and socialisation in the contemporary city: opposites, complementarities and instabilities, *Antipode* 34, 3, 405–26.

Gough, J. and Eisenschitz, A. (1996a) The construction of mainstream local economic initiatives: mobility, socialisation and class relations, *Economic Geography* 76, 2, 178–95.

— (1996b) The modernisation of Britain and local economic policy: promise and contradictions, *Environment and Planning D: Society and Space* 14, 203–19.

— (1997) The division of labour, capitalism and socialism: an alternative to Sayer, *International Journal of Urban and Regional Research* 21, 1, 23–37.

Grabher, G. (ed) (1993) *The Embedded Firm*, London: Routledge.

Granovetter, M. and Swedberg, R. (eds) (1992) *The Sociology of Economic Life*, Boulder, CO: Westview Press.

Greater London Council (1980) *London's Economy: Trends and Issues*, London: GLC.

— (1985) *London Industrial Strategy*, London: GLC.

— (1986) *London Labour Plan*, London: GLC.

Green, D. (1991) The metropolitan economy: continuity and change 1800–1939, in Hoggart and Green, 8–33.

Gregory, D. and Urry, J. (eds) (1985) *Social Relations and Spatial Structures*, London: Macmillan.

Gunn, R. (1989) Marxism and philosophy, *Capital and Class* 37, 87–116.

Habermas, J. (1976) *Legitimation Crisis*, London: Heinemann.

Hahnel, R. and Sherman, H. (1982) The rate of profit over the business cycle, *Cambridge Journal of Economics* 6, 185–94.

Hales, M. (1980) *Living Thinkwork*, London: CSE Books.

Halford, S. and Savage, M. (1997) Rethinking restructuring: embodiment, agency and identity in organizational change, in Lee and Wills.

Hall, P. (1962) *The Industries of London since 1861*, London: Hutchinson.

Hall, P., Breheny, M., McQuaid, R. and Hart, D. (1987) *Western Sunrise*, London: Allen & Unwin.

Hall, P., Thomas, R., Gracey, G. and Drewett, R. (1973) *The Containment of Urban England*, London: Allen & Unwin.

Hall, S. and Jacques, M. (eds) (1989) *New Times*, London: Lawrence & Wishart.

Hamilton, F. (1991) A new geography of London's manufacturing, in Hoggart and Green.

Hanson, S. and Pratt, G. (1995) *Gender, Work and Space*, London: Routledge.

Hargreaves Heap, S. (1980) World profitability crisis in the 1970s: some empirical evidence, *Capital and Class* 12, 66–84.

Harrison, B. and Bluestone, B. (1988) *The Great U-Turn*, New York: Basic Books.

Hartsock, N. (1987) Rethinking modernism: minority versus majority theories, *Cultural Critique* 7, 187–206.

Harvey, D. (1982) *The Limits to Capital*, Oxford: Blackwell.

— (1985a) *The Urbanisation of Capital*, Oxford: Blackwell.

— (1985b) The geopolitics of capitalism, in Gregory and Urry.

— (1989) *The Condition of Postmodernity*, Oxford: Blackwell.

— (1996) *Justice, Nature and the Geography of Difference*, Oxford: Blackwell.

— (2000) *Spaces of Hope*, Edinburgh: Edinburgh University Press.

Hayden, D. (1980) What would a non-sexist city be like? in Stimpson, C. *et al.*, *Women and the American City*, Chicago: University of Chicago Press.

Hayter, R. and Watts, H. (1983) The geography of enterprise: a reappraisal, *Progress in Human Geography* 7, 2, 157–81.

Hayter, T. and Harvey, D. (1993) *The Factory and the City*, London: Mansell.

Herod, A. (1997) From a geography of labor to a labor of geography: labor's spatial fix and the geography of capitalism, *Antipode* 29, 1–31.

— (ed) (1998) *Organizing the Landscape: Geographical Perspectives of Labor Unionism*, Minneapolis: University of Minnesota Press.

Hirst, P. and Zeitlin, J. (eds) (1989) *Reversing Industrial Decline?* Oxford: Berg.

Hodgson, G. (1984) *The Democratic Economy*, Harmondsworth: Penguin.

Hoggart, K. and Green, D. (eds) (1991) *London: A New Metropolitan Geography*, London: Edward Arnold.

Howitt, R. (1993) A world in a grain of sand: towards a reconceptualisation of geographical scale, *Australian Geographer* 24, 1, 33–44.

Hudson, R. and Sadler, D. (1986) Contesting works closures in Western Europe's old industrial regions: defending place or betraying class? in Scott and Storper.

Hutton, W. (1995) *The State We're In*, London: Jonathan Cape.

Hyman, R. (1987) Strategy or structure? Capital, labour and control, *Work, Employment and Society* 1, 1, 25–55.

Hyman, R. and Elger, T. (1981) Job controls, the employers' offensive and alternative strategies, *Capital and Class* 15, 115–49.

Hymer, S. (1972) The multinational corporation and the law of uneven development, in Bhagwai, J. (ed.) *Economics and the World Order*, New York: Free Press.

Isaac, L. and Christiansen, L. (1999) Degradations of labor, cultures of cooperation: Braverman's 'labor', Lordstown, and the social factory, in Wardell, Steiger and Meiksins.

Itoh, M. (1995) *Political Economy for Socialism*, Basingstoke: Macmillan.

Itoh, M. and Lapavitsas, C. (1998) *Political Economy of Money and Finance*, Basingstoke: Macmillan.

Jenkins, R. (1984) Divisions over the international division of labour, *Capital and Class* 22, 28–58.

Johnston, R. (1986) The state, the region, and the division of labor, in Scott and Storper.

Jonas, A. (1994) The scale politics of spatiality, *Environment and Planning D: Society and Space* 12, 257–64.

— (1996) Local labour control regimes: uneven development and the social regulation of production, *Regional Studies* 30, 323–38.

— (1998) Investigating the local-global paradox, in Herod.

Kaldor, M. (1982) *The Baroque Arsenal*, London: Deutsch.

Kelly, J. (1985) Management's redesign of work: labour process, labour markets and product markets, in Knights, Willmott and Collinson.

King, A. (1991) *Global Cities: Post-imperialism and the Internationalisation of London*, London: Routledge.

Knights, D. (1990) Subjectivity, power and the labour process, in Knights and Willmott.

Knights, D. and Collinson, D. (1985) Redesigning work on the shopfloor: a question of control or consent? In Knights, Willmott and Collinson.

Knights, D. and Willmott, H. (eds) (1990) *Labour Process Theory*, Basingstoke: Macmillan.

Knights, D., Willmott, H. and Collinson, D. (eds) (1985) *Job Redesign*, Aldershot: Gower.

Laclau, E. and Mouffe, C. (1985) *Hegemony and Socialist Strategy*, London: Verso.

Lappe, L. (1988) The use of technology and the development of qualifications: how the debate about the labour process is viewed in German industrial sociology, in Knights, D. and Willmott, H. (eds) *New Technology and the Labour Process*, London: Macmillan.

Lash, S. and Urry, J. (1994) *Economies of Signs and Spaces*, London: Sage.

Leborgne, D. and Lipietz, A. (1988) New technologies, new modes of regulation: some spatial implications, *Society and Space* 6, 263–80.

Lee, R. and Wills, J. (eds) (1997) *Geographies of Economies*, London: Arnold.

Leigh, R., North, D., Gough, J. and Escott, K. (1982a) *Monitoring Manufacturing Employment Change in London 1976–81: The Implications for Local Economic Policy, Vol.1: Main Report*, London: Middlesex Polytechnic.

— (1982b) *Monitoring Manufacturing Employment Change in London 1976–81: The Implications for Local Economic Policy, Vol. 2: Sectoral Studies*, London: Middlesex Polytechnic.

Lembcke, J. (1993) Class formation and class capacities: a new approach to the study of labor and the labor process, in Berberoglu.

Levidow, L. (1981) Grunwick: the social contract meets the 20th century sweatshop, in Levidow and Young.

Levidow, L. (1990) Foreclosing the future, *Science as Culture* 8, 59–79.

Levidow, L. and Young, B. (1981) (eds) *Science, Technology and the Labour Process*, Vol. 1, London: CSE Books.

Leys, C. (1985) Thatcherism and manufacturing: a question of hegemony, *New Left Review* 151, 5–25.

Leyshon, A. and Thrift, N. (1996) *Money/Space*, London: Routledge.

Lipietz, A. (1992) *Towards a New Economic Order*, Cambridge: Polity.

Littler, C. (1979) *The Development of the Labour Process in Capitalist Societies*, New York: Heinemann.

Lorenz, E. (1992) Trust, community and cooperation: towards a theory of industrial districts, in Storper, M. and Scott, A. (eds) *Pathways to Industrialization and Regional Development*, New York: Routledge.

Lovering, J. (1990) Fordism's unknown successor: a comment on Scott's theory of flexible accumulation and the re-emergence of regional economies, *International Journal of Urban and Regional Research* 14, 1, 159–74.

— (1991) The changing geography of the military industry in Britain, *Regional Studies* 25, 4, 279–93.

— (1999) Theory led by policy: the inadequacies of the 'new regionalism' (illustrated from the case of Wales), *International Journal of Urban and Regional Research* 23, 2, 379–95.

MacInnes, J. (1987) *Thatcherism at Work*, Milton Keynes: Open University Press.

Maddison, A. (1979) The long run dynamics of productivity growth, in Beckerman, W. *Slow Growth in Britain*, Oxford: Oxford University Press.

Maguire, M. (1988) Work, locality and social control, *Work, Employment and Society* 2, 383–400.

Mandel, E. (1968) *Marxist Economic Theory*, London: Merlin.

— (1986) In defence of socialist planning, *New Left Review* 159, 5–37.

— (1978a) *Late Capitalism*, London: Verso.

— (1978b) *The Second Slump*, London: New Left Books.

Mann, E. (2000) 'A race struggle, a class struggle, a women's struggle all at once': organising on the buses of LA, *Socialist Register 2001* 259–74.

Manwaring, T. and Wood, S. (1985) The ghost in the labour process, in Knights, Willmott & Collinson.

Marchington, M. (1992) Managing labour relations in a competitive environment, in Sturdy, Knights & Willmott.

Marchington, M. and Parker, P. (1990) *Changing Patterns of Employee Relations* Brighton: Harvester Wheatsheaf.

Marglin, S. (1978) What do bosses do? In Gorz.

Marsden, T., Lowe, P. and Whatmore, S. (1992) Introduction, in Marsden, Lowe and Whatmore *Labour and Locality: Uneven Development and the Rural Labour Process*, London: David Fulton.

Marshall, A. (1919) *Industry and Trade*, London: Macmillan.

Marshall, M. (1987) *Long Waves of Regional Development*, Basingstoke: Macmillan.

Martin, J. (1966) *Greater London: An Industrial Geography* London: G. Bell.

Martin, R., Sunley, P. and Wills, J. (1996) *Union Retreat and the Regions*, London: Jessica Kingsley.

Martinez Lucio, M. and Stewart, P. (1997) The paradox of contemporary labour process theory: the rediscovery of labour and the disappearance of collectivism, *Capital and Class* 62, 49–78.

Marx, K. (1976) *Capital*, Harmondsworth: Penguin.

Massey, D. (1976) *Industrial Location Theory Reconsidered*, Milton Keynes: Open University Press.

— (1984) *Spatial Divisions of Labour*, London: Macmillan.

— (1993) Power-geometry and a progressive sense of place, in Bird *et al.*

— (1996) Space/power, identity/difference: tensions in the city, in Merrifield, A. and Swyngedouw, E. (eds) *The Urbanisation of Injustice*, London: Lawrence & Wishart.

Massey, D. and Allen, J. (eds) (1988) *Uneven Redevelopment*, London: Hodder & Stoughton.

Massey, D. and Meegan, R. (1978) Industrial restructuring versus the cities, *Urban Studies* 15, 273–88.

— (1979) The geography of industrial reorganisation: the spatial effects of the restructuring of the electrical engineering sector under the Industrial Reorganisation Corporation, *Progress in Planning* 3, 155–238.

— (1982) *The Anatomy of Job Loss*, London: Methuen.

Massey, D., Quintas, P. and Wield, D. (1992) *High-Tech Fantasies*, London: Routledge.

McDowell, L. and Massey, D. (1984) A woman's place, in Massey, D. and Allen, J. (eds) *Geography Matters!*, Cambridge: Cambridge University Press.

McIntosh, A. and Keddie, V. (1979) *Industry and Employment in the Inner City*, London: Department of the Environment.

Meegan, R. (1988) A crisis of mass production?, in Allen, J. and Massey, D. (eds) *The Economy in Question*, London: Sage.

Mensch, G. (1979) *Stalemate in Technology: Innovations Overcome the Depression*, New York: Ballinger.

Meszaros, I. (1971) *Aspects of History and Class Consciousness*, London: Routledge and Keegan Paul.

Metcalf, D. and Richardson, R. (1976) Unemployment in London, in Worswick, G. (ed.) *The Concept and Measurement of Involuntary Unemployment*, London: Allen & Unwin.

Moore, B., Rhodes, J. and Tyler, P. (1982) Urban-rural shift and the evaluation of regional policy, *Regional Science and Urban Economics* 12, 1, 139–57.

Moran, J. (1998) The dynamics of class politics and national economies in globalisation: the marginalisation of the unacceptable? *Capital and Class* 66, 53–84.

Morgan, G. and Hooper, D. (1987) Corporate strategy, ownership and control, *Sociology* 21, 4, 609–28.

Moseley, F. (1999) The US economy at the turn of the century: entering a new era of prosperity? *Capital and Class* 67, 25–46.

Murray, F. (1987) Flexible specialisation in the 'Third Italy', *Capital and Class* 33, 84–95.

Myrdal, G. (1957) *Rich Lands and Poor*, New York: Harper & Row.

Newham Community Development Project (1977) *Growth and Decline: Canning Town's Economy 1846–1976*, London: National CDP.

Nichols, T. (2001) The condition of labour – a retrospect, *Capital and Class* 75, 185–98.

Nichols, T. and Beynon, H. (1977) *Living with Capitalism*, London: Routledge & Kegan Paul.

Noble, D. (1979) Social choice in machine design: the case of automatically controlled machine tools, in Zimbalist, A. (ed.) *Case Studies on the Labour Process*, New York: Monthly Review Press.

Nove, A. (1983) *The Economics of Feasible Socialism*, London: Allen & Unwin.

O'Connor, J. (1973) *The Fiscal Crisis of the State*, New York: St Martins Press.

BIBLIOGRAPHY

Ollman, B. (1993) *Dialectical Investigations*, New York: Routledge.

Palloix, C. (1976) The labour process: from Fordism to neo-Fordism, in Conference of Socialist Economists.

Peck, J. (1992) Labour and agglomeration: control and flexibility in local labour markets *Economic Geography* 68, 325–47.

— (1996) *Work-Place: The Social Regulation of Labour Markets*, New York: Guildford Press.

Peck, J. and Tickell, A. (1995) The social regulation of uneven development: 'regulatory deficit', England's South East and the collapse of Thatcherism, *Environment and Planning A* 27, 1, 15–40.

Peet, R. (1983) Relations of production and the relocation of United States manufacturing industry since 1960, *Economic Geography* 59, 2, 112–43.

Pelaez, E. and Holloway, J. (1990) Learning to bow, *Science as Culture* 8, 15–26.

Perrons, D. (2000) The new economy and uneven geographical development: towards a more holistic framework for economic geography, Institute of British Geographers Economic Geography Research Group Working Paper 00/01.

Perulli, P. (1993) Towards a regionalisation of industrial relations, *International Journal of Urban and Regional Research* 17, 1, 98–113.

Phizacklea, A. and Wolkowitz, C. (1995) *Homeworking Women*, London: Sage.

Piore, M. and Sabel, C. (1984) *The Second Industrial Divide*, New York: Basic Books.

Polanyi, M. (1967) *The Tacit Dimension*, London: Routledge & Kegan Paul.

Pollert, A. (1988) Dismantling flexibility, *Capital and Class* 34, 42–75.

— (ed) (1990) *Farewell to Flexibility?* Oxford: Blackwell.

Prais, S. (1978) The strike-proneness of large plants in Britain, *Journal of the Royal Statistical Society A* 141, 368–84.

Pratt, A. (1994) *Uneven Re-production*, Oxford: Pergamon Press.

Pratten, C. (1971) *Economies of Scale in Manufacturing Industry*, Cambridge: Cambridge University Press.

Pratten, C. (1976) *A Comparison of the Performance of Swedish and UK Companies*, Cambridge: Cambridge University Press.

Pred, A. (1965) The concentration of high value added manufacturing, *Economic Geography* 41, 2, 108–32.

Radice, H. (2001) Globalization, labour and socialist renewal, *Capital and Class* 75, 113–26.

Rainnie, A. (1984) Combined and uneven development in the clothing industry, *Capital and Class* 22, 141–56.

Resnick, S. and Wolff, R. (1987) *Knowledge and Class*, Chicago: University of Chicago Press.

Robinson, J. and Eatwell, J. (1973) *An Introduction to Modern Economics*, London: McGraw-Hill.

Rose, D. (1981) Accumulation versus reproduction in the inner city: the *Recurrent Crisis of London* revisited, in Dear and Scott.

Rose, M. and Jones, B. (1985) Managerial strategy and trade union responses in work reorganisation schemes at establishment level, in Knights, Willmott and Collinson.

Rosenbrock, H. (1977) The future of control, *Automatica* 13, 389–92.

Ross, R. (1983) Facing Leviathan: public policy and global capitalism, *Economic Geography* 59, 2, 144–60.

Roweis, S. and Scott, A. (1981) The urban land question, in Dear and Scott.

Rubery, J. and Wilkinson, F. (eds) (1994) *Employer Strategy and the Labour Market*, Oxford: Oxford University Press.

Sabel, C. (1989) Flexible specialisation and the re-emergence of regional economies, in Hirst and Zeitlin.

Sassen, S. (1991) *The Global City*, Princeton: Princeton University Press.

Sayer, A. (1985) The difference that space makes, in Gregory and Urry.

— (1995) *Radical Political Economy: A Critique*, Oxford: Blackwell.

Sayer, A. and Morgan, K. (1988) *Microcircuits of Capital*, Cambridge: Polity Press.

Sayer, A. and Walker, R. (1992) *The New Social Division of Labour*, Oxford: Blackwell.

Scott, A. (1988) *Metropolis: From Division of Labour to Urban Form*, Berkeley: University of California Press.

— (1998) *Regions in the World Economy*, Oxford: Oxford University Press.

Scott, A. and Storper, M. (eds) (1986) *Production, Work, Territory*, London: Allen & Unwin.

SEEDS Association (1987) *The South–South Divide*, Stevenage: SEEDS Association.

Sennett, R. (1998) *The Corrosion of Character: The Personal Consequences of Work in the New Capitalism*, New York: Norton.

Sheppard, E. and Barnes, T. (1990) *The Capitalist Space Economy*, London: Unwin Hyman.

Smith, C. and Thompson, P. (1999) Re-evaluating the labor process debate, in Wardell, Steiger and Meiksins.

Smith, N. (1989) Uneven development and location theory: towards a synthesis, in Peet, R. and Thrift, N. (eds) *New Models in Geography* Vol 1, London: Unwin Hyman.

— (1993) Homeless/global: scaling places, in Bird *et al.*

Smith, T. (1995) *Lean Production: A Capitalist Utopia?* Amsterdam: International Institute for Research and Education.

Soja, E. (1989) *Postmodern Geographies*, London: Verso.

Solinas, G. (1982) Labour market segmentation and workers' careers: the case of the Italian knitwear industry, *Cambridge Journal of Economics* 6, 331–52.

Spencer, D. (2000) Braverman and the contribution of labour process analysis to the critique of capitalist production – 25 years on, *Work, Employment, Society* 14, 2, 223–43.

Stedman Jones, G. (1971) *Outcast London*, Oxford: Oxford University Press.

Steiger, T. (1999) Forms of labor process and labor's share of value, in Wardell, Steiger and Meiksins.

Storey, D. (1988) *Entrepreneurship and the New Firm*, London: Routledge.

Storper, M. (1998) *The Regional World*, New York: Guilford Press.

Storper, M. and Walker, R. (1983) The theory of labour and theory of location, *International Journal of Urban and Regional Research* 7, 1–44.

BIBLIOGRAPHY

— (1989) *The Capitalist Imperative*, Oxford: Blackwell.

Sturdy, A., Knights, D. and Willmott, H. (eds) (1992) *Skill and Consent*, London: Routledge.

Swyngedouw, E. (1992) The mammon quest: 'glocalisation', inter-spatial competition and the monetary order: the construction of new scales, in Dunford, M. and Kafkalas, G. (eds) *Cities and Regions in the New Europe*, London; Belhaven Press.

— (1997) Excluding the other: the production of scale and scaled politics, in Lee and Wills.

Taylor, M. (1994) The business enterprise, power and patterns of geographical industrialisation, in Conti, S., Malecki, E. and Oinas, P. (eds) *The Industrial Enterprise and Its Environment*, Aldershot: Avebury.

Taylor, M. and Conti, S. (eds) (1997) *Interdependent and Uneven Development*, Aldershot: Ashgate.

Terry, M. (1989) Recontextualising shopfloor industrial relations: some case study evidence, in Tailby, S. and Whitston, C. *Manufacturing Change*, Oxford: Blackwell.

Therborn, G. (1983) Why some classes are more successful than others, *New Left Review* 138, 37–56.

Thernstrom, S. (1984) Socialism and social mobility, in Laslett, J. and Lipset, S. (eds) *Failure or Dream?* Berkeley: University of California Press.

Thompson, E.P. (1968) *The Making of the English Working Class*, Harmondsworth: Penguin.

Thompson, P. (1989) *The Nature of Work*, London: Macmillan, 2nd ed.

— (1990) Crawling from the wreckage: the labour process and the politics of production, in Knights and Willmott.

Thrift, N. (1988) The geography of international economic disorder, in Massey and Allen.

Urry, J. (1985) Social relations, space and time, in Gregory and Urry.

Vernon, R. (1966) International investment and international trade in the product cycle, *Quarterly Journal of Economics* 80, 190–207.

Vogel, L. (1983) *Marxism and the Oppression of Women*, London: Pluto.

Wainwright, H. and Elliot (1982) *The Lucas Plan*, London: Allison & Busby.

Walby, S. and Bagguley, P. (1989) Gender restructuring: five labour-markets compared, *Environment and Planning D: Society and Space* 7, 277–92.

Waldinger, R. (1986) *Through the Eye of a Needle*, New York: New York University Press.

Walker, R. (1989a) Machinery, labour and location, in Wood (1989a).

— (1989b) A requiem for corporate geography, *Geografiska Annaler* 71B, 1, 46–68.

Walker, R. and Storper, M. (1981) Capital and industrial location, *Progress in Human Geography* 5, 473–509.

Warde, A. (1988) Industrial restructuring, local politics and the reproduction of labour power, *Environment and Planning D: Society and Space* 6, 75–95.

— (1992) Industrial discipline: factory regime and politics in Lancaster, in Sturdy, Knights and Wilmott.

Wardell, M., Steiger, T. and Meiksins, P. (eds) (1999) *Rethinking the Labor Process*, Albany: State University of New York Press.

Watson, S. (1992) The restructuring of work and home: productive and reproductive relations, in Allen, J. and Hamnett, C. (eds) *Housing and Labour Markets*, London: Unwin Hyman.

Webber, M. and Ribgy, D. (1996) *The Golden Age Illusion*, New York: Guilford Press.

Weisskopf, T. (1979) Marxian crisis theory and the rate of profit in the postwar US economy, *Cambridge Journal of Economics* 3, 4, 341–78.

Williams, K., Williams, J. and Thomas, D. (1983) *Why Are the British Bad at Manufacturing?* London: Routledge & Kegan Paul.

Williamson, O. (1975) *Markets and Hierarchies*, New York: Free Press.

Wills, J. (1998) Space, place and tradition in working-class organisation, in Herod.

—— (2001) Community unionism and trade union renewal in the UK: moving beyond the fragments at last? Paper at the Association of American Geographers Conference, New York, February.

Wirth, L. (1938) Urbanism as a way of life, *American Journal of Sociology* XLIV, 1, 1–24.

Wood, E.M. (1986) *The Retreat from Class*, London: Verso.

—— (1991) *The Pristine Culture of Capitalism*, London: Verso.

—— (1995) *Democracy against Capitalism*, Cambridge: Cambridge University Press.

Wood, S. (ed.) (1982) *The Degradation of Work?* London: Hutchinson.

—— (ed) (1989a) *The Transformation of Work?* London: Unwin Hyman.

—— (1989b) The transformation of work? in Wood (1989a).

Zuege, A. (1999) The chimera of the Third Way, in Panitch, L. and Leys, C. (eds) *Socialist Register 2000*, Woodbridge: Merlin Press.

Index to Major Threads of the Argument

Note: This index gives section and chapter numbers, rather than page numbers.

labour process – absolute versus relative surplus value – cooperation and conflict between capital and labour – location – workers' organization   1.3, Chapter 3, 4.2, 4.4, 5.3, Part III, 10.4–10.7, 11.2–11.5, Chapter 12, 13.2–13.4, 13.7

labour process – capital–labour relation – labour market – reproduction of people – location – workers' identities   2.3–2.4, 3.6, 4.4, 5.3, 5.7–5.8, 6.5, 7.3, 7.6–7.7, 7.11–7.13, 8.5–8.7, 9.2–9.4, 10.1–10.3, 10.6, 11.3, 11.5, Chapter 12, 13.6–13.7

labour process – premises – land market – location   2.5, 4.4, 5.2, 5.7, 6.6, 7.4, 7.9–7.10, 8.2, 8.7, Chapter 10, 11.3, 12.4

labour process – products – technical rents – location – workers' identities   2.7, 3.4, 3.6, 5.2–5.6, 6.4, 6.7, Chapter 8, 10.5–10.6, 11.2, 12.4, 13.3–13.4, 13.6–13.7

labour process – rhythms of accumulation, cycles and waves – location – capital–labour relations – workers' competition   1.3, 2.8, 3.4, 4.3–4.4, 5.2, 5.6, 5.9–5.10, 7.8–7.9, 8.7–8.8, 9.6–9.7, Chapter 11, Chapter 12, 13.2, 13.7

labour process – sectoral competition (geography, price/quality, intensity) – workers' competition   1.4, 2.6, 5.3–5.5, 6.7, 13.2., 13.5

local socialization of production – local socialization of reproduction – disruptions of socialization – mobilities   1.3, 1.4, 2.1, 2.7, 2.8, 3.6, 4.2, 4.4, 5.2–5.8, 6.7, Chapter 11, 12.2, 13.7

London service and manufacturing sectors – surplus profits – high factor costs – reproduction of labour power   5.2–5.6, 6.4–6.5, 8.3–8.4, 9.4, 11.2–11.3, 13.6

scales – ubiquitous structures constituting them – inter-scale relations   2.1, Chapter 4, 5.2–5.3, 5.6, 5.9–5.10, 8.8, Chapter 11, 12.3, 12.7, 13.2, 13.5, 13.7

Subject and Author Index

armaments production 82, 102, 104, 105, 282

Braverman, Harry 30–1, 34, 52, 91n, 276–7
British economy 104–8
  class structure 76–7, 104–7
  manufacturing 82, 101, 103–8
  see also governments, British
Burawoy, Michael 34, 35, 91, 129, 248, 273, 273n, 276–7, 294
business cycle 245–68
  in Britain (1976–81) 13, 106–8
  and capital–labour relations 13, 106–8, 245, 255–8, 279–80
  and contradiction 248–50, 259–63
  in labour markets 130–3, 246, 250–1, 255–8
  and labour process 7–8, 12, 53, 148, 152–5, 159–60, 162–3, 170, 174–6, 178, 188, 195, 196–7, 201–4, 208, 246, 249, 251–63
  in London (1976–81) 12, 108, 112, 298–301
  origins of 247–50
  in output 246, 250–1, 253–5
  in profitability 246, 250–8
  and scale 246, 250–1, 255–8, 262
  and the state 12–13, 107, 248–9
  and switches in locational strategies 148, 258–9

capital accumulation
  and geography 10–11
  and labour process 8–10, 53, 67–9, 70–2, 205–9, 231, 264–7, 269–70, 291–2, 294
  and products 185–6, 188
  see also business cycle; fixed investment; overaccumulation; reinforcing accumulation; rhythms of accumulation; underaccumulation
capital intensity 219–20
capital–labour relations 4, 9–10, 27–31, 45, 49–50, 104–6, 151–2, 270–1
  and business cycle 13, 106–8, 245, 255–8, 279–80
  collaborative 14, 60–3, 171, 178, 206–7, 291
  collaborative versus conflictual 271–3, 280–3
  conflictual 34–5, 56, 218–19, 223–5
  consent 34–5, 56

as culture 5–6, 15–16, 34–5, 45, 59, 81–4, 105–6, 128, 132–3, 273–7, 282, 287–91
  disciplinary 45, 61–3, 80–1, 105–6, 132–3, 173–8, 237–8
  and geography 13–14, 237–8, 270–1
  partial versus universal sides of capitalism 8–9, 62–3, 208–9, 240–2, 291–2
  and relations between workers 3, 13–14, 30, 32, 151–2, 270–83
  relative and absolute surplus value 50–6, 199
  responsible autonomy versus direct control 61–2, 161, 190–1, 195, 197–200, 205–6, 219–26, 272
  subsumption of labour 34, 50–1, 160–1, 182, 195, 219–20
  see also class; employment; labour process; neoliberalism
case study 1, 18
  backwardness 119–22, 144–5
  and business cycle 251–62
  competition and profitability 139–42
  forms of capital 143–4
  labour power 126–33
  labour processes 115–20
    change in 151–230
  premises 134–9
  product activities 115–16, 118–22
  product industries 113–14, 116–20
  and rhythms of accumulation 231–68
  selection of panel 112–13
  trade unions 128–30
  uniqueness 11–12
Clarke, Simon 60n, 93n, 245
class, theories of 290–1
  see also capital–labour relations
Cohen, Sheila 34, 35, 278–80, 293
coherence, *see* socialization
competition 40
  of localities 14, 25–9, 41–2
  monopolistic 91–2
  price versus quality 41, 57–8, 60, 139–42, 181–2, 185–7, 291
  in product-industries 6–7, 10–11, 40–2, 67, 139–42, 280–3
  of workers 1–3, 5–6, 13–16, 41–2, 271–4, 280–3, 291–5
    and socialist strategy 15–16, 270–1, 280–3

components of change 71, 112–13, 302
cooperatives 291–2
cost cutting 54–6, 196–209
  diseconomies of scale 56, 177, 205–8
  economies of scale 56, 189, 203–4
  hours of factory operation 55, 202–3
  wage cuts 55, 197–202
Cox, Kevin 25, 43–4, 70, 71
cultures
  of industrial sectors 79–89
  of neighbourhoods 38, 42, 132–3, 287–9
  of workers 5–6, 15–16, 34–5, 45, 59, 81–4,
    105–6, 128, 132–3, 273–7, 282, 287–91,
    295–6

demand 42, 60, 294
  see also London manufacturing, demand for
design
  inter-firm collaboration 185–7
  labour process of 32, 58, 149, 171, 185–7
  rents, see technical rents
devalorization 240–2
  and relocation 165–9, 204, 241
  see also business cycle; long waves;
    overaccumulation
Devine, Pat 293
diseconomies of scale 56, 177, 205–8
disproportionality 235–6, 239
domestic work 36–7, 294

economies of scale 56, 189, 203–4
Edwards, Paul 11n, 33, 62, 112, 129, 218, 273
Edwards, Richard 34, 36, 91
Elger, Tony 13, 62
employment 4, 31–5
  in Britain 107, 298–9
  British manufacturing 106–7, 298–9
  ethnic minorities 5, 38–9, 54, 80, 128, 129,
    200, 286, 288
  gender divisions 38, 86, 88, 122–33, 143–4,
    171–3, 274–5, 294
  homeworkers 123–4, 128, 183–4, 200, 203
  hours worked 50, 54nn, 127, 163, 198, 202,
    293
  London manufacturing 88, 100–1, 108,
    113, 122, 298–301
  men's 83, 128–9
  security of 61, 81, 274, 293
  self-employment 127–8
  turnover of workers 124–5, 132, 163, 256–7
  unregistered 101n, 127–8
  women's 81, 86, 123, 126, 127, 163, 200
  youth 123, 200
  see also capital–labour relations; labour
    markets; labour power; unemployment;
    wages
ethnic minority communities 5, 38–9, 200,
  288

finance, relation to manufacturing 69n, 78,
  104–5, 139, 249n, 252n, 292–3

firms
  behavioural theory of 27, 32, 68
  form of capital 7, 80–9, 142–4
  inter-firm relations and division of
    labour 43–5, 81, 97, 103
    for design 185–7
    and radical product change 193–4
  and labour processes 7, 142–4, 178–9,
    207–8, 243n
  multisite 7, 143, 149, 165–8, 171n, 174–9,
    204
  new firms and entrepreneurs 71–2, 84, 143
  owner-managed 70–1, 207–8
  as private accumulation of capital 28–9,
    42, 185–7, 243n
  and products 7, 143–4
  quality of 84
  satisficing 207–8
  see also managers; workplace
fixed investment
  depreciation of sunk 55, 70–1, 174, 202–3,
    220
  extensive 95, 152, 249, 293
  hours of operation 55, 202–3
  intensive 95, 152–9, 249, 252–4, 293
  vintage 100, 138, 144
flexible specialization 60, 191, 291
  see also Fordism/post-Fordism
floor space intensity and labour process
    change 134–6
  and relocation 149, 166–8, 303
Fordism/post-Fordism as periods 60–1, 63–4,
  191, 227
Fothergill, Stephen 94, 100, 135–6, 167
Friedman, Andrew 31, 35, 61–2, 65, 91, 112,
  129

geography of production
  relation to time 263–4
  relations between economy and space
    10–11, 13–14, 16, 25–30, 214–15
  see also local economies; localities;
    relocation; scale; socialization, and/
    versus mobilities; spatial division of
    labour; spatial shifts; workplace
    location
Gibson-Graham, J.-K. 35, 128, 290
globalization 13–14
  see also mobilities
Gordon, David 15, 36, 63, 65, 70, 93, 175
governments, British
  Conservative (1970–4) 106
  Conservative (1979–97) 12–13, 107–8, 249,
    257
  Labour (1974–9) 106–7, 174, 237, 257
Gudgin, Graham 94, 100, 135–6, 167

Harvey, David 3, 16, 18, 25, 43–4, 46, 70, 95,
  136, 176–7, 202, 242n, 246–8, 259, 283,
  287, 291n

Herod, Andrew 34, 66
homeworkers 123–4, 128, 183–4, 200, 203
housing 37–9, 44, 77, 102, 123, 125–6
Hyman, Richard 62, 112

industrial districts 43, 63, 80, 82, 100, 102, 288
   see also local economies, socialization;
      London manufacturing, broad sectors
industrial relations, see capital–labour
      relations; employment; trade unions;
      workers
industries, see product-industries
institutionalist theory 27, 35, 174, 229
intensification of work, see labour process,
      intensification of work
investment, see capital accumulation; fixed
      investment

Japan 60, 104
Jonas, Andrew 25, 207
journey to work 37
   and gender 123–6
   in London 123–6, 287–8

Kelly, John 57, 273
Keynesian strategy 62, 106–7, 282, 283
Keynesian theory 27, 44n, 68, 136n, 174, 231

labour, see domestic work; labour markets;
      labour power; labour process; workers
labour markets
   and business cycle 130–3, 246, 250–1, 255–8
   local 36–9, 45
   in London 17, 77, 120–33
   in London manufacturing 79–89, 99–100, 122–33, 130–3, 145
   scales of 123–6, 255–8
   segmented 5, 15, 32, 36–9, 61, 112–16, 123–6, 163–4, 199–200, 274–5, 284
   and skill 32, 124–5, 129, 130–3
   training 125, 130–1, 293–4
   variation in Britain 170–4, 176–7
   see also employment; journey to work; wages
labour power
   abstract and concrete 70, 171
   and labour processes 5–6, 32, 35–6, 53–4, 130–3, 156–8, 162–4, 169–78, 190–3, 197–203, 205, 216–17
   skilled 30–1, 52–3, 61, 115–16, 123n, 197–202, 222–3, 228, 276–8, 291–4
      absolute versus relative change in skilling 156–8
   see also employment; labour markets;
      reproduction of labour power; workers
labour process 3–4, 9–10, 30–6
   aspects of 30, 49–52, 115

and business cycle 7–8, 12, 53, 148, 152–5, 159–60, 162–3, 170, 174–6, 178, 188, 195, 196–7, 201–4, 208, 246, 249, 251–63
and capital accumulation 8–10, 53, 67–9, 70–2, 205–9, 231, 264–7, 269–70, 291–2, 294
change in 11–12, 49–64, 213–29
   approach to explanation 150, 217–18
   aspects of initial labour process constructing 218–19
   blockages to 218–28
   by initial labour process 148–209, 213, 216–29
control of work process 31–5, 49–53, 56, 92, 133, 161, 183–4, 205
cost cutting 54–6, 196–210
definition 3, 30, 33
of design 32, 58, 149, 171, 185–7
and devalorization of capacity 165–9, 204, 240–2
diseconomies of scale 56, 177, 205–8
disintensification of work 163, 183, 197–8
dynamic tendencies or potentials of 150, 217–18, 247
economies of scale 56, 189, 203–4
floor-space intensity of 134–6, 149, 166–8
and form of capital 7, 143–4, 178–9, 207–8, 243n
and geography 10–11
homeworking 123–4, 128, 183–4, 200, 203
and hours of factory operation 55, 202–3
in situ change and/versus relocation 69–71, 148, 151–2, 178, 193, 195, 196, 213, 216–26, 232, 239–40, 258–9, 262
increase in labour discipline 174–8, 205–8
intensification of work 3, 159–62, 203, 209, 277–8, 293–4
   via change in workforce 162–4, 169–74
   relation to mechanization 49–54, 160, 178
and labour power 5–6, 32, 35–6, 53–4, 130–3, 156–8, 162–4, 169–78, 190–3, 197–203, 205, 216–17
   continuity of workers' experience 61, 163, 171, 178, 200, 234, 236
   and skill 30–1, 52–3, 61, 115–16, 123n, 197–202, 222–3, 228, 276–8, 291–4
layout of premises 137–8, 158–9, 222
and localities 9–10, 17, 36–46
in London manufacturing 17, 79–93, 96–103, 115–20, 144
and long waves 12, 60, 93–8
material and/versus social aspects (forces and/versus relations of production) 33–4, 46, 50–1, 62, 228–9
mechanization (process technology) 152–8, 165–6, 182–3, 189–91, 219–21, 228–9, 277, 279, 280, 293–4
on-site work 83–4, 127, 141, 149, 171

labour process – *continued*
  and overaccumulation 235–8, 239–40
  and premises 6, 10, 39–40, 134–9, 168–9
  in product-industries 116–20
  and product-industry competition 10,
    40–2, 91–3, 139–42, 196, 198, 201–3,
    208–9
  productivity increasing 132–3, 151–80
  and products 6, 10, 35, 57–61, 85, 89–91,
    115–16, 118–22, 132, 139–42, 188–95,
    221–2, 229
    radical technical change in
      products 193–4
  and quality of production 53, 57, 132–3,
    181–5
  and reinforcing accumulation 232–5,
    239–40
  and relocation 165–77, 184–5, 191–3, 195,
    200–2, 204, 206, 213–15, 226–8, 234,
    237, 239–41
    logical relations between 214–15
  and reproduction of labour power 5–6,
    10–11, 29–30, 37–9, 45, 132–3, 178,
    198–9, 227, 232–3, 235–7, 238–40,
    287–8
  and rhythms of accumulation 7–8, 43–6,
    67–9, 103–4, 130, 231–43, 263–7, 291–2
  in services 286–7
  and socialist strategy 269–73, 275–80
  and 'structured paralysis' 239–40
  and technical rents 139–42, 195, 282,
    285–7, 288–9
  and technological change 30–3, 50–4,
    115–6, 169, 228–9, 292
  timeliness of 80, 83, 92, 118, 141
  typology of 11–12, 115–17
  and underaccumulation 238–9
  use value versus exchange value of 8–9,
    33–6, 40–2, 46, 62, 104–6, 134–9, 159,
    219–21, 228–9, 234, 242, 249, 264–7,
    279–80, 291–2
  and wage cuts 55, 197–202
  and workers' identities 5–6, 15–16, 34–5,
    45, 59, 81–4, 105–6, 128, 132–3, 273–7,
    282, 287–91, 295–6
  see also capital–labour relations;
    employment; managers; workers
labour productivity, *see* productivity
left strategies, actually existing 15–16, 263,
    269–70
  see also Keynesian strategy; social democratic
    strategy; socialist strategy
Levidow, Les 31, 63
local economies 10, 14, 25–48
  contradictions and disruptions of 44–6,
    66–7
  cultures of 43–6
  demand 42
  and global economy 14, 25–9
  infrastructures 45
  inter-firm relations 43–5

  see also industrial districts
  inter-local competition 41–2
  labour markets 36–9, 45
  and labour processes 9–10, 36–46
    diversity in 17, 44–5
  and long waves 93–4
  overaccumulation in 45–6, 77, 94, 101,
    103, 167, 235–6
  policies for, mainstream 132n, 133–4,
    272–3
  premises 39–40, 135–6
  reinforcing accumulation in 43–4, 96–8,
    101, 232–3
  rhythms of accumulation in 43–6
  socialization of 8, 14, 42–6, 63–4, 96–8,
    272–3
  underaccumulation in 45, 98, 101, 235–6,
    238–9
  see also localities; London; regional policy
localities 9–10, 17n
  disruption of 38–40, 43, 46
  and reproduction 36–9, 42, 263, 289n
  socialization of 14, 42–6
  and worker collectivity 1, 16–17, 38–9
  see also local economies; London economy;
    metropolis
location theory 25, 65
London economy
  consumption and demand 77–8, 288–9
  core sectors 16, 76–8, 88, 94–5, 102, 295–6
  housing 77, 102, 123, 125–6
  labour power 17, 77, 120–33
  land market 77, 134–9
  and rhythms of accumulation 16, 77, 79,
    122, 132–3
  ruling class in 77, 288–9, 296
  and socialist strategy 284–9
  socialization and political regulation 77–8,
    88, 145
  transport 78, 81, 87, 88, 99, 102, 173
  unemployment 125, 126, 130, 256–7, 300
  wages 17, 122–3
London manufacturing 1–3, 17
  backwardness 100, 121, 144–5
  broad sectors 79–89, 101–2, 113–14, 124
    craft capital goods 81–2, 89–90, 96, 99,
      107, 113–14, 124, 128–9
    craft consumer goods 78–80, 99, 101n,
      102, 113–14, 124, 128–9
    Fordist 85–7, 96–100, 106, 113–14, 129
    jobbing 83–4, 98, 114
    materials processing 87–8, 96–8, 113–
      14, 129
  demand for 139–42, 187
    in London 79–80, 83, 87, 95–6, 282,
      288–9, 296
  design and technical innovation 78–82,
    87, 92, 99, 118, 144
  employment 88, 100–1, 108, 113, 122,
    298–301
  form of firm 80–9, 142–4

historical development 78–91, 94–103, 135–6
inter-firm relations 81, 97
labour power 79–89, 99–100, 122–33, 144–5
  reproduction of 99–100, 102–3
  and skill 130–3
  training 125, 130–1
labour processes 17, 79–93, 96–103, 115–20, 144
and land use planning 102
long waves in 16, 94–8, 101
premises 87, 134–9, 168–9
prices of 134–6, 139, 142, 145
products 89–91, 118–20
profit rates 100, 136, 142, 145
socialization and politics 88, 96–8, 100–3, 131, 145
spatial expansion 98–101
specialization 79–89, 92, 96–8, 118–22
surplus profits 82, 92–3, 142, 282, 288–9
trade unions 86, 88, 96, 128–30
see also case study; London economy
long waves
  and dominant ideologies 12–15, 292
  in London manufacturing 16, 94–8, 101
  relation to other accumulation rhythms 264–7
  and scale 93–8
  of stagnation (1970s on) 13–15, 60–1, 94, 101, 103, 106–8, 245
  theory of 93
Lovering, John 46, 63, 82, 281

managers
  relations between 207
  strategies of 34, 36, 112, 130, 159n, 240, 260–2
  views, knowledge and theories of 112, 133, 138–9, 170, 173–4, 218
Mandel, Ernest 53, 93, 103, 106, 202, 242nn, 246n, 247–9, 248n, 265, 293
manufacturing, definition of 75–6
  see also services
market socialism 291–2
Marshall, Michael 78n, 93–6, 246, 246n
Marx, Karl 50–1, 54n, 57, 242n, 247–8, 284
Marxist political economy 15, 27–9, 42–3, 46, 46n, 51, 57, 65, 93, 195, 231, 274n
Massey, Doreen 11, 14, 16, 25, 56n, 65, 70, 80, 95, 100, 158, 160n, 169, 175, 204, 215n, 237–8, 241, 242n
Meegan, Richard 11, 56n, 65, 70, 85, 95, 100, 158, 160n, 169, 175, 204, 215n, 237–8, 241, 242n
method, see theoretical approach
metropolis 284–9, 294–5
  see also London
mobilities and/versus socialization 8, 14, 63–4, 70–1, 87, 105–6, 249, 272–3

neoclassical economics 26, 27n, 40, 42, 44n, 45, 68, 69, 70, 133, 174, 202
neoliberalism 1, 13–14, 107, 263, 269, 290, 292
new regional economics 43, 46, 63, 65–6, 243n, 291
Nichols, Theo 88, 129, 278

Ollman, Bertell 9, 27–8
overaccumulation 7–8, 28, 103, 235, 247–8
  definition 45–6
  and labour process, summary 235–8, 239–40
  and long waves 93, 94
  within local economies 45–6, 77, 94, 101, 103, 167, 235–6
  within a product-industry 24–3
  within workplaces 69, 149, 206, 236, 239–42, 250–1
  see also business cycle

partial versus universal sides of capitalism 8–9, 62–3, 208–9, 240–2, 291–2
Peck, Jamie 15, 36, 46, 63, 103
philosophy, see theoretical approach
politicization 105–6, 292–6
  see also neoliberalism
postmodern theory 29–30, 35, 128, 290–1
premises, industrial 6, 39–40, 133–9
  constrained location hypothesis 134–6
  floor-space intensity of employment 134–6, 149, 166–8
  and labour process 6, 10, 39–40, 134–9, 168–9
  and land market 134
  layout of 137–8
product-industries
  in case study 113–14, 116–20
  definition 40
  forms of competition 6–7, 10–11, 40–2, 67, 139–42, 280–3
  typology of (Groups 1–5) 139–42
  and labour processes 116–20
  and labour processes change 10, 40–2, 91–3, 139–42, 196, 198, 201–3, 208–9
  profit rates 40, 139–42, 196, 208
  see also spatial division of labour
productivist strategy 106–7, 291–2
productivity
  change, differences between labour processes 155, 164–5
  conflict with quality of production 181–5, 195
  and price changes 155n, 165n
  and socialist strategy 293
  value, see products and product change
  volume 49–54, 151–80
  and value productivity, definitions of 59
products and product change
  and capital accumulation 188
  commissioned and bespoke 185–6

products and product change – *continued*
  cycle theory 58, 63
  diversification and economies of
    scope 187–8, 192
  and labour process 6, 10, 35, 57–61, 85,
    89–91, 115–16, 118–22, 132, 139–42,
    188–95, 221–2, 229
    first cut 57–9
    and relocation 184–5, 191–3, 195
    second cut 89–91, 118–20
    third cut 188–93
  ownership of design 185–6
  radical change in technologies of 193–4
  specialization 188, 192
  and technical rents 6, 59, 82, 91–3, 185–7,
    195
  timely 80, 83, 92, 118, 141
  vertical integration 188
  and worker identities 6, 59, 288–9
profit rates 40–2, 94n, 103, 242
  British manufacturing 106–7
  over business cycle 246, 250–8
  at different scales, relation between 256–7
  of firms 198, 208
  London manufacturing 100, 136, 142, 145
  in product-industries 40, 139–42, 196, 208
  see also surplus profits

racism 37, 274–5
rationalization of capacity 165–9, 204, 241
regional policy 99–100, 102, 134
regulation theory 15n
reinforcing accumulation 7–8
  definition 43–4
  and labour process, summary 232–5,
    239–40
  within local economies 43–4, 96–8, 101,
    232–3
  within workplaces 67–8, 149, 171, 178–9,
    203–4, 233–5, 239–42
relocation of workplaces 149, 302–3
  to change labour process 165–77, 184–5,
    191–3, 195, 200–2, 204, 206, 213–15,
    226–8, 234, 237, 239–41
    better premises 138, 168–9, 240
    and changes in floor space 149, 166–8,
     303
    cost cutting 200–2, 204, 206
    improved mechanization 165–6
    increased productivity 165–78
    increased discipline of labour 174–8,
     237, 240
    intensification 169–74
    product change 184–5, 191–3, 195
  contractionary and expansionary 149,
    165–9
  and devalorization 165–9, 204, 241
  first cut explanation 214–17
  and labour markets 169–78, 200–2, 237–8
  second cut explanation 226–8
  see also workplace location

reproduction of labour power 5, 36–8
  cultures of 38, 42, 132–3, 287–9
  domestic work 36–7, 294
  housing 37–9, 44, 77, 102, 123, 125–6
  and labour processes 5–6, 10–11, 29–30,
    37–9, 45, 132–3, 178, 198–9, 227, 232–3,
    235–7, 238–40, 287–8
  local socialization of 4, 10, 37–8, 102–3,
    133n
  and socialist strategy 287–8, 294–5
rhythms of accumulation 3, 12, 16, 46
  different temporalities of 263–7
  and labour processes 7–8, 43–6, 67–9,
    103–4, 130, 231–43, 263–7, 291–2
  and scale 232–43, 263–7
  and socialist strategy 281–2, 291–3
  see also business cycle; capital accumulation;
    devalorization; long waves;
    overaccumulation; reinforcing
    accumulation; underaccumulation

Sayer, Andrew 28, 41n, 53, 76, 194, 243n,
  269, 281, 291
scale, geographical 10–11, 13–14, 25–9, 41,
  66–7, 99–100, 108–9, 207, 282–3
  and the business cycle 246, 250–1, 255–8,
    262
  and long waves 93–8
  and rhythms of accumulation 232–43,
    263–7
  see also firms, multisite; globalization; local
    economies; localities
services, labour processes in 286–7
skill, *see* labour markets; labour power; labour
  process
Smith, Neil 25, 207
social democratic strategy 291–2
  see also Keynesian strategy
socialist strategy 3, 243, 269–96
  and the business cycle 279–80
  and competition between workers 15–16,
    270–1, 280–3
  and differences between workers 15, 270,
    275–80, 282, 285–9
  and employment contracts 276
  and intensification 277–8, 293–4
  and mechanization 277, 279, 280, 293–4
  and metropolises 284–9
  and non-capitalist countries 293n
  and planning of investment 243, 267, 277,
    281–3, 292–5
  and relative versus absolute surplus value
    strategies 272–3, 281–2
  and reproduction of people 287–8, 294–5
  and rhythms of accumulation 281–2,
    291–3
  and skill 276–8, 291–4
  and spatial division of labour 291–4
  and technical rents 282, 285–7, 288–9
  and wages 276, 278–80, 282, 293

socialization 242–3
and/versus mobilities 8, 14, 63–4, 70–1,
87, 105–6, 249, 272–3
of local economies 8, 14, 42–6, 63–4, 96–8,
272–3
disruption of 44–6, 66–7
of localities 14, 42–6
disruption of 38–40, 43, 46
of production 43, 63, 104–6, 232, 264–7
of reproduction of labour 4, 10, 37–8,
102–3, 133n
within firms 243n
south-east England, rest of (ROSE) 77,
99–103, 123, 170–1
spatial division of labour 41–6, 63, 118–20,
139–42, 167, 193–4, 200, 215, 291–3
spatial shifts 13, 44, 72, 97–8
see also mobilities
state intervention 103, 104, 287
see also governments; local economies,
policies for; regional policy
Storper, Michael 43, 63, 65, 68, 69–70, 97–8,
242n, 243n
structured paralysis 239–40
surplus profits 83, 91, 136, 142
and employment relations 91–3, 142
from spatial monopoly 92
technical rents 6, 59, 82, 91–3, 139–42,
185–7, 195, 282, 285–7, 288–9
from timeliness 80, 83, 92, 118, 141
survey, see case study
Swyngedouw, Erik 14, 37

technical rents 92
and labour process 139–42, 195, 282,
285–7, 288–9
in London manufacturing 82, 91–3,
139–42
and product strategies 6, 59, 82, 91–3,
185–7, 195
theoretical approach
abstract and concrete 17–18, 40, 117, 150,
226n, 258, 295
agency 9, 30, 34, 62, 218, 262–3
contingency, necessary relations and
tendencies 11, 150, 217–18
contradiction 28, 30, 33, 38, 62–3, 108–9,
218, 238, 239–40, 248–50, 259–63,
289–91
dialectics 29–30
difference and/versus commonality 26,
29–30, 63, 290–1
internal and/versus external relations 11,
25–30, 41–2, 51–2, 109, 133, 136–9,
144–5, 174, 208, 215, 238, 250–1
'structure' 9, 28, 30, 34, 49, 66–7, 289
spatially effective structures 37–8
theory and practice 269, 293
Thompson, Paul 30, 34, 35, 36, 41, 53, 57n,
229

trade unions 14, 16, 106–7, 174, 277n
in London manufacturing 128–30, 162,
163, 174–8, 205, 223–5, 237, 286

underaccumulation
definition 45
and labour processes, summary 238–9
within local economies 45, 98, 101, 235–6,
238–9
within workplaces 68–9, 149, 239
unemployment 293
in Britain 13
in London 124–5, 126, 130, 256–7, 300
United States capital 82n, 105–6

value, see devalorization; labour process, use
value versus exchange value; profit
rates; surplus profits; wages

wages
in Britain 13, 107
cuts 55, 197–202
by changing the workforce in situ
199–200
by relocation 201–2
differences in 199, 274
and inflation 197
in London 17, 122, 197
and socialist strategy 276, 278–80, 282, 293
and surplus profits 91–3, 142
Walker, Richard 53, 65, 68, 69–70, 76, 97–8,
193, 194, 242n, 243n
Wood, Ellen Meiksins 15, 34, 35, 104–5, 290,
295
work identities see worker identities
work relations, see labour process, control
workers
antagonism between 274–5
see also employment, gender divisions;
racism; workers, competition
collective organization, militancy and
consciousness 9, 14–16, 128–30,
223–5, 255–7, 271–3, 284, 287–8, 295–6
and space 15–16, 26, 176–8, 271–3, 284,
287–8
competition 1–3, 5–6, 13–16, 41–2, 271–4,
280–3, 291–5
and socialist strategy 15–16, 270–1,
280–3
differences and commonalities between
1–3, 8–9, 15–17, 228, 270, 273–80, 285–
91
and socialist strategy 15, 270, 275–80,
282, 285–9
fragmentation 1, 14–16, 32, 295
identities and culture 5–6, 15–16, 34–5, 45,
59, 81–4, 105–6, 128, 132–3, 273–7, 282,
287–91, 295–6
individual sale of labour power 1, 13, 28–9,
284–5, 289–90
long-term mobility of 43, 272

workers – *continued*
  relations between workers within labour
    process   31, 52, 293–4
  subordination to capital   34, 291–2, 295
  see also capital–labour relations,
    subsumption of labour
  see also capital–labour relations;
    employment; reproduction of labour
    power; trade unions
workplace and workplace location   65–72
  and the labour process   69–72, 148, 151–2,
    178, 193, 195, 196, 213, 216–26, 232,
    239–40, 258–9, 262
  location switches over business cycle   148,
    258–9

openings of   71–2
overaccumulation in   69, 149, 206, 236,
  239–42, 250–1
reinforcing accumulation in   67–8, 149,
  171, 178–9, 203–4, 233–5, 239–42
relation to larger scales   25–9, 66–7, 70–1
theory of location   25, 65
underaccumulation in   68–9, 149, 239
see also relocation of workplaces
workplace, size of   116, 118, 143
  and change in floor space intensity   134–6,
    149, 166–8, 303
  diseconomies of scale   56, 177, 205–8
  economies of scale   56, 189, 203–4

For Product Safety Concerns and Information please contact our EU
representative GPSR@taylorandfrancis.com Taylor & Francis Verlag GmbH,
Kaufingerstraße 24, 80331 München, Germany

Batch number: 08158403

Printed by Printforce, the Netherlands